HISTORY OF
AMERICAN LITERATURE

From 1910 to the Present

HISTORY OF

American Literature

FROM 1910 TO THE PRESENT

Martin S. Day, Ph.D.

PROFESSOR OF ENGLISH
AT THE UNIVERSITY OF HOUSTON

A College Course Guide

DOUBLEDAY & COMPANY, INC., GARDEN CITY
NEW YORK
1971

PREFACE

This volume offers the reader a very complete and convenient survey of American literature of the twentieth century. As the title indicates, it covers the years from 1910 to the present. It is a companion volume to the author's *History of American Literature from the Beginning to 1910.* The two books have been written so that they may be used entirely independently of one another. But together they give a continuous account of our literature; and the pattern and treatment are alike in the two.

American literature in the twentieth century has brought us many major novelists, poets, dramatists, and prose writers of unusual interest. Such names as Hemingway, Fitzgerald, Wolfe, Steinbeck, Faulkner among the novelists; Robinson, Frost, Sandburg, William Carlos Williams, Wallace Stevens among the poets; Eugene O'Neill, Tennessee Williams, Arthur Miller, Edward Albee among the dramatists—these give only a suggestion of the wealth with which this book is concerned. In this volume we give full attention to them and many other important writers, discussing their background and distinctive characteristics, and presenting summaries of their chief works, with critical or explanatory comment wherever it seems helpful.

The book, however, does not limit itself to the major writers. It is an inclusive survey, with thoughtful sections on lesser writers who have made valuable and varied contributions. Writers who are often grouped together because of a shared approach—such as the Imagists, the Agrarians, and later the Projectivists, the Beats, the Black Poets, and the New Critics—are introduced by information about their joint objectives and then considered individually.

The book consists of two Parts:

Part One focuses upon the years from 1910 to the end of the Second World War.

Part Two is devoted to the writers of mid-century and up to the present.

It is important to point out that some writers who are considered in Part One continued to do important work into mid-century, yet we present their later writings in Part One, in order to keep the discussion of each writer at one place. Conversely, there are a few writers who by date of birth would seem to belong to Part One but whose influence has been more strongly felt in the later years; they are therefore reserved for Part Two, where both their earlier and more recent works are considered as a unit.

A word should explain the choice of 1910 rather than 1900 for the starting point of this volume. The opening decade of the century in the field of literature tended to round out the writing of the later nineteenth century. It was in the second decade that new voices began to be heard. A few writers who were already prominent in the nineteenth century but continued well into the twentieth are presented, including their later writings, in our companion volume, *American Literature from the Beginning to 1910.*

One technical point which is of some interest: where a work was written in one year and published or produced (if a play) somewhat later, the date of composition is given in italics and the date of publication in roman type. For example, *The Great God Brown (1925,* 1926) indicates that this O'Neill play was completed in 1925 but not produced until 1926.

The author has been assisted in many ways by a large number of people. He would like especially to express his thanks to Lawrence W. Lamm, Patricia White, Ellen L. Glascock, Harriet Supnick, Ralph W. Hodges, Jr., and J. Oscar Lieben.

June 1971   Martin S. Day

CONTENTS

PART TWO
AMERICAN LITERATURE IN
MID-CENTURY

PART ONE

American Literature in the Early Twentieth Century

CHAPTER ONE

The Novel in the Early Twentieth Century

THE ASCENDANCY OF THE NOVEL

More than any other form of literature, the novel has proved to be the truly representative expression of American literature in the early twentieth century. The mere mention of such names as Ernest Hemingway, F. Scott Fitzgerald, William Faulkner, Theodore Dreiser, Thomas Wolfe, Sinclair Lewis, Willa Cather, Sherwood Anderson, and John Steinbeck immediately indicates the great wealth of creative and distinctive fiction which appeared and won recognition during those years.

Toward the end of the nineteenth century and in the opening years of the twentieth, there had been a definite trend toward realism in American fiction, with emphasis upon fidelity to the facts of everyday life in various fields of activity. Some writers of this period, both here and in Europe, moved toward inclusion of the more sordid and violent aspects of life in their factual presentation of characters and events, and the term "naturalism" is applied to this extension of realism. The influence of the realistic and naturalistic approaches is apparent in the work of several of the major novelists of the years from 1910 to mid-century.

A rather different type of realism, sometimes spoken of as classicism, shares the viewpoint of Henry James and is seen in the novels of Edith Wharton and some others who became prominent in the first decade of the twentieth century. As our present volume starts essentially in 1910, we have considered the writing of this group of classical realists in a section of the last of the chapters on fiction in the first volume of this two-volume history of American literature. Some of these novelists wrote notable and highly valued novels in the period discussed in the present chapter; but we have felt that their later works could be more effectively appreciated if grouped with their earlier novels in our first volume.

Realism in the nineteenth century was to a degree a reaction against the later expressions of romanticism, which no longer had the imaginative impact of the earlier romanticism. In the twentieth century, although the trend to realism continues, it is not surprising to find equivalents of romanticism from time to time appearing perhaps in the more subtle form of symbolism, or in reflective or experimental fiction, and sometimes as sheer fantasy.

In the present chapter the novelists each make their contribution as individuals rather than as representatives of a specific approach. The order in which they appear is not rigidly chronological, but seeks rather to provide ready comparisons between writers, some of whom have elements in common and others who provide striking contrasts.

MAJOR NOVELISTS OF THE EARLY TWENTIETH CENTURY

Sherwood Anderson (1876–1941). Born in Camden, Ohio, Sherwood Anderson was taken at the age of eight to Clyde, Ohio, which was to become the basis for the Winesburg of his stories. In 1896 he went to Chicago where he worked in a warehouse until enlisting in the Army in 1898 during the Spanish-American War. From 1900 to 1912 he tried a twofold career as a paint manufacturer in Elyria, Ohio, and as an author. In the latter year a nervous breakdown caused him to drop his manufacturing activities. He proceeded to Chicago, determined to devote himself wholly to a literary career. Becoming a prominent figure in the "Chicago Renaissance," he achieved a mounting reputation, reaching a peak in *Winesburg, Ohio*. Anderson visited Paris in 1921 and upon his return resided at various places until settling down upon a farm near Troutdale, Virginia, in 1926. *Dark Laughter* (1925) was the last of his works to be widely read. He died at Colón, Panama Canal Zone, while on a good-will tour to South America.

Anderson's range was limited as compared with that of some of his contemporaries, but he had an extraordinary gift for conciseness and a sensitivity to often unexpressed aspects of character in individuals. Motivating all his writing was essentially one theme remarkably parallel to that of the Southern Agrarians: Deploring modern mechanization and materialism, he yearned for a "unity of things" in which all men would be brothers by nature. He was more successful in his shorter pieces than when he attempted novelistic studies of such subjects as collectivism in *Marching Men* (1917) or sexuality in *Many Marriages* (1923). Many of his short stories are of such classic excellence as to be indispensable anthology selections down to the present. Few authors seem capable of matching Anderson at his best in depicting the spiritual self-discovery of the provincial Midwesterner and the groping, pathetic emergence of awareness in underprivileged, inarticulate, starved natures. Hemingway, Wolfe, and many other novelists of the last fifty years are deeply indebted to Anderson. Faulkner asserted that Anderson was "the father of my generation of American writers and the tradition of American writing which our successors will carry on."

Winesburg, Ohio (1919) is thematically related to Edgar Lee Masters' *Spoon River Anthology*, but where Masters (see Chapter 2) had observed satirically, Anderson studied with abundant sympathy and understanding. Postimpressionist painting (Anderson was a gifted amateur painter) and the writings of Gertrude Stein (see Chapter 4) were also influential.

The people of Winesburg seem at first to be quite ordinary figures, but as we are drawn beneath the surfaces of their outward lives we become intensely aware that each one has within him some core of passion, some life impulse struggling to be free. They try to reach out and touch others who want to be touched though there is always some wall between them which usually prevents contact. Many of them soon grow tired of trying and failing, and hide themselves behind a cloak of ordinariness or eccentricity. Even so, high moments in each of their lives do occur when they truly touch another human being; and if these moments are soon over, whether they be filled with dread or joy, there is within them a nucleus of truth that can suddenly be grasped and held and shared.

George Willard, young newspaper reporter on the Winesburg *Eagle*, is a constantly recurring figure throughout the stories. He is Anderson himself, the observer, the person who must make sense out of and unify the many isolated moments in the lives of the people of Winesburg. It is his presence that gives the stories a sense of wholeness, and makes the reader feel that these lives have not existed in a vacuum. We are reassured of this in the last story, "Departure," when George finally leaves Winesburg and looks out the train window: "the town of Winesburg had disappeared and his life there had become but a background on which to paint the dreams of his manhood."

There is a central conflict around which many of the stories revolve: The old want to communicate the truth which they have found in life to the young, who, in turn, want to experience life for themselves. Elizabeth Willard, the mother of George, tries to tell her son in "Mother" that within him "there is a secret something that is striving to grow . . . the thing I let be killed in myself." But when a confrontation comes she cannot find words to express this feeling and there is only an air of strained embarrassment between them. The old eccentric Wing Biddle-baum in "Hands" tells George, "You must begin to dream. From this time on you must shut your ears to the roaring of the voices." He reaches out to touch George's hair but then he runs away because years ago he had been destroyed when he had tried to dream and to touch others.

In the story "Tandy" an old drunken stranger arrives in town and becomes a friend of Tom Hard, who has a five-year-old daughter. The stranger says that he is "a lover and have not found my thing to love." Thus he has created an imaginary world in which there is a woman with the courage to be loved, whom he calls Tandy. The stranger looks at Tom Hard's daughter and thinks that she may one day be the woman of his dreams. He tells her, "Be brave enough to dare to be loved. . . . Be Tandy." The stranger leaves and the little girl passionately declares that she wants to be called Tandy and there is nothing that Tom Hard can do to cure her of this desire. There seems to be a communication between the old stranger and the very young girl, the kind of communication that seems impossible between adults in the other stories.

The Triumph of the Egg (1921) contains some outstanding, un-forgettable short stories.

"I Want to Know Why" is a story of the awakening of an adolescent boy. The boy has been raised in the thoroughbred race-horse country of Kentucky and runs away with three other boys to see the races at Saratoga. He knows and loves the beautiful horses and feels that men should show the same strength of character that these animals seem to radiate. He idolizes the trainer of Sunstreak, who wins the big race, and afterward goes to seek him out. The boy sees the trainer with a group of men in a whorehouse cursing and bragging, and he cannot understand how the trainer, "who knows what he does, could see a horse like Sunstreak run, and kiss a woman like that the same day. . . . What did he do it for? I want to know why." The boy has been introduced to the paradoxes of adolescence and has begun the process of discovering the differences between men and women and between human beings and horses.

"The New Englander" describes one of those moments of self-dis-covery around which Anderson formed so many of his stories. From a stony New England farm thirty-five-year-old Elsie Leander and her parents travel west to Iowa and a new life. During the train journey through the broad plains Elsie senses new emotions working within her, emotions that for so long had been suppressed in the old closed society of New England. On the Iowa farm Elsie's life is outwardly much the same as it had been before, but she is aware of strong feelings that she does not understand. As the corn grows high in the fields she hears the voices of unborn children in the rustling of the tassels and "she wanted something but did not know what it was." One night as she lies in the cornfield below an approaching storm she sees her young girl cousin embrace and kiss a farm hand, and then Elsie is alone. The storm breaks and "the storm that had for years been gathering in her also broke."

Elsie's awakening to life and to sexuality takes on a simple and primitive beauty, for Anderson does not tamper with the natural course of events by confusing them with language but rather allows the senses to be the instructor in the mysteries of life. Elsie becomes aware of the resources within herself through the observation of life and growth around her and thus can make the step from the life of a closed-in, civilized New Englander to the acceptance of the free and natural passions which the Western prairie has awakened in her.

Horses and Men (1923) is another excellent collection of short stories. The best Sherwood Anderson short stories often consider the awakening of adolescent boys to the joys and pains of life. Anderson asserted that he sang the ugliness of life, the strange beauty of life pressing in on the mind of a boy. "I'm a Fool," frequently reprinted, is related by a middle-class youngster of nineteen who is working as a lowly swipe at the race tracks. In the grandstands he meets Wilbur Wessen and his lovely sister Lucy, whom the boy tries to impress by claiming that his father owns a stable of horses. By lying, the youth slams the door upon a renewal of this acquaintance. The narrator realizes his stupidity but fails to comprehend the forces at work. Commonplace standards are warring within him against the adventurous, "unrespectable" racing world. His need for social position conflicts with his need for love, and vitiates his chances to gain either. The fool blames himself without understanding that he is a victim of powerful social pressures.

Many Marriages (1923) is a strangely personalized novel set in the favorite Anderson locale of a small Midwestern community.

John Webster, a washing-machine manufacturer in a small Wisconsin town, lives a respectable and quite ordinary life with his wife and daughter. One day at the office a strange mood comes over him; he is suddenly more aware of his senses and the events going on around him than ever before. He realizes that he loves his secretary, Natalie Schwarz, and that she loves him, and he determines to leave his wife. But before he leaves he decides to tell his daughter, Jane, his reasons for leaving and the new vision of life that he has seen so that she will not fall into the same spiritual and physical malaise as her mother has. The major portion of the novel deals with Webster's bizarre confrontation with his wife and daughter. For several nights he moves about naked in his candlelit bedroom before a picture of the Virgin. Finally one night his wife and daughter walk in. Webster begins a series of reminiscences of his first meeting with his wife. A crushing feeling of horror takes hold of his wife as Webster examines their relationship in detail. When Webster leaves, his wife commits suicide. Jane is comforted by the family servant.

As in so many of his other works, Anderson is concerned in *Many Marriages* with the power of a single moment to change the course of a life. He explores several of these moments. The first one occurs in Webster's office, and it comes without any warning. Some mysterious power has taken hold of him and all he can do is submit to it. At first he is somewhat hesitant, but when he sees the revelations that are within his grasp in the new life style that forms in his mind, he willingly embraces the transformation.

The moment of confrontation in Webster's bedroom has powerful elements in it; in too closely defining the circumstances which led to the scene, however, Anderson loses that "sense of the moment" which he was able to achieve with so much more power in his short stories. Jane, the character who is most briefly defined, nevertheless emerges as the most powerful character, for she grasps the moment as fully and completely as she grasps the stone which her father leaves her as a remembrance. After Webster leaves she lies on her bed and is suddenly gripped by fear. In her mind she sees her mother drinking poison from the bathroom cabinet. And when she discovers that this has really happened she is not surprised. She has needed no language or physical senses to perceive a moment of death that is close by. This ability to transcend the ordinary modes of perception is something which John Webster understands but which he cannot fully experience because his mind is too cluttered with moral contradictions of society. He rejects his old concept of sexuality, but the habits of the old order prevent him from fully embracing his new life with Natalie.

Theodore Dreiser (1871–1945). Theodore Dreiser was the son of the superintendent of a mill in Terre Haute, Indiana. His older brother Paul, who changed his surname to Dresser, was one of the best-known writers of popular songs ("On the Banks of the Wabash" and "My Gal Sal") around the turn of the century. Dogged by family poverty, Theodore had a sketchy education which ended after his freshman year at Indiana University. The religious fanaticism of his ailing father and a priest's interdict on his reading of skeptical scientific and philosophical works caused his bitter renunciation of Roman Catholicism. He began a newspaper and magazine career in 1892, moving to various cities until settling in New York in 1895. His fellow workers and especially his brother Paul encouraged him to write fiction. His first novel, *Sister Carrie*, was suppressed shortly after its 1900 publication, but issued again later. The years following 1910 saw the completion and publication of a group of powerful novels. Of all his works, *An American Tragedy* (1925) was the most widely read. Dreiser visited Russia in 1927–28. He received the Award of Merit from the American Academy of Arts and Letters in 1944.

Intended as the definitive statement of Dreiser's philosophy, "The Mechanism Called Man" remained incomplete at his death and is still unpublished. The novels, however, effectively expound his naturalistic concepts. Life, he felt, is an inevitable tragedy. In modern America, he concluded, materialism is the primary motivating force and compels an individual to push for ever greater financial distinction. The overemphasis upon the money drive is countered by a moral puritanism rigorously repressing the sex drive and severely punishing transgressors. Puppets of these forces, some Americans may by chance be thrown to the top, but in this relentless competition happiness is a transitory, unlikely happenstance, while frustration and unhappiness are certainties.

Dreiser's prose is often cumbersome and awkward, the syntax and idiom frequently tortured and bungling, and the detailed description of every material fact about every character becomes heavy-footed. But the intense sincerity of the man makes him one of literature's mightiest truth seekers. Sinclair Lewis, in receiving the Nobel Prize, said of Dreiser: "Without his pioneering I doubt if any of us could, unless we liked to be sent to jail, seek to express life, beauty and terror."

Sister Carrie (1900) was anathematized with indignation at its appearance, but has since become a milestone in American literature. In 1889 at the age of eighteen Carrie Meeber leaves Columbia City, Wisconsin, for her sister's Chicago home. She is accosted on the train by Charles Drouet, a salesman and enthusiastic roué, who attempts to captivate her with a picture of urban delights. She is resistant at first, but a term of sweatshop labor in a shoe factory so discourages her that she forms a liaison with him. Through Drouet she meets George Hurstwood, manager of a Chicago saloon. The infatuated Hurstwood, who is already married, ruins himself for Carrie, stealing from his employer and fleeing with her to Montreal. Finally, without funds, the two descend upon New York. Hurstwood becomes a chronic ne'er-do-well, and Carrie tries the theater as a source of livelihood. Under the name Carrie Madenda she achieves a celebrated stage career, by which time she has abandoned Hurstwood, who falls to begging and commits suicide. Carrie, on her side, hardly recognizes that the magnitude of her achievement and eminence of her position afford her remarkably little satisfaction.

Dreiser's quarter-of-a-century struggle in support of *Sister Carrie*'s publication typifies his own epic dimensions and giant determination. The novel's ultimate acceptance dramatizes a significant shift in attitude from ideas prevalent at the century's outset. By previous standards every fallen woman of fiction ought to pay the penalty, yet Carrie appears to have thrived on sin. However, it is only appearance. Dreiser sees "the illusion of the self-made" as the ironic epitome of all illusions. *Sister Carrie* is unsettlingly deterministic. Its active principle is less the individual personality than the interaction of mass-generated economic forces that push, squeeze, and propel the characters along unchosen paths. As if in obedience to inexorable physical laws Carrie rises and Hurstwood sinks because each has accumulated a certain velocity in that direction. Carrie exploits her sex and modest talents for material gain, but the factors principally responsible for her success are random ones, such as time and place. Even her physical charms are accidents of birth, and the use she puts them to could have had any number of other consequences.

Jennie Gerhardt (1911) did not appear until a full decade later due to the poor reception accorded *Sister Carrie.* More than any other work, it draws upon the actual life of the Dreiser family.

Because William Gerhardt, a stern Lutheran glass blower, is unemployed, his wife works as a charwoman in the best hotel of Columbus, Ohio, in 1880. The laundry she does for a hotel resident, Senator Brander, is delivered by her daughter, eighteen-year-old Genevieve (Jennie). Brander seduces Jennie and he dies of typhoid while she is pregnant. The elder Gerhardt angrily drives out Jennie, who goes to live in Cleveland. As a maid in the home of the wealthy Bracebridges, Jennie proves attractive to their house guest, Lester Kane. Against the wishes of his upper-class family Lester makes Jennie his mistress, but pressure from the Kanes, especially the will of Lester's father, finally forces him to break with Jennie and marry Letty Gerald of his own class. Some years later he summons Jennie as he is dying.

Unlike the heroine of *Sister Carrie,* Jennie has an unlimited capacity for selfless affection. It is her warm, outgoing nature that sustains her and at the end leaves her more content with a broken life than Carrie was in seeming triumph. The stern patriarch, her father, is one of Dreiser's memorable characterizations; finding that Jennie alone among his children genuinely loves him, he grows close to her as his life draws to an end. Although Lester Kane's intentions toward Jennie are admirable, Lester is a modern skeptic without any fixed convictions, who eventually realizes that he cannot "fly in the face of society."

The Financier (1912) begins the Cowperwood trilogy, collectively designated as the *Trilogy of Desire.* Evoked by the era of "muckrakers," this series is based upon the career of the real Charles T. Yerkes, a mogul who dominated the finance of late nineteenth-century Chicago and then attempted equally spectacular coups in London, England.

Frank Algernon Cowperwood is born of a Philadelphia family that regards life "as a business situation or deal." At ten he observes a lobster slaying a squid in a fish tank and concludes that all existence is the overcoming of the weak by the strong. If squids are preyed on by lobsters, "men lived on men." Gigantic in his appetite for power and sex, Cowperwood competes ruthlessly, manipulates everything to his will, and at last leaves Philadelphia for the more challenging and lucrative environment of Chicago.

Cowperwood is the American success story, not in the Horatio Alger mode, but very much as it actually was. Indeed, Dreiser's account is generally more credible than Gustavus Myers' factual *The History of the Great American Fortunes* (1910), to which it was considerably indebted. "Never fail, never get caught" is Cowperwood's motto. Cowperwood is caught once—in the business panic of 1871—and is sent to prison, but he bounces back imperturbably. While maintaining an outward appearance of respectability, Cowperwood is a heartless buccaneer in high finance and a libertine in private life. His socially correct marriage to Lillian Semple is thrust aside by the attraction of Aileen Butler, the strong-willed daughter of an Irish political boss. The very absence of any spirituality in Cowperwood, along with his remarkable ability to accept and ride with changes, makes him perfectly adapted to the self-interested scramble for wealth. It almost seems that Dreiser had a secret admiration for his hero and his sort of flamboyant success.

The Titan (1914) continues the Cowperwood narrative in Chicago and New York settings.

With Aileen Butler now his wife after his divorce from Lillian Semple, Cowperwood joins the economic elite in Chicago. His speculation in grain and stocks is only a prelude to a massive take-over of Chicago public utilities. Cowperwood adopts the guise of philanthropist and presents an astronomical observatory to the University of Chicago. His trips to Europe result in a huge and expensive collection of art objects. By now he has tired of Aileen and pursues other women, especially Berenice Fleming, the daughter of an ex-proprietor of a bordello. Berenice accompanies him to Europe when competitors weaken his position in American finance.

This novel, though impressive, is not the equal of *The Financier*. Dreiser's biggest difficulty lies in amplifying the character of Cowperwood to accommodate his enlarged stature in business. The details of financial transaction on the corporation-building scale become more abstract and less dramatic than Cowperwood's former infighting. He has a succession of mistresses. Aileen, neglected by husband and Chicago society, takes to drink and pathetic flirtations. Cowperwood continues to forge onward, essentially unchanged. The final book of the trilogy, *The*

Stoic, appears later in the present discussion, as it was not published until 1947.

The "Genius" (1915), in part essentially autobiographical, should have been one of Dreiser's masterpieces, but it suffers from closeness to the subject and from undigested masses of experience.

Eugene Tennyson Witla has artistic yearnings quite inappropriate to his native town, Alexandria, Illinois. He proceeds to Chicago where he works in the art department of a newspaper and becomes engaged to Angela Blue. He goes to New York, and rises there as an illustrator. There, too, he carries on several love affairs, the most important with a concert singer, Christina Channing. She rejects him in favor of her career, and he marries Angela. Overwork, dissipation, and complications in his married life cause a nervous breakdown and dry up his sources of artistic inspiration. Eugene changes his career and works up to the post of managing director of a large publishing firm. Concurrently he falls in love with a debutante, Suzanne Dale. Suzanne's mother crushes the affair, and Eugene is discharged for his indiscretion. Angela dies in childbirth, and the repentant Eugene rededicates himself to artistic attainment and the care of his baby daughter.

The theme is a mighty one: the contest between artistic integrity and the impulses that threaten to distract it. To counter his undisciplined sexual drives Eugene seeks the stability of marriage, but the sort of ordered existence Angela offers is not one to which he can adjust. Her decent, solid, conformist way of life acts as a check upon his imagination; yet he begins to feel the gnawings of guilt. Eugene's final rehabilitation as an artist occurs after a period of objective self-evaluation, in which he begins to realize the limitations he must place upon his life if it is to be effective.

An American Tragedy (1925), Dreiser's best-known novel, is based upon the 1906 drowning murder of pregnant Grace Brown in Big Moose Lake, upper New York, by her lover, Chester Gillette. Of several parallel slayings Dreiser considered this the most typical and most dramatic.

Clyde Griffiths, the young leading character of *An American Tragedy,* grows up in Kansas City where his parents operate an impoverished evangelist mission for drunkards and derelicts. Clyde has no sympathy for his parents' fervent piety, is embarrassed when forced to take part in the street theatrics they stage to attract converts, and ashamed of the sordidness of their daily existence. As a bellhop in a large hotel Clyde is introduced to the spectacle of affluence, and soon begins spending his earnings and tips on good clothes and luxuries for himself. He becomes involved—as a passenger—in an automobile accident in which a little girl is killed. Fearing the consequences of guilt by association, he takes pains to avoid the police interrogators, leaves town, and finally gets a job as a bellhop in Chicago. At this time a prosperous uncle in Lycurgus, New York, offers Clyde work in his collar factory, which he accepts. Before long many of his leisure hours are devoted to an affair with Roberta Alden, a quiet but responsive mill hand from his department at the factory. Suddenly after a brief meeting at a dinner party in his uncle's house, Clyde discovers himself the recipient of attentions from Sondra Finchley, a debutante belonging to the town's best society. Sondra has been a good friend of Gilbert Griffiths, Clyde's cousin whom he resembles in looks. The attraction between Clyde and Sondra ripens, and Clyde realizes that he stands on the immediate threshold of wealth, position, and marriage to a desirable young woman. Then Roberta informs him that she is pregnant and expects him to marry her. Clyde senses a deep conflict within himself and sees no ready solution. He feels that he must rid himself of Roberta's claim on him. Finally, inspired by a newspaper article, Clyde hesitantly commences to plot Roberta's murder. Knowing that she cannot swim, he rows her to a remote area of Big Bittern Lake, intending to capsize the boat. His determination deserts him at the last moment, but the boat overturns by accident and Clyde watches passively as his object is fulfilled. When he is apprehended and tried, however, a reconstruction of his movements prior to the drowning transparently reveals Clyde's original design. He is condemned to die. During the trial the Lycurgus Griffithses prevent an insanity plea, which they feel might reflect upon the family. And the Finchleys are able to keep Sondra and her name out of the proceedings.

In the last days remaining to him before his execution Clyde finds comfort in his mother's presence and the guidance of a minister; and he arrives at something like an understanding of the nature and magnitude of his guilt, his lack of moral strength, and his indifferent attitude toward this deficiency.

In calling this tragedy American, Dreiser stresses his strong conviction that the emphasis upon material success in American life is a constant danger and frequently the cause of tragic events.

The Bulwark (1946) had been conceived as early as 1910 and was announced for publication as early as 1917. Nonnaturalistic, it reflects the strong religious bent of Dreiser's later period.

Solon Barnes, son of Quaker parents, is taken from his native Maine to a New Jersey Quaker community, a suburb of Philadelphia. Unshakable in his principles of religion and morality, he rises high in Philadelphia banking. To his chagrin, his children rebel against their austere background and, in Solon's eyes, go forth to sin. After the suicide of his son Stewart and his wife's painful death, Solon resigns from the bank and falls into despondency. Etta, a daughter who had adopted a bohemian way of life, returns to comfort him. Before his death Solon finds a philosophy of love for all living things, faith in God and revelation, and resignation to his sufferings.

The title is ironic. To his coreligionists the undeviating Solon (named for the ancient Greek lawgiver) indeed seemed a bulwark, and for his business associates he was a sturdy façade of moral rectitude behind which they could indulge in irresponsible speculation and suspicious business practices. But he could not protect his family and eventually himself from the worst buffets of life. His denunciation of the practices of his fellow directors evokes the laconic comment that Solon's principles are "too high for these days." Dispirited, Solon finds a transcendental faith in the *Journal* of John Woolman. Though cosmic patterns are beyond understanding, Solon observes: "Surely there must be a Creative Divinity, and so a purpose, behind all of this variety and beauty and tragedy of life." Etta has the last word, and it is Dreiser's too. Her brother Orville is surprised that his once rebellious sister should weep at Solon's death. She replies, "Oh, I am not crying for myself, or for Father—I am crying for *life*."

The Stoic (1947) was begun about 1914, worked upon over a period of many years, and was still not in final form at the novelist's death. Although it completes the Cowperwood series, it is properly considered separate from the two earlier volumes in the series because it is the work of the older Dreiser, and is less naturalistic.

Cowperwood, now in London, has plans to create a monopoly out of the London underground (subway). However, as he ages he suffers increasingly from Bright's disease. Estranged from his wife, Aileen, he lives with his mistress, Berenice Fleming, while continuing to involve himself with other women. Contemplating his approaching death, he hopes to immortalize his name with a Cowperwood Art Gallery and a Cowperwood Hospital. When he returns to die in New York, the angry Aileen refuses him sanctuary. He expires in a large hotel. All his grandeur fades away as lawsuits—the fruit of his questionable business ventures—eat up the estate. Aileen dies and is buried with Cowperwood. Berenice spends five years in India, where she becomes a convert to Hindu philosophy. She returns to raise the money for a Cowperwood Hospital.

The first two volumes of the trilogy present the thesis that the "superman," abundantly endowed for the "survival of the fittest," will dominate and mold his fellows regardless of prevailing moral attitudes and conventions. The concluding volume contends that after using him for her purposes Nature will impersonally destroy the superman and all his works. The final novel of the series has weaknesses. Dreiser does not develop the London setting with the solidity that confers impressive weight upon his American episodes.

The *Best Short Stories of Theodore Dreiser* (1947), edited by Howard Fast, includes famous Dreiser short stories of almost four decades. Many are naturalistic, such as "The Second Choice," about a working girl who throws over a drab clerk to whom she is engaged in favor of a much more attractive man, who quickly discards her. The most frequently anthologized story is the atypical "The Lost Phoebe." In this poetized account a bereaved and mentally unbalanced old man searches for his wife whom he cannot believe dead, and eventually pursues a hallucination of her over the edge of a cliff to his own death.

Willa Cather (1873–1947). Willa Sibert Cather was born near Winchester, Virginia, in 1873, but grew up in Nebraska. Her first writings appeared in a student literary magazine, which she edited while at the University of Nebraska, 1892–95. Also during her college days she wrote for a Lincoln, Nebraska, newspaper and in 1896 she went to Pittsburgh, Pennsylvania, as editor of the *Home Monthly*. From 1901 to 1906 she taught English in a Pennsylvania high school. Starting with *McClure's Magazine* in 1906, she rapidly rose to the post of managing editor. In 1912 she quit journalism to devote all her subsequent time to fiction writing. Never marrying, she traveled extensively but maintained residence in the East.

The first Cather novel, *Alexander's Bridge* (1912), is somewhat in the manner of Henry James. Subsequently Willa Cather found her characteristic approach in a style based partly upon the Greco-Roman classics, but largely upon the French masters, especially Flaubert. Her subject in several of her early novels is the reaction of the soul of Europeanized man to the environment of the New World, generally to the Western prairies. Whereas Rølvaag treats comparable material in an epic-romantic fashion, Willa Cather prefers a calm, restrained handling of a small, fully controlled canvas.

O Pioneers! (1913) has some of the qualities of Hardy's pastoral novels.

John Bergson, an emigrant from Sweden to Hanover, Nebraska, has died and left his daughter, Alexandra, in her twenties, as the mainstay of the farm and the family: her unresourceful mother and her brothers Lou, Oscar, and Emil. Alexandra becomes attracted to Carl Linstrum, but chooses to remain single for the sake of her dependent relatives. She befriends a Czech girl, Marie Tovesky, who marries the farmer Frank Shabata. Disastrously, Emil Bergson falls in love with Marie, and both are killed by her husband. When Linstrum returns, Alexandra at last agrees to marry him.

Alexandra's will and tenacity are a mighty force, but their potential is inadequately realized. She has a recurrent dream of a giant figure who effortlessly carries her swiftly across the fields. This represents the total unconscious psyche confident of vast creative power. The people with whom Alexandra must live and whom she must sustain offer no fulfillment. Her brothers Lou and Oscar demonstrate the vulgarization that the local scene can inflict upon newcomers. Alexandra must make do with what is around her, and accept her incessant responsibilities. Her resilient personality carries her through both boredom and bereavement. Alexandra's only equal is the immemorial earth of the great plains with its ceaseless rhythms.

The Song of the Lark (1915) is the story of Thea Kronborg of Moonstone, Colorado, in the desert section of the state, who has won recognition in her small town for her splendid singing voice. Railway worker Ray Kennedy, who dies in an accident, leaves the money for her to escape her coarse family and dreary community to study music in Chicago. She gains attention but falls ill. Wealthy Fred Ottenburg helps her to recuperate, but they are prevented from marriage by Fred's estranged wife. Later Thea becomes a noted Wagnerian soprano at the Metropolitan Opera. Finally she marries Fred, but her career continues to be of first importance.

Thea and many other Cather characters are skilled in one of the fine arts. These talented Cather people are, first of all, escapees from the stifling towns and austere acres of the prairie. Like the novelist herself, they yearn for an aesthetic, cultured life. The fascination of the life of an artist is eloquently developed. But Thea pays a price for her success. Devotion to art demands of her a stark asceticism which for a long time prevents any hope of fulfillment as a wife.

My Ántonia (1918), often considered Cather's best novel, employs a narrator, Jim Burden, who has little direct influence on the action.

The Shimerda family from Bohemia, like many pioneers in that raw Nebraska country, have a poor farm and live in a cave. Mr. Shimerda, a gifted musician who yearns for the past and the cultural centers of Europe, puts an end to his own life. His daughter Ántonia tries to hold the family together on the soil. Later, in the town of Black Hawk, Ántonia works as a hired girl, is involved in an affair, becomes pregnant, then is cast aside. She returns to the countryside, where her illegitimate child is born. Subsequently she marries Anton Cuzak and enthusiastically enters upon a home life of her own.

Narrator Burden is an intellectual disgruntled with provincial Nebraska; because of his restlessness his path crosses Ántonia's at successive stages of life. Mr. Shimerda has the frail, sensitive temperament of the artist; his new homeland offers hardship without intellectual satisfactions. It is revelatory that he dresses himself meticulously as he prepares to kill himself. Ántonia is an epitome of hope and liveliness, but duty and human suffering compel her to stick to the task. Burden last sees her in middle age, the mother of a numerous brood, content amidst her surroundings.

Youth and the Bright Medusa (1920) collects the best Cather short stories, ranging as far back as *The Troll Garden* (1905), her first published volume. These stories are all concerned with the appeal of art—the Medusa is the attractive and sometimes fatal allure of art to youth. "Paul's Case" tells of a Pittsburgh slum boy desperately dreaming of an artistic life. He steals money to live in high style in New York until pursuers begin to catch up with him; then he commits suicide. "The Sculptor's Funeral," probably Cather's most famous short piece, stigmatizes the narrow life of the Kansas home town to which the artist's corpse is returned for burial. Townsfolk scorn the artist as a local boy who went wrong in the purlieus of sinful art. Among those gathered around the coffin, only the town's alcoholic lawyer is able to recognize and speak out about the envy and distrust that underlie the community's contempt for genius.

One of Ours (1922) received the Pulitzer Prize in 1923. Cather appreciated the award, as she considered Claude her favorite hero.

Gopher Prairie, Nebraska, seems confining to young Claude Wheeler, although it is quite to the taste of his brother Bayliss, a farm-machinery salesman. Family finances prevent Claude from completing the college education that he wants, and he is maneuvered into marriage with the fanatically religious Enid Royce. In her zeal for good works she soon deserts him to tend a sick relative in China. Claude stagnates in Gopher Prairie for a time, and then joins the Army to fight in France during World War I. Through friends there he acquaints himself with French culture, but he dies in battle before he is able to explore the new possibilities open to him. The home community can satisfy Bayliss, but the seeker for aesthetic order, like Claude, can find little of importance there.

A Lost Lady (1923) marks two important developments in Miss Cather. First, her attitude toward the modern age of mechanization and materialism has grown from antipathy to revulsion. And, second, stylistically she has hewn to more rigidly classical diction and structure; her own term was the "novel *démeublé*," stripped of all superfluities and tightened to the point of demanding functional value for every episode and sentence.

From his boyhood Niel Herbert is enraptured with the vivacious Marian Forrester, the wife of Captain Forrester, an aging pioneer railroader in Sweet Water, Colorado, a railroad town. Marian seeks diversion, but as time passes she finds she must settle for less and less.

Her affair with the eligible Frank Ellinger is terminated by his marriage. After Forrester's financial failure and death, she takes up with Ivy Peters, an unsavory businessman who chooses to marry elsewhere and appropriate the abandoned Forrester mansion for himself. Marian marries an Englishman of some means and settles with him in South America.

To the censorious small town, Marian is a "lost lady" because of her escapades. She possesses unquestionable charm, an outgoing, affectionate nature, telling the narrator, "I feel such a power to live in me, Niel." He, however, cannot forgive her because "she preferred life on any terms."

The Professor's House (1925) tells the story of a turning point in the life of Professor Godfrey St. Peter, a middle-aged historian. The title refers to the old dwelling that St. Peter clings to when his wife insists on moving to a newer abode.

As an escape from the dissatisfactions of his personal life it has become Godfrey St. Peter's solution to lose himself in antiquarian pursuits. His specialty is the Spanish period of American history. St. Peter cherishes fond memories of his finest student, Tom Outland, a casualty of World War I, who had come to him after discovering an ancient cliff dwelling while working in the Southwest. As he edits Outland's writings the professor rediscovers his own youthful self, his "twin." But his disaffection with his present circumstances is still so great that he almost lets himself succumb to the seeping gas from a defective outlet in the old house's attic. The intervention of a faithful old servant sets him on the path of rededication to his principles.

The new house built at his wife Lillian's instigation has become what he most abhors. Disinherited of the land, the professor indulges himself in reveries of the past of which the Outland account is an actual, concrete manifestation. Fortunately, a demonstration of simple human affection is able to revive his spirits and his determination to persevere.

Death Comes for the Archbishop (1927) is one of the great gems of classic art in American fiction. Although the novel is based on documentary accounts, the historical Bishop Lamy of Santa Fe is renamed Jean Marie Latour and his historical vicar-general Macheboeuf becomes Father Joseph Vaillant.

In 1851 two French priests arrive in Santa Fe: Father Latour, appointed Vicar Apostolic of New Mexico, and his close associate, Father Vaillant. The hostile Mexican priests force Latour to journey to Durango to get authorization documents. Back in his diocese he struggles with Christian patience and fortitude against all obstacles: the huge empty land, villainous gringos like Buck Scales, the apathy of civil authorities, and the enmity of inefficient and corrupt Mexican clerics. Latour is successful, culminating his efforts by the building of the cathedral of Santa Fe. Vaillant becomes the first Bishop of Colorado, dying there. Latour becomes an archbishop and dies satisfied with his labors for the faith. With incisive, economical strokes, Miss Cather limns the successive layers of Southwestern culture: the primitive paganism of the Indians, the decayed aristocracy of the Mexican grandees and the animal-like grip upon the land by the peons, and the pragmatic vigor of the *Norteamericanos*. Latour and Vaillant are noble representatives of the civilizing force of European society. Their mission is to elevate the spirit; they wish not to supplant but to integrate and to inspire. Consequently, whatever the adversities and even the incomplete accomplishments, Latour and Vaillant are never frustrated souls, like many previous Cather characters.

In that setting, that age, that faith, Miss Cather finds a wholeness and grandeur implicitly stigmatizing the "divided aims" and "palsied hearts" of today.

Shadows on the Rock (1931) is a novel of the early Canadian wilderness. The town of Quebec at the time is a tiny stronghold of European civilization in a vast and wild land. Cécile Eclair, the young daughter of apothecary Euclide Eclair, is caught up in the middle of two cultures—the old culture of France with its long-held traditions and laws, its political and religious arguments, and the new and unformed culture of the wilderness with its violence and hardship. The culture of France had been deeply ingrained in Cécile by her dead mother and by her father. But Pierre Charron, the young fur trapper, tells her of another side of the wilderness. There is a natural beauty and a wild freedom to be found there. He disdains the veneer of civilization, and those habits of thought and action which Cécile had believed to be so necessary to life. Cécile and her father had always assumed that they would be returning to France one day, but upon the death of the old Governor General of Canada in whose service Eclair has been, they are forced to stay in Canada. And Cécile knows that that is what she really wanted. She marries Pierre and has four sons by him. They will be the "true Canadians," the pioneers of the new land who will have no memories of the old order to follow them into the wilderness.

Obscure Destinies (1932) contains three notable novellas of Nebraska life. "Neighbor Rosicky" tells of an aged Czech farmer dying of heart trouble; his daughter-in-law, impatient with country life because of her small-town background, learns from him a sense of the primordial relationships of man to the earth. "Old Mrs. Harris" concerns a Virginia grandmother brought to Nebraska by her daughter Victoria; when the old woman can no longer work, her annoyed daughter neglects her, but Mandy, the servant girl, compassionately aids Mrs. Harris. "Two

Friends" pictures a child's desolation when two elderly men, long friends, quarrel and part.

Not Under Forty (1936), essays by Miss Cather, stipulates her credo of classic art and her deep dissatisfaction with modern life and literature.

Sinclair Lewis (1885–1951). Harry Sinclair Lewis was the son of a physician in Sauk Center, Minnesota. After a year at Oberlin College, he transferred to Yale where he received his A.B. in 1908. His first literary efforts appeared in Yale undergraduate publications; and during his senior year he worked for a time at Helicon Hall, Upton Sinclair's socialistic colony. From 1908 until 1916 (when he began to give all his time to writing) he held various editorial posts in Iowa and in the East. In 1930 he was the first American to receive the Nobel Prize for literature. His first wife was Grace Hegger, and his second, the well-known columnist Dorothy Thompson. His later years were saddened by his own illness and by the death in World War II of his son, Wells. Sinclair Lewis died in Rome, Italy.

Lewis was probably the most highly appreciated American novelist of his day. The scope of his work was wide and ambitious enough to encompass many aspects of our national life, and he was wittily critical of much that he treated. His principal targets were the smug ignorance and intransigent provincialism of the American small town, and the hypocrisy resulting from the ubiquitous profit motive. His weapon is caustic but intelligently balanced satire that exposes meanness and pettiness. He wrote four lesser novels prior to *Main Street,* the work that brought him instant and abundant recognition.

Main Street (1920) is a barbed critique of a small town similar to the one in which Lewis himself was raised. It marks an epoch in American literature. This was the first novel to attack a beloved American institution and still become a best seller.

A recent college graduate, idealistic Carol Milford has an abiding faith in the worth of a literary education. When she marries Dr. Will Kennicott and accompanies him to Gopher Prairie, Minnesota, she pits herself against the intellectual indolence of the town. The inertia of the townspeople and her uncompromising overzealousness combine to defeat her every project. Disheartened, Carol leaves her husband to go to Washington and help in the war effort. Finally she comes back to Gopher Prairie with a more realistic and patient attitude.

The phrase "Main Street" for a long time acquired specific connotations from this novel, altering the image of the small town from the good-natured, equitable bulwark of American democracy to a moral and cultural backwater. The dominant theme of the book is disillusionment as Carol is repeatedly overpowered by the limited outlook of

Gopher Prairie, while the townsfolk boast of their progressive spirit. Their vaunted morality comes from narrow minds capable of cruelty toward any deviation from their rigid conformity. Lewis is rather fair even in his realistic satire. Will Kennicott manifests the worst and the best characteristics of Gopher Prairie. He and the town have enormous powers of endurance, and in their rigid way get each day's job done and keep the earth reassuringly revolving upon its axis. The concluding lines of the novel dramatically confront the romantic actions of Carol with the matter-of-fact solidity of Will and Gopher Prairie.

Babbitt (1922) is one of the few American novels to contribute a word to the language. Drawing upon the chief character in Lewis' novel, the expression "a babbitt" is a bit harsh and oversimplifies the man who gives the title to the novel. In this general sense, a babbitt has come to mean a man who conforms unthinkingly to prevailing standards and has no appreciation for artistic or intellectual values.

George F. Babbitt is a reasonably successful real estate salesman in Zenith, "the Zip City," in the state of Winnemac (Wisconsin, Minnesota Michigan). He is continually praising the American way of business life and the local chamber of commerce, and most admires those personal qualities that make a man an effective sales representative and a lively companion on a train trip. He lauds his job and his city to himself and anyone who will listen. Of art and similar subtle gratifications of the spirit he is oblivious.

Babbitt hardly thinks of himself as a dull fellow, and believes the practice of a little mild hypocrisy is innocent, even appropriate, in a man of his position and temperament. Although vocally devoted to law and morality he is proud of the Prohibition-interdicted liquor he can offer his guests; from the safe distance of an out-of-town convention he is frolicsomely unfaithful to his commonplace wife and two uninspiring children. But at forty-six, a bit overweight and slightly balding, he pauses to question the real significance of his life. His more reflective friend Paul Riesling is of no avail to Babbitt in this identity crisis. Riesling, floundering, turns upon his own wife and murders her.

Babbitt strikes up an affair with Mrs. Tanis Judique, but the anxieties of socially compromising behavior soon frighten him away. This is the last episode in Babbitt's brief, abortive search for new values. He has hopes, however, for his son, Ted, who has bolted from the conformist path to make his own way in the world.

The story considers Babbitt in his middle years. The stirrings within him demand some psychic satisfaction; but taste, value, beauty, sex, religion, art, soul do not exist for him. He does achieve a sort of self-realization in coming to understand that he actually contributes nothing to society. His is a typical parasitic job. His daily existence offers him extensive material comforts but the competitive fever of making money really provides no genuine gratification, only status. At the novel's outset Zenith, whose very name means the highest pinnacle, is labeled a city "for giants." The next hundred pages minutely detail one day in George Babbitt's life, a life anything but gigantic. Individualism and independence are verbally extolled, but stifled in practice. In Lewis' depiction of Midwestern capitalism there are more victims than villains, which substantiates his statement, "I wrote *Babbitt* not out of hatred for him but out of love."

Arrowsmith (1925), the story of an idealistic medical crusader, reflects the Lewis family's close association with the medical profession and its early influence upon Sinclair. His brother as well as his father were physicians. The novel was written in collaboration with Paul de Kruif, a popularizer of modern science who supplied technical details.

Martin Arrowsmith, a young medical student, displays a devotion to his studies so rare that he attracts the attention of Dr. Max Gottlieb, the university's irascible specialist in research. He becomes Gottlieb's protégé and is taught, in addition to laboratory technique and scientific method, contempt for the sloppy and profit-seeking medicine he sees around him. After graduation Martin finds himself married to a loyal and adoring wife, Leora, and practicing in a small Midwestern town, where his patients are smug, superstitious, and resistant to progressive ideas. In frustration Martin moves on to Nautilus, Iowa, and directorship of the town's public-health department. When he opposes the laxity of his predecessor and presses for genuine reform he makes powerful enemies who force him to leave. A brief term at Chicago's prestigious Roncefield Clinic shows him medicine in its most mercenary form. Finally he finds refuge in New York at the McGurk Institute, where his old mentor Gottlieb has offered him a post.

At McGurk, Martin is free to undertake meaningful independent research and is soon on the verge of developing an important new method of immunization. But by his reluctance to publish prematurely he loses credit for the discovery to a European researcher, and must content himself with empirical testing of the antitoxin. He goes with Leora and Gustaf Sondelius, a celebrated epidemic fighter, to the West Indies to combat an outbreak of bubonic plague. His aggressive attack on the disease eventually succeeds, but it first takes the life of his devoted Leora and then of Sondelius.

Martin returns to New York to stagnate for a time at McGurk. A second marriage to a society woman becomes increasingly irksome. At last he and a like-minded friend, Terry Wickett, cloister themselves in a

Vermont forest cabin to give themselves entirely to medical investigations.

Lewis' criticism of many aspects of the American medical profession is probably more caustic and one-sided than any position in his other major novels. The various unworthy physicians that appear in the pages of *Arrowsmith* are not misguided victims of an empty-valued society, but knowing exploiters of that society.

In the case of Martin, Lewis has attempted a balanced appraisal. Like Gottlieb, Martin can be peevish, overdemanding, and acerbic when the sanctity of his calling is slighted or misapprehended. But where Gottlieb brings to his work the realism and personal detachment that science demands, Martin tends to petulance if recognition is slow or lacking. His admiration for Sondelius, who is more quarantine enforcer and water boiler than pharmacologist, reveals his vision of medicine to be unduly romantic. He basks in the adulation of a beautiful woman while his wife dies elsewhere, but when celebrity status is his he is unprepared and unappreciative. As the book ends he seems ready to embark on a new and important part of his career.

Elmer Gantry (1927) in its satire of evangelical Protestantism was occasioned by the furor over the Scopes "monkey" trial in 1925 and the careers of Billy Sunday and Aimee Semple McPherson.

Elmer Gantry is a clergyman who uses huckstering techniques in public preaching and in his private sex life. Ordained as a Baptist, he escapes from Lulu and from a conventional pulpit to be a revivalist with the lady evangelist Shawn Falconer. He becomes a Methodist, feels restive in marriage to Cleo, manages to thwart Hettie (who threatened him with public exposure). In the last sentence Gantry solemnly intones, "We shall yet make these United States a moral nation."

Lewis brilliantly describes the orgy of a revival meeting, an unattractive church picnic, the political jockeying of clerics. "The book I wrote," Lewis declared, "is what I saw." What he saw was the death of religion in the scoundrel Elmer Gantry. Gantry actually has no religion, as the Reverend Andrew Pengilly (one of the few commendable clerics pictured in the novel) astutely observes. Exhibitionist religiosity is only the means of Gantry's drive for sex, fame, money, and power. Gantry is close to a naturalistic character, molded by his background and compelled by forces he does not understand. Gantry has sympathetic traits, his vigor and brashness, and he rides to success. Lewis considers only one aspect of religion, evangelical fundamentalism, and he offers no substitute for the charlatanry of Gantry. Thus he is unable to give the book the truly tragic quality which his theme seems to demand.

Dodsworth (1929) is generally considered the last major novel by Lewis.

Samuel Dodsworth, an able engineer, builds the Revelation Automobile Company into an industrial success and sells it to the Unit Automotive Company. He then yields to his wife Fran's desire for a trip abroad. In France, Dodsworth lags behind his wife in *savoir-faire* and feels awkward in the salons and social gatherings. Leaving Fran immersed in her manifold activities he makes a brief trip back to the United States, returning to find that Fran's new sophistication has encouraged her to take Arnold Israel for a lover. She repeats this performance in Berlin with Kurt Obersdorf and requests a divorce. Sam acquiesces on the condition she delay for a reasonable period, and goes himself to Italy where he finds the understanding he seeks in Edith Cortwright. When Fran's romance with Kurt is overturned she attempts a reconciliation with Sam, but he has seen too much of her superficiality and instead chooses to continue with Edith.

Fran had come to feel that the average American male is too preoccupied with business and money-making to prove a good lover or good husband. Sam recognizes the cultural heritage of Europe, but considers Europeans just as materialistic as Americans. Americans, he asserts, are now thinking deeply and growing culturally.

Basically the novel is a story of American married life. Sam is a quiet, considerate chap who long endures but at last rebels against the snobbish, superficial, sexually frigid Fran whose sole interest in life seems to be social climbing. The trip to Europe becomes a journey of self-discovery and discovery of America by Sam Dodsworth. Sam is Lewis' most attractive character. *Dodsworth* demonstrates the author's ability to write a novel as a story and not a tract.

Unfortunately, the later Lewis novels never fulfilled the promise of *Dodsworth*. Nevertheless, they had many readers, especially: *Ann Vickers* (1933); *It Can't Happen Here* (1935), about the possibility of a Fascist coup in the United States; and *Cass Timberlane* (1945).

F. Scott Fitzgerald (1896–1940). Francis Scott Key Fitzgerald was a direct descendant of the writer of our national anthem, for whom he was named. He was born at St. Paul, Minnesota. On both sides of the family there had been wealth, but the novelist's father had limited means. Even so, the family made it possible for Fitzgerald to enter Princeton in 1913; but illness and low grades caused him to leave in 1917 without a degree. He served as an army lieutenant from 1917 to 1919 without going overseas. Upon his discharge, he worked for an advertising agency, writing fiction at night. Following the success of his first novel in 1920 he married Zelda Sayre. With a good income he lived extravagantly, moving constantly to different spots here and in Europe. During these years he was in Paris at the time that Ernest Hemingway was there and they knew each other well. In 1927 he began extensive writing for Hollywood, and in the same year his wife began to suffer from mental illness which thereafter kept her in sanatoriums for much of the rest of the novelist's life. This personal problem was paramount in Fitzgerald's "crack-up" of 1935–37 when alcoholism and his own illness stymied most of his writing.

Fitzgerald popularized the label "Jazz Age" for the 1920s. As Sinclair Lewis was the great analyst of the 1920s' middle class, Fitzgerald was the great observer of the ways of the wealthy, whose habits seemed to exemplify the spirit of the twenties. In the 1930s many dismissed Fitzgerald as merely the chronicler of the previous decade, but since World War II his reputation has continually soared. He is now recognized as one of the notable stylists of the American novel, though a traditionalist rather than an innovator. He is also considered one of the few American novelists with a deeply penetrating concept of love, a concept which is often a departure point rather than the focus of American fiction. He is also seen as a significant critic of modern American culture.

This Side of Paradise (1920), his first novel, was described by Fitzgerald as "a somewhat edited history of me and my imagination."

Amory Blaine, spoiled scion of wealth, enjoys Princeton life, although he is too puny for football. His fun is dampened by the death of a fellow student, Dick Humbird, in an automobile accident. After war service, 1917–19, Amory works in an advertising firm. Rosalind Connage returns his love but rejects him in favor of a much wealthier suitor. In Maryland he is intrigued by Eleanor Ramilly, a madcap Southern aristocrat, who involves him in wild escapades. The death of Monsignor Darcy, once a beau of his mother, causes Amory to mold himself into "one on whom people can depend."

This Side of Paradise depicts the generation thrust from the quietly adventurous opening years of the century into World War I and its aftermath, the "lost generation." The unhinging of the Blaine fortune was the least of the surprises encountered by a youth bred to those halcyon prewar years. Initially puzzled by some objections to the social castes represented in the Princeton clubs, Amory eventually becomes imbued with socialistic ideas. From the orthodox religious background of St. Regis (the Newman School in Fitzgerald's own life) Amory proceeds to doubting, until "there was no God" in his heart. At the focus of the book is the "questioning of moral codes" by a new generation as it breaks with the Victorian concept of conduct and standards. By Fitzgerald's own statement this is a "quest novel," depicting the struggle to achieve purpose and direction by a young man in an age of radical change. Amory is an unforgettable picture of the modern American starting as "Romantic Egotist" (original title of ms.) and groping toward self-realization in the unromantic realities of the present.

Tales of the Jazz Age (1922), a collection of short stories that Fitzgerald wrote for contemporary magazines, imposed its title upon the era. "May Day" depicts the general hysteria of that spring (1919) which inaugurated the Jazz Age. Anticipating the technique later employed by Dos Passos in *U.S.A.*, Fitzgerald presents a kaleidoscopic backdrop of a victory-celebrating New York against which individuals demonstrate the destruction of modern values and the overthrow of inhibitions. Gordon Sterrett, defeated and disillusioned, commits suicide amidst the wild merrymaking. "The Diamond as Big as the Ritz" may be the one flawless jewel created by Fitzgerald. Its theme is the Fitzgerald contention that great wealth has a core of horrible corruption. John T. Unger is initially overawed by the Braddock Washington magnificence, erected upon a great diamond mountain in Montana. This material splendor is the present apotheosis of the American dream, but its glory is turned to ashes in destruction by bombing. In symbolic power, this story evidences Fitzgerald's artistry.

The Beautiful and the Damned (1922), based in part upon Fitzgerald's marriage to Zelda, has contributed in its title another characterizing label for the period.

Playboy Anthony Patch marries Gloria Gilbert and with her participates in a wild spree of drinking, gambling, and carousing that causes his puritanical grandfather to disinherit Anthony. Rejected for a commission, young Patch enlists as a private and at a Southern army post seduces small-town girl Dot. When his grandfather dies, Anthony and Gloria successfully contest the will and end up with several million dollars. The rival claimant kills himself. Anthony is finally broken in health, confined to a wheelchair.

Grandfather Patch represents that older generation of wealthy Americans who gained their wealth by hard work and hard bargains, while clothing their rapacity with generous folds of pious morality. The younger generation of wealth, in revolt, totally discards the overlay of Victorian morality, and despising work, parties uproariously while waiting around for its inheritance. Anthony's only function is to be heir, and Gloria's to be his beauteous spouse. Initially lovers, they drift apart because their meaningless existence cannot provide the basis for a viable marriage and a significant life.

The Great Gatsby (1925) is perhaps Fitzgerald's most rounded work.

Narrator Nick Carraway, a Midwesterner selling bonds in New York, is a neighbor of Jay Gatsby in West Egg, Long Island, in 1922. Gatsby too is a Midwesterner, formerly James Gatz but now a prosperous bootlegger throwing enormous, costly parties. Gatsby attempts to renew his old love affair with Daisy Fay, now the wife of Tom Buchanan. Driving Jay in his car, Daisy in a hit-and-run accident kills Myrtle Wilson, Buchanan's mistress. Myrtle's husband, George, assuming that Jay is the guilty party, kills Gatsby and then himself. Nick is among the tiny handful at Gatsby's funeral.

The sustaining power of the novel is Gatsby as the mythic American hero. Gatsby is the modern parody of the Horatio Alger success story. From humble origins he has risen to magnificent wealth and splendor; all the "in" people, including the star goddesses of Hollywood, flock to his parties. His whole drive to status and affluence was actually to prove to Daisy and to himself that he was worthy of her. But Daisy is a shallow, empty creature; and his riches, produced by illegal booze, can buy neither friends nor happiness. Destroyed in a sordid affair because of a stupid misunderstanding, Gatsby is unmourned by the "ins" who will now sponge upon someone else. Pathetically, his father, Mr. Gatz, not knowing the truth, is sure that his son was a great and good man.

With the frontier gone, men of Midwestern origin like Nick and Gatsby find that their energies throw them eastward, where a corrupt and decadent society uses and destroys the innocents. At the end, Nick abandons the East to seek the more promising region of his origin.

Tender Is the Night (1934) takes its title from Keats's "Ode to a Nightingale," implying that joy of life is threatened by rapid disillusionment and destruction. The material was strongly suggested by Fitzgerald's European residence with Zelda and by her mental breakdown.

Dick Diver, a young American psychologist, is a successful partner in a Zurich clinic. Nicole Warren, a wealthy American girl, suffers from schizophrenia, which had evidently developed because she had been a victim of incest. Diver marries her out of pity, determined to cure her. As she strengthens, he weakens. He carries on an affair with a movie actress, Rosemary Hoyt, and drinks excessively. Nicole turns to Tommy Barban and after her divorce marries Barban. Diver returns to general practice in New York, drifting eventually to a seedy futility in a small town.

Tender Is the Night communicates a stronger feeling of decadence than Fitzgerald's other works. The structure of the plot is X shaped, with Diver going from ebullience and achievement down to despair and emptiness, while Nicole rises. Diver is another American innocent in Europe, but his downfall is caused not by Europe but by America and by himself. It is American money that makes possible the Zurich clinic, and it is American money that vitiates those who possess it selfishly and purposelessly. Diver is presumably capable of better things, but his talent and spirit are helpless against the obstacles he encounters.

The Last Tycoon (1941) remained unfinished at the novelist's death.

The narrator is Cecilia Brady, daughter of a Hollywood executive locked in a power struggle with his dynamic rival, Monroe Stahr. Cecilia is herself enamored of Stahr, but he is interested in Kathleen Moore. Stahr is eventually driven to plot the murder of Pat Brady, Cecilia's father, but abandons the scheme and later dies in a plane crash.

It is difficult to criticize an unpolished fragment, but the complete novel might well have been close to the best of Fitzgerald. The tinselly, make-believe world of the movies can perhaps best convey the Fitzgerald concept of the vulgar debasement of the American dream. Stahr is the last of the old-style executives, self-made and autocratic but also paternalistic and fair. To the feverish compulsion of business he subordinates all else in his life. He must be viewed with a mingling of distaste and respect. Stahr is larger in stature than any other Fitzgerald character and convincing even for the melodramatic plot assigned to him.

The renewed interest in all of Fitzgerald's work and the increased recognition of his artistic skill are present-day tributes to a novelist of unusual gifts.

Ernest Hemingway (1898–1961). Ernest Miller Hemingway was the son of a physician in Oak Park, Illinois, a suburb of Chicago. As a youngster he accompanied his father on extensive hunting trips in northern Michigan. While in the local high school he was an outstanding boxer and later worked as a sparring mate for a professional pugilist. In 1918 he volunteered as an ambulance driver in Italy; he was severely wounded and was twice decorated by the Italian government. Back in America he became a reporter for the Toronto *Star*, which sent him to Europe as a foreign correspondent.

In the 1920s he was prominent in the group of American expatriates who formed a colony of writers and artists in Paris. F. Scott Fitzgerald also belonged to this group, and a frequent focal point was the home of Gertrude Stein, patron of modern art, experimental writers, and artists in Paris. From 1928 to 1938, Key West, Florida, was the base for Hemingway's writing as well as for his vigorous life as sportsman and athlete.

Out of love for Spain and its people, Hemingway raised $40,000 on personal notes to procure ambulances for the Loyalists during the Spanish Civil War, which he covered as a correspondent for the North American Newspaper Alliance. With the outbreak of World War II he became a war correspondent in China. Upon his return he settled in Cuba. After Pearl Harbor he served in anti-submarine patrols in the Caribbean. In 1944 he proceeded to England, reporting upon his actual flights with the Royal Air Force in combat. With the U. S. 4th Division he participated in the Normandy invasion, receiving the Bronze Star for bravery in battle. In 1953 he revisited Africa, survived two plane crashes that fostered reports of his death, and emerged, receiving the Nobel Prize in 1954. His death by gunshot in Ketchum, Idaho, was very evidently self-inflicted.

Hemingway had been married four times, divorced from his first three wives and survived by his fourth wife. By the first marriage he had one son, and by the second, two sons.

Embracing as it did the extremes of the active and the reflective, Hemingway's life expressed itself in a literature peculiarly brawny, masculine, economic, consciously avoiding literary airs and poses. The events of this life—the wars, safaris, deep-sea fishing, hunting, boxing, and bullfighting—were his frequent subject matter, and all Hemingway's writing is essentially autobiographical. It is perhaps in his style that Hemingway has been most influential. Its great hallmark, a terse, absolutely concrete representation, denies abstractions and commentary in order to present events with a stark, uncompromising conciseness that seems to strip the world down to actual, elemental experience.

Hemingway first attracted attention as a depicter of the "lost generation" (a term coined by Gertrude Stein), the spiritually exhausted survivors of World War I to whom it had been revealed that modern life is no fair contest, affording neither satisfaction in victory nor honor in defeat. His characters are often lonely, isolated beings, sustained by their personal honor, who grimly endure for the sake of associating themselves with pursuits and causes that promise a degree of individual dignity and self-respect.

In Our Time (1925), the first Hemingway book published in this country, contains short stories written mostly in Europe but chiefly centered about the American Nick Adams, an alter ego of the author. Reader response was generally slight, but Fitzgerald was enthusiastic. Subsequent critics have found these among the most notable American short stories, containing the germs of virtually all later Hemingway writing.

"Indian Camp" tells of Nick Adams' physician father performing an emergency Caesarean delivery upon an Indian woman in a primitive hunting camp of northern Michigan. Although the operation is successful, the woman's husband panics at her agony and cuts his own throat before the boy's eyes. It is a classic of the initiation story, the sudden violation of a boy's innocence as he must confront the harsh realities of suffering and violence.

"The Doctor and the Doctor's Wife" is a story of the obligatory decisions in life. A patient purposely starts a quarrel with the boy's father so that he will be ejected and thereby escape paying the physician's bill. Nick's Christian Scientist mother, unwilling to believe that human beings consciously promote injustice and wrong, consequently gets into an argument with her husband. The physician walks out, and Nick joins him.

"The Three-Day Blow" concerns Nick's juvenile love affair with a girl named Marjorie. He and his friend Bill arrive at the male decision not to let themselves be trapped but to keep the affair "in reserve." Contrasting their real experience of sex with the sentimental novels of the prewar era, they choose the natural and the practical.

"Big Two-Hearted River" is a two-part account of Nick Adams, who has returned to America from the World War I battlegrounds to recover from a nasty spine wound and to fish in northern Michigan. The character of Nick is representative of a whole generation, deeply marked by war and disillusionment. In the immemorial rituals of the hunt he soothes a battle-ravaged spirit. He is actually profoundly sensitive, and seeks in liquor and blood sports a release from the pain of human bruisings. By being tough with himself he acquires armor against the world.

The Sun Also Rises (1926) takes its title from the first chapter of Ecclesiastes where the Preacher sadly contemplates the vanity of human existence.

In postwar Paris, Jake Barnes is an American correspondent emasculated by a war wound. He is interested in Lady Brett Ashley, an English noblewoman whose moral standards are being replaced by a cynical hedonism. She is awaiting a divorce which will permit her to marry Michael Campbell, a bankrupt, war-shattered alcoholic. Also interested in Brett is Robert Cohn, a Jewish novelist and expert boxer. This group descends upon northern Spain for the bullfights. Jake goes fishing in the Spanish mountains with friend Bill Gorton while Mike Campbell and Robert Cohn spar over Brett's attentions. Brett falls in love with the matador Pedro Romero but eventually gives him up. Robert takes out his resentment by thrashing Jake, Mike, and Romero. Brett settles for Mike and leaves the other men to flounder as best they can.

The Sun Also Rises is essentially a study of the aftermath of World War I, but in its Spanish setting it bypasses the physical destruction wrought by the conflict to focus on the human casualties. Of these, Brett, Mike, and Robert Cohn are the most unfortunate, having retained not even the illusion of a goal or purpose. Instead of living they are marking time, and death is the only significant incident awaiting them in their individual futures. Their lassitude is such that they cannot emulate Romero, who courts death ceremoniously as an art; they merely try to fill the interim with the pursuit of frenetic sensuality and petty combativeness.

The fourth casualty is Jake, whose war wound has left him without his powers of generation. This deprivation becomes a symbolic state, and Jake realizes he is without influence over the course of events in the world. This is less a catastrophe for him than for those such as Brett, who as a Hemingway heroine is at bottom instinctively dependent on the masculine principle. With Romero in a state of innocence and Jake incapacitated, there remain only Mike and Cohn, spiritual vacuums who dissipate and cheapen her femininity. Her release of Romero is a laudable act, but Brett is without the resources for many more such gestures; indeed, her future role in life with Mike will be primarily parasitic.

As sterile as he is for others, Jake is still of some benefit to himself. His affinity for nature, his sense of brotherhood, and his resignation to his limitations become for him the necessary prerequisites for a satisfactory existence, and Jake will presumably persevere until the wounds on the face of the land have begun to heal. Hemingway declared that his novel was not "a hollow or bitter satire, but a damn tragedy with the earth abiding forever as the hero." This remark, together with the cyclic description of the cosmos in the cited passage of Ecclesiastes, suggests there is some potential for a salutary if temporary rebirth.

Men Without Women (1927) collects short stories written after *In Our Time,* most of them first printed in magazines. Hemingway explained that "the softening feminine influence" is virtually absent in each of these stories.

"The Killers" is a great classic of callous, uncompromising realism. Two gangsters, Al and Max, have come to a small Michigan town in pursuit of Ole Andreson, an aging, fugitive boxer who has somehow offended powerful Chicago gambling interests. At the lunch counter where Nick Adams works they are arrogantly open about their intent to commit murder. Nick takes it upon himself to warn Anderson, but the older man is resigned. The story reflects upon political fascism and the inability of mankind to raise defenses against its inhumanity.

"In Another Country" is set in Italy, in a hospital, but the title suggests a different philosophy as well as a different locale. A young

American undergoing therapy for a leg wound is a tyro for whom an Italian major with a withered arm is tutor. As a professional the major seeks to live precisely and cleanly, avoiding losses so far as possible. His stricture against marriage is seen to be motivated by the recent death of his own wife.

"The Undefeated" tells of the last *corrida* of Manolo Garcia, an aging bullfighter. His only meaning in life is the code of the matador, and he manages to retain the *coleta* (the matador's symbolic pigtail) by demonstrating unqualified courage in killing the bull even though severely injured.

A Farewell to Arms (1929) was the first Hemingway volume to win due popularity.

Frederic Henry, an American volunteer in the Italian ambulance corps, enters into a seemingly casual affair with Catherine Barkley, an English nurse. When he is hospitalized for leg wounds their romance flowers, and at his return to duty they are man and wife by mutual agreement. In the catastrophic retreat from Caporetto, the Italian Army falls apart and Henry finally becomes a deserter. He and Catherine flee to Switzerland where she dies in childbirth, leaving him alone and despondent.

The ambiguous title indicates the two themes of love and war, which are interwoven and counterpointed throughout the novel's beautifully constructed length. Henry begins as a rootless American with a cavalier attitude toward both love and war. The abnormal and unnatural war successively intrudes upon him until he is overwhelmed with its meaninglessness and peremptorily quits. This leaves a vacuum, which is filled as normal and natural love gradually sweeps over him. But the death of Catherine closes this episode and reminds Henry that society and its incessant pressures cannot be evaded.

The description of the Caporetto disaster has been widely praised. An orderly retreat at the outset gradually degenerates into total rout. Friend and foe are inextricably mixed up and impartially slain. Hemingway employs landscape and weather throughout to harmonize with the inner moods of his characters.

Death in the Afternoon (1932) is a nonfictional analysis of Spanish bullfighting, the best in English and, it has been said, the best in any language. On the practical level it is a superb exposition of every movement in the spectacle. More importantly, it comprehends the aesthetic experience of the bullfight as an Aristotelian tragedy arising from deep in the Spanish soul, a tragic vision of life. In the bullfight, Hemingway discovered the "feeling of life and death and mortality and immortality." The matador is the exemplar of Hemingway's ritual hero.

Winner Take Nothing (1933) collects Hemingway short stories written during several years after *Men Without Women*.

"A Clean, Well-Lighted Place" concerns a young waiter and an older waiter in a Spanish café late at night. The one remaining customer, a deaf old man, orders another drink. The young waiter wants to close up and go home to his wife, but the older waiter realizes that for the lonely old man, who has recently attempted suicide, and for himself, the café is a clean, well-lighted refuge from nothingness.

Green Hills of Africa (1935) is a nonfictional description of an African big-game safari. Like *Death in the Afternoon*, it is a novelist's work of selectivity, here exploring the ritualistic code of the hunt as art amidst nature. The country and the people are fully the representatives of intense living. Inflicting pain and death is acceptable if it is done cleanly and quickly. Hunting is a decent business in comparison with the moral and spiritual degradation of civilization.

To Have and Have Not (1937), though minor as a novel, marks an important development in Hemingway's thought.

Economic setbacks compel Harry Morgan to use his Key West sportfishing boat illegally. On one occasion to escape detection he is forced to slay a go-between in a deal to smuggle Chinese into the United States. When he becomes involved with Cuban bank robbers, he realizes that they will kill him to keep him silent. He manages to slay them but is fatally wounded in the fracas.

This is Hemingway's "depression" novel. Morgan is interpreted as the self-reliant American brought to destitution by economic forces beyond his control. In trying to earn a living he is pushed to extremes in which there is no place for moral standards.

The Fifth Column and the First Forty-nine Stories (1938) collected earlier Hemingway stories. Two stories of particular significance appeared here in book form for the first time. We shall consider them now. (*The Fifth Column* is a play about the Spanish Civil War.)

"The Short Happy Life of Francis Macomber" grew out of Hemingway's African safari of 1933–34. The principals are Francis and Margot Macomber, a handsome American couple, and Robert Wilson, their hunting guide. Francis has had chronic difficulty asserting himself in life, and his beautiful but shrewish wife tends to take advantage of this. While confronting a wounded lion Francis puts on a spectacular display of cowardice that provokes Margot's most scathing contempt. She plays him off against Wilson, going so far as to sleep with the latter during the night. The following morning Francis encounters a charging water buffalo and is on the point of acquitting himself manfully when a bullet from Margot's gun strikes and kills him. Wilson, who has had previous experience with American women, believes the shot was deliberate—Margot's response to the self-confidence and mastery she saw Francis acquiring during his "short happy life."

"The Snows of Kilimanjaro" begins with prefatory enigma: A dead leopard is discovered near the snowy peak of Kilimanjaro, the mighty African mountain which the Masai tribe believes is the house of God. The story itself concerns American novelist Harry who is dying of a hunting wound on the plain before Kilimanjaro. As he sits in camp awaiting the inevitable, there is little to do but ruminate over the details of his past: the advantageous marriage that chained him to luxury; the neglected potential of his own artistry. But more often his mind drifts back to scenes that were fresh, meaningful, and spiritually invigorating.

He recalls the women he had known, the good times that he had in Paris and in Constantinople, and the horrors of war he had witnessed. He feels a great regret that he did not write all the stories that he was capable of. He considers the life of luxury he has been living and how it has prevented him from being a good writer. The contrast of the present—the hot, heavy torpor of the plain and the gangrenous festering of his leg—reinforces the bitterness of his recollections and rouses him to spiteful outbursts against his wife, Helen. The next morning a plane arrives to transport him to Nairobi, but once he is aboard, it turns aside to approach the snowy summit of the great mountain. The reader is soon to realize that the flight is hallucinatory, for that same morning Helen finds Harry dead in his tent. His symbolic journey is his imagination's reply to his yearning for cool cleanliness, purity, and the rarefied heights of significant achievement.

For Whom the Bell Tolls (1940), widely read and acclaimed, may be Hemingway's greatest novel.

Robert Jordan, an American college professor, a strong advocate of democracy, decides to help the Loyalists of Spain resist the fascistic incursions of General Franco. In a mountain cave he meets the guerrillas he will supervise in detonating a bridge and thereby isolating the Loyalists from a fascist counterattack: Pablo, the bibulous leader whose courage has run thin; his wife Pilar, the real source of spirit and determination behind the band; young Maria, a refugee from fascist degradations; and the pious, aging Anselmo. Jordan and Maria find a fitful escape from events in a love that grows between them, but as the day of the mission approaches, all begin to see the inadequacy of the Loyalist strategy and organization and the precariousness of their own position. Pablo is particularly fretful, and at the last moment he cripples the undertaking by making off with the explosives. Jordan decides that grenades can be substituted, and despite a sense of futility and foreboding proceeds with the plan. It is a success, but costs the life of Anselmo and disables Jordan. His sense of purpose is still intact, however, and in a last gesture he awaits the fascist advance on a hillside with a loaded machine gun.

Telling much of the story through the mind of Jordan, reminiscing about the past, and debating with himself his personal and ideological problems, and through the accounts by the guerrillas of many previous events, Hemingway widens this local engagement to epic and universal dimensions. The epigraph from John Donne's "Meditation 17" is the keynote of the theme: "Never send to know for whom the bell tolls; it tolls for thee." The death of any one is to a degree the death of each of us. The human struggles of one are the struggles and tragedies of every human being.

Hemingway's work offers neither a black-and-white interpretation of the combatants nor an assurance that right will triumph. Anselmo with his Christian ideals and Jordan with his political ones are the only combatants consistently above self-interest, and even they are serving their own sense of what a man should be. The Loyalist cause is upheld for a variety of reasons, not all commendable, and the behavior of the Republicans is often highly reprehensible. Pilar's description of a bestial massacre of fascists by enraged peasants is the most vivid example. The support received from the cynical Russian communists is needed but hardly welcome. Jordan knows almost from the first that the overall strategy, of which his fatal mission is but a tiny piece, is certain disaster. Nonetheless, he gives his life for the cause which, with all its shortcomings, represents the better of human choices. A man must give full commitment to his fellows and to the principles that are meaningful to him. There are causes, Hemingway indicates, worth dying for.

Hemingway intends the affair of Jordan and Maria as primarily the mystic bond of love. Jordan dies in the manner of epic tragedy; Maria, borne off by Pilar, will give birth eventually to Jordan's child.

Deeply in love with the Spain that he considered betrayed, Hemingway assails the senses with the surging impact of the land. Of the characters, Pilar is pre-eminent. A fervent and valiant patriot, she also understands the supreme importance of individual happiness and fulfillment, thereby bringing together Maria and Jordan.

Across the River and into the Trees (1950) ended a decade of fictional silence during which Hemingway was heavily involved with war reporting and actual fighting.

The novel is predominantly a string of reminiscences by a fifty-year-old American colonel, Richard Cantwell. Cantwell, a veteran of both great wars, recounts experiences that parallel those of Hemingway, and the judgments he passes on men and events are evidently derived from the same source. Hemingway makes of his book a novel rather than a commentary by providing a setting—Venice—and a few other characters as conversational foils, in particular the young Renata, a countess involved in a romance with Cantwell.

Cantwell would then seem to be little more than Hemingway's idea of himself as a retired soldier, replete with the insight and expertise that is the author's trademark. Accordingly he is allotted a soldier's death, with the last words of General Stonewall Jackson from which the title is taken still on his lips. The book has its moments of interest and descriptive power, but on the whole it is too permeated with Hemingway's ego.

The Old Man and the Sea (1952), a novella or long short story, confirms the undiminished genius of the later Hemingway. It is based upon an actual incident learned of by Hemingway during his fishing experiences in Cuba.

Santiago, a grizzled old Cuban fisherman, depends for his livelihood and dignity on the catch he brings back from the sea each day. Recently he has met with many reversals, and in order to recoup his losses he rows out beyond his usual distance. There he hooks an enormous marlin, and a great contest of strength ensues. Santiago's palms are repeatedly torn by the fast-running lines; in the few periods of rest he is allowed, he collapses into exhausted reveries of his youth. The next day he is finally able to bring the huge fish alongside his smaller skiff and lash it securely. But during his return to land the persistent sharks attack again and again until his catch is stripped down to the skeleton. Later he is found, broken and prostrate in his hovel, by the young boy who alone remains loyal to him.

Hemingway said of this work that it "would mean many things." The concord and conflict of man with Nature is perhaps the primary theme, and it has been treated here in a manner both realistic and poetic. Because he is old and alone, or possibly because he has upset a delicate balance by presuming to appropriate a creature too magnificent for his modest needs, Santiago is bested by the irresistible strength of the sea after he has expended his own powers to their limit. The story is tragic in the purest sense; although Santiago will not return to the sea again, there is greatness in what he has attempted and affirmation in his defeat. The didactic and emotional force of the ordeal will not be lost on the boy, who stands in the place of a son to Santiago and is his spiritual heir.

The story operates on the religious level as well. The stigmata on Santiago's palms, his laboring beneath the mast of his boat as he stumbles to his hut, and the outspread arms of his final prostration are all readily recognized symbolically. But these touches evidently do not attempt anything more than to suggest universality.

As a narrative *The Old Man and the Sea* acquires grace from its tight construction and clear, direct style, as well as lyricism from its lucidity and visual imagery.

Thomas Wolfe (1900 38). Thomas Clayton Wolfe was born in Asheville, North Carolina, the "Altamont" of his writings. His father, a stonecutter, recited Shakespeare to him and encouraged him to read Bancroft and similar American historians. His mother ran a boarding-house in Asheville. At the University of North Carolina, from which he graduated in 1920, he wrote several plays, in one of which, *The Return of Buck Gavin* (1919), he acted the title role. Baker's famous 47 Workshop lured him to Harvard in 1920, where he received his M.A. in 1922. When professional production of his dramas was not forthcoming he began to teach English at New York University in 1924. Except for occasional trips to Europe he taught at New York University until 1930. Thereafter he labored indefatigably at mountains of manuscript until his untimely death, which came about as a result of a cerebral infection developed after a long siege of pneumonia.

Physically Wolfe was a giant of a man, standing six and a half feet tall and weighing about 250 pounds. From his early days at the University of North Carolina he was recognized as potentially a major American novelist, because of his stupendous energy (working fifteen hours a day), his panoramic sweep, and his exuberant lyricism.

Look Homeward, Angel: A Story of the Buried Life (1929), Wolfe's first novel, was cut down from a 300,000-word manuscript by Maxwell Perkins, the great editor at Scribner's. The first part of the title is a quotation from Milton's "Lycidas," urging the protector angel St. Michael to turn from foreign concerns to weep for tragedy at home, in this case the Gant household of the novel. Wolfe's father for some time had a stone angel, made in Italy, upon the porch of his stonecutting shop—a symbol for the artistic creativity that the father yearned to achieve but never did. The second part of the title is quoted from Matthew Arnold's poem of the same title. In an era when fiction strongly concentrated upon the reportorial quality of a Sinclair Lewis, Wolfe insisted upon a romantic exploration of the secret life, inimical to the outside world but perhaps the wellspring of meaning and selfhood.

The first part of the novel deals with the life of Eugene Gant to his twelfth year and is closely autobiographical. Wolfe's stonecutter father appears as W. O. Gant, given to rhetoric and drinking; his mother as Eliza Gant. Their backgrounds are described as being exceedingly disparate. W.O.'s heritage is bound up with inveterate wandering, whereas Eliza is of a family inclined to establishing firm roots. W.O.'s frustration at being tied down is manifest in his drunken carousing and irrepressible tirades. What he perceives as Eliza's pettiness is a torment to his expansive spirit. Eliza has a consuming interest in money and real estate, minuscule detail and picky economies. Inevitably she is constantly upbraiding W.O. for his prodigality and thoughtlessness, and thereby reaping the whirlwind of his gargantuan temper.

Into this environment Eugene is born, in 1900, in the town of Altamont (Asheville) of the state of Old Catawba (North Carolina). Eugene's siblings consist of two sisters, Daisy and Helen, and three brothers, Steve, Luke, and Ben. Only Ben, bearing the name of one of Wolfe's real brothers, shares deep feelings and thoughts with Eugene. Eliza leaves her incorrigible husband to run the "Dixieland" boardinghouse. Young Eugene is torn between these two strong, irreconcilable personalities.

The second part traces Eugene's progress in a private school run by John and Margaret Leonard. The life of art and thought strongly appeals to the youth, who feels increasing isolation from his nonintellectual family. To Margaret, more than he ever could even to Ben, he reveals his buried life of imaginative dreams.

The third part begins with the sixteen-year-old Eugene at the state university at Pulpit Hill (Chapel Hill). At first the object of ridicule, he distinguishes himself in his senior year, but is haunted by inner struggles. Eugene has an unhappy love affair with one of his mother's boarders, Laura James, who leads him on. During World War I he works in Norfolk, Virginia, and finds that he can survive by himself. During the flu epidemic of 1918 his brother Ben dies, sundering his last firm tie with the Gant family.

Wolfe explains his theme in the opening pages: "that we are born alone—all of us who ever lived or will live—that we live alone and die alone, and that we are strangers to one another, and never come to know one another." Later in *The Story of a Novel* (1936) he suggested "search for a father" as the key to his entire writing. Central certainly to Wolfe's first novel is the spiritual pilgrimage, the groping of a sensitive soul for props to sustain him amidst searing and tumultuous existence. Eugene is abnormally perceptive of all experience and abashed by the crudities and humiliations in his family and in his narrowly provincial community. Contrarily, he is a voracious giant, huge in appetites of all sorts, driven by a stupendous lust for life. Schooling with the Leonards and later at Pulpit Hill expands his horizons, helps him to see in perspective the sufferings and disillusionments of his earlier years, and consecrates him as "beauty's miser" to see in art the expression of the totality of life.

Among the most effective parts of the novel are the larger-than-life portraits of the Gant family, especially W. O. Gant with his temper and gusto; Eliza with her endless reminiscences; Steve who possessed all his father's vices and none of his magnificence; stuttering, feckless Luke; strong Helen, who even as a child was alone capable of controlling W.O.; and sullen yet sympathetic Ben, whose potentialities were doomed to early extinction.

Amidst the determinedly prosaic accounts of most contemporary fiction Wolfe interposed a heady draught of lyric intensity. Poetic symbolism carries through the entire novel, most obviously in the angel of the title. Perhaps the most distinctive Wolfean symbol is the train, abiding with Eugene as the "gateway to the lost world." Mountains familiarly suggest Eugene's wish to escape and rise to higher ground. Constantly recurring is the triple symbol of "a stone, a leaf, a door." The stone, associated with Gant's angel, is the almost intractable substance of the world to which the artist must give form and life. The leaf is the transitory human existence. Most frequently invoked is the door, through which Eugene must pass to artistic and spiritual realization.

Of Time and the River; a Legend of Man's Hunger in His Youth (1935), Wolfe's second novel and the last to be published during his lifetime, picks up on the day following the end of *Look Homeward, Angel* and takes Eugene Gant through the years 1920-25. Eugene, continuing his search for life's meaning, is broadly likened to questing heroes of legend.

Book I. Orestes: Flight Before Fury. Eugene leaves Altamont for Harvard. In Baltimore he visits his father, dying of cancer in a hospital. The train trip evokes a now famous incantation upon the vast, lonely landscape of America.

Book II. Young Faustus. Yearning and grasping for all knowledge, Eugene feverishly reaches for the intellectual wealth of the Harvard library and roams the Boston streets. He studies playwriting with Professor Hatcher (Baker), in whose class there are a number of aesthetic poseurs. A fellow student, Francis Starwick, has an artistic bent that attracts Eugene; Starwick's talent is overdelicate and unvigorous, however. Visits to Uncle Bascom Pentland, his mother's brother, offer Eugene a welcome escape from cramped routine. Perhaps the most impressive passage of the novel describes the death of W. O. Gant.

Book III. Telemachus. Awaiting a decision about a play he has written, Eugene returns to Altamont. After a drunken spree he is briefly confined in a South Carolina jail. An outstanding passage is the paean to October (the original manuscript title of the work was *October Fair*), the month of eternal return.

Book IV. Proteus: New York. To finance his playwriting, Eugene teaches freshman English at a New York college where he is annoyed by stupid students and even more by an intelligent one, Abe Jones. Visiting the idyllic country estate of wealthy Joel Pierce, he is appalled at evidence of narrow-mindedness and contempt for art.

Book V. Jason's Voyage. Eugene (Jason) journeys to Europe (Colchis) in search of the lost father (Golden Fleece) preparatory to a return when he will reclaim his America (throne of his father). At Oxford he is annoyed at finding Americans bogged down by an inferiority complex in the presence of the culture of the Old World. In Paris he joins in the revels of Starwick and Starwick's two American woman friends. Eugene has an amusingly unsuccessful love affair with one of the women, Ann; and he violently breaks with Starwick, who has revealed himself as a homosexual.

Book VI. Antaeus: Earth Again. A country train trip from Paris to Orleans re-establishes Eugene's contact with earth's realities after the previous nightmares.

Book VII. Kronos and Rhea: The Dream of Time. Rambling through provincial France, Eugene tries to define the essence of American life. He would establish a concept of time in the art of fiction.

Book VIII. Faust and Helen. On the ship back to America Eugene meets Esther (Mrs. Aline Bernstein). Smitten with love, Eugene returns home with a joyous anticipation in his heart.

Both time and the river (space) symbolize the American wanderers. The search for the father is the search for America, and Eugene can only find America by leaving it to gain perspective and then returning as the artist determined to epitomize it in lyrical prose. Most of all, the artist discovers America within himself.

The headlong rhapsodies upon New York City, the recollections of Old Catawba, and more widely of the giant American continent represent to many people the most memorable and characteristic achievement of Wolfe. These passages suggest comparison with Walt Whitman. At the same time, *Of Time and the River* contains striking satire upon college life and would-be sophisticates.

The Web and the Rock (1939), posthumously published, forms—together with *You Can't Go Home Again*—the George Webber story. Wolfe's own life is still the subject, but the treatment departs much more from autobiographical fact than do the Eugene Gant novels.

George Webber is born in Libya Hill (Asheville) in 1900. Early in his life his father deserts his mother for another woman, and George is brought up by his mother's family, the strait-laced Joyners. In 1916 he is sent to a staunchly Baptist institution, Pine Rock College. From this provincial milieu George proceeds to New York with vague dreams of becoming a writer. He spends the last of his inheritance on a European trip. Returning, he meets Esther Jack (Mrs. Bernstein) on the ship and falls in love. Needing money, he teaches at the School of Utility Cultures. The love affair with Esther cools as he accuses some of her artistic friends of being pretentious frauds. Back in Europe, he is badly beaten up in a German beer hall. Regarding himself in a hospital mirror, George attempts to come to terms with the insatiable drives of the spirit and the humble limitations enforced by the body.

The Web of the title refers to all entanglements that prevent a man from realizing his nature and capabilities— the puritanical Joyners, the backwoods college mentality, and eventually the affair with Esther. *The Rock* is not the stone of the previous novels but New York City, that cynosure of the young and the ambitious. The contrast of the two symbols is in the static quality of the rock and the constantly changing, expanding nature of the web. Contrast dominates the volume —the floundering George of the first three books as opposed to the later artist-creator; the earlier small-town culture and the big-city atmosphere; the Protestant ethos at the outset and the cosmopolite Jewish spirit later on; the young and innocent George versus the mature sophistication of Esther (who is at least fifteen years his senior). Wolfe himself explained the novel as "one man's discovery of life and of the world . . . discovery through a process of finding out." The end product is supposedly George's dropping of romantic conceptions in order to look "calmly and sanely forth upon the earth." The novel contains frequent digressions, many of them fascinating in themselves.

You Can't Go Home Again (1940) picks up George Webber in New York in April of 1929.

On a return to Libya Hill for the funeral of Aunt Maw Joyner, who brought him up, George finds the community caught in a hysterical wave of real estate speculation. Once again in New York, he reacts with disgust at the decadence and futility of the New York intelligentsia at a party given by Esther Jack and her husband. George's novel, *Home to Our Mountains* (i.e. *Look Homeward, Angel*), meets with critical approval but arouses a hornet's nest of protest from the burghers of Libya Hill. The stock market crashes and the Great Depression begins. George quits his teaching job and rents a nondescript Brooklyn flat from whence he observes the suffering of his fellows. His one friend now is the editor Foxhall Edwards (Maxwell Perkins), a brilliant yet disillusioned man and a loyal admirer of George (Wolfe). George spends some time in England and visits Germany for the Olympic games. The rise of Nazism horrifies him, and he becomes obsessed with a need to warn his countrymen about this threatening virus and to exhort them to uphold their own basic philosophy. His concluding letter to Edwards announces his break with the editor's pessimism and his own confidence in the American dream. This is an episodic book, and evolves from a spiritual quest rather than a plot format. In succession George examines and rejects: allegiance to the provincial community; the pursuit of wealth; the rigors of the competitive system; the luxuriating of the well-to-do; love on the terms of privilege and servility; ephemeral adulation of the fashionable; cruelty and self-aggrandizement at the expense of others; and, finally, a cynical acceptance of the unrighteous state of things. At the end he proclaims a Whitmanesque confidence in "mystic evolution," and he reaffirms his conviction that the America of his day points to the promise of the future.

The Hills Beyond (1941) contains short fiction belonging to the Gant and Webber cycles. Most interesting are the ten chapters of an incomplete novel bearing the book title. These carry the Joyner family (Webber's maternal ancestors, possibly identical with the Pentlands of the Gant series) from the pre-Civil War days in Old Catawba through the Reconstruction era. Wolfe for the first time was attempting to go beyond his own autobiography to an accurate historical appraisal of the South. Though generally sympathetic, even amusing, this projected novel asks the Southerner to recognize his real, unaristocratic origins and see the Civil War without the glamorous incrustations of legend.

Some critics consider both Thomas Wolfe and his works tragic fragments: giants that were shattered before form and definitive meaning could be imposed. But a greater number unite in saluting Wolfe's importance. He may be said to represent a major purpose of the American novel, to evoke the feel of American life, the sense of struggle and wonderment in its small towns and its megalopolises, the still compelling force of the American dream, and the frustration and disillusionment of its everyday existence.

John Steinbeck (1902–68). John Ernst Steinbeck, Jr., was born in Salinas, California, the locale of much of his writing. He left Stanford University in 1925 without a degree and went to New York where he found employment in various trades while seeking to find himself as a writer. Disgruntled with the indifference of the editors he met, he returned to California where he continued to write with only small financial success. While living at Pacific Grove he became a friend of Ed Ricketts, the manager of a biological supply laboratory, who was thereafter a close associate of the novelist; and the two men shared a view of all life as essentially one organism. In the mid-thirties Steinbeck began to win recognition, and before long he achieved national prominence. During World War II he reported for the New York *Herald Tribune* from European battlefields. After the war Steinbeck resided principally in or near New York. He was awarded the Nobel Prize in 1962. In 1966–67 he acted as a war correspondent in Vietnam. The next year he was ill for a time before his death.

The Pastures of Heaven (1932), one of Steinbeck's early works, is a group of interrelated short stories about the inhabitants of a green and fertile valley in California. In this book Steinbeck deals with many of the themes and characters that he was to develop further in some of his best novels. His major focus is upon the struggle between man and nature. This struggle, he indicates, is often humorous and ironical, for man is constantly trying to infuse into nature qualities that exist in his own mind.

In the second episode or story this idea becomes clear. The people of the Pastures of Heaven believe that the abandoned Battle farm is cursed, "for lands and houses that have been deserted seem always sodden with gloom and with threatening . . . the trees which grow up around a deserted house are dark trees and the shadows they throw on the ground have suggestive shapes." One inhabitant of the house, John Battle, is seen as a man whose "life was devoted to the struggle with devils." At night he searches out demons in the brush around the farm. One evening he encounters a snake, and, believing it to be the devil, he attacks it. "The snake struck him three times in the throat. . . . He struggled very little and died in a few minutes." There is a grim humor in this account but Steinbeck colors it with a deep sympathy for the ways of men.

If civilized man has made nature his enemy, he has also made his enemy those men who act in harmony with nature. Episode IV tells of Tularecito, a deformed creature with the brain of an infant but the strength of a man. He lives in a state of gentle friendship with men and animals until he is forced by the law to attend school. The schoolteacher fills his head with myths and sends him out digging for "the little people who live in the earth," from whence Tularecito thinks he came. One night Tularecito attacks a man who fills in the holes that he has dug and he is committed to the insane asylum.

In all, the book consists of twelve episodes.

Tortilla Flat (1935), the first Steinbeck work to bring him fame, is gay and fantastic in its spirit. The title refers to a fictitious slum community of Monterey, California, inhabited by Mexican-Americans.

Upon his return from World War I, Danny finds that he has inherited from his grandfather two shacks in Tortilla Flat. He rents one to his friend Pilon and lives in the other. Pilon can pay no rent, and after his hovel burns down, moves in with Danny, along with two other friends. They admit a half-wit, the Pirate, because of his bag of quarters, but respect his little treasure because with it he plans to buy a golden candlestick to St. Francis. A latecomer, Joe Portagee, steals the Pirate's bag, but the group recovers the money. In a wild bacchanalian orgy Danny falls to his death in a ravine. His remaining friends ritualistically burn down his house.

On the surface the bizarre eccentrics of Tortilla Flat appear to be parasites; scrounging, begging, stealing for their only desires—wine and women. But these amoralists are sympathetically viewed as seeking a hedonistic existence untrammeled by the materialistic standards of contemporary America. Thus they are not without standards; in their opposition to commonplace society, they have their own different and equally cherished sets of values and behavior.

Steinbeck consciously drew upon and varied a theme from Malory's *Morte d'Arthur,* aiming to show in *Tortilla Flat,* as in the case of the Round Table, a well-intentioned group forming a social organism. Danny and his friends do no gainful work and live essentially by the labors of others. There is really no place in a fixed civilization for such characters as Danny and his mob; but such an individualistic and irresponsible way of life has been a secret yearning of many men in many advanced civilizations.

In Dubious Battle (1936), telling of a labor strike, is written in a coarse and forceful style. Its title is a quotation from Milton's *Paradise Lost.*

Jim Nolan, an innocent bystander at a radical demonstration, is beaten up by the police and cashiered from his job in San Francisco. Angered, he joins the Communist Party and is assigned to Mac, a fanatical party member, who is working to foment a strike of fruit pickers in the fictitious Torgas Valley. The strike is smashed by bloody force, and Mac uses the murder of Jim to incite prospective adherents to communism.

A product of the bitter Depression years, the novel is a two-edged sword. Steinbeck obviously opposes the entrenched capitalists who want simply to exploit labor. Equally, however, he opposes Communists who lust for power, heedless of the individual. A spokesman for the novelist is the physician Doc Burton who, refusing to join the Communist Party, tells Mac: "I don't believe in the cause, but I believe in men." This man of good will simply vanishes, for the tragic implication of the work is that in this wholly dubious struggle of our time the righteous, balanced spirit is at best ignored and often consumed by the system.

Continuing to think of Milton, Steinbeck places this local battle in "heaven"—a gloriously beautiful and fertile valley of central California. It is appropriately from apple orchards that the strikers are driven out by the emissaries of law at the command of the landowners controlling the valley. Satan is the Communist Party, tempting the workers with freedom, power, and knowledge, but actually seeking self-aggrandizement. Capitalism triumphs as does Milton's God; but Steinbeck leaves unanswered the question: Is this a tyrant deity or a just god who must fulfill good purposes through violence and evil?

Of Mice and Men (1937) takes its title from the Burns poem "To a Mouse"—"The best-laid schemes o' mice an' men / Gang aft agley." Carefully limited in locale, number of characters, and concentration upon one significant problem, *Of Mice and Men* displays some of the most artful precision and selectivity in the American novel. Steinbeck was consciously experimenting with an almost wholly dramatic exposition.

Two migratory farm workers, George Milton and his huge, moronic companion, Lennie Small, have long shared a dream of owning a little place of their own. To George it represents independence and the good life; to Lennie it means having and tending the soft, furry animals he has always been attracted to but too often kills with his overpowering caresses. Candy, an old hand at the farm where they work at the time, offers the small sum he has put aside if he can be included in the plan, and for the first time George's dream seems more than an empty fantasy. But there is trouble ahead in the form of Curley, the boss's arrogant son, and his promiscuous wife. Drawn to Lennie's enormous size and strength, she encourages his attentions, with the result that Lennie inadvertently crushes her to death. Afterward, fearful of George's displeasure, Lennie takes to the woods. Curley is quick to organize a manhunt, but George is able to arrive at Lennie's hiding place before the posse. There he is obliged to shoot his friend to forestall the lynching Curley intends.

This work is the most naturalistic of Steinbeck, suggesting a determinism that renders futile the vanity of human wishes.

Of Mice and Men lent itself well to dramatization; and the play based on it was acclaimed.

The Long Valley (1938), a collection of short stories all set in the Salinas Valley, offers some of the best-crafted examples of American short fiction. The central theme is the frustrated life of ordinary people. In this garden paradise they embrace dreams of order and meaning that are cruelly assailed by the realistic world. Although contemporary readers catalogued Steinbeck as the outstanding novelist of social consciousness, only "The Raid," about a Communist agitator preparing for a workers' meeting, is genuinely topical.

"The Chrysanthemums" shows how the unscrupulous manipulate the dreams of others for selfish reasons. Elisa Allen, lonely wife of a rancher, believes an itinerant tinker shares her passionate love of flowers. He gets from her the money he is seeking, and accepts the chrysanthemum shoots that she urges on him. Later Elisa finds the flowers carelessly thrown away by the road. She is left in bitter disillusionment, unable then to communicate with her decent but uncomprehending husband.

"The Vigilante" tells of a man returning to his home after participating in a lynching. His shrewish wife accuses him of having been out with another woman. The man realizes that his inclination to share in the violence of the lynching had arisen from bored frustration and that the fact of action has aroused in him renewed sexual desire.

"Johnny Bear" concerns a mentally retarded character, a favorite subject of Steinbeck. Half-witted Johnny Bear has marvelous powers in mimicry and can capture the exact intonations of conversations he overhears, often without understanding their meaning. He uses his talent to procure himself drinks from paying customers at the town saloon. There is universal horror when he reproduces the dialogue of two highly respected spinsters, one of whom, illegitimately pregnant by a Chinese worker, commits suicide with the connivance of the other. Johnny Bear unknowingly faithfully depicts a community and disrupts its cherished idolatries with the light of reality.

"The Red Pony," actually a novella in four episodes, tells of Jody Tiflin's initiation into adulthood. His rancher father is a stern disciplinarian with good intentions but little perception; his mother is a practical housewife and not especially communicative; the cowhand Billy Buck is Jody's true mentor and idol. In "The Gift" Jody is given a red pony that dies despite his and Billy Buck's unstinting efforts to save it. The impact of the loss banishes Jody's childhood. In "The Great Mountains," an old Mexican named Gitano wanders onto the Tiflin ranch with the story that the land once belonged to his family. Rebuffed in his request for a job, the old man steals a useless horse and goes off on it to die. The story is a dramatic representation of the passing of Spanish California. In "The Promise," Jody finally gets the horse he so desires—a newly foaled colt which is given birth at the bloody cost of its dam's life. In "The Leader of the People," Jody's grandfather visits the ranch and recounts stories of the heroic pioneering days of his youth. Jody is fascinated, but his father registers impatience at the garrulous oldster and his tendency to live in the past. Thus Jody's education is completed. He has witnessed birth and death and their attendant woes in nature and in man.

The Grapes of Wrath (1939) arises from Steinbeck's own experience.

In 1937 he joined "Okie" migrants (from Oklahoma) on the trek westward and worked with them in the fields of California. The book is generally considered Steinbeck's best-rounded work; it was awarded a Pulitzer Prize.

A combination of starved soil, dust storms, and the pinch of the Depression is ruining Oklahoma farmers. Banks foreclose on mortgages, evict the tenants, and bunch the properties together for more economical tractor farming. The dispossessed Joad family, comprising three generations at the start of the novel, has seen pamphlets advertising work and good pay in California. Like many others they decide to embark on a westward migration, their number augmented by Connie Rivers, husband of young Rosasharn (Rose of Sharon), and Jim Casy, a disillusioned minister who has abandoned the cloth.

The journey overland in a dilapidated panel truck is hard; Grampa and Granma Joad die on the way, one of the children disappears, and the remainder of the family begins to learn that it must cooperate with other travelers in order to get by. Their destination proves to be a greater discouragement. The farmers find they are pawns in a scheme to saturate the labor market and drive wages down. They are molested by peace officers and herded into squalid refugee camps. There is no work. Some of the Joads, among them Tom, stiffen their resolve and strive to obtain sustenance and self-respect; others desert, like Connie, who leaves behind his pregnant wife, Rosasharn. After numerous vicissitudes the Joads locate something like steady employment at the Hooper fruit ranch, only to learn they are being used to break a strike organized by Jim Casy. There is an outbreak of violence in which Casy is killed; and Tom, in avenging him, becomes a fugitive. Soon afterward heavy rains interrupt the work at the ranch and the Joads are forced from their refuge in an abandoned railroad car by rising flood waters. Once again on the move, possessing no more than the will to live, the family pauses while Rosasharn suckles a starving man with the milk her stillborn baby will never need.

The novel's story is one of individual and collective growth. The earliest epiphany belongs to Jim Casy, who has lost his vocation, but found faith and worth in the service of mankind's sufferers. His apostle, Tom Joad, is a wanted man who in his enforced wanderings will find ample opportunity to carry on Casy's work and teach an understanding of the potent social forces that oppress the poor. Something of this vision is vouchsafed all the Joads. Their family unit is cohesive and energetic, but much too small to do effective combat with the giant capitalist complexes that seek to exploit it. Steinbeck's organistic concept of mankind here discovers concrete expression in the labor unions he evidently believes should be formed to protect the rights of the migrant farmer. Such unionization would be based upon social consciousness, broader acceptance of responsibility, and sympathetic sharing—qualities that are demonstrated in Rosasharn's concluding act of generous compassion.

Steinbeck's portrait of the Joads is not the sympathetic rendering of a propagandist. They are coarse, unlovely people with a narrow, foreshortened perspective on matters that come to affect them intimately. The symbolic thread of the book identifies them with the refugee children of Israel coming up out of the bondage of Egypt into the desert. The Promised Land which they seek will be hard won, and is contingent upon a long interval of wandering and painful mastering of the lessons of the world.

Steinbeck is not a revolutionary. He does not seek an overthrow of capitalism but its reformation. As a student of biological science, he interprets the struggle of human organisms as an ecological conflict that must be resolved to the mutual benefit and harmony of all members. But he realizes that the basic reform must originate in the enlarging and ennobling of the individual heart.

Sea of Cortez (1941) treats of a 1940 exploration of the living things in the Gulf of California by Steinbeck and his friend Ricketts. The second part of the volume is a scientific treatise by Ricketts, while the first part is a log of the expedition by the novelist. Intrinsically a fascinating account of a little-known and unusual area, the Steinbeck portion casts considerable light upon the major concepts of his fiction.

As we mentioned above, Ricketts and Steinbeck shared a "biological" view of life as one great organism, in which all living things are caught up. Coupled with that broad concept is Steinbeck's recognition of the importance of the individual in spite of this and his feeling that individuals have strong commitments to one another. Steinbeck indicates that the way of the modern world tends to make misfits and outcasts of many, but that farmers and laborers when not pressed by materialistic motives tend to lead essentially contented and satisfying lives.

Steinbeck sees man's condition on earth as being governed by an ethical paradox. Man praises as good the virtues of kindness, tolerance, altruism, generosity; but those who manifest these qualities generally fail in human society. Ironically the successful humans possess an abundance of bad traits that seem to constitute survival capability.

Cannery Row (1945) demonstrates the ethical paradox in a study of the waterfront skid row in Monterey, California. The central character Doc is obviously Ed Ricketts. In a sense the novel reflects the wholesale disillusionment that surfaced at the close of World War II. By implication, however, it is a potent criticism of the contemporary America that exalts status, property, commercial values, relentless pace, and suffers the resultant malaise. The human flotsam and jetsam of Cannery Row cannot compete on life's material level, but Steinbeck suggests that they are the pure in spirit. Often inept and bungling (they almost ruin Doc in their desire to "do something" for him), with all their amorality (Madame Dora maintains an exemplary brothel) they are more the sons of light than are the respectable gentry.

The Pearl (1947) is a lyric parable, "a folktale," in Steinbeck's words, that he based on a story heard during his Gulf of California exploration. Desperately poor, Kino, a pearl diver, finds a huge and valuable pearl. He expects to provide for his family and be wealthy, but the avaricious and unscrupulous whom he approaches make his life a nightmare. Finally he heaves the pearl back into the sea. Kino has sold his soul for great riches and finds them bitter ashes.

East of Eden (1952) has a title that recalls a line from Milton's *Paradise Lost,* and refers to the land where Cain dwelt after the murder of his brother, Abel. The novel treats a modern version of this biblical legend through the course of two generations. The first generation is that of Charles and Adam Trask, who quarrel over their father's favoritism toward Adam. Eventually Adam moves to the Salinas Valley and fathers twin sons, Caleb and Aaron. The latter of the two boys is Adam's favorite, and by way of revenge Caleb tells him the truth about their mother, Cathy. Aaron had remembered her lovingly and thought her dead. Caleb reveals the fact that Cathy had been a prostitute and had deserted their father and them to return to her old profession. Aaron meets her, and in shock at the destruction of his ideal tries to escape by enlisting in the Army, only to die in the war. Adam is grief-stricken at the loss of Aaron and dies soon afterward. His bequest to the surviving Caleb is the Hebrew word *Timshel,* which is taken to mean "Thou *mayest* rule over sin."

The main plot is fundamentally a description of ways in which sin or evil operates. Steinbeck's theme is an ambitious one, and the story struggles under its weight. Nevertheless it is sufficiently dramatic to make possible its rendering as a powerful motion picture.

Other noted Steinbeck novels are *The Wayward Bus* (1947) and *The Winter of Our Discontent* (1961).

William Faulkner (1897–1962). William Cuthbert Falkner was born at New Albany, Mississippi. His great-grandfather, who bore the same name, had achieved some reputation as a novelist in the past century. The Falkner family moved in 1902 to Oxford, Mississippi, thereafter the novelist's residence for most of his life, and under the name of Jefferson, the locale for much of his fiction. In 1918 he enlisted in the Royal Air Force in Toronto, Canada, later receiving an honorary commission as second lieutenant. During 1919–20 he attended the University of Mississippi but left to go to New York for a time. While working at various jobs in Oxford from 1922 to 1924, he published a work of nonfiction, using the spelling "Faulkner" on its title page and on all subsequent works; and it became the accepted spelling of his name. In 1925–26 Faulkner was in New Orleans and in Europe. His first novel, *Soldiers' Pay,* appeared in the latter year. With successive novels, he achieved wide recognition. He received the 1949 Nobel Prize for literature.

Faulkner may be compared with Balzac and Dickens as a novelist of superabundant fertility who by intense concentration upon the world he knew brought to full life an entire time and place, and in the process illuminated the entire human situation. Furthermore, like these men Faulkner had the gift of superlative storytelling ability and a deep concern for suffering humanity.

The most frequent setting of Faulkner's novels is the fictional Yoknapatawpha County, freely adapted from the real Lafayette County, Mississippi. Yoknapatawpha (accented on "taw") has become as famous a literary area as Hardy's Wessex, which it resembles in being the locale for an essentially tragic vision; but where Wessex was cursed with blind cosmic happenstance, Yoknapatawpha is blighted by the blindness of man. Simplified and modified from Faulkner's approved map, Yoknapatawpha looks roughly like the drawing opposite.

The county is approximately 2400 square miles in area. Population at the time: whites 6298, blacks, 9313. Oxford, the actual seat of Lafayette County, is located about forty miles away from its imaginary counterpart, Jefferson. The real and fictional counties share the Tallahatchie River. The river to the south of Lafayette County is Yocana, in old records Yocanapatafa, which Faulkner explains as Chickasaw for "water runs slow through flat land." It must be understood that Yoknapatawpha County is no mere depiction of a regional or provincial society. "An organic community," as Cleanth Brooks labels the county, "it is a microcosm of all humanity." Faulkner himself said, "I don't see too much Southern legend in it."

Sartoris (1929) is the first Faulkner novel upon Yoknapatawpha County, and the first work in the vein in which he would write his great novels.

In 1919, after the death of his twin brother, John, an aviator in World War I, Bayard Sartoris III returns to his home in Jefferson and begins a routine of dissipating his youthful energy through fast driving. Shortly after his marriage to Narcissa Benbow, who was also courted by Byron Snopes, a worker in the Sartoris bank, Bayard has an auto accident in which his grandfather dies. Bayard disappears from Jefferson

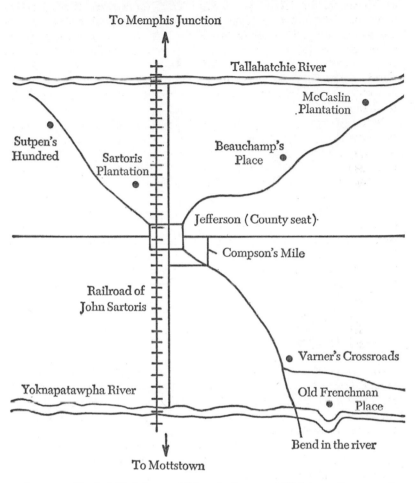

YOKNAPATAWPHA COUNTY

To Memphis Junction

Tallahatchie River

McCaslin Plantation

Sutpen's Hundred

Sartoris Plantation

Beauchamp's Place

Jefferson (County seat)

Compson's Mile

Railroad of John Sartoris

Varner's Crossroads

Yoknapatawpha River

Old Frenchman Place

Bend in the river

To Mottstown

and eventually is killed in an Ohio airplane test flight on the very day his son is born.

In the genealogical tables which follow, a marriage is indicated by =, while an illegitimate liaison is indicated by ≠. (N.) means Negro. (part N.) means someone who can pass as white though containing Negro blood. While Faulkner is remarkably consistent, inevitably some allusions in his works are at variance with these standardized schemes of genealogy.

GENEALOGY OF MAJOR SARTORIS FIGURES

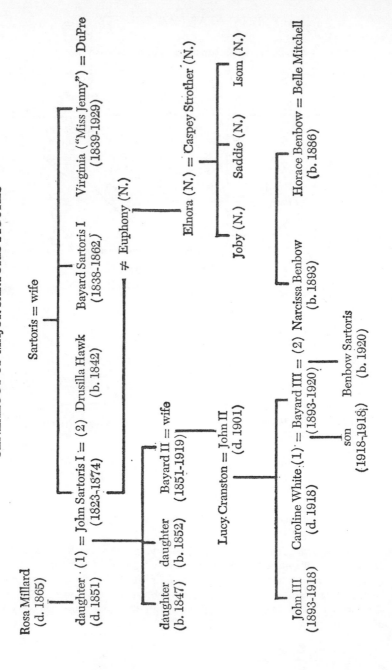

Rosa Millard
(d. 1865)

Sartoris = wife

daughter · (1) = John Sartoris I = (2) Drusilla Hawk
(d. 1851)   (1823-1874)   (b. 1842)

Bayard Sartoris I
(1838-1862)

≠ Euphony (N.)

Virginia ("Miss Jenny") = DuPre
(1839-1929)

Elnora (N.) = Caspey Strother (N.)

Joby (N.)   Saddie (N.)   Isom (N.)

Horace Benbow = Belle Mitchell
(b. 1886)

daughter   daughter   Bayard II = wife
(b. 1847)   (b. 1852)   (1851-1919)

Lucy Cranston = John II
(d. 1901)

Narcissa Benbow
(b. 1893)

Caroline White (1) = Bayard III = (2) Narcissa Benbow
(d. 1918)   (1893-1920)

John III
(1893-1918)

son
(1918-1918)

Benbow Sartoris
(b. 1920)

GENEALOGY OF MAJOR SNOPES FIGURES

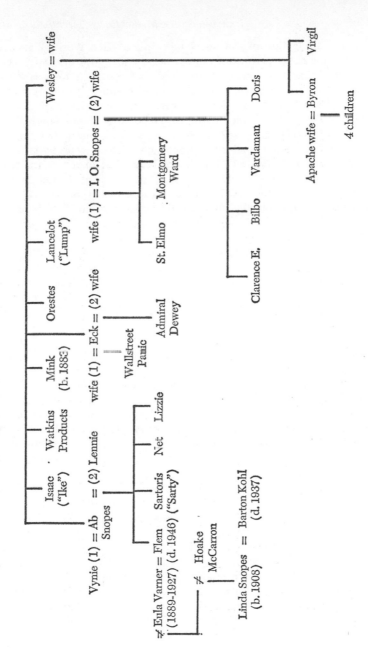

Though the action of the novel takes place after World War I, the subject is the entire *mythos* of the Sartoris family, with the Old Colonel, dead for almost half a century, the dominant figure. *Sartoris* as a word suggests "tailored elegance," and the clan is legendary in the county for swashbuckling energy and color. But there is a large element of exaggeration here; for example, the fabled Bayard I died ignominiously in the Civil War while stealing anchovies from a Union mess, but time has blown up his deed to valorous proportions. The recent Sartoris men are haunted by the legend of their forebears, but in a modern setting their tradition is only partly valid; it is death oriented, and its static rigidity undermines the new generation. The death of Bayard III comes about when he misguidedly attempts to practice the old Sartoris bravado in the new mechanical age. Miss Jenny, not addicted like the male Sartorises to a treasured dream of family glory, actually represents the most solid and sustaining virtues of the bygone era. A bit of the future is presaged in Flem Snopes's ascension to the vice-presidency of the bank run by Bayard II (the "Young Colonel"). The Snopes clan represents the low-born, unprincipled opportunists whose shrewdness and effrontery are proving surer keys to success than the ante-bellum honor and valor of the Sartorises.

The Sound and the Fury (1929) by a detailed scrutiny of four days casts extraordinary illumination upon thirty years of the Compson family history.

7 April 1928. Benjy Compson, a thirty-three-year-old idiot, loves but three things: his sister Caddy (Candace), the pasture which his father sold in 1909 to the golf club to pay his brother Quentin's way to Harvard, and fire. Benjy's young Negro helper, Luster, takes him to see the golfers and brings him back home to attend his birthday party. Benjy, through his moronic consciousness, is the narrator of this section of the novel.

2 June 1910. At Harvard, Quentin, eldest son of the Compson family, muses upon his sister Caddy who had been seduced by Dalton Ames. Quentin has failed in trying to avenge Caddy's honor, and Caddy has since effected a brief marriage of convenience with Sydney Head, an Indiana banker. At the end of the day Quentin goes out to commit suicide. All is told through Quentin's hypersensitive intellectuality.

6 April 1928. Jason, the brother between Quentin and Benjy, has his problems with Caddy's illegitimate daughter (she is named Quentin). She promises to be as ungovernable as Caddy and is therefore locked in her room at night. The most mercenary of the Compsons, Jason, whose consciousness presents this section, offers the clearest narrative of the volume.

8 April 1928. Dilsey, the Negro cook and mainstay of the household,

GENEALOGY OF MAJOR COMPSON FIGURES

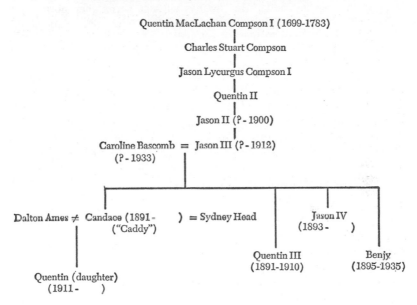

Quentin MacLachan Compson I (1699-1783)

Charles Stuart Compson

Jason Lycurgus Compson I

Quentin II

Jason II (?- 1900)

Caroline Bascomb = Jason III (?-1912)
(?- 1933)

Dalton Ames ≠ Candace (1891-   ) = Sydney Head   Jason IV
                    ("Caddy")   (1893-   )

                                                    Quentin III   Benjy
                                                    (1891-1910)   (1895-1935)

Quentin (daughter)
(1911-   )

finds Quentin (Caddy's daughter) gone. Jason discovers that the girl rifled his money box before fleeing. The pursuit fails to catch up with the girl. This section is related by an omniscient observer.

The title is taken from Macbeth's famous words: "[Life] is a tale / Told by an idiot, full of sound and fury, / Signifying nothing." To the consciousness of the perceivers of the first three sections such indeed seems the case. The errant Caddy is the center of all the characters' attention. Benjy's account is quite literally "told by an idiot." To him Caddy smelled like trees; she meant innocent love, and he cannot mentally let her grow up to normal sexuality. Benjy is a depiction of modern man as a sterile moron (Jason IV had insisted upon his castration in 1913 when the idiot scared some schoolgirls). To Quentin III, Caddy is the repository of the family honor according to the moral code of the Old South. Emotionally immature and unstable, he cannot properly uphold the old code or transfer his allegiance to a new one. Suicide is both a way of escaping the dilemma and a gesture to appease his wounded pride. Jason is angered because Caddy's downfall has blackened the family cloak of respectability; moreover, she was divorced from Sydney Head within a year of her marriage. Both of her actions have militated against Jason's securing lucrative employment. Perhaps the greatest sufferer is Caddy. Her family will not permit her normal development, so she explodes in conduct that will blight her relations and make her own life naught but "sound and fury." Although the Compsons do not realize it, Dilsey is the focal point and binding force of the family. For her the world is not mere "sound and fury" but an arena of sorrow and compassion.

The vast riches of this novel have elicited even vaster studies. For example, some studies have emphasized the water symbolism of this novel—purification for Caddy (she washes off her perfume so that Benjy can find her treelike smell again) and death for Quentin (who cannot face the challenge of the waters of life). Existentially, human freedom requires the prospect of the open future, while each of the Compsons is self-trapped in the past.

As I Lay Dying (1930), a favorite of the novelist, is remarkable for its grotesque blending of disparates: rough comedy and deep tragedy, romantic heroism and coarse naturalism. As another experiment in technique, the novel is told in forty-nine sections of the interior monologue of the seven Bundrens and eight "outsiders."

Finding marriage to Anse Bundren loveless, Addie Bundren has a son, Jewel, by preacher Whitfield, after bearing her husband two sons, Cash and Darl. Subsequently she gives Anse a daughter, Dewey Dell, and another son, Vardaman. Addie has extracted from Anse the promise that she will be buried in Jefferson with her kinfolk. When she dies, Cash, who has become a carpenter, prepares his mother's coffin and the whole family takes part in carrying her body by wagon. In addition to their ostensible mission in Jefferson, Anse wants a set of false teeth, Cash wants to buy a phonograph, and pregnant Dewey Dell (aged seventeen) wants abortion pills. After surmounting such major obstacles as floods and an accident in which Cash's leg is broken, they lay Addie to rest as she had requested. Anse acquires new teeth and a new wife, and Darl is committed to a mental hospital. Cash's broken leg is properly set; Dewey Dell's pregnancy continues.

The Bundrens are "poor whites": coarse, selfish, squalid, and generally stupid. Nonetheless, they have their sense of honor and display heroism like their betters, the Sartorises and the Compsons. They do not use the highflown language of the aristocrats and cannot realize the symbolic meanings of their journey.

Faulkner here contemplates man's capacity for action and suffering. Like the "outsiders" we are uncertain whether to laugh or cry, for the Bundren heroic adventure is at once monumentally impressive and abysmally appalling. Their motives for making the journey to Jefferson are greatly varied, and the stresses of the endeavor explore the basic aspects of each character. After her death Addie's sons must search for their own meaning, independent of her. Anse and Dewey Dell are the most shallow personalities, have the fewest emotional ties to Addie, and at the end remain the least altered. Cash, agonized by his broken leg, reveals stoic courage in his ordeal. Jewel's rescue of the coffin from a flooded river and later from fire enhances his stature. Vardaman, only nine, begins to grasp the harsh realities of the adult world. Darl, the most intelligent and most realistic of all, is broken asunder by the events and ends his quest for identity by descending into madness. The center of the family, holding it together and willing it to concerted epic effort until she lies buried, is Addie, a great Earth Mother. In her assent to life she denies the mere words that bandy about ideals and hypocrisies, whether the pious mouthings of neighbor Cora Tull or the false protestations of love from Anse. For Addie the sole reason for living is the "duty to the alive."

These 13 (1931) is the first, and many believe the best, collection of Faulkner short stories. Perhaps Faulkner had in mind Balzac's *Histoire des treize*, but almost certainly he was thinking of the popular superstitious aversion to the number 13. The first four stories evoke the pity, terror, and irrationality of World War I. Most famous of this group is "All the Dead Pilots," an anecdotal account of John Sartoris' competition with a British flyer, Captain Spoomer, for the favors of a French girl. Sartoris plays a mad prank upon Spoomer and as punishment is transferred to another squadron, dying in action soon after. The next six stories spring from Yoknapatawpha and range from such subjects as aborigine Indians to modern-day Jefferson. Probably the most discussed of all Faulkner short stories is "A Rose for Emily." Following the Civil War, Emily Grierson's father discouraged all her suitors, presumably because the good men had been killed off. After his death she took up with a Yankee construction foreman, Homer Barron, whom she killed when in danger of losing him. After Emily's death the townsfolk of Jefferson invade the old house and to their astonishment find that Homer's corpse has shared her bed for all those years. The rose is an ironic accolade for Emily.

Sanctuary (1931) was Faulkner's first novel to be widely read.

The story is set in Yoknapatawpha County and revolves around a murder committed at the Old Frenchman Place, a dilapidated plantation that is headquarters for Lee Goodwin, a bootlegger, and his guest Popeye, a depraved and sexually impotent gangster from Memphis. Temple Drake, the college-aged daughter of the prominent Judge Drake, is abandoned at the plantation by her inebriated escort Gowan Stevens, leaving her only the simple-minded young Tommy as protector. When Popeye sees his opportunity he kills Tommy, rapes Temple (with a corncob, it is later discovered), and transports her to Memphis, where she is kept prisoner in a bordello and made to cater to Popeye's voyeuristic fancies. Back in Yoknapatawpha, Goodwin has been arrested for Tommy's murder and his defense has been undertaken by Horace Benbow, an attorney dominated by his wife and his sister and also by his search to find himself. Benbow's case is careful and clean-cut, but is overthrown when the terrorized Temple perjures herself at the trial. (Popeye has since committed another murder to maintain his hold on Temple.) The convicted Goodwin becomes the victim of mob justice. Judge Drake takes his daughter to Europe to recover from her ordeal. Popeye is later tried and executed for a murder in Alabama of which he is innocent.

The title is scathingly ironic, for there is no sanctuary, unless it lies in empty conformity. Justice has been led astray by certain self-interested parties in Yoknapatawpha. Goodwin has been lynched, and Benbow, weak though intellectual, returns to his domineering spouse. The blame for the injustice rests largely with the good ladies of Jefferson, led by Benbow's militant sister, who want to ignore evil or decorously cover it up. On the other hand, the most apparent victim of events, Temple Drake, has displayed an avid nymphomania, although she parades a façade of outraged womanhood, during her confinement in the Memphis brothel, and she bears much responsibility for the sordid happening.

In establishing his theme of general guilt, Faulkner makes most of the characters in *Sanctuary* two-dimensional, rather than fully rounded individuals. For each of them there is no place to hide; not even in the obscure rural haven of Yoknapatawpha. And the crowning tragedy is the failure of almost everyone to realize what has happened.

Light in August (1932) is the longest and most experimental Faulkner novel. The two major characters never meet, but in a period of ten days constantly draw all the other characters into intense involvement.

From Alabama, Lena Grove comes to Jefferson in search of her lover, Lucas Burch, who made her pregnant. She arrives on the day that Joanna Burden, a forty-four-year-old spinster of New England origins, has been murdered. The accused is Joe Christmas, a thirty-six-year-old drifter who was Joanna's lover. Joe's father was a "Mexican" circus hand suspected of being part Negro. Joe's whole life has been fractured by his worries over his racial affiliation. He has actually killed Joanna in self-defense but takes flight anyway, only to be captured in Mottstown. After being returned to Jefferson, Joe is brutally slain by a mob led by a fanatical deputy named Percy Grimm. A sawmill worker, Byron Bunch, has meanwhile been assisting Lena to find her lover, who has changed his name to Joe Brown and become implicated in the crime. After he had revealed that Joe Christmas had some Negro ancestry the townsfolk were persuaded of Christmas' guilt and released Brown. Now Byron is able to arrange a meeting between Lena and her child's father, but the latter is still unwilling to undertake responsibility and decamps once more. When her baby is born, Lena placidly accepts Byron's companionship and the trio wander off into the countryside.

From well-intentioned, educated Gavin Stevens, the district attorney, to the savage avenger Percy Grimm, the town of Jefferson is characterized by a Calvinistic rigidity. Without pity or discrimination, the community cruelly lacerates the deviator: Gail Hightower, an unfrocked cleric, is ostracized because of his unorthodoxy; Joanna Burden is stigmatized as a "nigger-loving" Northerner; Joe Christmas never knows whether he is black or white, and in this community all must be unequivocally one or the other. Once his origins are understood, the community discards reasoned consideration and asserts its convenient cliché: Joanna has been assaulted by the embodiment of dark passion. Though not quite the Christ figure suggested by his name (given because he was left at an orphanage on Christmas Eve), Joe is the scapegoat. As he epitomizes the death thrust of his society, symbolized in darkness and terror, Lena epitomizes the life impulse, light and placidity. Her name is a diminutive of Helena, in Greek meaning "a torch" or "a light one." As Faulkner explained the title, it is "a luminosity older than our Christian civilization" suggested by the brilliant August days in Mississippi. By coming to her assistance, Bunch escapes from his vacuous existence into a sense of meaningful service. The most deeply affected is the Reverend Hightower, who helps Lena at her childbirth and attempts vainly to keep Grimm from killing Joe. Hightower had taken the second path explicated by Faulkner ("I will not participate"), as Bayard Sartoris III and Quentin Compson III had followed the first path ("I will take death"). Hightower now realizes that no man can live only for himself. Although readers often infer that the injured Hightower will die shortly after the novel's end, Faulkner himself insisted that the renegade clergyman would survive with the possibility of a regenerated, outgoing life.

The two paths which we have mentioned are the first two of the three stages of man's response as outlined by Faulkner, later at the University of Virginia: "The first says, I'll have no part of it, I will take death first. The second says, I don't like it, I can't do anything about it, I will not participate in it myself. The third says, I'm going to do something about it."

Pylon (1935) is one of the few Faulkner novels set entirely outside Yoknapatawpha County. The work centers about the death of a flyer, Roger Shumann, in the air contests inaugurating Feinman Airport (Shushan Airport) at New Valois (New Orleans). By entitling his next-to-last chapter "Lovesong of J. A. Prufrock," Faulkner underlines his indebtedness to T. S. Eliot. New Valois is to Faulkner the wasteland of modern society, and he is never quite at home in the metropolis. He conceives of the aviators as "ephemera on the face of the contemporary scene." Unconventional in their moral outlook, the flyers form a "family unit" about the pilot. Although Roger is the legal husband of Laverne, her children's actual fathers could be any of the aviators. Roger dies in seeking money for Laverne's latest child, and with his death the family unit is dissolved.

Absalom, Absalom! (1936) in its title quotes David's heartbroken lament in the Bible for his deceased favorite son, who had rebelled against him.

In the early nineteenth century, mountaineer Thomas Sutpen was bent upon acquiring wealth, position, and a proud line of descendants. In the West Indies he made a fortune and married the daughter of a Haitian sugar mogul. Finding that his wife had Negro blood, Sutpen divorced her and renounced her son, called Charles Bon. In 1833 Sutpen bought a hundred square miles of Yoknapatawpha soil from the Chickasaw chief Ikkemotubbe, and married Ellen Coldfield. By her he had a son, Henry, and a daughter, Judith. At the University of Mississippi Henry Sutpen became a friend of Charles Bon who had grown up cultured, worldly, and exotic. In time Charles began to court Judith. Thomas forbade the union, which would combine incest and miscegenation. Henry fights alongside Charles during the Civil War and admires him, but in the end he defers to the color bar and kills the friend who is his half brother. Thomas Sutpen returns from the Civil War as a colonel of the 23rd Mississippi Infantry and is determined upon a new male heir. His callousness toward Milly Jones causes Wash Jones, Sutpen's poor-white handyman, to kill Thomas, Milly, and their illegitimate child. Judith Sutpen, unmarried, and Clytie (Thomas Sutpen's daughter by a Negro slave) have brought up Charles Etienne De St. Velery Bon, son of Charles Bon by his octoroon mistress. Although he was white in appearance, the younger Bon considered himself a Negro and married a Negress who bore him an idiot son, Jim Bond. In 1884 Etienne and Judith died of yellow fever. In 1909 Rosa Coldfield, sister-in-law of Thomas Sutpen, discovers Henry in hiding on the old Sutpen plantation. Mistakenly believing that Henry is still sought for the murder of Charles Bon fifty years before, Clytie burns down the house. Only Jim Bond, the idiot, remains as a descendant of Sutpen amidst the ashes of his mansion.

Three narrators present the account: Rosa, in a highly charged, romantic Old South diction, reminiscent of Jacobean drama; Jason Compson III, in a world-weary tone of *fin de siècle* decadence; Quentin Compson III, in the realistic voice of an intelligent young Southerner

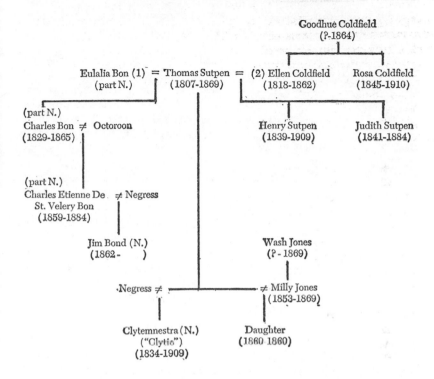

trying to comprehend his background. An important element in the novel's structure is Shreve McCannon, the Canadian roommate of Quentin at Harvard, who tries to grasp the American South through this story. No one person can extract the final truth from these materials, but Quentin and Shreve apparently come closest.

Initially Quentin considers Thomas Sutpen an upstart and monomaniacal monster. Gradually he comes to regard the man as a tragic hero destroyed by the cultural patterns to which he attempted conformity. Sutpen was driven by the compulsion to material values and infatuated by the code of aristocratic dynasty. He had carved a rich plantation out of the Chickasaw wilderness and ornamented it with a sumptuous mansion. But Sutpen came to an inglorious end, and all he hoped for in the future was obliterated: his mansion reduced to charred ruins and his dynastic expectations ironically descended to nothing but an idiot. His social and racial intolerance hopelessly blighted his relations with his sons and eventually blotted out the entire line in blood. However,

Quentin feels that Thomas Sutpen was superior in strength and vision to any of the Compsons or the Sartorises, and that his fate is genuinely tragic.

The Unvanquished (1938) consists of seven short stories narrated by Bayard Sartoris II. The subject of all is the Southern mystique as viewed by Bayard. The first story, "Ambuscade," is set in 1862 when the narrator is twelve. From a romantic youngster at the outset, Bayard proceeds through successive tales to mature and critical adulthood in the last story, "An Odor of Verbena," set in 1874 when he is twenty-four. The first six stories, originally written for magazines, use the Sartorises to exemplify the gallantry and sentimentality of the Old South. The last story, written especially for book publication, provides perspective and dimension. Bayard II in the final narrative is summoned home from legal studies at the University of Mississippi because his father has been slain by a former business associate, Ben Redmond. His stepmother Drusilla and almost everyone else expect Bayard to follow the code of the duello and kill Redmond in vengeance. Repudiating his father's code, Bayard faces Redmond unarmed. After one wild shot at Bayard, Redmond quits Jefferson permanently. Bayard's restraint is a product of his determination to act as a man and not as a performer in a ritualistic act of violence. Thus the traditional concept of honor embodied in his father has undergone a skeptical re-evaluation by the young man.

The Wild Palms (1939) is another of the few Faulkner works not associated with Yoknapatawpha. In the original printing, chapters of the Harry and Charlotte account were alternated with chapters about a convict caught in the Mississippi flood of 1927. In subsequent editions the convict's story was assembled in a unit called "Old Man" (actually he was twenty-five). Critical opinion has frequently deemed the "Old Man" section superior to the Harry Wilbourne part of the story. Briefly, the plot entails the elopement of a young medical interne, Harry Wilbourne, with Charlotte Rittenmeyer, a married woman. Incurably romantic and seeking "natural" love, they escape New Orleans for Chicago, and then to a Utah mining camp, and finally to the Mississippi Gulf Coast where Harry bungles an abortion operation upon Charlotte. She dies and he is sentenced to fifty years in prison.

In contrast is the tale of the "Old Man," a convict who braves a perilous flood to save a pregnant woman and eventually brings her and her infant to safety, only to be returned to prison. The old man is an unthinking naïf who survives and works commendable good, but he is just as trapped as the illicit lovers.

The Hamlet (1940) is the first volume of what has come to be called the Snopes trilogy (continued later in *The Town* and *The Mansion*). Frenchman's Bend, down in the southeast corner of Yoknapatawpha

County, demonstrates the trend of economic and social change in the South. Its big plantations of older days have been broken up into small, seedy farms; these in turn have come under the control of Will Varner, a small businessman. But the Varner acquisitiveness is quite surpassed by the cold rapacity of Flem Snopes, who arrives early in the 1900s. By shrewd, unscrupulous deals Flem moves upward to dominate French-man's Bend, and at the end moves to Jefferson in search of new worlds to conquer. Flem's wife is Eula Varner, a local siren who marries him to make legitimate her daughter Linda (whose actual father is Hoake McCarron). Another Snopes, the idiot Ike, has a fantastic love affair with a cow. Mink Snopes kills a neighbor in a feud and is sentenced to life imprisonment. His brother Flem pointedly refuses to come to his aid.

The work is a series of loosely connected episodes containing boisterous comedy in the tall-tale tradition, macabre horror, and brutal naturalism. Unity is achieved partly by the device of the narrator, V. K. Ratliff, a sewing-machine salesman, but chiefly by the contrast of economic man with natural man. Ratliff is the normal, relatively balanced man gazing upon the extremes of Snopesism. Idiot Ike is the natural man, the lover, even if a cow is his love object. Flem is the economic man, representa-tive of the breed that will oust the old families (Sartoris, Compson) and rule the New South.

Faulkner evidently dislikes the Snopeses as a whole, regretting that with their fertility of offspring and especially their powerful economic orientation they are the winners of today and the inheritors of tomorrow. When the novelist comes to grips with individual Snopeses, however, he makes them genuine people, not mere stereotypes. The Snopeses fall below the old families chiefly in being more vulgar and trivial and in lacking any humanitarian or community values.

Go Down, Moses (1942) consists of seven separate stories that form a unit because almost all treat of descendants of Lucius Quintus Carothers McCaslin.

"Was," set in 1859, is largely seen through the eyes of Cass Edmonds, then nine, as he watches the twin bachelors, Uncle Buck and Uncle Buddy, pursue Tomey's Turl, who has run off to the Beauchamp planta-tion to visit his sweetheart, Tennie. Although the brothers oppose slavery, they continue the ritualistic patterns of plantation life, including this comic parody of the pursuit of the runaway slave in *Uncle Tom's Cabin*. Uncle Buck narrowly escapes matrimony with spinsterish Sophonsiba Beauchamp, and the McCaslins buy Tennie as a spouse for Tomey's Turl. For Cass it is initiation into the practices of ante-bellum life.

"The Fire and the Hearth" is a reference to the sanctity of the home. The story is set in 1941. Lucas Beauchamp, the Negro grandson of old

GENEALOGY OF MAJOR WHITE McCASLIN FIGURES

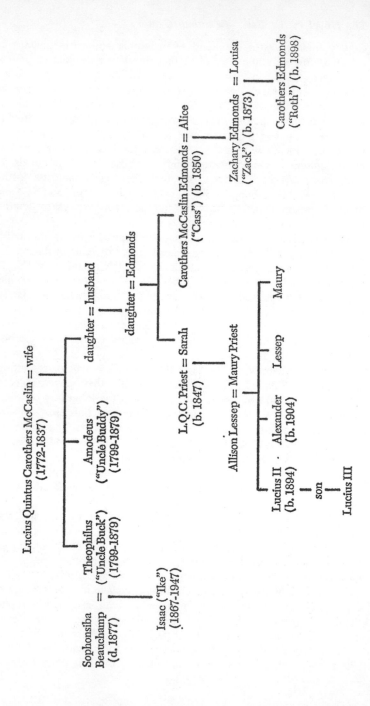

GENEALOGY OF MAJOR NEGRO McCASLIN FIGURES

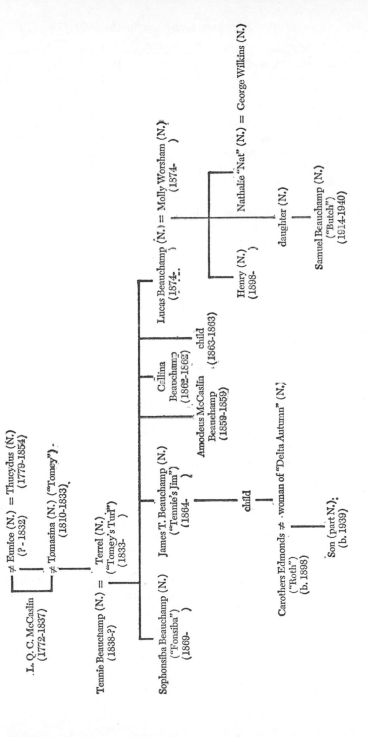

L. Q. C. McCaslin, is involved in distilling moonshine with his son-in-law, George Wilkins, and in treasure-hunting with a mine-detector salesman. In the course of these activities an older story reveals itself. Back in 1898 Lucas had had his wife taken and held by Zack Edmonds after Zack's wife died in giving birth to young Roth. Lucas asserted the honor of his home and insisted that the white man's code of respecting another man's marital rights be extended to him. He got his wife back, but as Roth grew up he grew away from his childhood associations with Lucas' son Henry. As a result, Roth was quietly ostracized as his Negro relatives retreated into racial isolation.

"The Old People" is the initiation in 1879 of Ike McCaslin into the ritual of the hunt by Sam Fathers. The old man's name is a shortening of Had-Two-Fathers. His actual father was Ikkemotubbe, a Chickasaw chief, who made a quadroon slave pregnant and married her to a Negro, the second father of Sam. Then Ikkemotubbe sold the octoroon mother and the infant to L. Q. C. McCaslin in 1809. Ike McCaslin kills his first buck and in ceremonial fashion is marked with the animal's blood by Sam. Then Sam shows Ike a huge buck, the emblem of life and nature.

"The Bear" has been the subject of an unusual amount of critical discussion. Within this novella one may find Faulkner's views on the South in transition.

The locale is the northern part of Yoknapatawpha County in the virgin timberland along the Tallahatchie River bottom. This tract, formerly part of Sutpen's Hundred, fell to Major Cassius de Spain by foreclosure. A shack has been turned into a hunting lodge by the Major, who conducts two-week hunting parties there every November.

Sections I, II, and III are a chronological account of the hunting of a legendary bear, Old Ben, who has grown old and wise during his years of eluding various pursuers. Ike McCaslin, entering upon his early teens, has become intimate with the ways of the woods and on one occasion, having voluntarily left gun and compass behind, he encounters the hoary old animal and they regard each other significantly. The experience establishes a mystic bond between boy and beast, so that Ike is never able to raise a weapon against the bear on subsequent meetings. Yet Old Ben's days are numbered. In Ike's sixteenth year (1883) Sam Fathers captures a courageous wild dog which he trains to the hunt, and after a series of headlong chases the Major's men corner the bear, which is dispatched by Boon Hogganbeck, a mixed blood (part white, part Indian) whom the Major employs as an unofficial gamekeeper. The dog Lion is fatally clawed in the melee, and Sam Fathers is mysteriously stricken at the moment of Old Ben's death. When Sam dies some days after, he is buried in Chickasaw Indian fashion along with Lion and a paw cut from the bear.

Section IV, the most difficult, takes place when Ike turns twenty-one. He has decided to relinquish his right to the McCaslin plantation, explaining this act in a long debate with his cousin McCaslin Edmonds. Isaac's (Ike's) argument is a history of the South itself as land entrusted by God to men to be overseen. Instead, generations from the Indians on have seized, ravaged, bought, sold, and bartered it, and the land is cursed for their sins. Ike sees the Civil War as God's painful breaking of the hold of avarice and himself one of the first to respond by laying down his hereditary claim. In several flashbacks he examines old ledgers kept by his father and uncle, abounding in curt, semiliterate entries that suggest a long history of suffering and sexual exploitation undergone by the slaves and ex-slaves of the plantation. Elsewhere Ike recalls a journey to distribute what remained of the McCaslin wealth among the illegitimate, half-Negro heirs his grandfather begat. In the last pages of the section he takes up the trade of carpentry, rents a room, and marries, refusing his wife's demand that he repossess the McCaslin lands.

Section V, the last, recounts Isaac's final return to the Major's hunting camp, which has been sold along with the surrounding forest to a lumber company. As he journeys by logging train and finally on foot he muses on hunting incidents of the past. After a visit to Sam Fathers' grave, where he imagines the creatures buried there restored and resurrected as they merge with soil and tree, he goes on to the rendezvous with Boon Hogganbeck. Ike finds Boon hysterically destroying his rifle and loudly announcing his ownership of the woodland creatures to all within earshot.

"The Bear" is rich in interpretational possibilities that call for examination on several levels. Most prominently, the saga of Old Ben conforms to the pattern of the South's epic history, its instinctive nobility and primeval courage, as related in the crucial fourth section. Boon Hogganbeck, and especially the dog Lion are the offspring of the raw woodlands they unite to overthrow. After the Civil War, what is left falls into the hands of the lumber-company carpetbaggers. Sam Fathers, for one, prefers to die as his world passes away, while Boon Hogganbeck persists in trying to perpetuate the old order by enslaving it.

The symbolic force of heredity is most elaborately displayed in the case of Isaac McCaslin. His decision to live in rented quarters and work with his own hands is more quixotic than realistic, more motivated by conscience and nostalgia than a clear realization of purpose. He yearns for the elemental simplicities of an earlier heroic age when men sought a complementary position in Nature's scheme, and does not care to accept the fact that his race has irrevocably outgrown its own world.

"Delta Autumn" takes place in the 1940s when Ike McCaslin is over seventy. Roth Edmonds asks Ike to give money and a farewell message to a Negro whom Roth has made pregnant. To his astonishment Ike learns that she is the granddaughter of Tennie's Jim, the grandson of L. Q. C. McCaslin. He bequeaths to her coming child the old hunting horn that General Compson had left to him, thus symbolizing the wilderness heritage of both the black and the white descendants of old McCaslin. But Ike cannot overcome his prejudice and succumbs to the bonds of his social conditioning.

"Go Down, Moses," taking its title from a Negro spiritual, tells of the grief of Molly Beauchamp for the death of her grandson Samuel ("Butch"). The young Negro had been executed for murder in Chicago, and attorney Gavin Stevens had kept the story out of the local newspapers. The chant of the mourning woman is the instinctive emotional outpouring of someone living far deeper than the intellect or the consciousness. The death of Butch is felt as a symbol of the enslavement of the race; and there is the suggestion that the Negro awaits a Moses to lead him out of the land of bondage. Roth Edmonds, the owner of the plantation that Ike repudiated and where Butch was raised, represents the white man's oppression of the black.

Intruder in the Dust (1948) and subsequent volumes, while of notable merit, in some respects lack the brilliance of Faulkner's earlier work.

The Negro Lucas Beauchamp, accused of murdering Vinson Gowrie, is about to be lynched in Jefferson, but "Chick" Mallison and his uncle Gavin Stevens prove that Crawford Gowrie, brother and business partner of the murdered man, was the actual slayer.

This novel in large part belongs to the genre of the detective story, as do the short pieces of *Knight's Gambit,* but there are social implications that exist within the machinery of the plot. When Chick Mallison was twelve years old, Lucas rescued him when he fell in a creek, and always thereafter Lucas maintained their relationship as man to man rather than black to white. This attitude irritates Chick, who misses the respect usually accorded the color of his skin. The townsfolk are similarly exasperated by Lucas' recalcitrance, and relish this opportunity to put him in his place. Ironically, in trying to pay a debt to Lucas and thereby reassert his white superiority, Chick undermines the ordered structure of the South. The disgruntled whites must accept Lucas at his own valuation as a man.

Knight's Gambit (1949) consists of six detective stories involving the attorney Gavin Stevens.

The series shows Gavin Stevens, a product of Harvard and Heidelberg, learning persistence and humanity in his dealings with even petty and vicious people. Stevens is often considered a spokesman for Faulkner, but the author frequently smiles at the garrulity and romanticism of the lawyer. With all his expanded sensibilities, Stevens does not arrive at the

GENEALOGY OF MAJOR STEVENS FIGURES

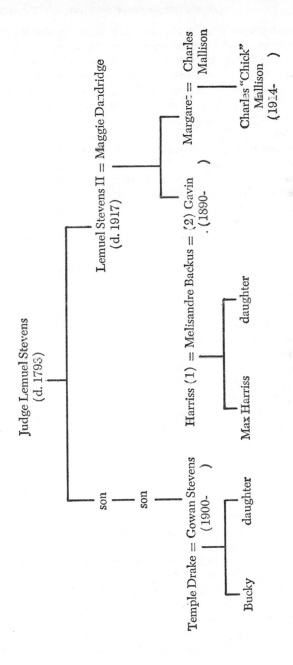

Judge Lemuel Stevens
(d. 1793)

son son

Lemuel Stevens II = Maggie Dandridge
(d. 1917)

Temple Drake = Gowan Stevens
(1900-   )

Bucky   daughter

Harriss (1) = Melisandre Backus = (2) Gavin
(1890-   )

Max Harriss   daughter

Margaret = Charles
Mallison

Charles "Chick"
Mallison
(1914-   )

broadly humanistic viewpoint of his creator. In the title story, Stevens prevents Max Harriss from causing the death of Captain Gualdres, an Argentinian horseman who had jilted Max's sister. Subsequently Stevens marries Max's widowed mother. The title refers to a chess move in which a knight threatens both queen and castle; the logical response is to save the queen and let the castle go. Stevens in saving the Harrisses and Gualdres from irreparable harm proves himself a large-spirited and able man.

Requiem for a Nun (1951) takes place eight years after the events of *Sanctuary*.

Gowan Stevens has married Temple Drake and established residence in Jefferson. Nancy Manningoe, their Negro nursemaid, has been sentenced to die for smothering their infant daughter to death. Gowan's uncle Gavin Stevens induces Temple to drive with him to Jackson and intercede with the governor in Nancy's behalf. It seems that Temple had planned to elope with the brother of Red, her former lover in a Memphis brothel, and Nancy had killed the child to prevent the breakup of the home. Despite Temple's evidence, the governor refuses to stay the execution.

Nancy, the "nun" of the title, is portrayed as having sought to save the soul of Temple. Gavin Stevens is the heart of the novel as he forces Temple to face the truth and for once act with consideration for another. "The past is never dead," states Gavin. "It's not even past." Although she claims now to be the wholly respectable Mrs. Gowan Stevens, Temple still bears the burden of her earlier sin and continues to act to the dire injury of others.

A Fable (1954), another of the rare Faulkner removals from Yoknapatawpha County, earned him his first Pulitzer Prize, a belated recognition of his total stature. The work is based upon the "false armistice" of May 1918, and the purported appearance of a Christ figure in the front lines to preach peace to both combatants.

The Corporal, illegitimate son of the Marshal, was even born on Christmas Day in 1885. At the age of thirty-three in 1918, he proclaims his message of love and peace, calling for the armies to cease fighting. He has twelve followers, one of whom, Polchek, betrays him, while another, Pierre Bouc, denies him. The Marshal fruitlessly tempts him with secular power. His half sisters Marya and Marthe parallel Mary and Martha. After he is slain like Christ between two criminals, his body is taken to a farm by Marya and Marthe. By chance the body of the Corporal is chosen as the Unknown Soldier to be buried at the Arc de Triomphe. The Runner who tries to continue the mission of the Corporal is a twentieth-century Paul, and is martyred as Paul was. This work must be viewed as the parable its title proclaims it to be.

Its lineage is of John Bunyan and Jonathan Swift. The writing of *A Fable* began shortly after "The Bear," and its focal point is the conversation between the Corporal and the Marshal, as the focal point of "The Bear" is the discussion between Ike and Cass. The Marshal, like Cass, represents human law and order, social respectability and authority; the Marshal and Cass demand the continuance of the *status quo*, working for betterment within the framework of things as they are. The Corporal, like Ike, stands for spiritual truth, but, as "Delta Autumn" clearly indicates, Ike is so weakly mortal that he fails to attain for himself the full spiritual renovation he desires. In contrast, the Corporal is a true Christ who resolutely goes to his martyrdom.

The Town (1957), the second of the Snopes trilogy, presents characters of less stature than appear in most other Faulkner works. Critics frequently object to a patchwork effect arising from the stitching together of pieces written separately over a period of twenty years.

In 1909 Flem Snopes leaves Frenchman's Bend for the greater opportunities of Jefferson. His voluptuous wife, Eula, dazzles the entire male population and encourages them to be flirtatious. Gavin Stevens is an ineffectual courtier, but the mayor Manfred de Spain makes Eula his mistress. Flem pretends ignorance of his wife's derelictions but uses the affair as the lever to superintendency of the local power plant. He also brings a plague of Snopeses upon Jefferson, as his relatives flock in. After the death of Bayard Sartoris II, De Spain becomes bank president with Flem as vice-president. When the time is ripe, Flem springs a trap, utilizing the scandal of De Spain and his wife to oust De Spain and become president of the bank himself. Eula commits suicide; and Linda, her illegitimate daughter, departs for New York.

As the title indicates, this novel centers about the community of Jefferson, making the reader aware of the day-by-day existence of its citizens. Three narrators explore the rise of Flem Snopes, their differing viewpoints suggesting the many faces of truth. V. K. Ratliff, the sewing-machine salesman of *The Hamlet*, is a shrewd, laconic speaker, fully acquainted with the nefarious Snopeses of Frenchman's Bend. Gavin Stevens, the intellectual man of principle, struggles unsuccessfully against the Snopes invasion. Chick Mallison is consciously the voice of the general community. Respectability is Jefferson's credo, but its morality is so weak and compromised that the rapacious Flem easily maneuvers his way to the economic and social heights of the town. Gavin Stevens, romantically imbued with old-fashioned Southern tradition, cannot lead the community, which tacitly has accepted the Snopes philosophy as its own. Gavin is so concerned with public opinion and his quixotic allegiances that he makes a fool of himself and effectively helps no one.

The Mansion (1959) concludes the Snopes trilogy. The title refers to the most handsome house in Jefferson, formerly the property of De Spain but now the proud residence of his dispossessor, Flem Snopes.

In 1946, after thirty-eight years in prison, Mink Snopes comes to Jefferson intent upon killing Flem (see *The Hamlet*). Linda also returns after a ten-year absence. Her husband, Barton Kohl, a Jewish sculptor, was killed during the Spanish Civil War and she was deafened by an exploding shell. Gavin Stevens marries the widowed Melisandre. After killing Flem, Mink is aided in his escape by Linda.

There is much tidying up of the Yoknapatawpha cycle, and many pieces of the jigsaw are fitted into place, such as what happened to Benbow Sartoris and Benjy Compson. Though less omnipresent than in *The Town*, Jefferson is still a prominent part of the narrative. But the pervasive theme seems to be the thwarted, isolated lives of individuals. Linda is a rootless modern who returns to Jefferson only because she has no longer any alternative to her early pattern of life. Gavin Stevens ineffectually supports the ideals of an older South only to end up living in the luxury bequeathed to Melisandre by her first husband, a prosperous bootlegger. Snopesism has so triumphed in its pliant, opportunistic manipulations that Flem seems a rather pitiful superannuate waiting around for his murder. Incredibly, Mink (called by Ratliff "the only out-and-out mean Snopes") compels the reluctant admiration of the reader. The basic sin of Snopesism is lack of integrity. Although he is coarse and animal-like, Mink nonetheless stands apart from his fellow Snopeses in his cherishing of the traditional concept of honor. Flem had broken the deep clan obligations of kinship. A lifetime of suffering, during which immediate family and all else had been lost to him, is consecrated by Mink to one act of vengeance.

The Reivers (1962), the last Faulkner novel, won the novelist's second Pulitzer Prize. The mood of this story is quite different from that of most of Faulkner's work. The title employs an archaic word meaning "plunderers."

In 1961 Lucius Priest II (see the McCaslin genealogy) reminisces about a wild escapade of 1905. In his grandfather's car Lucius, then eleven, is taken to Memphis by Boon Hogganbeck and Ned McCaslin. Boon has the boy go with him to visit Corrie, a prostitute in Miss Reba's brothel. Ned swaps the car for a race horse named Lightning, and they then must win the race to regain the car. After vast excitement Grandfather Priest gets back his automobile, losing $500 en route. Corrie is persuaded by Lucius to renounce her profession and become Boon's wife.

Though bawdy and slack-twisted, the fairy-tale world here re-creates more than half a century later a world of lost innocence. Here all men, black and white, accept their roles contentedly, and most are warmhearted, simple, and natural. It is a somewhat dreamy land in which an eleven-year-old boy reforms a prostitute. Lucius undergoes initiation into the adult world, but does not enter it with the burdens of Ike McCaslin or Quentin Compson; the tragic undertones are drowned out by the notes of lusty comedy. From his grandfather, Lucius learns the lesson that "a gentleman accepts the responsibility of his actions and bears the burden of their consequences." In his *vale* to Yoknapatawpha, Faulkner casts about his county the aura of a golden age.

In appreciating Faulkner and his work it is important to realize that when his earlier novels appeared there was a tendency to look upon them as examples of sordid naturalism replete with the pettiness and obscenity of weak and vicious men. More and more the depth and breadth of Faulkner's achievement came to be recognized. And Faulkner himself stated his essential faith in memorable words in acceptance of the Nobel Prize in 1950: "I believe that man will not merely endure: he will prevail. It is [the artist's] privilege to help man endure by lifting his heart, by reminding him of the courage and honor and hope and pride and compassion and pity and sacrifice which have been the glory of his past."

VARIOUS DISTINCTIVE NOVELISTS OF THE PERIOD

SOME IMPORTANT REALISTIC AND NATURALISTIC NOVELISTS

James T. Farrell (1904–). James Thomas Farrell was the son of a Chicago Irish teamster. Because of the family's poverty he was brought up principally by his mother's parents. He worked at numerous jobs that included cigar-store clerk and filling-station attendant, as well as newspaper work. From 1925 to 1929 he attended the University of Chicago, paying his own way. During 1931 and 1932 he lived in Paris where he was encouraged by Ezra Pound. Since then, New York has been his home. During 1936 and 1937 he held a Guggenheim fellowship in creative writing.

In the 1930s, with the vogue of proletarian fiction, Farrell was thought of as one of the major American novelists. He has continued writing to the present but his earlier work is considered his most important. An avid disciple of Dreiser, he is an outstanding naturalist in his own right. In each of his three major multivolume works he is preoccupied with a "psychological life cycle," minutely exploring every aspect of representative twentieth-century young Irishmen encountering growth, self-discovery, and frustration in American cities. Farrell has been regularly attacked by both left-wing and Christian critics, idealists, and academicians, but his vast structures are impressive as detailed anatomies of urban life in American fiction. Farrell has said that the theme of his fiction is the American way of life.

The Studs Lonigan trilogy, composed of *Young Lonigan* (1932), *The Young Manhood of Studs Lonigan* (1934), and *Judgment Day* (1935), examines the highlights in the second half of Studs Lonigan's life from June 1916 to his death in August 1931 at the age of twenty-nine. It is set in industrial Chicago. The account is given in Studs's own words, his own actions, his own patterns of thoughts and feelings. Studs comes from a middle-class background, and is initially imaginative and sensitive. In the first volume he rejects learning and the healthy influence of Lucy, a young girl who takes an interest in him, in favor of joining the ruffians of the Prairie Avenue gang and asserting what he considers his masculinity with a more promiscuous girl, Iris. In the second volume he is truly on the way down, succumbing to his surroundings and regarding conventional mores and attitudes with a fierce mixture of bitterness and contempt. In the concluding volume, Studs is an inconsequential laborer, and at last unemployed. A girl named Catherine tries to take a hand in his moral refurbishment, but his only real response is to make her pregnant. When he finally dies of heart disease he has all but arrived at the very bottom. Studs's descent is the result of his environment. His only defense is to toughen himself against its abrasions, but this tactic forms him to its own world.

The Danny O'Neill pentalogy *A World I Never Made* (1936), *No Star Is Lost* (1938), *Father and Son* (1940), *My Days of Anger* (1943), and *The Face of Time* (1953) follows Danny O'Neill from 1909 to 1927. Although the Studs Lonigan trilogy is Farrell's most famous work, the Danny O'Neill work is certainly his richest and is strongly autobiographical. The last volume in the series treats of the earliest years of Danny. Danny is Farrell himself, starting from the matrix of Studs but winning his way out of his oppressive background. In *My Days of Anger*, chronologically the last of the series, he breaks with all his traditions, determined to infuse humanitarian values into Studs's bleak universe. He leaves the University of Chicago and his home to become a writer in New York. Danny is the consciously evolving and increasingly perceptive artist emerging from a limited background. Although less dramatic than the Studs Lonigan series, the Danny O'Neill pentalogy is an even fuller indictment of urban mentality.

The Bernard Carr trilogy originally began as *Bernard Clare* (1946), but the name was changed because of a libel suit brought by a man bearing this name. The series was completed with *The Road Between* (1949) and *Yet Other Waters* (1952). Bernard is a Chicagoan transplanted to New York during the years 1927 to 1936. He matures against the backdrop of New York intellectuals and writers during the period of strong Communist influence. A brief dabbling in Marxism liberates Bernard from his provincial origins, but he realizes in disillusionment that the Communists are just as much trapped as was Studs. He finally achieves an artist's integrity in isolation. The most ambitious of Farrell's cycles, the Carr trilogy is actually at its best in the Chicago interpolations. The cultural world of New York is shadowy in comparison to Farrell's recalling of the Chicago of his early years. Especially, in trying to depict the independent artistic mind, Farrell cannot achieve the stark objectivity of Studs's world. Farrell stated elsewhere that he did not want culture to conceal reality.

John Dos Passos (1896–1970). John Roderigo Dos Passos was the son of a Chicago attorney, but his early schooling took place in the vicinity of Washington, D.C. After graduating *cum laude* from Harvard in 1916, he went to Spain to study architecture. In 1917 he volunteered for ambulance service in France and Italy, and later served in the U. S. Army Medical Corps. After discharge in 1919, he traveled in Europe and the Near East until 1922. In the mid-1920s he was closely associated with the Greenwich Village literary circles of New York. In 1927 he was briefly jailed for picketing in favor of Sacco and Vanzetti. In 1928–29 he visited Russia, responding favorably to what he saw there. In addition to extensive fiction writing he had done extensive reportorial work.

Later Dos Passos made an unusual odyssey from the political left to the far right. Rebellious in the 1920s, he turned early in the Depression era to the radical left, although maintaining his independence against Marxian dogmatism. In 1932 he voted Communist, but gradually mellowing, he supported Franklin Roosevelt with enthusiasm in 1936. Increasingly he found the "New Deal" too collectivistic for his tastes, and by 1944 was voting for Republican Thomas E. Dewey. By 1954 in *Most Likely to Succeed* he was satirizing the radicals and bohemians of the 1930s, and in *Midcentury* (1961) his conservatism expressed strongly anti-union sentiment. In 1964 Dos Passos favored Goldwater.

Dos Passos conceives of humanity not as an aggregate of individuals but as conflicting social forces. From the technique of the movies Dos Passos took montage effects that photographically record people at the everyday business of living. Dos Passos seeks not the trim traditional novel of plot but the very flow and cadence of life's continuum.

His first trilogy is collectively unnamed but may well be termed "The American Perspective." The major theme is the evaporation of the American hope of individual fulfillment through the crystallization of institutions in a materialistic society.

Three Soldiers (1921), influenced by Crane's *Red Badge of Courage*, is a powerful expression of the intellectual's horror of World War I. The three soldiers of the title are all spiritually broken by the war: Dan

Fuselli, an Italian from San Francisco, who sought material success but has been walked over by the more calculating and ruthless; Chrisfield, an Indiana farm boy who kills a sadistic officer; John Andrews, a Harvard graduate who deserts and is picked up by the Military Police. War, Dos Passos indicates, is the negation not only of civilization but of living itself.

Streets of Night (1923) is derived from Hawthorne's *Fanshawe,* even to the extent of presenting as a character a scholarly aesthete named Fanshaw. A puritanical social heritage here effects the stultification of American life, resulting in the suicide of David Wendell. The past is a rigid tyranny. The novel's scene is Cambridge and Boston in 1910–19.

Manhattan Transfer (1925) owed debts to Dreiser's *Sister Carrie,* but marked a flowering of Dos Passos' technique and gained the first widespread audience for the novelist. Of about three-score characters the chief are Ellen Thatcher, a talented actress; Jimmy Herf, a newspaperman with ambitions for creative writing; Stanwood Emery, a thwarted architect; Congo Jake, a French ex-seaman and successful bootlegger. The central subject, however, is New York City from 1890 to the mid-1920s. A whirlpool of apparently chaotic scenes throws up figures, bumps them together momentarily amidst the city's frenetic pursuit of material success, and impersonally crushes them all. All except Jimmy. In the final scene he leaves Manhattan after giving Ellen her divorce. Penniless he pushes away from the city to find himself. By its newsreel technique this novel dramatically captures the staccato pace and syncopated cadence of the great metropolis.

The second trilogy was collected in 1938 as *U.S.A.* Its dominant theme is a Marxist interpretation of the America of the period. In its attempt at a broad and multifaceted panorama of the United States from the turn of the century to the onset of the Depression in 1929, it was praised as epic in its scope. In contrast to the first trilogy, *U.S.A.*'s components, *The 42nd Parallel* (1930), *1919* (1932), and *The Big Money* (1936), constitute a continuous narrative, and many of the hundred and more characters appear in each volume. The historical framework is established first by "Biographies," a series of impressionistic sketches that range in subject from Thorstein Veblen to Henry Ford and Woodrow Wilson; and second by prose poems describing actual events, most notably the Wright brothers' first airplane flight. The social framework is established by "Newsreels," collections of newspaper headlines, billboard advertisements, radio broadcasts, even snatches of everyday conversations by anonymous passersby. The individual vision of the controlling artist is established by "The Camera Eye," impressionistic sketches of the personal observation of Dos Passos.

Dos Passos sees virtually all his Americans as emerging from a nineteenth-century idealism of "democracy." The pre-eminent national problem in this century, he believes, is achieving industrial democracy. Lost, he feels, is the cohesive family unit and the community spirit that previously maintained stability and traditional values. Most of the fictional personalities begin rather appealingly as children still imbued with the older idealism, but their growth to maturation becomes increasingly unattractive. J. Ward Moorehouse uses the money of his first wife, Annabelle Strang, to rise in the world and then discards her for Gertrude Staple; he becomes a prosperous advertising executive. Eleanor Stoddard achieves success in interior decoration, becomes the mistress of Moorehouse, and finds affluence to be sterile and arid. Richard Savage drops his artistic ambitions for lucrative employment with Moorehouse. Fenian McCreary, a printer, loses his job and wanders around the country as a vagrant until taking refuge in Mexico. Joe Williams deserts the navy and serves in the merchant marine until he is killed in a tavern brawl in St. Nazaire. Benny Compton, a Jewish boy from New York, is sentenced to the Atlanta penitentiary for his labor agitation. Paralleling Jimmy Herf, he emerges without job or prospects but is the only clear-eyed searcher for purpose and life.

The third trilogy was collected in 1952 as *District of Columbia,* but is often referred to as "the Spotswood trilogy." This trilogy, covering the national scene from the 1920s through World War II, lacks the impact of Dos Passos' earlier work, but it indicates his later point of view. *Adventures of a Young Man* (1939), *Number One* (1943), and *The Grand Design* (1949) are tenuously linked to the nation's capital and to the careers of two generations of the Spotswoods. In the first volume Glenn Spotswood goes to his death in Spain as a pawn of the Communists. In the second, Glenn's older brother, Tyler, is the intellectual motive force behind a demagogic politico. In the concluding book Herb Spotswood, father of Glenn and Tyler, is a Washington radio commentator whose liberalism is worn thin by the abrasion of aspects of the New Deal and by a catastrophic war. *The Grand Design* in title and statement makes clear the later thesis of Dos Passos: Not change but preservation is now his purpose. The grand design of American life is the ideal of individualistic democracy.

Zona Gale (1874–1938). The only child of a railroad engineer, Zona Gale was born in Portage, Wisconsin. After graduating from the University of Wisconsin in 1895, she worked on newspapers in Milwaukee and New York until again making Portage her home in 1904. A fervent liberal, she was active in La Follette progressivism, in support of Glenn Frank as the president of the University of Wisconsin, and in behalf of Sacco and Vanzetti. At the age of fifty-four, she married William L. Breese, a Portage stocking manufacturer.

Miss Gale's writing career dramatically exemplifies the rapid transformation in the twentieth-century American novel. Portage remained her subject throughout her career, but in 1918 her interpretation underwent a fundamental change. From her first novel, *Romance Island* (1906), to *A Daughter of the Morning* (1917), a predominant locale is Friendship Village, a sentimentalized small town of the type dear to the pre-World War I romancers. With *Birth* (1918) the community is transformed to Burage, a bleak, ugly town inhabited by petty people. The amiable denizens of Friendship Village give way to spiteful, grasping Buragers, and the prose eschews the earlier attempts at lyricism in favor of a stark, unadorned diction appropriate to characters and locale.

Miss Lulu Bett (1920) was published in the same year as Sinclair Lewis' *Main Street* and, like Lewis' novel, attracted wide attention.

A spinster at thirty-three, Lulu Bett performs all the drudgery of the Dwight Deacon household, where she is a neglected sister-in-law. Dwight's visiting brother Ninian marries her and later drops her to return to his legal wife. In spite of hostility and gossip, Lulu marries Neil Cornish, a music-store proprietor.

The portrayal of Lulu as caught in her limited world is effective; but the best of the novel is the depiction of the Deacon family, a sour representation of the traditional middle-class American home. Dwight is the clichéd respectable businessman, a mouther of platitudes and oblivious to anything but the trivia of Warbleton. Ina, Lulu's sister, is his futile, simpering spouse. Older daughter Di is a quite unpleasant would-be sophisticate, and younger daughter Monona is a pest. The novel offers a presumably happy ending, but a dramatization the year after the novel was published stuck to more consistent realism in having Lulu flee the Deacon household for an unknown future after learning of Ninian's bigamy.

Erskine Caldwell (1903–). Erskine Preston Caldwell was born in White Oak, Georgia. He attended Erskine College, the University of Virginia, and the University of Pennsylvania. His extraordinary range of occupations has included newspaper writer, cotton picker, stagehand, professional football player, book reviewer, editor, lecturer, scenario writer, foreign and war correspondent.

The violence, coarseness, incest, miscegenation, and general lack of amiability among the lower-class whites of the South is the focal interest of Caldwell, and he portrays this vividly. Caldwell knows his Georgia "crackers" as well as Faulkner knew the sharecroppers of Yoknapatawpha, and his dialogue for the squalid, hard-bitten red-necks is just as authentic. But Caldwell in style, perspective, theme, and mythic concept lacks Faulkner's vision of the examined life, the questing soul. Also, while rich in gusto, Caldwell's comic sense of life never permits a tragic concept. His characters are grotesques, caricatures, even subhumans incapable of spiritual growth. They are so locked in by the poverty-cursed clay around them that their only pathetic outlets are Ford cars and fornication. Caldwell is more the naturalist than any other Southern author except William March.

Tobacco Road (1932) in its stage version of 1933 enjoyed one of the longest runs of Broadway history.

Desperately loving his worn-out soil, Georgia farmer Jeeter Lester lives in hopeless poverty with his mother, his ailing wife Ada, son Dude, and harelipped daughter Ellie May. Pearl, another daughter, has become the child bride of railroader Lov Benson. Jeeter's widowed sister, Bessie Rice, lures Dude into marriage by giving him an automobile which Dude wrecks, killing his grandmother. Pearl runs away from Benson, and Ellie May takes her place. The Lester shack burns down, killing Jeeter and Ada.

The theme is the deterioration of a once-fertile farm and a once-vigorous family, but the chief interest in the book has been the riotous cavortings of the degenerate Lesters. Shiftless and improvident, low in mentality and morals, they are in an advanced state of depravity. But Caldwell is quite fascinated with the humorous and stoic attempts of these characters to adjust to their hostile environment. Impressive as the novel is in its depiction of the depressed rural South, the absence of any larger perspective, whether mythic or philosophic, keeps it from a higher appraisal.

God's Little Acre (1933) takes its title from Ty Ty Walden's allocation to the church of the income from one of his run-down acres of Georgia hill country. According to the needs of the moment, the location of the acre is conveniently shifted.

Ty Ty Walden is obsessed with the belief that there is gold underneath his land. He sends his loose-moraled daughter Darling Jill and her fat suitor Pluto Swint to Scottsville, where her sister Rosamund and brother-in-law Will Thompson live. Since the mill workers are on strike, the Thompsons agree to help dig for gold. At the farm Rosamund almost kills Will for sleeping with Darling Jill. Griselda, the wife of Buck, another son of Ty Ty, accompanies the Thompsons back to Scottsville. After possessing Griselda, Will dies in a riot of the striking mill workers. Jim Leslie, eldest son of Ty Ty, also tries to seduce Griselda but is slain by Buck, who commits suicide. Ty Ty resumes his digging.

Momentarily out of character, Ty Ty ruminates: "There was a mean trick played on us somewhere. God put us in the bodies of animals and tries to make us act like people." Ty Ty is just so tricked. He has not even the Jeeter Lester love of earth, only a mad dream of finding nonexistent wealth, which he undoubtedly would not know how to use if he got it. Devoid of values, traditions, or purposes, he is an indestructible, innocent monomaniac. His family consists of oversexed grotesques rivaling the Lesters but developed into slightly more rounded characters.

SOME IMPORTANT NOVELISTS OF SOCIAL CONCERN

Dorothy Canfield Fisher (1879–1958). Dorothy Canfield (the name she still employed for some years after her marriage) was the daughter of a professor at the University of Kansas at Lawrence, Kansas. She received a bachelor's degree from Ohio State University (1899) and a Ph.D. from Columbia University (1905). In 1907 she married John R. Fisher, and they made their home principally in Vermont on a site which had belonged to Dorothy Canfield's family from 1762. During World War I, Mr. and Mrs. Fisher went to France for volunteer service with the wounded and the orphaned. Returning, she and her husband devoted much of their lives to humanitarian causes. She was again active during World War II, especially with the Crusade for Children.

Dorothy Canfield drew to a considerable degree upon her own background in *The Bent Twig* (1915), one of her earlier novels which deals intimately with the life of a family, the Marshalls, in a Midwestern college town. It is most especially the story of Sylvia, one of the two daughters of the Marshalls, and tells of her early years, then about cross-currents in love; and it includes a memorable visit to Paris and the French countryside nearby. There is a traditional quality about *The Bent Twig*, a leisureliness of pace, a strong feeling for moral values. In *Hillsboro People* (1915) somewhat the same quality infuses a group of short stories about Vermont people.

The Brimming Cup (1921), set in Vermont, concerns Marise Crittendon, who at thirty-eight is shaken by a grand passion for Vincent Marsh. She recognizes that her marriage to Neale Crittendon has given her the satisfaction of children and a conventional way of life, but feels that it has been far from complete. Worldly wise, urbane Vincent almost wrecks the Crittendon marriage, but Marise finally decides that duty and her husband's solid though unspectacular virtues surpass the allure of Vincent. She learns, too, more about herself and the age-old problem of a spouse in the "mid-channel" of marriage. *Rough Hewn* (1922) doubles back to the earlier years of Marise and Neale when they drifted into marriage.

The Deepening Stream (1930) is largely autobiographical. Matey Gilbert, daughter of a Midwestern professor, finds life in the eastern states more traditional and pleasantly cultured. She and her husband, Adrian Fort, go to France for volunteer service in World War I. Their early idealism is considerably dimmed by the war's sordid realities. In a world on the brink of madness, personal relationships are the only meaningful support.

Booth Tarkington (1869–1946). A native of Indianapolis, Indiana, Newton Booth Tarkington attended Purdue University, then Princeton, where he founded the Triangle Club but left without graduating. Although many of his novels were written early, his later works are decidedly in the spirit of the twentieth century. *The Gentleman from Indiana* (1899), about a crusading editor who effects needed reforms by service in the state legislature, won him quick fame. Tarkington himself was an Indiana state legislator in 1902–3. One of the very popular American authors during the first quarter of the century, he wrote several plays and a large number of novels. His eyesight failed in 1930, and was only partially restored by operations.

Among early popular successes for Tarkington was his historical romance *Monsieur Beaucaire* (1900), which he later rewrote as a play.

Booth Tarkington was a capable artist of the novel who was interested in conditions of life, the theme of the realists in fiction; but by temperament he was inclined to re-evaluate these conditions in friendlier terms, which brought him closer to the romanticists. *The Conquest of Canaan* (1905), for example, contains genuinely powerful scenes of narrow-mindedness and brutality in its small-town Indiana setting, while its main plot eventually conforms to romantic literary conventions. Tarkington's novels often reveal much about middle-class Americans of his era.

Penrod (1914) is a splendid depiction of a boy's childhood. Twelve-year-old Penrod has the riotous imagination and the strange inward dignity appropriate to his years. In an uncomprehending adult world, only his great-aunt Sarah seems to understand him. Herman and Verman, the Negro youngsters, are comic masterpieces. An excellent ear for juvenile dialogue and a captivating ingenuity give the book its attractiveness.

Seventeen (1916) continues the same theme of growing up. Billy Baxter is a slightly older but less clearly perceived Penrod. His absurd and hopeless infatuation with the summer visitor, Miss Pratt, is wondrously amusing but is not approached penetratingly.

The Magnificent Ambersons (1918) is a treatment of two generations of middle-class Midwesterners.

Isabel, heir of old Major Amberson, falls out with her beloved, Eugene Morgan, and marries stodgy Wilbur Minafer. Her son, George Amberson Minafer, comes home from an eastern university to find Morgan establishing an automobile factory. Snobbish George estranges most of the community and succeeds in preventing his widowed mother from marrying the widower Morgan. With family fortune vanished,

George must work in the chemical factory. After an automobile accident he wins Lucky, Morgan's daughter.

The older Midwestern families at the top of the social ladder fall before the new tycoons, as Morgan comes to occupy the former heights of the Ambersons; and George, to the glee of many townsfolk, is reduced to employee rank. Nostalgically, Tarkington imparts to the old Major from the Gilded Age a good breeding and solid certainty in his social position that contrast with the insufferable snobbery of young George.

Alice Adams (1921), is a more sober and realistic work, which found favor with a changing postwar reading public.

Alice Adams tries to encourage the attentions of Arthur Russell, but her gauche family causes the young man to lose interest in her. Alice's father miserably fails in his own business, and her dice-shooting brother Walter steals from his employer and leaves town. Mrs. Adams has to take in boarders, and Alice starts secretarial studies at Frincke's Business College.

Tarkington penetratingly communicates Alice and all her embarrassment and frustration as she desperately tries through Arthur to rise in social status and transcend the crudeness of her family. Failing, she matures and faces up to her limited world.

Tarkington was awarded Pulitzer Prizes for both *The Magnificent Ambersons* and *Alice Adams*.

Ellen Glasgow (1874–1945). Ellen Anderson Gholson Glasgow was born in Richmond, Virginia, which was her permanent residence. Illness gave her a lifelong difficulty in hearing, which was chiefly responsible for her education at home. From 1896 until 1937 she frequently traveled in Europe. Her first novel, *The Descendant* (1897), began a long sequence culminating with *In This Our Life* (1941). Because of two unhappy love affairs she never married. In her later years she was recognized as one of the most prominent citizens of Richmond and received honorary degrees from a number of Southern universities.

The realistic rebellion led by Ellen Glasgow against the chivalric, aristocratic legend of the South is imperfectly appreciated today. Even as a girl Ellen Glasgow planned a "solitary revolt" against what she called the "sanctified fallacies" of her area. Although she resolutely depicts the actualities of Southern life, her major characters achieve spiritual triumphs as the characters of most of her realistic contemporaries do not.

Barren Ground (1925) is generally regarded as her most powerful novel.

The life of Dorinda Oakley, the daughter of a poor but upright farm family of Pedlar's Mill near Richmond, is traced from 1894 when she is twenty until 1924. Her first love was Jason Greylock, who was pressured by his family into marrying Geneva Ellgood. Dorinda flees to New York where she loses her child by Jason. She returns to transform her father's run-down "Old Farm" into a thriving dairy enterprise. Her marriage of convenience to Nathan Pedlar is moderately happy, but she is widowed by his death in a train wreck. Jason's marriage is a failure. Geneva drowns herself and Jason dies a broken man.

The very real people of this novel offer a detailed sociological analysis of a small Southern community. The Greylocks are decadent aristocrats whose weakness will ruin them and possibly others. The Oakleys are small landowners who can fall below the level of respectability, as does Joshua, Dorinda's father, or can by determined industry become sturdy yeomen, as does Dorinda herself, thus superseding the declining Greylocks and Ellgoods. The "New South" also manifests itself among the Negroes, represented by the ambitious and capable Fluvanna; aging Aunt Mehitable, an ex-slave, is a holdover from an older, superstitious past. As the first name of Dorinda's lover indicates, the novel has a mythic antecedent in the story of Jason and Medea in classic Greek legend. The details do not follow the myth, but as in a Greek drama, one's own character is one's fate. Dorinda is made of stern stuff and rides out her personal tragedy to gain material position and spiritual fortitude. But her stoic calm has been bought at a terrible price—a life wasted by the absence of love.

The Romantic Comedians (1926) is simultaneously a delicious comedy of manners and an allegory of the Old versus New South. The time is the 1920s.

After the death of his first wife, sixty-five-year-old Judge Gamaliel Honeywell of Queenborough (essentially Richmond) marries twenty-three-year-old Annabel Upchurch. In time his pleasure-loving young wife runs off to New York with Dabney Birdsong. Honeywell is unsuccessful in trying to get Annabel to rejoin him. He becomes seriously ill with influenza. But spring returns and the aging judge begins to look with kindling interest upon the attractive young nurse attending him.

This is a masterful example of the comedy of December's marriage to May. Miss Glasgow's characters are neither paragons nor monsters, but beings of human foibles and follies. Annabel accepts the judge because he can give her and her mother the wherewithal they lack and yearn for. When she tries to change him and his surroundings, the aging man insists on living as he always had lived. Defying convention and tradition, Annabel kicks up her heels and flees to a modern environment. In a superb change of pace Ellen Glasgow here abandons the solemn tragedy of *Barren Ground* for a comedy of wit. With smiling tolerance she leaves the old judge reasserting his illusions in the concluding lines.

The Sheltered Life (1932) to many academic critics seems Miss

Glasgow's best work of art. In contrast to *The Romantic Comedians* it is a tragedy of manners, set again in Queenborough early in this century.

Modern industry has brought grime and dilapidation to once-fashionable Washington Street, but the aristocratic Archbalds and Birdsongs try to maintain their establishments there in an unchanged fashion. Jenny Blair Archbald lives with her grandfather, General Archbald, her widowed mother, and her aunts Etta and Isabella. Homely Etta is thwarted from marriage, while Isabella marries beneath her, to Joseph Crocker, a Baptist carpenter. Eva Birdsong is the idealized Southern Lady, but her feckless husband, George, is faithless to her. As she grows up, Jenny becomes infatuated with George. Ailing Eva sees George in Jenny's arms and kills him.

All the lives in this novel are misshapen by the code of gentility, which no longer brings happiness to anyone. George cannot endure the task of being husband to the perfect Southern lady and takes clandestine refuge with other women, especially his mulatto mistress, Memoria. But it is the women who suffer most in this life sheltered from realities. Unattractive Etta seeks release in endless French novels and latent lesbianism. Isabella kicks over the traces and falls from grace, even though a proper genealogy is concocted for Crocker. Beneath her radiant exterior Eva writhes in frustration. Jenny starts as a charming ten-year-old but is sheltered into a selfish adolescent, affecting airs and mannerisms. Circumstances drive toward inevitable tragedy, and the hysterical Jenny can only throw herself into her grandfather's arms, protesting, "Oh, Grandfather, I didn't mean anything! . . . I didn't mean anything in the world." In its sensitive perception of character and motive and its pervasive but discreet irony, this is one of the great American novels of tragic illumination.

Floyd Dell (1887–1969). Born to a very poor family in Barry, Illinois, Floyd Dell had a variety of jobs until he became a newspaper reporter in Davenport, Iowa, in 1905. In 1908 he moved to the Chicago *Evening Post,* becoming editor in 1911. In 1914 he went to New York where he was editor of *The Masses* and its sequel, *The Liberator,* until 1924.

The American literary capital of the 1920s may have in actual fact been the left bank of the Seine, as so many American writers then lived the life of expatriates in Paris. But for the American writer who stayed at home it was Chicago and New York's Greenwich Village. Dell was the spokesman and chronicler for those who stayed in the United States. As a socialistic critic he proved highly significant through a broadly Marxian interpretation of American life in *Intellectual Vagabondage* (1926). Perhaps his best work was *Love in the Machine Age* (1930), exploring the new sexual morality, its origins and its consequences.

Moon-Calf (1920) is clearly autobiographical in its account of the vicissitudes of Felix Fay. Disgruntled with his small town and an unsuccessful love affair, Fay goes to Chicago where he plunges into the literary maelstrom of the Chicago Renaissance. Fay must break the narrow restraints of his early years, discover the real world which is free of the concepts implanted by his background, and prepare himself for the meaningful vision of the true artist.

The Briary-Bush (1921) takes Fay to Greenwich Village where he is exposed to the avant-garde. Although annoyed at American conventions and hypocrisies, he finally effects a moderate position, achieving a viable marriage and a successful literary career.

Homecoming (1933), a nonfiction autobiography, penetratingly reexplores the ground of the two novels. Dell diagnoses his function as the artist liberating America from the bonds of middle-class torpor. Never concerned with structure but always with ideas, he is not a top-rank novelist, but his position seems virtually unchallenged as a depicter of the American literary man in his native habitat during the tempestuous 1920s.

J. P. Marquand (1893–1960). Born in Wilmington, Delaware, John Phillips Marquand came of a distinguished New England ancestry that included Margaret Fuller and Edward Everett Hale. In 1907 he went to school in Newburyport, Massachusetts, and in 1911 proceeded to Harvard to receive his A.B. as a science major in 1915. After brief newspaper experience in Boston he served with the American Expeditionary Force in France. Returning to America, he worked for the New York *Herald Tribune* and an advertising agency until deciding in 1921 to devote himself wholly to fiction writing. During World War II he was again in the Army, this time in the Pacific.

Marquand's most significant novels follow the great tradition of Thackeray and Trollope as intimate realistic scrutinies of the contemporary upper strata of society.

The Late George Apley (1937) was the first of Marquand's social comedies and won him a place among the prominent novelists.

Supposedly delivered as a prose epitaph by his fellow Bostonian, Horatio Willing, the novel traces the life of the title character from birth in 1866 to death in 1933. George was born at the zenith of Boston's grandeur. While at Harvard, where there had been an Apley in every generation since 1662, he fell in love with Mary Monahan, a lower-class Irish girl, but his family quashed this attachment. He married the proper Catherine Bosworth, and because he was not an astute businessman, was set by the family to a life of coupon clipping. His daughter Eleanor irked George by marrying a journalist, and his son John married a divorcée. George was especially annoyed by all the modernism of the twentieth century, and although not financially ruined by the Depression, died in perplexity and disappointment.

The theme of the book is the decline of the Boston Brahmins, whose way of life had, until World War I, been deemed the exclusive apex of American culture. Santayana's *The Last Puritan* (see Chapter 4) is more profound and poetic, but Marquand's work is more skillful as a novel. Unconsciously, Horatio Willing satirizes himself too, in revealing his attitudes as those of a Back Bay conformist. George Apley is a decent, well-intentioned man endowed with a genuine sense of responsibility to a society which is relegating him and his sort to oblivion.

Wickford Point (1939) also studies the New England decline in this most autobiographical of Marquand's novels. Jim Calder, a popular fictionist, is patronized and exploited by his relatives the Brills, who live upon the reputation of their ancestor, John Brill, confrere of Hawthorne, Emerson, and Thoreau. Loving the New England heritage, Jim nonetheless learns that one must live not in the past but from the past. The technique is a clever use of flashbacks, and in Bella Brill the novelist created a classic portrait of a female shrew.

H. M. Pulham, Esquire (1941) considers another George Apley type, though with emphasis upon the private life of love and marriage.

On the occasion of his twenty-fifth reunion at Harvard, Harry Pulham examines his past life. While working on a soap campaign for a New York advertising agency, Pulham had fallen in love with career girl Marvin Myles, but Bostonian pressures forced him into a marriage with Kay Motsford. Tempted years later to elope with Marvin, Pulham reconsiders. Kay has tried an adulterous fling, but they reconcile and seek to make a go of it.

Although Pulham's world is not as fully explored as Apley's, Harry appears to be a more subtly observed Bostonian and a more percipient character. When he scrutinizes his life, Harry realizes that with all its frustrations and inadequacies he had lived "the only sort of life for which I was really fitted." Although he had yearned for Marvin with "passion and wish," he now knows that life cannot supply fulfillment of our dreams. We must make do with what we have and what we are.

So Little Time (1943) takes place during the early years of World War II before America entered the conflict.

Jeffrey Wilson is a successful "play doctor" and lives a comfortable life in New York City with his wife, Madge, and his younger children Charley and Gwen. His older son, Jim, is a student at Harvard just as Jeffrey had been many years before. Jeffrey looks back on what he has done and how he has lived, and tries to evaluate his life. This section tells of the years when he was in college, and how later he wrote a play, worked on a newspaper, and served in World War I as a pilot. The book is focused around the relationship between Jeffrey and Jim and their attempts to communicate with each other. Jeffrey is suddenly needed in Hollywood to work on a script, and he goes unwillingly for he feels he should be with Jim at this time. While in Hollywood he has a brief love affair with Marianna Miller, an actress with whom he has worked for many years. When he comes back to New York, Madge begins pestering him about Jim's love affair with Sally Sales, a girl whom Madge does not approve of. Jeffrey's great fear for the past year has been that America will soon enter the war and that Jim will be called into the Army and perhaps be killed before he has had a chance to live. Jeffrey tells Jim and Sally to get married right away and to enjoy as much of life as they can while there is still time. When the Japanese attack Pearl Harbor, Jeffrey tries to enlist but when he is offered the same sort of job that he has been doing as a civilian—working on scripts for public-relations movies—he decides to give up the idea. In the end he seems to have weathered his period of spiritual crisis and is ready to accept his life with Madge.

Point of No Return (1949) is another study of the upper middle-class society which Marquand knew so well. Charles Gray, an assistant vice-president in a bank, suddenly reflects on his own life and wonders whether the endless cycle of boredom and anxiety which come with ambition are justified by the material pleasures which seem to be the only reward. But Charles is trapped within his world and lets his wife, Nancy, prod him into the vice-presidency of the bank and into an acceptance of the competitive jungle of the American business world. The novel also is a study of the class system of Gray's native New England community of Clyde (Newburyport) and of Gray's longing for the life that he rejected there to find success in New York City. He had loved a girl, Jessica, in Clyde, but he now realizes that he has crossed the "point of no return," that Jessica is forever lost to him and that he does not possess the will to go back to Clyde. Marquand as a realist does not pass judgment on Gray's decision but rather shows that he no longer has the ability to choose.

Sincerely, Willis Wayde (1955) is a novel centered specifically on the American businessman.

Willis Wayde graduates from Boston University (not Harvard) and has to settle for a marriage to Sylvia Hodges rather than Bess, the heiress of the prosperous Harcourt mills of Clyde. Slowly he ascends the managerial ladder until he becomes president of Simcoe Rubber Hose and Belting, picking up the Harcourt interests as a subsidiary. Willis closes down the Harcourt mills, ostensibly as an expediency, but perhaps for revenge. As a result Bess Harcourt pointedly snubs Willis, whose wife comforts him with tranquilizers.

In this story of usurpation by the lower middle class, the Harcourt interests represent the old individualistic family concerns doomed to annihilation amidst the flexing of giant corporate muscles. Willis represents the new wave of corporation managers. He is a model American, loving home and family, going to church devoutly, and supporting worthwhile civic organizations. But Willis never proves capable of the examined life, as do other Marquand characters. He has been molded and conditioned by the corporate images of the era. Expensive cars and respectable golf scores take the place of substance. His pet words are "basically" and "sincerely." Willis believes that he is indeed sincere in his relations with everyone.

A MASTER OF FANTASY

James Branch Cabell (1879–1958). The scion of a distinguished Richmond family, Cabell considered himself first a Virginian and secondly a writer. While still an undergraduate at William and Mary (A.B., 1898), he published verse and taught French and Greek to lower classmen. From 1898 to 1901 he worked on newspapers in Richmond and New York. For the next ten years he worked as a professional genealogist in this country and in Europe. Rather astoundingly, from 1911 to 1913 he worked in West Virginia coal mines.

Cabell's most acclaimed works are fantasies, of which he wrote a long, interconnected series. The imaginary locales of his plots, Poictesme and Storisende, are marvelously conceived microcosms in which various adventurous and romantic episodes comment allegorically on art, morality, love, and other human affairs. V. L. Parrington praised him as "a self-reliant intellectual rich in the spoils of all literature," and his perverse originality endeared Cabell to such men as H. L. Mencken and Mark Twain. Indeed, he is a prime exemplar in American literature of the comic myth-maker. Although he enjoyed an enthusiastic following during his most creative years—the scandal over unaccustomedly outspoken sexual suggestiveness in *Jurgen* (1919) put him in the spotlight—the later tendency for a time has been to consider him something of an anomaly. The realistic trend of this country's literature found it difficult to accommodate a writer to whom life is a wild and wondrous game to be played by a gentleman gambler. Yet his skill as a stylist, his imaginative inventiveness, and his refreshing disregard for the tribulations which are the theme of the realists and naturalists give him a very distinctive place in American literature and point to the likelihood of continued renewed interest in his writings.

Biography of the Life of Manuel is the collective title that Cabell chose for the eighteen-volume Storisende edition of his works (1927–30). The apparently redundant words in the title indicate a study of a life stream of vital force. Dom Manuel is a swineherd in the pseudo-medieval kingdom of Poictesme (combining the names of the real French places Poitiers and Angoulême) located, he indicates, between France and Spain. As a count in later volumes, Manuel founds the Fellowship of the Silver Stallion, which resembles Arthur's Round Table. Manuel is not the paragon of Tennyson's *Idylls* but an Everyman, a fusion of coarseness and idealism, practicality and occasional lunacy, wisdom and nonsense. He is quester for the right way of life, and out of his blunderings and strivings emerges a myth. Maps of Poictesme can be filled in as fully as those for another imaginary land, Yoknapatawpha County; and genealogies—Cabell was a professional here—can stretch from the eleventh century to the present, since Cabell's later novels, including those set in Virginia, follow descendants of Manuel.

In their wide ranging, the volumes of the series play numerous variations on a group of three philosophies.

The first, the "chivalric view," interprets life as spiritual testing. At its best the chivalric ideal represents a "vicarship," in that men conceive themselves earthly maintainers of divine order. Hence the tradition of public service by the aristocrat. To women is accorded what Cabell called *domnei:* the respect properly shown to noble ladies as exemplars of beauty and virtue. Strength of will is the most prized human quality.

The second, the "gallant view," considers life a sportive toy to be enjoyed to the utmost. This hedonistic ideal produces consummate manners and libertine morals. The gallant praises intelligence above all other human attributes.

The third, the "poetic view," deems life the raw material challenging men to creativity. For the poet, imagination is the transcendent faculty of man.

The organization of the Storisende edition does not follow the chronology of initial publication but essentially this three-fold approach of Cabell. Thus *Chivalry* (1909) is fifth in the collected series and keynotes this major consideration of the middle of the series. *The Certain Hour* (1916) is the eleventh volume and lengthily examines the poetic view of life, which dominates the latter portion of the series. Of course, the three different drives appear in every book, and the thoroughly skeptical Cabell will not let any of these approaches gain complete domination.

Figures of Earth: A Comedy of Appearances (1921), a chivalric view, is second in the collected series. The subtitle reveals the theme attendant upon Manuel's quest. His chivalric goal is on the level of monster killing and maiden rescuing, but the naïve knight-at-arms finds the world quite otherwise than it seems. All experience is ambiguous. For example, a wizard provides Manuel with a magic sword to rescue an imprisoned princess; actually the princess is the wizard's wife, he is bored stiff with her, and convention of course prevents him from getting rid of her except by a traditional romantic champion to bear her off. Freydes is the ideal female to whom Manuel can display *domnei*, but he cannot forever endure her and finally accepts misery in order to get back the bossy Niafer. In his palace at Storisende, Manuel belatedly realizes that this supposedly solid, real world of the senses is mere deceptive appearance.

Jurgen: A Comedy of Justice (1919), a gallant view, number six in the collected series, is Cabell's best-known work. Its initial fame arose from the attempts by moralists to ban the book. The New York Society for the Suppression of Vice shut down publication for eighteen months until a jury in 1922 absolved Cabell of obscenity. The objectionable passages no longer seem sensational, and now *Jurgen* can be appraised solely on the basis of its art, which stands high.

A middle-aged Poictesme pawnbroker, Jurgen, out of whimsical perversity defends the Devil (Koschei), who as a favor spirits off Dame Lisa, Jurgen's loquacious wife. Gradually coming to yearn for Lisa's return, Jurgen undertakes an odyssey to find her. The Centaur Nessus gives him a bright shirt that restores his lost youth. As a young man of twenty-one, Jurgen has titillating adventures with Queen Guenevere (faith), Queen Anaïtis (Morgan Le Fay, or desire), and Queen Helen (vision). In Hell he marries a vampire. In Heaven he conducts metaphysical arguments with the God of his grandmother. Eventually he persuades Koschei to restore Lisa, and Jurgen resumes his wonted existence as a middle-aged pawnbroker.

Jurgen is catapulted into situations satirically echoing many of the Western myths, notably his visit to the land of Cocaigne, his relations with Dorothy la Désirée, and his reunion with Lisa. The ironic subtitle means that Jurgen finds all of life a gross injustice. Through most of the novel he pursues the gallant way of life but with insuperable handicaps. He retains his middle-aged mind and memory while enjoying a vigorous, youthful body. The combining of the two ages in Jurgen produces not happiness but an intensified bitterness and skepticism. Eventually he concludes that we can only accept our beleaguered lot and live with actuality in the here and the now.

The Cream of the Jest: A Comedy of Evasion (1917), a poetic view, number sixteen in the series, deals with an American, Felix Kennaston, who escapes a disenchanting marriage and the ennui of his existence through a magic talisman, the "sigil of Scoteia." He is transported back in time to the land of Storisende, where he once bore the name of Horvendile and loved an idealized woman, Ettarre, an "ageless, lovable, and loving woman of whom all the poets had been granted fitful broken glimpses." She bears him company as he explores many other romantic periods of history, but remains inviolate and incapable of being possessed. At last Kennaston's periodic journeys to Storisende are terminated when upon the death of his wife, Kathleen, he discovers to his amazement that the sigil of Scoteia is no more than the lid from a jar of cold cream.

Ettarre is the stuff of dreams, the supreme and elusive beauty for which the poetic soul eternally yearns. Dwelling upon her, Kennaston finds his actual life increasingly humdrum and uninteresting. Escapism becomes infinitely more precious to him than real existence. Ironically, he finally realizes that the talisman was a familiar domestic item. Whatever magic and satisfaction that life can afford is not truly in these poetic flights. Thus he comes to realize that Kathleen was his Ettarre, or at least the nearest, best thing to Ettarre that fate can afford. The sad "cream of the jest" is that Kennaston has learned this truth too late.

In *Beyond Life* (1919) Cabell ascribes to significant literature the "virtues of distinction and clarity, of beauty and symmetry, of tenderness and truth and urbanity." Exemplifying these criteria in his own fiction, he may well gain his place among the most gifted novelists of our literature; but many Americans find him alien to their expectations. He is concerned with the human experience rather than the specifically American experience. Above all, he is the prime (and most bewildering) example in American letters of a serious novelist cavorting in the buffoon pose of a Rabelais or a Laurence Sterne.

HISTORICAL AND REGIONAL NOVELISTS

Joseph Hergesheimer (1880–1954). A native Philadelphian, Joseph Hergesheimer originally planned to be a painter. After studies at the Pennsylvania Academy of Fine Arts, he maintained studios in Italy at Florence and Venice. Returning to the United States in 1902, he devoted himself to fiction, but his first novel, *The Lay Anthony*, did not appear until 1914. Personally shy and retiring, he strove for vivid romance in his writings.

There has been some tendency to label Hergesheimer's baroque, languid, and luxurious novels anachronistic and overly romantic. As a good friend of his, James Branch Cabell, pointed out, Hergesheimer in time let his romantic leanings drift him into the best-seller scramble, but he wrote two early novels that have persisted as classics of American fiction.

The Three Black Pennys (1917) traces a dynasty of Pennsylvania iron founders from colonial times to the outset of the twentieth century. A Welsh strain in the Pennys seems to account for the appearance in different generations of a rebellious son, disdainful of restraint and convention. We meet Howat Penny when he is twenty-five, Jasper Penny when he is middle-aged, and the second Howat Penny when he is an old man. The misdeeds of each seem to be mirrored in the next black Penny, until in the end the second Howat Penny is "the husk of a passion that had burned out all vitality." Whether conventional or unconventional, the Penny family has gradually declined from its original vigor and talent.

Java Head (1919) takes its title from the name of a high black rock that overlooks the Sunda Strait in the East Indies. To Jeremy Ammidon, a merchant-captain in the days of the clipper ships, it is the "symbol of the safe and happy end of an arduous voyage," and consequently he bestows the name on his home in Salem, Massachusetts. Jeremy's son Gerritt returns to this house with his beautiful Chinese wife, the high-born Taou Yuen. Assaulted by the lustful Edward Dunsack, Taou Yuen commits suicide. Gerritt marries his former love, Nettie Vollar, the niece of Dunsack, and sails back to the Orient. Hergesheimer portrays an exotic symbol of beauty and serenity introduced into a crassly materialistic society and destroyed as a result. The novel conveys the receptiveness of the New England of those days to the mystery and beauty of the Far East.

Ring Lardner (1885–1933). Ringgold Wilmer Lardner was born at Niles, Michigan. His formal education ended with a brief stay at Armour Institute in Chicago in 1902. In 1905 he began a journalistic career, first with the *Times* of South Bend, Indiana, and subsequently with newspapers in Chicago, St. Louis, and Boston. Until 1913 most of his writing was sports journalism, chiefly about baseball, but in that year he began a column for the Chicago *Tribune* and started to write popular short stories. Magazines vied with each other for his work, which finally encompassed many volumes.

Viewed by many primarily as a humorous writer, Ring Lardner is indeed a bitingly satiric commentator upon American life as he knew it. He presented the commonplace world of everyday Americans doing ceaseless battle with the routine minutiae of existence. Under an exterior of rough comedy, the perceptive reader can find penetrating scrutiny of egotism, vanity, narrow-mindedness, self-deception, and heartless rejection of or interference with others.

You Know Me Al (1916) brings together a group of related stories appearing in the *Saturday Evening Post,* commencing in 1914.

Jack Keefe is a semiliterate baseball pitcher who writes to his boyhood friend Al Blanchard of Bedford, Indiana, about his vicissitudes on and off the diamond. Keefe moves up to Chicago in the major leagues from the Central League, is briefly dropped back to the West Coast League, but returns to pitch for Chicago. After several somewhat grotesque romantic adventures he marries plain Florence, the sister-in-law of a teammate. Florrie leaves him in a huff but eventually returns and presents him with a son that Jack fears may turn out to be a southpaw. At the end Jack prepares to accompany the White Sox and the Giants on their famous world tour of 1913–14.

The ludicrous misspellings and inept phrasings of Keefe stem from the native tradition of the folk philosopher. Keefe believes and wants Al to believe that he is a man of character and courage, wit and wisdom. Unknowingly he reveals that he is a liar, a cheat, and a crude, selfish bungler. Keefe always blames others for his own shortcomings and failures. Most pathetic is his total inability to understand and criticize himself.

The Love Nest (1926) and *Round Up* (1929) reveal Lardner at his height in the short-story form.

The title piece of *The Love Nest* exemplifies one of the major themes of the later Lardner. Although apparently quite happy in his own family life, Lardner was greatly concerned with marital discord. Lou Gregg of "Love Nest" is a wealthy man who marries Celia Sayles, a rising young movie star, so that he will have a lovely wife to show to the world and to bear him attractive children. Celia is equally scornful of motherhood and wifehood, and had wedded Lou merely to further her career. Gregg's mania for money and status deforms Celia into a bitter, thwarted woman, and an alcoholic on the sly.

"Haircut" is one of the most frequently anthologized of American short stories. In its depiction of Jim Kendall, a practical joker, it offers one of the most devastating indictments of the cruel small-town spirit that finds funny the embarrassment and emotional agony of others. Because Julie Gregg has ignored him, Jim Kendall maneuvers her into revealing her love for Doc Stair, and he does this for the amusement of his cronies. Kendall is killed while hunting, supposedly by accident, but almost certainly in vengeance. The barber-narrator chucklingly recalls Kendall as a "card," but unwittingly stigmatizes the spiteful, nasty pettiness in this village cut-up, and a deplorable lack of basic human decency in his fellow townsmen.

Ole Rølvaag (1876–1931). A native of Norway, Ole Edvart Rølvaag emigrated to America in 1896. He received his A.B. from St. Olaf College (Minnesota) in 1905 and his M.A. in 1910. In 1908 he became an American citizen. From 1912 he taught at his alma mater. Although written in America and dealing with this country, his novels were all originally written in Norwegian.

Giants in the Earth (Norwegian 1924–25, English translation 1927) is a true epic of the American pioneer and a great tribute to the American soil.

Per Hansa brings his wife, Beret, to a sod hut in South Dakota in 1873. Exultant in the promise of the new land, he names his son Peder

Victorious. Beret, however, is oppressed by the vast empty land and turns to a stern Calvinism and even to deep ancestral Norse superstition. At her urging, Per Hansa hesitatingly breasts a February blizzard to get the parson for a dying friend and never returns. In the late spring of the northern prairie Per Hansa's body is found seated, his face staring westward.

Rølvaag's immigrant background did not keep him from an unsurpassed feeling for the epic conquest of the continent—and the price it exacted. Per Hansa revels in the challenge, but the natural forces of this raw land strike down even this invincible Viking. The greatest achievement of the novel is its portrayal of the "sick soul" of Beret, desperate for the comfortable homeland far away, brooding amidst the huge silences of a dark land, and seeking refuge in an uncompromising faith. From experience as a laborer, Rølvaag knows every fiber of these people, and his evocation of the emptiness and impassivity of the vast Dakota plains is superb. Two sequels, *Peder Victorious* (1929) and *Their Fathers' God* (1931), continue the account to form a trilogy.

Upton Sinclair (1878–1968). Born in Baltimore, Maryland, Upton Beall Sinclair received his A.B. from City College of New York in 1897. In 1906 he exploded upon the nation as the author of *The Jungle* (1906), a novel of the Chicago stockyards which accused meat packers of holding workers to starvation wages and distributing unwholesome food to the American consumer. *The Jungle* spurred quick passage of the Pure Food and Drug Act. With the proceeds of this immensely successful novel, Sinclair established a socialistic community, Helicon House, in New Jersey, where Sinclair Lewis worked briefly. In the same year (1906) Upton Sinclair was an unsuccessful candidate for Congress from New Jersey on the Socialist ticket. Upon his move to California he was a frequent Socialist candidate for political office. In 1934 as a Democratic candidate in an EPIC (End Poverty In California) campaign he almost won the governorship.

A late, reissued book of his octogenarian years, *The Cry for Justice* (1963), could stand as a title for Sinclair's entire life. Although he received the Pulitzer Prize for *Dragon's Teeth* (1942), critics have never taken him very seriously as a novelist. His importance is rather as the archpropagandist for social justice. When coal miners suffered from dangerous working conditions and shabby treatment from employers, Sinclair wrote *King Coal* (1917); when the Sacco-Vanzetti case rocked the nation, Sinclair seethed with indignation in *Boston* (1928); while Prohibition ruled, Sinclair railed in *The Wet Parade* (1931).

From *World's End* (1940) to *The Return of Lanny Budd* (1953) a dozen novels chronicled the amazingly fortunate presence of Lanny Budd at all the great crises of contemporary events. This imaginary son of a Connecticut millionaire munitions maker is the man that Sinclair would like to have been. Lanny participates in all the significant conferences and deliberations surrounding World War II, is the intimate of Roosevelt and Churchill and all the other greats of the time. Lanny gives Sinclair abundant opportunities to voice his opinions upon almost all the world's problems.

Margaret Mitchell (1900–49). Margaret Mitchell was born in Atlanta, Georgia. She wrote only one novel, but that has proved to be the most widely read novel issued in this century, *Gone With the Wind* (1936). The heroine, Scarlett O'Hara, is the advantaged daughter of a wealthy plantation owner. She has beauty, charm, and a sharp, avaricious intelligence. Nonetheless she is disappointed in her romantic hope of marrying Ashley Wilkes, who takes Scarlett's virtuous and sweet-tempered cousin Melanie Hamilton to the altar. Scarlett is financially overturned by the Civil War and subsequent Reconstruction. It requires all her wits and two successive loveless marriages to useful husbands for her to fight her way back into some semblance of her previous affluence. At critical moments she is aided by Rhett Butler, the Byronic and opportunistic hero. Inevitably she eventually weds Rhett; their marriage is passionate and tempestuous, and ends with Rhett's deserting her, at least for the time. Scarlett realizes too late that her drive to achieve and possess has been blind to values and realities of greater price.

The novel pictures the ante-bellum South, lamenting the passing of an idealized plantation society of chivalry and idyllic charm. Miss Mitchell's skill expresses itself in bringing to life the grace of the plantation before the war and equally the wartime care of the wounded in Atlanta. The characters in *Gone With the Wind* are effectively conceived and well contrasted, and this is true not only of the central figures but the many lesser ones as well.

Sholem Asch (1880–1957). A native of Poland, Sholem Asch lived in various European countries before coming to the United States in 1910. He was naturalized in 1920. For a few years in the mid-1920s he again resided in Europe, but returned, he stated, because he believed that this country had become an outstanding literary center. He proved one of the most potent figures in Yiddish-American culture, writing for the *Jewish Daily Forward* and producing plays for the Yiddish theater in New York as well as writing novels in Yiddish.

Some of Asch's novels deal with Jewish-American life, such as *East River* (1946), which treats the Davidowsky family of 48th Street. Most memorably, however, he wrote of Jews in Central Europe from *Mottke the Vagabond* (1917) onward. In his later years he presented a warmly sympathetic treatment of Jesus and of Christianity in a trilogy: *The Nazarene* (1939), which represents Jesus as the last of the great Hebrew prophets; *The Apostle* (1943), which offers the viewpoint, held by many of the Jewish faith, that Christianity is largely the creation of St. Paul; and *Mary* (1949), which gives the story of Jesus' mother. Implicit throughout is a plea for a tolerant mutual understanding between Christian and Jew, and a profound respect for all men of faith and good will.

Oliver La Farge (1901–63). Oliver Hazard Perry La Farge, son of Christopher La Farge, a noted architect, was born in New York City. Among his ancestors he counted Benjamin Franklin and his namesake, Commodore Perry. At Harvard (A.B. 1924, M.A. 1929) he specialized in anthropology, subsequently doing field work in the American Southwest and in Guatemala. From 1931 to 1933 he was research associate in anthropology at Columbia University and for many years from 1932 served as president of the Association on American Indian Affairs. In 1936 he assisted the Hopi Indians in preparing a constitution and forming a tribal organization. As an officer in the Air Transport Command during World War II he detailed the story of that unit in *The Eagle in the Egg* (1949).

Laughing Boy (1929) was his first novel. The incentive for this work was La Farge's deep interest in acculturation, or the transfer of culture from one people to another.

A skillful Navajo silversmith, Laughing Boy, loves Slim Girl, who is confused and bitter because of her American schooling. The two elope, but Slim Girl continues to meet her white lover. Laughing Boy wounds both the clandestine lovers and later is reconciled with Slim Girl. Slim Girl is killed in an ambush and Laughing Boy, after a due funeral vigil, resumes his tribal role.

Laughing Boy is a prose lyric to natural love in a primitive setting, and to the tragedy of mixed cultures. Effectively introduced are detailed, accurate descriptions of Navajo life and activities, particularly various forms of native art.

B. Traven (1890–1969). Berick (or Bruno) Traven Torsvan Torsvan, if that is his name, is the mystery man of twentieth-century American letters. Scrupulously shunning all publicity, he even left in doubt his national origin. Apparently he was born in Chicago and spent most of his life abroad, chiefly in Mexico. His popularity is greatest in foreign countries, probably because of his strenuous attacks upon capitalism.

The Treasure of the Sierra Madre (1935), the basis for the excellent Hollywood film of 1948, is a striking contemporary parable on the futility of human greed. Three American gold seekers battle natural hardships and Mexican bandits to extract the precious ore from the Mexican mountains. Eventually the gold ore falls into the hands of the bandits, who, ignorant of its value, let it be blown by the winds back to the mountains from whence it came. Most memorable is the depiction of the raw wilderness of the Mexican land that draws forth violence and brutishness from man. The principal character Dobbs is a perpetual underdog, undone by his own background and low nature.

Pearl Buck (1892–   ). The missionary parents of Pearl Sydenstricker were on furlough from China when she was born in Hillsboro, West Virginia. From the age of five months until she was seventeen, when she returned to America to enroll at Randolph-Macon College, she lived in China. After graduation in 1914 she went back to China, married John L. Buck in 1917, and taught in Chinese universities. Since 1932 the United States has been her permanent residence. After divorce from her first husband she married Richard J. Walsh in 1935. In later years she headed a group dedicated to the care of Asian and Asian-American children in America. Her publications have extended from 1922 to the present, but her fame in the world of letters rests largely upon one novel, *The Good Earth* (1931). This moving book has been translated into more than thirty languages, and has been widely read in China.

Wang Lung, the son of a poor farmer, loves his land with peasant tenacity and endures famine and poverty with his plain, faithful wife O-lah. Eventually he is able to accumulate some wealth, his holdings increase, and he can afford a pretty second wife, Lotus. The great House of Hwang has vitiated itself over the years by luxurious living; Wang Lung buys it out and settles his growing family as the most prominent in the region. But his children lack his sense of attachment to the soil; and at his death they sell the family acreage and move to the city.

The novel's primary fascination is Wang Lung and his passionate hold upon the immemorial earth. To retain his few acres Wang Lung will persevere at anything from back-breaking toil to the wily manipulation of his bandit-allied uncle, neutralizing that troublemaker by getting him addicted to opium. To reproduce the dignity and timelessness of Chinese speech, Pearl Buck employs a biblical phrasing and sonority that suggest not merely the enduring power of the Chinese peasant but the continuity of all life. The two Western-minded sons and the revolutionary son represent the sundering from the soil and the dispersion afflicting China of the 1920s and, in fact, all the recent world. *Sons* (1932) and *A House Divided* (1935) continue the family chronicle and complete a trilogy collectively named *The House of Earth*.

In 1938, Pearl Buck was awarded the Nobel Prize.

SOME IMPORTANT REFLECTIVE AND EXPERIMENTAL NOVELISTS

Thornton Wilder (1897–   ). Born in Madison, Wisconsin, Thornton Niven Wilder was taken to China in 1905 when his father was designated American consul general of Shanghai and Hong Kong by Theodore Roosevelt. From 1910 to 1915 he continued his education (started in Chefoo, China) in California and during the latter year entered Oberlin College. He transferred to Yale and after wartime service in the Army completed his A.B. in 1920. Following a year's study of archaeology at the American Academy in Rome, he returned to teach at the Lawrenceville School. While there he worked on an M.A. at Princeton and received it in 1926. He achieved fame with his novel *The Bridge of San Luis Rey* in 1927, and was able to quit teaching and to travel in Europe. From 1930 to 1936 he lectured at the University of Chicago. Thereafter writing occupied him except for service with the U. S. Air Force (1942–45) and occasional lectures. In 1962 he went to Arizona to live in retirement for a time.

Wilder is important both as a novelist and a dramatist. (In this chapter we shall consider only his novels. His plays will be discussed in Chapter 3.) In his novels as in his plays he is virtually unique in the contemporary literary scene—essentially an optimist and humanist. Socially minded critics have bitterly assailed Wilder for ignoring immediate problems. Wilder, however, is concerned with the broader patterns of Western culture, and like a true classicist seeks the universal and the essential that lie beneath the changing surfaces of life.

The Cabala (1926) received little attention because an era absorbed in realistic-naturalistic art could not appreciate a novel of ideas told with remarkable wit.

A young American scholar (nicknamed "Samuele") becomes a confidant of an aristocratic clique in modern Rome, headed by Cardinal Vaina. The American is induced to exert his puritanical influence upon Prince Marcantonio, but the noble youth commits incest with his sister and then suicide. Samuele's pedantic American friend James Blair rejects the love of the Princess d'Espoli. Aristocratic Frenchwoman Astrée-Luce has her faith undermined by the Cardinal and tries to murder him. Samuele returns to America for a fresh start.

Wilder is fascinated with the intellectual and cultural threads of European society but finds them badly worn and frayed. The cabalists clutch pitifully at an outmoded aristocratic view, and the arid scholarship of Blair is equally deadly. The one great force of life is the ancient humanism personified in the Roman poet Virgil, who is perhaps the dominant character of the entire work. At the end Virgil appears to Samuele with the abjuration: "The secret is to make a city, not to rest in it." The American comes back to New York with the sense of challenge and opportunity.

The Bridge of San Luis Rey (1927) brought Wilder wide recognition. On July 20, 1714, five persons were upon the osier-woven bridge, the only crossing of a valley on the way between Lima and Cuzco, Peru. A Franciscan monk, Brother Juniper, horrified at seeing them fall to their death as the bridge collapses, asks himself what patterning of Providence would arrange such a tragedy. His scrutiny of all that he can discover makes him certain that divine will had intervened to take these five at the climactic moment when for each no other solution was possible. All are victims of hopeless love. The Marquesa de Montemayor loved her daughter Clara, who had escaped her by marrying and going to Spain. Pepita, companion to the marquesa, desperately pined for the Abbess in the convent where she had been brought up. Esteban dearly loved his twin brother, Manuel, who had been removed from him by the actress Camila and by the great remover, Death. Uncle Pio had helped to make an outstanding actress of Camila, who became better known as La Périchole. Uncle Pio loved not the woman but the entry into beauty and art that she represented. She banished him when she abandoned her career in favor of respectability and it was closed anyway by the ravages of smallpox upon her face. Jaimé, illegitimate son of Camila, was also banished because he was sickly and annoying to the mother whom he adored.

Was this tragedy blind fate, the will of an all-seeing deity, or perhaps in some fashion an end desired and brought about by the victims themselves? In the mystery that is life there is no absolute answer. Wilder is least sympathetic to the dogmatism of Brother Juniper, who looks solely to external evidence which he handles pseudoscientifically to assert a theological belief. The internal evidence shows that all five had willed themselves to that risk at that time. While Brother Juniper may have learned all too little, those who were close to the five are profoundly affected. As the Abbess sadly states, "All of us have failed." She, Clara, and Camila all perceive the inadequacies of their love. Each of the five who died on the bridge was himself or herself a bridge, and we who live must make of ourselves firmer bridges of love for our fellows.

The Woman of Andros (1930), which harks back to the *Andria* of Terence, is set in ancient Greece. Its classic, gemlike beauty was lost upon the Depression era.

Chrysis, a hetaera from the island of Andros, conducts a witty salon on the isle of Byrnos that intrigues the local young men. She is genuinely drawn to Pamphilus, whose father, Simos, prefers that the youth marry the proper Philumena. Pamphilus turns his affections to Glycerium, the younger sister of Chrysis, and she soon becomes pregnant. Chrysis dies, partly from chagrin over the Pamphilus-Glycerium liaison; her property is sold, including her sister. Simos recognizes the loveliness of Glycerium and buys her from the slave dealer for Pamphilus. But the girl dies in childbirth and the child with her. Pamphilus in his sorrow seeks to gain courage from the memory of Glycerium and of Chrysis. While the story fully recognizes the shortcomings and brutalities of pagan Greece, these are offset by a sense of the gloriously transparent air of Greece and the spirit of Platonism. Chrysis is imbued with the classical humanistic spirit, seeking to live the noble life and to discover the eternal religious values. Yet she and the other notable characters are unable to effect a harmony between their inner ideals and the coarse real world in which they live.

Heaven's My Destination (1935) surprisingly is one of the few American novels upon religion as religion. Wilder's George Brush is a Midwestern Baptist sincerely intent upon following the true Christian path.

In the Depression-ridden Midwest of 1930–31 George Brush is a traveling salesman thoroughly absorbed in a fundamentalist faith and in the nonviolence concept of Gandhi. Intent upon the good life amidst an America consecrated to materialism, George is frequently insulted, beaten up, and arrested. Eventually his health and his faith fail, but the influence of a Roman Catholic priest, Father Paszieski, another totally good man, restores his confidence, and he returns to his evangelical path.

George is annoying to his fellows because he envisages man solely as a product of God. Wilder suggests that man should be viewed only as man. Nonetheless, he feels that society desperately needs the Brush values as a corrective to the modern bondage of flesh and money. George's greatest defect is intellectual immaturity. Although he has not embraced the humanistic ideal at the end, he has purged himself of the worst of his narrowness and ignorance. He is a seeker and has the potential thereby to move forward. Wilder profoundly loves George and loves Americans. Heaven is our destination, but it is heaven right here, if we will only mature enough to see it and make it so.

The Ides of March (1948) is true to Roman classic antiquity, just as *The Woman of Andros* was true to ancient Greece. Instead of telling history by fictionalizing the extant documents, Wilder concocts imaginary documents as "primary sources" for the life of Julius Caesar; only some verse from Catullus and the Suetonius description of the assassination are actual quotations. Reacting to the recent phenomenon of dictators, Wilder chose to study the most famous dictator of them all, but his Julius Caesar differs sharply from the recent tyrants. This is not a historical novel seeking to explain events of the past so much as it is an attempt to explain the nature of the soul of a great figure of history. Caesar is torn between the pulls of public responsibility and the deep personal need for an inner life of wholeness and contentment. He is too wise to be enraptured with power for itself. He learns of life by living it; and with clear eyes goes undeviatingly to his fate.

The Eighth Day (1967) shows a return by Wilder to the themes similar to those of his early novels and plays.

In 1902 John Ashley of Coaltown, Illinois, is tried for the murder of his friend Breckenridge Lansing, a murder which, it is later revealed, he did not commit. He is summarily tried, found guilty; and on his way to be executed he is rescued by six armed men whose identity he never finds out. Ashley makes his way to New Orleans and finally to Chile where he becomes a mining engineer, a profession he had worked in at Coaltown. Meanwhile Ashley's wife and daughters raise themselves from poverty with a courage and resourcefulness which seem inherent in the Ashley nature. Ashley's son Roger goes to Chicago and is destined to become famous. When Roger returns for a visit to Coaltown he finally learns the true story of the murder and the escape. Lansing was killed by George, his own son, who now writes a confession and escapes to Russia. John Ashley was rescued by members of a church which he had attended as a child; and later he secretly contributes money to it. Ashley's name is now cleared, but though it is believed that he is living in Chile he is never seen again.

Wilder, as in *The Bridge of San Luis Rey* and the play *Our Town,* writes in terms of the universality of human experience that lies beneath the changing surfaces of reality and the impossibility of men's attempts to understand the meaning and the plan of Nature. As in *Our Town,* he uses the particular events of a small town to serve as a microcosm for the continuous flow of human life. The title of the novel is ironic. Dr. Gillies, the town philosopher, says on the eve of the twentieth century, "The Bible says that God created man on the sixth day and rested. Man is not at an end but a beginning. We are at the beginning of the second week. We are children of the eighth day." Then Dr. Gillies' thoughts are revealed. "Dr. Gillies was lying for all he was worth. He had no doubt that the coming century would be too awful to contemplate—that is to say like all the other centuries."

Wilder feels that there are deep mysteries of existence which are simply beyond the capacities of men's minds, and whatever happiness men can achieve can be achieved through acceptance of those mysteries. The story of John Ashley is a reminder of this idea, showing that men believe what they want to believe. To the citizens of Coaltown, Ashley is a murderer, and this belief about him is destructive to him. But the destruction is mysteriously balanced in a surge of life and renewal by his family. There seems to be no way of explaining the whole chain of events in the novel, for they often are quite fantastic and illogical; yet Wilder points out that this story must be looked upon as only one of millions of stories, all of them perhaps bits of a larger pattern.

George R. Stewart (1895–   ). George Rippey Stewart was born at Sewickley, Pennsylvania. He received his A.B. from Princeton in 1917, the M.A. from the University of California in 1920, and the Ph.D. from Columbia University in 1922. From 1923 until retirement in 1962 he taught English at the University of California. Stewart's books tend to be unconventional. *Doctor's Oral* (1939) is a definitive portrayal of the pains and pleasures of the university graduate student. *Storm* (1941) covers twelve days in the life of its protagonist, a giant typhoon spawned in the far Pacific and spinning its way eastward to lash California. The contemporary practice of giving girls' names to hurricanes is attributed to the young meteorologist of this novel, who whimsically names the storm after his sweetheart, Maria. *Fire* (1948) is a similar treatment of the life of a large forest fire, from its ignition by a bolt of lightning to its final extinguishment. The people organized to fight the blaze add their moments of drama to the narrative. In particular, John Bentley, the fire boss, is ironically discharged only hours before a change in the weather turns the tide against the fire. Neither *Storm* nor *Fire* derives from a specific occurrence but they are clearly backed by careful research and documentation.

Stewart's nonfiction includes some exceptionally interesting volumes, accurate in scholarship and imaginatively conceived: *Names on the Land* (1945), a study less of the derivation of American place names than of the mind-sets that governed those choices; *Man, an Autobiography* (1946), which treats the cultural career of mankind as though all our species was one individual; *U.S. 40* (1953), which is the biography of a highway.

OTHER NOVELISTS OF THE PERIOD

HISTORICAL AND SEMIHISTORICAL NOVELISTS

Kenneth Roberts (1885–1957). Kenneth Lewis Roberts, in a series from *Arundel* (1930) to *Lydia Bailey* (1946), won recognition as outstanding among historical novelists of this era. His own native Maine is the jumping-off place for all these works, ranging in setting from 1759 in *Northwest Passage* (1937) to the War of 1812 in *The Lively Lady* (1931) and *Captain Caution* (1934). General readers are excited by a series of stirring episodes, while serious historians are impressed by the painstaking and authentic re-creation of America's past. Perhaps Roberts' most penetrating novel is *Oliver Wiswell* (1940), which sympathetically studies in its title character the Tory attitude during the American Revolution.

Hervey Allen (1889–1949). William Hervey Allen, a native of Pittsburgh, Pennsylvania, produced one of the most popular novels of the century in *Anthony Adverse* (1933). The novel carried its title character from an illegitimate birth in 1775 in an Alpine village to death in the American Southwest in 1825. Violence, sex, pure kinetic action, and rapid shifts of fortune and locale are its strongest merits and have appealed to a wide readership. Perhaps the best Allen novel is *Action at Aquila* (1938), which seeks to explain the American reactions to the Civil War chiefly through the experiences of a Pennsylvania cavalryman, Colonel Franklin. Allen's most ambitious project was a contemplated five-volume series upon an eighteenth-century New Yorker, Salathiel Albine, brought up by Indians to become a frontiersman in an early Pennsylvania settlement near Pittsburgh. *The City in the Dawn* (1950) collects the three novels of this series completed before Allen's death.

Edna Ferber (1887–1968). A native of Kalamazoo, Michigan, Edna Ferber wrote of many places and periods in American life. *So Big* (1924) shows the struggle of the widowed Selina De Jong, in Illinois, to provide for herself and her infant son Dirk. *Show Boat* (1926) romantically follows three generations of entertainers on the Mississippi River. It was the basis for the famous musical in 1927 with songs by Jerome Kern and lyrics by Oscar Hammerstein. *Cimarron* (1930) traces the degeneration of the colorful Yancey Cravat from a leading role in the Oklahoma land rush of 1889 to obscurity. *Saratoga Trunk* (1941) commences in New Orleans and takes its chief characters to Saratoga Springs, New York, in the eighties, when this spa was the great gathering place for social adventure and intrigue. *Giant* (1952) is a story set in Texas; and *Ice Palace* (1958) has Alaska as its scene.

Charles Bernard Nordhoff (1887–1947) and **James Norman Hall** (1887–1951). Nordhoff and Hall collaborated upon the trilogy *Mutiny on the Bounty* (1932), *Men Against the Sea* (1934), and *Pitcairn's Island* (1934). All three derive from the mutiny against the eighteenth-century Captain Bligh led by Fletcher Christian. Of particular interest is the South Seas locale in days of pagan and supposedly idyllic primitivism. The first of the trilogy was made into a notable movie.

MacKinlay Kantor (1904–   ). A native of Webster City, Iowa, Kantor did his first writing for the local newspaper. He went to England as a war correspondent during World War II, but having volunteered for combat duty, flew many missions as an aerial gunner.

Long Remember (1934), which established Kantor's reputation, is one of the finest Civil War combat novels since Stephen Crane. Certainly its graphically realistic picture of the Battle of Gettysburg has a shattering and unique immediacy.

Andersonville (1955) ranks high among historical novels written in this century. Its entire setting is the infamous Confederate prison camp in Georgia where almost fourteen thousand Union prisoners died in the closing years of the Civil War. Kantor follows the lives of several score of characters on both sides, sparing the reader none of the bestiality and suffering that killed so many and brutalized captive and captor alike. Over all, however, broods a spirit of deep compassion for tortured mankind; and even in this hell Dr. Elkins, the Confederate medical officer, struggles desperately to help, while Union prisoner Nathan Dreyfoos laments the senseless waste of lives. The conclusion achieves a feel of classic serenity after the anguish.

REGIONAL AND LOCAL NOVELISTS

Elizabeth Madox Roberts (1886–1941). Born at Perryville, Kentucky, Elizabeth Madox Roberts was taken while an infant to Springfield, Kentucky, where she resided most of her life. After some years as a schoolteacher she attended the University of Chicago, receiving her Bachelor of Philosophy degree in 1921. She was afflicted with poor health, especially after 1931.

Miss Roberts, like DuBose Heyward and Harper Lee, belongs to the romantic wing of the Southern Renaissance. Her first published volume, the verses of *Under the Tree* (1922), suggests that she was basically a poet. While her novels are usually models of structure and development her primary gift was a poetic insight into human personality.

The Great Meadow (1930) is a novel on the pioneer settlement of Kentucky. The book covers the tempestuous war years from 1774 to 1781 when the Indian allies of the British ravaged the American pioneer outposts in Kentucky. Diony Hall is induced by the intrepid Berk Jarvis to leave her Tidewater Virginia home and venture into the wilderness. Miss Roberts conceives of her novel as the westward saga from a woman's viewpoint. Diony takes her name from the Titaness Dione, symbolic of elemental love in a raw new world. Diony is the archetypal pattern of order and perpetuity, as necessary in civilizing the wild land as the masculine strength of Berk Jarvis and Daniel Boone.

Louis Bromfield (1896–1956). Born in Mansfield, Ohio, Louis Bromfield became an agrarian romantic, most of whose significant novels chronicle the decline of American individualism and Jeffersonian democracy. His best work, *The Farm* (1933), traces four generations from 1815 to 1915 upon the Bromfield family farm in Ohio. Immensely popular after *The Green Bay Tree* (1924), he won a Pulitzer Prize for *Early Autumn* (1926). Probably his most memorable writing concerns Malabar Farm, a one thousand-acre area near his birthplace, which he purchased in 1939 and made into an international showpiece of agricultural planning. Volumes from *Pleasant Valley* (1945) to *Animals and Other People* (1955) are notable contributions in their portrayal of intelligent, self-sufficient husbanders of the soil.

Conrad Richter (1890–   ). Conrad Michael Richter, born in Pine Grove, Pennsylvania, first won recognition with *The Sea of Grass* (1937), about Lutie Brewton, the daughter of a cattle baron, who leaves her family for an eastern lawyer but is drawn back to the huge sprawling ranch of the Old Southwest. His other novels deal chiefly with his native Pennsylvania community, notably *The Trees* (1940), *The Fields* (1946), and *The Town* (1950), which together form a trilogy.

Glenway Wescott (1901–   ). Born in Kewaskum, Wisconsin, Glenway Wescott attended the University of Chicago from 1917 to 1919. His first publication, *The Bitterns* (1920), consisted of poems. He spent most of the 1920s in Europe and has resided in New Jersey since 1934.

The Grandmothers (1927) is a strong example of American realism. In France, Alwyn Tower reflects upon the lives of his three grandmothers (his paternal grandfather was married twice) in mid-nineteenth-century Wisconsin. With the familiar love-hate syndrome of Midwestern authors, Wescott bares their often bleak and frustrated lives but perceives the spiritual exaltation of their puritanism as well as its narrow restraint.

Andrew Lytle (1902–   ). Andrew Nelson Lytle was born in Murfreesboro, Tennessee. After graduating from Vanderbilt University in 1925 he was a member of the famous 47 Workshop at Yale and later an actor in New York. He returned to Tennessee to contribute to *I'll Take My Stand* (1930) and take a prominent place among the southern Agrarians. He has held three Guggenheim fellowships and has taught at the universities of Iowa, Harvard, and Florida. Since 1961 he has been professor of English at the University of the South and editor of the *Sewanee Review*.

The late maturing of Lytle has militated against the reputation of a novelist who has been likened to Faulkner by critics. *Bedford Forrest and His Critter Company* (1931), written while Lytle was a history teacher, presents in nonfictional form the same Forrest that Faulkner depicts, a product of Southern frontier life in all its valor and violence. Lytle's concern is Faulkner's—the downfall of the family and rural tradition of the South before a ruthlessly competitive industrial society. This concern is mirrored in *The Long Night* (1936), a novel about the battle of Shiloh, and in *The Velvet Horn* (1957), about Tennessee in the 1870s. A notable achievement is *A Novel, a Novella and Four Stories* (1958). The long work in this collection, "A Name for Evil," is a ghost story. The ghost of the former owner, Major Brent, haunts a decaying house and induces the young writer residing there to murder his wife.

Lillian Smith (1897–1966). A native of Jasper, Florida, Lillian Smith moved with her family to Clayton, Georgia, in 1915. She attended Piedmont College, the Peabody Conservatory, and Columbia University without receiving a degree, but this deficiency has been rectified by subsequent honorary doctorates from Oberlin, Howard University, and other institutions. For three years she taught at Huchow, China. From 1936 to 1945 she was coeditor of *South Today,* a famous liberal journal. Miss Smith has proved one of the most vocal advocates of human freedom and brotherhood, especially in *Killers of the Dream* (1949).

Strange Fruit (1944) has elicited accolades of approval. The plot concerns a refined, educated mulatto girl in love with a white man, a theme already familiar before in Boucicault's *Octoroon*. Murder and lynching are the tragic outcomes of the romance. Miss Smith's convincing opposition to prejudice gives great strength to her novel.

DuBose Heyward (1885–1940). A direct descendant of Thomas Heyward, a signer of the Declaration of Independence and a scion of aristocratic Southern society, DuBose Heyward was born in Charleston, South Carolina. His first publication was *Carolina Chansons* (1922), a collection of poems by himself and Hervey Allen.

Porgy (1925) is set in Charleston's Catfish Row, which had degenerated from the one-time residence of the city's fashionable elite to a dilapidated Negro quarter. While watching a crap game, Porgy, a crippled beggar, witnesses a murder committed by Crown, a belligerent stevedore. Crown immediately goes into hiding. When Crown's girl friend Bess turns up searching for him, Porgy offers her shelter, and soon a feeling of love grows up between the gentle cripple and the rather sophisticated and somewhat cynical girl. Crown learns of this and sneaks back to reclaim Bess; but Porgy summons his strength and is able to kill Crown. Porgy is thrown into jail for the crime, and the disillusioned Bess turns to the lure of New York.

Despite the squalor and degradation of the Negro quarter, life is irresistibly vigorous and poetic in Catfish Row. With wonderful music by George Gershwin and lyrics by his brother, Ira, the novel was made into *Porgy and Bess* (1933), universally admired as an American operatic masterpiece.

Claude McKay (1880–1948). A native of Jamaica, British West Indies, Claude McKay served in the native constabulary before coming to the U.S.A. in 1912. He was the chief figure in the "Negro Renaissance" of the 1920s. Marxism attracted him briefly, but he was disillusioned by a visit to Russia.

Home to Harlem (1928) is the first significant novel to treat of the Negro ghettos of Northern cities. The account shows the bewilderment and frustration of a black soldier back from France in Harlem after World War I.

NOVELISTS OF VARIOUS SPECIALIZED INTERESTS

Vardis Fisher (1895–   ). Alvero Vardis Fisher was born of Mormon parents in Annis, Idaho. Living as he did in wild, remote mountains, he obtained his education at considerable difficulty. After service in the Army during World War I, he attended the University of Utah, receiving his A.B. in 1920. The M.A. (1922) and Ph.D. (1925) followed from the University of Chicago. Except for teaching at New York University (1928–31), where he was a close friend of the novelist Thomas Wolfe, he has resided in his native Idaho.

Children of God (1939) won prompt recognition. This depiction of the early history of Mormonism, although repudiated by the Mormon Church, was widely hailed for its fairness. It is robust and rich in the color and feel of the pioneer West. Fisher's ambitious project, a twelve-volume series, *Testament of Man*, began with *Darkness and the Deep* (1943) and was completed with *Orphans in Gethsemane* (1960). This long sequence seeks to trace the evolution of the human soul from its earliest stirrings down to the present. Vardis Fisher had earlier in his career written the Vridar Hunter tetralogy (1932–36), a group of autobiographical novels that interpret the individual as torn between two opposite forces: selfless or social drives and selfish or personal drives.

Frederic Prokosch (1906–   ). Frederic Prokosch's father, Eduard Prokosch, was one of the most distinguished philologists of this century, serving as president of the Linguistic Society of America and of the Modern Language Association. The novelist was born at Madison, Wisconsin, and was educated largely at European schools. He received an A.B. from Haverford College in 1926 and an M.A. in 1928, an M.A. from Cambridge University, England, in 1930, and a Ph.D. from Yale in 1931. He taught at Yale and New York University from 1931 to 1937. Subsequently he resided in various parts of Europe, although returning during World War II to work for the Office of War Information and later for the American Legation in Stockholm.

From *The Asiatics* (1935) to *The Wreck of the Cassandra* (1966) Prokosch has been an evoker of the exotic. His novels set in America, such as *Night of the Poor* (1939), are less convincing. His forte has been the intrusion of Europeans, occasionally Americans, into the most remote and bizarre regions—central Asia, the heart of Africa, the mountain fastnesses of South America. The picaresque framework embodies the themes which Prokosch explains as *"search* for a meaning in life, for peace, and for self-fulfillment; *flight* from stagnation, from imprisonment, mental or spiritual." His characters must learn about themselves and the integration of their personalities amidst stark or demonic landscapes and extraordinary hardships. This travail is recounted in a notably poetic style.

Ludwig Lewisohn (1883–1955). Born in Berlin, Germany, Ludwig Lewisohn was brought to Charleston, South Carolina, at the age of seven. He received bachelor's, master's, and doctor's degrees from the College of Charleston. From 1911 to 1919 he was a professor of German language and literature at Ohio State University. From 1919 to 1924 he was an editor of *The Nation.* For many years he was one of the most distinguished free-lance critics of European and American literature. From 1948–55 he served on the faculty of Brandeis University. *Up Stream* (1922) and *Mid-Channel* (1929) are autobiographical.

His earlier novels, beginning with *The Broken Snare* (1908), were generally sensitive studies of incompatible marriages. Later novels, starting with *The Island Within* (1928), concentrated upon problems of Jewish life. Interestingly, Lewisohn attempted in *The Last Days of Shylock* (1931) to follow Shakespeare's famous character after *The Merchant of Venice* ends; Shylock finds solace in the Hebrew faith and proclaims Zionism for his people.

William McFee (1881–). William Morley Punshon McFee was born at sea on *Erin's Isle,* a British ship. He received brief education in England and was apprenticed at the age of seventeen to a firm of mechanical engineers in London. From 1906 to 1911, when he settled in the United States, he served on British ships. During World War I, he returned to England for duty with the Royal Navy; but afterward came back to this country, becoming a naturalized citizen in 1925.

Although he has objected to the narrowness of the categorization, McFee is known almost exclusively as a novelist of the sea. Joseph Conrad had told many of his stories by the device of a narrator, Marlowe; and in somewhat the same way McFee has Chief Engineer Spenlove. In his wide-ranging voyages Spenlove meets numerous interesting and unusual people whose lives he scrutinizes with the knowing eye of an old salt. Beginning with *Casuals of the Sea* (1916), McFee's observations of men and women are shrewd and sympathetic, often ironic. One of McFee's best novels is *Command* (1922), where a commonplace sailor is stirred to heroism during World War I when his freighter is torpedoed by a submarine near Saloniki.

Walter van Tilburg Clark (1909–   ). Born at East Orland, Maine, Walter van Tilburg Clark moved west with his family. He received an A.B. in 1931 and an M.A. in 1932 from the University of Nevada, where his father was president. In 1934 he received an M.A. from the University of Vermont. He has taught at Montana State University, San Francisco State College, and the University of Nevada. During 1960–61 he was fellow in fiction at the Wesleyan University Center for Advanced Studies.

The Ox-Bow Incident (1940) is the one unquestioned example of the Wild West novel transformed into a work of art. In 1942 it appeared as a memorable motion picture. In 1885 citizens of Bridger's Wells, Nevada, pursue alleged rustlers, and lynch Donald Martin and his two ranch hands. Deputy Mapes leads the posse for his own glory; rancher Tetley, ex-Confederate officer, is driven by his desire for revenge; Gil Carter goes along to allay suspicion that he is one of the rustlers; sadistic Farnley relishes the killing. After the incident Sheriff Risley refuses to arrest any of the lynchers, though it is demonstrated that they killed innocent men. Gerald Tetley, sensitive son of the rancher, who has participated unwillingly, commits suicide, as does his father.

The force of the novel is in its sense of the tragic; a cruel land of cruel men breeds violence and misery. As a study of mob psychology it underlines the contest between liberal democratic justice and totalitarian destruction.

The Track of the Cat (1949) is set in early twentieth-century Nevada. The primitive mythic symbol of evil is attributed by Indian Joe Sam to a savage black panther. His rancher employers, the Bridges family, are infected with Sam's superstitious dread, brothers Arthur and Curt both dying in pursuit of the beast. This is a taut psychological drama of the inner war of primeval dark animism with the light of twentieth-century day.

John Erskine (1879–1951). A native New Yorker, John Erskine received from Columbia University the A.B. (1900), A.M. (1901), and Ph.D. (1903). From 1903 until 1909 he taught English at Amherst College, and thereafter until 1937 taught at his alma mater. He took occasional leaves of absence for lecture trips, and in 1919 served as educational director of the American Expeditionary Force University in Beaune, France. His musical career was almost as important to Erskine. He performed as a piano soloist with symphony orchestras of New York, Detroit, Minneapolis, and Chicago. In 1927 he became a trustee of the Juilliard School of Music and served as the president of that institution from 1928 to 1938. His many books range from poetry and short stories to opera librettos, scholarly studies, and four witty volumes of autobiography. The best known of his works present famous legendary characters satirically in modern dress.

The Private Life of Helen of Troy (1925) is an example of professorial wit without professorial pedantry. This imaginary account of Helen's readjustment problems upon her return to Greece after the Trojan War is told in colloquial English of today. Actually, the concerns of the 1920s—the aftermath of war, the position of women, the breakdown of moral standards—are topics which lend themselves to discussion in the setting of the ancient world. The era relished this work as a surprise and a droll satire playing upon the dignity of classical heroes and heroines.

Galahad (1926) is one of several other Erskine novels treating famous legends in the same lighthearted manner.

Carl Van Vechten (1880–1969). A native of Cedar Rapids, Iowa, Carl Van Vechten took a Ph.D. at the University of Chicago in 1903. In 1904 he published his own musical compositions. Thereafter as critic, composer, patron, and historian, he enjoyed a distinguished career in music. After devoting himself to fiction in the 1920s he shifted his interests to photography in 1932, and quickly became very prominent in his new field. During World War II he was a leading spirit in the American Theatre Wing and the Stage Door Canteen. He was the literary executor for Gertrude Stein.

A renewed interest in his era, acclaim to Van Vechten in his octogenarian years, and recent reissues of his novels have established his position as a novelist. He is a gifted writer of light comedy, writing of sophisticated characters who make wit and urbanity the keynotes of their existence.

The Blind Bow-Boy, a Cartoon for a Stained Glass Window (1923) proved one of the prime "shockers" of its iconoclastic, tradition-flaunting era. The title, taken from a Mercutio speech in *Romeo and Juliet*, suggests the astounding and irrational effects of love. Harold Prewett, after a very prim upbringing by an aunt, is summoned to New York by a father he had never known. His father lets Harold explore New York's most unconventional and uninhibited social set, presumably to counterbalance his puritanical background. When Harold finds out that his father had expected such flings to turn him against dissolute living, he angrily plunges deeper into wild abandon. Campaspe Lorillard is the novel's most fascinating creation, a determinedly libertarian, narcissistic woman.

Parties (1930) is the literary finale to the great upheaval in behavior that was the 1920s. In New York, Van Vechten examines the social whirl with bubbling gaiety. David and Rilda Westlake, their speakeasy cronies, and their bootleggers indulge in wild, no-holds-barred parties, desperately seeking an escape from the routine and pointlessness of it all. **Kay Boyle** (1903–   ). Born in St. Paul, Minnesota, Kay Boyle spent most of her early years in the East and in Europe. During the 1920s she was active in the magazine world (*Dial, Poetry, Broom*) as author and editor. In 1934 and in 1961 she was awarded Guggenheim fellowships. Her excellence in short-story writing is widely recognized.

Since most of her life has been lived in Europe and since her first and third husbands have been Europeans, Miss Boyle has devoted most of her notable fiction to the American, usually the American woman, in the Old World, beginning with *Plagued by the Nightingale* (1931). She refuses both of the clichés: that of the older concept of the American innocent in the corrupt Old World and the more recent version pointing to the corrupt American amidst Old World innocence. Her focus is upon the heightened perspective achieved by the two cultures in conflict. Loyalty and betrayal are her themes throughout. Her mastery of style and structure has made her pieces consistent anthology selections.

Damon Runyon (1884–1946). Alfred Damon Runyon was born in Manhattan, Kansas, but grew up in Pueblo, Colorado, where his first publications appeared in local newspapers. Although only fourteen, he enlisted in the Army during the Spanish-American War by lying about his age, and saw service in the Philippines. In 1911 he became a reporter for the New York *American,* and in its pages and in popular magazines he quickly became famous for his highly imaginative accounts of New York characters. His private life knew much unhappiness.

Guys and Dolls (1932) creates a memorable folklore for New York City. Runyon's subject is a fascinating melange of big-city sharpers, wise guys, parasites, sassy dames, and other characters, portrayed in a wildly slangy diction of outrageous metaphor and murderous English, relating almost everything in the present tense. The book is actually a collection of related tales. It was the basis for a delightful musical by Frank Loesser. Other Runyon volumes are equally lively in theme and style.

Vincent McHugh (1904–   ). Born in Providence, Rhode Island, Vincent McHugh was educated at Providence College. A free-lance writer, he wrote reviews for *The New Yorker,* directed the Federal Writers' Project in New York City during the New Deal years, taught college courses in creative writing at New York University and elsewhere, and wrote motion-picture scripts for Hollywood. In 1949 he won the literature award of the National Institute of Arts and Letters.

Caleb Catlum's America (1936) has bewildered some critics and many readers because it attempts to recapture the "tall tale" spirit of

America between the War of 1812 and the Civil War. Caleb is the archetype of the American wanderer and relator of "whoppers." Born in 1798, he details the first century of his life, during which Daniel Boone, Davy Crockett, Mike Fink, and John Henry were his roistering friends. He panned for gold, fought in our wars, popped up wherever hard liquor and exuberant talk were flowing. The extravagant stories are matched by extravagant language, often using regional and local terms and expressions. Few other twentieth-century works so uproariously capture the free-swinging gusto of a lost America.

CHAPTER TWO

Poetry of the Early Twentieth Century

NEW TRENDS IN POETRY

The seeds of a new poetry were fitfully growing in America and at the same time in England in the early years of the twentieth century. The great Romantic thrust of the early nineteenth century had worn itself out; the fiercely imaginative language of Blake, Wordsworth, Coleridge, Shelley and Keats was followed by men of rather more academic mold on both sides of the Atlantic. In America, Longfellow, Whittier, Lowell, and Bryant, as also Tennyson in Victorian England, held for the most part to rigidly conventionalized forms and chose chiefly traditional subjects even when dealing with regional matters. But one poet, Walt Whitman, sang out in free rhythms that were uniquely American. And Emily Dickinson spoke in a soft and starkly simple language that disdained the rhetorical conventions of mid-century. It was largely to these two poets, and to certain new trends in Europe, that the American poets of the twentieth century would look for inspiration.

From 1900 to 1910 there was little important activity in American poetry. However, the trend away from romanticism and the turning toward realism, which is so marked in American fiction of the period, is seen in such a poem as "The Man with the Hoe" by Edwin Markham, a starkly realistic portrayal of an impoverished farm laborer.

Around 1910 a group of poets called the Imagists formed in London. The group included the Americans Ezra Pound, Amy Lowell, Hilda Doolittle (H.D.), and John Gould Fletcher. The sharp precision and clarity in their poems had an effect quite similar to Japanese or

Chinese poetry. They sought a poetry that would aim directly at the senses and rejected traditional metrical form in favor of the shifting rhythms of free verse. In the manner of the French *symbolistes* they tried to suggest a feeling through the simple and direct presentation of a brilliant image rather than to express that feeling concretely or to comment on it. The Imagists strongly influenced a whole generation of poets, and through the vehicle of the little literary magazines, their poems reached a large and growing public. Among the Americans who were influenced by the Imagists were William Carlos Williams, Wallace Stevens, Marianne Moore, and, in some earlier works, Hart Crane and Carl Sandburg.

Sandburg, in another characteristic phase, became the leader in the use of free verse as he sang of the power of the industrial Midwest. Robert Frost and Edwin Arlington Robinson used a searching, if more traditional, language in their poems set largely in New England. Suddenly America possessed a new body of distinctive poetry.

The initial thrust of modern poetry perhaps reached a climax with T. S. Eliot's *The Waste Land* (1922). The poem "The Waste Land" and others by Eliot influenced a new generation of poets, most notably those of a Southern group called the Fugitives. Poetry appeared to have come a long way since the short bell-like songs of the Imagists. Feelings of emptiness and disillusionment began to be expressed by poets as they looked at the evils of a commercialized and often barbaric America. The probings of the subconscious by Freud had opened up new mysteries about the inner life of man; and Robinson Jeffers, among others, was deeply affected by the dark powers which science had uncovered.

The Depression of the thirties witnessed a decline in poetry. Poets tried to reach the common man and to express the fears of the laborer and city dweller. But the common man, used to a diet of radio, movies, and magazines could no longer understand the poet. The rise of the European dictatorships and the Spanish Civil War added to the confusion among the poets and they became more abstract, often experimenting in surrealism and Dada. Somewhat surprisingly, humorous and light verse flourished during this period, exhibiting versatility and skill. Finally, the inevitable Second World War arrived, and the serious poets shouted out their anger though few could hear them over the sounds of marching feet. After World War II, poetry in America was to strike out in many new directions, as we shall see in Chapter 6. We turn now to poets of the earlier part of the twentieth century.

MAJOR POETS OF THE EARLY TWENTIETH CENTURY

Edwin Arlington Robinson (1869–1935). Shortly after Edwin Arlington Robinson's birth in Head Tide, Maine, the family moved to Gardiner, Maine, the "Tilbury Town" of his poems. From 1891 to 1893 he attended Harvard but was forced to leave because of his family's financial plight, which also caused other disruptions in the family. One brother took to alcohol and drugs, the other to disastrous speculation and death from tuberculosis. Robinson's mother died suddenly of black diphtheria, and his father turned to spiritualism, "cutting my universe clean in half," the poet stated. Since editors ignored his verse, Robinson printed his first volume, *The Torrent and the Night Before* (1896), at his own expense. The next year he went to New York, where he was to spend most of his life in simple but adequately comfortable lodgings. Briefly in 1898 he held a clerical job at Harvard but was back in New York in 1899, where whiskey provided the only solace amidst his small means and virtual anonymity. Desperate, he was working as a timekeeper for a subway construction crew when in 1905 President Theodore Roosevelt became interested in Robinson's poetry and gave him a sinecure in the New York Custom House. With the Taft administration in 1909, however, Robinson was again jobless. In 1911 he spent the summer at the MacDowell Colony in New Hampshire, and thereafter made this his annual summer residence until his death.

It was not until 1927, when *Tristram* brought him financial success, that he could rely on his writings for economic support and could pay off his long-standing debts. Robinson is a consummate craftsman, essentially intellectual and tending to avoid sensuous imagery. Robinson's philosophy, "immediate pessimism plus ultimate optimism," is represented by the "dark" of everyday life and the "light" of the ideal. His short early poems employ generally time-honored poetic forms of the nineteenth century, but their "anti-poetic" expression was appropriate to a disjointed era no longer responsive to previous optimism. In his later life his long poems attempted to create a new myth for a depersonalized age.

The Children of the Night (1897) is considered the first "public" volume of Robinson's verse. It presents with alterations and additions *The Torrent and the Night Before* published privately the previous year. Although the earliest writing of Robinson, many of these short pieces are among his best. The book received relatively little attention, but critics later recognized the power of so many of these poems and of comparable later Robinson poems, which are brief, precise psychological studies of people who are failures but have a power of endurance akin to that of New England granite.

"John Evereldown" in stanzas of questions and answers tells of the lure of woman that irresistibly pulls even this aging man to Tilbury Town. Refrain and incremental repetition impressively delineate the treadmill of desire upon which man is doomed to run out his life.

"Luke Havergal" hauntingly illuminates the loneliness of a bereaved lover contemplating suicide.

"Her Eyes" tells of a painter estranged from his beloved by "that strife so grim." He abandons the world to paint her portrait and lives contemplating the expressive eyes in the painting. Memorable is the gray tone of the poem.

"Villanelle of Change" takes this elaborate French form, generally the vehicle for light verse, and makes of it a solemn statement, using the glory of ancient Greece as a symbol of the irretrievability of departed grandeur.

"Richard Cory," a favorite anthology selection, is unusual for Robinson in its surprise ending. Cory is portrayed as the American ideal in appearance, in manner, and in wealth. But in spite of being the envy of all, he commits suicide. The standard criteria of success do not necessarily add up to happiness.

"Calvary," expressing distress at mankind's failure for nineteen centuries to heed the message and agony of Christ, is the first sonnet printed in Robinson's volumes. He wrote many notable sonnets, all but one of which use the Italian form.

"Aaron Stark," also in sonnet form, is a sharp vignette describing a miserly misanthrope, self-alienated from his fellow men.

"Cliff Klingenhagen," another sonnet, wonders if the speaker, who is given wine, will be as happy as Cliff himself, who with a smile drinks the bitter wormwood of life.

"The Clerks," a sonnet, states a frequent Robinson theme: the lives of undistinguished ordinary people may gain and retain some worthy qualities not attainable by the ambitious and famous.

"Credo," in sonnet form, indicates Robinson's adherence to metaphysical idealism. Convinced that matter is only a manifestation of thought, he writes "I feel the coming glory of the Light."

Captain Craig (1902) received, like its predecessors, little recognition at the time. Its chief emphasis is upon the relation of the individual to society.

"Captain Craig," the title piece and Robinson's first extensive employment of blank verse, is his best blank verse according to many critics because of its supple, conversational ease and brilliant variety. The poem is not a narrative but a lengthy character sketch based upon Alfred Louis, an acquaintance of Robinson. The teller of the poem picks up the erudite old failure Captain Craig and provides for him until the aged man's death. Self-knowledge is Craig's motto, and knowledge has amply revealed to him the follies of mankind. Laughter is his response, not the sardonic humor of the cynic, but the laughter of wisdom that teaches resignation to fate. For his funeral Craig specifies a brass band and trombones. Life must go on.

"Isaac and Archibald," another blank-verse delineation of character, plays with remarkable subtlety and perception upon the opposite worlds of childhood and age. In retrospect the narrator tells of one afternoon of his boyhood when both the aging New England farmers named in the title separately confided to the youth the belief that the mind of the other was weakening. The boy lived in a world of constant discovery and of days seemingly infinite in length; the old men lived in a constantly diminishing, familiar world of ever-shortening days. Yet in poignant backward glance the mature narrator realizes that Isaac and Archibald found a tang rather than a taint in brevity and the mundane. The poem arose from an actual experience about 1900 when two aging friends of Robinson separately told him of their worries about each other.

"The Klondike" is an experiment in octameter to suggest the flow of the river and the irresistible but futile lure of gold.

"The Book of Annandale," a moderately long blank-verse narrative, begins shortly after the death of Annandale's young wife. In the first section Annandale meditates upon their happily married years, his deep grief, and the book which he had written but had never shown her. In the second section the widowed Damaris worships the memory of her dead husband, Argan. Gradually we learn that Annandale had loved Damaris, had written his book for her, and married another when she refused him. At the end Annandale and Damaris look to reunion. Robinson's intent is to show the necessary changes and often surprising realignments which are part of experience. He insists that the life force calls for resolute facing of life and accepting what happiness it has to offer.

The Town Down the River (1910), reacting to criticism of the previous volume, abandons blank verse. Reception, however, continued to be meager.

"The Master" is one of the notable poems on Lincoln and at the same time a bitter commentary on commercialism. "The shopman's test of age and worth" was the criterion by which Lincoln in his time was judged. The people on this basis subjected him to ridicule, never perceiving his greatness.

"The Town Down the River," the title poem, is related by a dispassionate "Watcher by the Way." Most of mankind, marching down the riverside to the sought-for town, finds no satisfaction, yet for a possible few life can provide shining lights.

"Miniver Cheevy," a perennial anthology favorite, depicts an alcoholic lamenting these humdrum days and wishing he had lived in spirited medieval times. Technically a masterpiece of ironic humor, the poem is especially skillful in the short last line of each quatrain with its feminine ending; the anticlimax superbly contrasts the golden dream of Miniver with the tawdry reality in which he lives.

"Two Gardens in Linndale" tells the story of two brothers, Oakes and Oliver, who split their inheritance and erect a fence to separate their parcels of land. They live separate but tranquil lives until Oakes dies. It is right, suggests Robinson, that each person does as he wishes and maintains his own identity.

The Man Against the Sky (1916), containing some of the best Robinson short poems, at last received strong critical support and marked him as an established poet, though not popularly acclaimed.

"Flammonde" tells of a Tilbury townsman eminently superior to his fellows in human relations. Though himself of minor attainments, Flammonde altruistically aids others and by human sympathy settles a number of difficult personal problems.

"The Clinging Vine" is a dramatic monologue in the manner of Robert Browning. An enraged wife verbally belabors her husband for his philandering and after dissecting their unsuccessful marriage stomps away from it.

"John Gorham" uses heptameter not for its usual lushness but for chilled hostility. With mounting insistence Jane Wayland asserts her love, and in alternate stanzas Gorham coolly brushes her off because unwittingly she had deeply wounded his vanity.

"Hillcrest" celebrates the benefits derived from residence at the Mac-Dowell Colony for writers and artists. The surroundings of this retreat permit meditation and re-evaluation and realization that humility and endurance are the best responses to the vicissitudes of life.

"Old King Cole" is a tragicomic depiction of a man whose two sons have turned out badly. Even though townsfolk rebuke the father, he refuses to be glum and censorious. As an individual he has his rights to happiness.

"Ben Jonson Entertains a Man from Stratford," the one blank-verse poem in this collection, is one of the most highly regarded of Robinson works. In a dramatic monologue Jonson talks on about his friend and fellow dramatist Shakespeare. Jonson reveals himself as a sturdy, hard-driving personality and offers a convincing and friendly picture of the actual, human Shakespeare. Jonson favored and wrote by classic precept, but he admits awe for the poet from Stratford who followed the dictates of his own genius and created his characters in the image of living men.

"Eros Turannos" ("tyrant love") tells the story of a promiscuous male who has yielded to "tradition" and the affections of an in-

telligent, mature woman. He marries her, and later resumes his phi-
landerings. Knowing him for what he is, his wife nonetheless remains
a hopeless prisoner of love.

"The Man Against the Sky," the title poem, illustrates Robinson's
metaphysical pessimism. It opens with a description of a solitary man
crossing a hilltop into the setting sun, evidently to life's end. Robinson
explores every conventional philosophy of life from dogmatic faith
to nihilism, finding all inadequate. We perceive the Word, the Deity,
only in fragmentary, imperfect fashion.

Merlin (1917) is Robinson's first long poem. It begins his trilogy
upon the Arthurian legend, retold as an analysis of the world Robinson knew. The characters in this poem are not pictured as medieval;
they take on a timeless quality. (The names appear in the form used by
Robinson.)

Wizard and wise man, Merlin is enthralled by the charm and beauty
of Vivian, an intelligent but self-centered woman. He leaves his post
as counselor to King Arthur and lives for ten years with Vivian at
Broceliande Castle in Brittany. Arthur summons him back because of
impending civil war. Modred, Arthur's child by his own sister, desires both the kingdom and Queen Guinevere. The queen, however,
is attracted to the handsome knight Lancelot and runs off with him.
Unable to do anything about the conflict now raging in the country,
Merlin sadly departs.

Robinson's account is closer to Malory's *Morte d'Arthur* than is
Tennyson's *Idylls of the King*. Tennyson, suppressing the sin of Arthur
in fathering Modred, makes of the King a paragon, defeated by the
viciousness of others. Robinson places the blame for the downfall
upon Arthur himself, thereby creating a human and genuinely tragic
figure. The central theme sees man as a selfish being with limited
vision, incapable of disciplining himself for the sake of enduring
righteousness.

Merlin is the poet-philosopher who can only be a rueful spectator,
clearly prophesying the inevitable course of events but helpless to
check them. Robinson sees Merlin as pointing out through Arthur
and his realm that nothing can stand on a false foundation. Merlin
is the inwardly divided intellectual, himself fated to unhappiness amidst
the turmoil. Yet Merlin is loyal to Arthur, and this causes Vivian to
turn away from him in jealousy. Vivian's "golden shell of exile," the
alluring aesthetic existence, is in its way as inadequate as Arthur's
insecurely based world. The work suggests the plight of the artist in
the confusion of the twentieth century, while at the same time it
recounts the great Arthurian legend with a modern sense of reality.

Lancelot (1920) re-examines much of the *Merlin* narrative from the viewpoint of Lancelot.

In Arthur's absence Guinevere urges Lancelot to come to her. Haunted by thoughts of the Holy Grail and contemplating a withdrawal to religious asceticism, Lancelot joins the queen reluctantly. Arthur's absence was actually a stratagem, and the suspicious monarch stealthily returns to surprise the lovers together. Lancelot fights his way out, taking Guinevere with him to Joyous Gard. Arthur wages inconclusive war against Lancelot until the Pope demands the safe return of the queen to Arthur. Motivated by a desire for the higher life, Lancelot agrees. But Guinevere goes uncomprehendingly to a nunnery. Modred rises against Arthur, and Lancelot unexpectedly comes to Arthur's aid, but too late. With both the King and Modred dead, Lancelot visits Guinevere. Smitten again, he urges their elopement, but meditation has convinced Guinevere that Lancelot was right earlier in advocating leaving her. Lancelot, too, seeks such a higher life.

In this version, the sins of Guinevere and Lancelot are not chiefly responsible, as other writers have assumed, for the downfall of Arthur and the Round Table. Merlin advises Arthur that Modred is the real danger and that, reprehensible as the illicit lovers are, Arthur should give his attention to the major threat. Robinson's poem is therefore a valedictory to the romantic tradition. Lancelot and Guinevere, torn by inner struggles and vacillations like those that beset the twentieth century, show that the passions and wars of mankind must be superseded by a new spirit. For the lovers it shall be the peace of God. The depiction of Lancelot's gradual lifting and backsliding is a very subtle and penetrating rendering of the famous knight.

The Three Taverns (1920).

"The Dark Hills," an anthology favorite, evokes the sorrow and wonder of receding splendor, lyrically depicting the sunset as emblematic of all passings and all eventual endings.

"The Three Taverns" is a dramatic monologue by St. Paul to Christians meeting him on the approach to Rome. The apostle offers an answer to the conundrum of "The Valley of the Shadow." The world is a "spiritual kindergarten," painful to all, hopeless to the fainthearted. Spiritual advancement is our goal, attainable only through suffering and endurance.

"On the Way" is a dramatic dialogue ascribed to Burr and Hamilton in 1794, before their falling out. Small-minded, selfish Burr is jealous of Washington. Hamilton perceives the greatness in the first President and the necessity of curbing one's own ambitions so that the nation may be led by its very best men.

"John Brown" resembles "The Three Taverns." In a dramatic monologue to his wife on the eve of his execution, the Kansas abolitionist expresses the need for patience and faith.

Avon's Harvest (1921).

"Avon's Harvest" is a study of obsession. When in boarding school at the age of sixteen, Avon was pestered by an obnoxious youth who attached himself to him. When Avon learns that his unattractive companion has injured another student by lying, Avon beats up the youth. Maliciously the youngster vows to haunt Avon until his death. Avon receives an implicitly threatening postcard from the chap each year on his birthday until the sinking of the *Titanic*. Avon then thinks himself free, but later in a Maine cabin while slumbering he is convinced that his enemy attacks him with a knife. A year later on his birthday Avon dies, apparently of fright. The horror in Avon's life poses more questions than it answers in Robinson's indirect and cryptic blank verse. Is Avon a normal man unjustly pursued by evil, or is he mentally unbalanced, conjuring up imaginary terrors?

"Mr. Flood's Party," justly one of the most famous Robinson pieces, portrays the loneliness of a solitary drinker on his way home from Tilbury Town one night. The old man pauses at the top of a hill conversing with himself "with two moons listening." After a fleeting moment of fulfillment, he realizes that there are only strangers in the town where once his friends lived.

"Lost Anchors," displaying Robinson's lifelong skill with the sonnet, uses an old sailor's tale of a reputed treasure ship that contained only anchors as a symbol of the ancient sea, often ungovernable and disappointing to man's fond hopes.

"Rembrandt to Rembrandt" is a blank-verse soliloquy delivered by the famous painter to a self-portrait painted early in his career. Much of its power derives from Robinson's identification of himself and his fortunes with the seventeenth-century Dutch artist. At the height of his genius Rembrandt is poor and obscure, with no prospects. Although the world passes him by, he asserts his conviction in the quality and rightness of his work. But he is assailed by even greater doubts about the point of any human endeavor. His final affirmation is faith in a supernatural force whose service provides ample motive for all life and creativity.

The Man Who Died Twice (1924) tells of a promising composer, Fernando Nash, who has ruined his talents through profligacy and lost his friends because of his arrogance. Converted to a Salvation-Army brand of religion, he becomes a drummer at street-corner revivals. Dying, he hears in his mind the monumental symphony that he had meant to do but had never composed. Once his genius had died through dissipation. Now facing a second death, he receives Divine

Grace, experiencing the great symphony and departing with the certitude that his life was not wasted. The blank-verse description of the symphony is one of the masterful attempts in English poetry in its conveying of musical effects.

Dionysus in Doubt (1925) is the last major assembly of short Robinson poems. *Nicodemus* (1932) collects some later short poems; but Robinson's chief works after 1925 were longer and in blank verse.

"Dionysus in Doubt" is a satiric diatribe immediately occasioned by Prohibition, understandably disturbing to the god of wine. Since Robinson's social philosophy is emphatic individualism, he is stoutly opposed to legislation upon private morality. Government should exist for the fullest self-development of individuals rather than for the restriction of lives, no matter how well-intentioned the state may be.

"Karma" takes its name from the East Indian concept of the impersonal cosmic principle governing all operations of the universe. The ironic application in this sonnet is to a businessman who financially ruins a friend, but salves his conscience by giving a Salvation-Army Santa Claus a dime.

"Maya," whose title is another Indian word suggesting the illusionary world of sense and thought, is a companion to "Karma." The soul of man tells the mind about the latter's being chained to earth and its inability to ascertain transcendent truth.

Tristram (1927) brought Robinson public acclaim.

Wounded in Ireland, Tristram of Lyonnesse is nursed by Isolt whom he later conducts to Cornwall as bride for his uncle, King Mark. Too late Tristram realizes his love for the Irish princess. Andred, his cousin and a minion of King Mark, surprises Tristram with Isolt and is wounded by Tristram. Banished, Tristram proceeds to Brittany and there marries another Isolt (Isolt of the White Hands). Summoned to be a knight of the Round Table, Tristram is reunited with Isolt at Joyous Gard, Lancelot's castle, when King Mark conveys his dying queen back to Cornwall and relents enough to permit her a brief meeting with Tristram. Andred stabs Tristram, and the lovers die in each other's arms. Dismissing the magic potion of the traditional story of Tristram and Isolt as an "impossible and wholly superfluous concoction," Robinson determined to relate the tragedy in purely human terms, largely following the Malory account. Robinson here as never before offers a lyric cry for thwarted passion. Speaking in the language of his time, he uses the techniques of psychology in analyzing the overwhelming attraction of the central pair. The tale is told against a background of sea imagery. Emery Neff and some other critics rate this as the best Tristram account in our language because of its poignant account of the tug within Tristram of the two Isolts—one attainable and therefore easily ignored, the other unattainable and consequently the aching desire of the heart's core. Notable also is Robinson's characterization of King Mark and of Isolt of Brittany. They are forced to contemplate the irretrievable loss of all dear to them and must seek within themselves some consolation and fortitude.

Cavender's House (1929) and subsequent long blank-verse narratives are generally considered less significant than Robinson's earlier works. He continues his previous themes, often with deepened psychological insight, but the poetic lyricism diminishes and readers are increasingly perplexed by indirection and cryptic phrasing. This poem deals with the mental turmoil of a man who has slain his wife. Robinson contends that no human or divine law but the conscience of the individual will enforce punishment.

The Glory of the Nightingales (1930) brings Malory to the mansion of the invalid Nightingale, intent upon killing him for wrongs to the dead Agatha. Nightingale disarms Malory and kills himself with Malory's gun, leaving his fortune for a hospital to be headed by Malory. Thus Malory is turned from a destructive urge toward an individual to a constructive purpose for society. At the same time he is confronted by an ambiguous benefactor who has greatly injured him and whom he cannot definitively appraise as either good or evil.

Matthias at the Door (1931) was labeled by Robinson as "transcendentalism." The "door" is a natural rock formation which symbolizes death to other figures in the poem but to the title character it is the door to a reborn spiritual life.

Amaranth (1934) in title refers to "the flower that never fades," i.e., truth. Fargo is an atrocious painter who learns through harrowing visions presented by Amaranth that he would better have been a plumber. Robinson's familiar theme of the inferior artist results not in pessimism but in self-knowledge and acceptance of the right, though humble, bent of life.

King Jasper (1935) was completed on the poet's deathbed. The idea for this "treatise on economics" occurred to Robinson upon the day of the first inauguration of FDR, and conveys many of Robinson's fears about the consequences of the Depression. Jasper was the name of the ill-fated mine that years before had swallowed up the last monies of the Robinson family. Jasper (capitalism) is the monarch of an industrial empire built by exploiting the elder Hebron (the common man). The younger Hebron (revolutionary zeal) brings about the downfall of Jasper but perishes also in his unbalanced fanaticism. Surviving is Zoë (broad intelligence) who points out the way to the future through altruism.

Thus the themes and moods and hopes of Robinson continue to the very end.

Robert Frost (1874–1963). Robert Lee Frost, born in San Francisco, was the son of a New Englander whose sympathies had been with the South. After his father's death, Frost at age eleven was brought back to New England where he attended school in Massachusetts and college briefly at Dartmouth and Harvard. When his grandfather left him a farm near Derry, New Hampshire, on the condition that he keep it for ten years, Frost began to supplement his farm income with teaching. He seemed destined to failure in all these efforts, so in 1912 he decided to become a full-time poet and moved his family to England. There he found quick success with his first two books of lyric poems, *A Boy's Will* (1913) and *North of Boston* (1914). When the Frosts returned to New England in 1915, Robert Frost's reputation was already established. Settling again on a farm in New Hampshire, Frost soon was called on to accept invitations to give public lectures and readings around the country. Many honorary degrees were conferred upon him. He was the only poet to take part in the ceremony of a presidential inauguration; he read one of his poems at the inauguration of John F. Kennedy in 1961.

While other poets of his time, W. B. Yeats, T. S. Eliot, and Ezra Pound, invented elaborate myths and structures for their poetry, Frost found innovation possible by purifying simpler forms. He sometimes used classical conventions but adapted them to his New England idiom.

Frost's Nature often epitomizes beauty, peace, and simplicity, but the poet discards the idea of transcendentalism in Nature. His readers share his delight in New England's farms and forests, but beyond these landscapes Frost catches deeper levels of meaning. By setting the elemental human passions in an idiom essentially puritan American, Frost is at once native to New England and highly original.

A Boy's Will (London, 1913; New York, 1915) takes its title from the Longfellow poem. Though rooted in the soil of New England, many of these lyrics show the influence of earlier poets. The prevailing tone is wistful unrest. The collection includes Frost's first published poem, "My Butterfly" (1894), and others written through 1912. The book represents a poet's youthful growth and his subjective moods.

"Stars" perceives in the celestial heavens not the master plan therein predicted by Dante but instead the absence of design, nonetheless awesome in its majesty.

"Storm Fear" looks like free verse but is an effective employment of varying iambic lines to suggest unresolved fears during a blizzard.

"The Vantage Point" indicates the dissociation of Nature and man. Humans are considered in the first stanza, Nature in the second. Frost refuses to say that either is better, for at will he may cling to either.

"Mowing," though an early poem, remains one of his most popular. The mower of this sonnet denies the nineteenth-century transcendentalism of Nature. He denies also the conventional justifications of work for financial profit or as a subsidy of later idleness. The poetry of labor is pragmatically doing and greatly relishing the job just for its very self.

"Going for Water" employs simplicity and exquisite crafting to catch a moment of deep perception of natural beauty, shared by two fetchers of water. A recurring theme in Frost is puritan devotion to a job and being rewarded when Nature unexpectedly bestows its gift of beauty.

North of Boston (1914) has a major place in American literature and contains much of the finest of Frost's work. He here speaks no longer in the manner of the earlier Romantics but in his own mature voice. His first volume had no dramatic poems whatsoever, but looming large here are monologues and dialogues. Blank verse now generally supersedes the stanzaic pieces of *A Boy's Will*. The predominant note is of man's isolation and alienation from his fellows. Yet humor occurs frequently.

"Mending Wall" wryly contemplates the difficulty of human communication. As the poet and his neighbor perform the annual ritual of restoring the stone fence between their farms, they argue amiably about the wall's necessity. The stolid neighbor insists upon maintaining traditional barriers. Frost whimsically questions their need when friendship exists.

"The Tuft of Flowers," refreshingly points out that by sharing the same sensitivities and by doing the same sort of task, "Men work together. . . . Whether they work together or apart."

"The Demiurge's Laugh" refers to the Platonic *demiurgos*, the first maker and destroyer, who is beyond all love or hate. Seeking the riddle of Nature, the poet finds that the cosmic order is utterly heedless of man or man's hopes.

"The Death of the Hired Man" is one of Frost's best dramatic poems, and has often been cited as one of the finest genre pictures in American poetry. Silas, a farm laborer, returns to the home of Warren and Mary to die. Warren doesn't want the old man, who was an unreliable and inferior worker (his one commendable skill lay in building a load of hay). Mary tries to win her husband to her own sympathy for Silas, while Warren attempts to instill his own practicality in her. As Mary argues, the hired man (never physically on the scene) becomes the embodiment of the stanch New Englander, cherishing self-respect when he has little else. Now that his proud independence has dwindled to a polite fiction, all that remains for him is death. Warren moves somewhat toward the compassion of his wife, yet maintains a certain separateness.

"The Mountain" indicates a remarkable but momentary rapport established between the narrator and a farmer near Lunenburg, Vermont.

The farmer gradually senses that the stranger has a poetic mind and therefore partly opens up to reveal his own romantic dream. Although living a lifetime in the shadow of Hor (which Frost names after an Old Testament mountain where the priest Aaron died), the farmer has never climbed the mountain to observe upon its summit a spring reputedly "Warm in December, cold in June." His practical mind tells him that the apparent difference of the water's temperature is only relative to the seasonal air temperature. But his poetic soul cherishes this magic spring and refuses to let him destroy the mystery by actually scrutinizing it. Embarrassed at revealing so much, the farmer turns back abruptly to his mundane tasks.

"Home Burial" (referring to the old practice of interring dead babies in the garden) is a penetrating dialogue, deeply revelatory of male and female psychology. A farm wife is about to leave her husband, who forces her to talk out their problem. She has completely retreated from him after he himself buried their dead infant; she scorns him as insensitive. He tried to assuage his grief in performing accustomed and necessary work; he wants future children to blunt their mutual pain. The poem breaks off as she is at the door, both at emotional peak. Perhaps the airing of their troubles will help in resolving them, but full understanding seems almost impossible.

"The Black Cottage" offers a brief framework for a monologue by a liberal country parson who accompanies the narrator to a deserted home. The theme is the valiant but pathetic desire of men for unchanging truths amidst a changing world. The aged woman who had last inhabited this home saw unswerving truths in Jeffersonian democracy, the cause of the North in the Civil War (for which her husband died in battle), and old-fashioned religion. The clergyman too would like a Utopia of unalterable truth and must respect the old lady's rocklike certitude. When, however, is truth true? Life and earth seem alone the persistent truths.

"After Apple-picking" masterfully employs irregular line length to suggest the sleepy surfeit after the fragrant harvest. Some critics suggest that the harvest is emblematic of writing poetry, but it seems sufficient that perfection can be reached in joyous achievement with Nature.

"The Code" in title is ambivalent, implying both an ethical standard and a way of communicating. Both meanings emerge. A city-bred farmer, urging his two hired hands to added effort in cocking hay before an approaching storm, is astonished when one worker quits and leaves. The other carefully explains the Yankee attitude that the farmer's statement was an implied criticism of the worker's ability and integrity, challenging his independence and self-respect.

"The Generations of Men" brings together a boy and a girl at the reunion of the Stark clan. They "consult the voices" of a brook, but Frost in his usual vein suggests that we ourselves are the makers of any meaning in Nature or human history. The conversation gradually builds an intimacy between the two, but in reticence they merely plan a second meeting.

"The Housekeeper" is a dramatic monologue by an elderly woman who keeps house for a man with whom her daughter Estelle had long lived as a common-law wife. On the previous day Estelle had gone off with another man, who promised marriage. We gradually learn from her mother that Estelle's sudden act arose not from distress at her questionable social status but from sheer resentment against the man who could not make up his mind to marry her.

"The Fear" seems almost a continuation of the previous poem. Having left one man, a woman is living with another on a lonely farm. Returning one night, she glimpses a strange face which she fears is that of her first lover come for her. By lantern light she ascertains that it is a casual passer-by, but, unnerved, she drops the lantern.

"The Wood-pile" brings the poet into a frozen swamp where he chances upon an abandoned and rotting pile of cut wood. To him it suggests that human creativity cannot expect Nature to protect it; and that it is man who imposes meaning upon Nature.

Mountain Interval (1916) offers a mixture of lyrics and dramatic dialogues and contains some of Frost's most characteristic pieces. "Interval" here means the low land between hills.

"The Road Not Taken," one of Frost's best-known works, is an image of choices of life. Its mood depicts the uncertain melancholy that may accompany the decision that has to be made upon little concrete basis. Of the various paths, Frost took "the one less traveled by."

"An Old Man's Winter Night" reveals the weakening grasp on life of an aged man alone on a frosty farmstead. Although Nature maintains its wonted rounds, man in consciousness gives order and organization to the world.

"Hyla Brook" celebrates a brook's natural beauty while mildly teasing in the concluding lines about other romantic poems (especially Tennyson's "Brook"). "We love the things we love for what they are" instead of seeking transcendental consolation.

"The Oven Bird," though fourteen lines, is not a sonnet. Frost made other experiments in this length that suggest the sonnet form while deviating from it. The bittersweet note of this poem suggests the very human sorrow for opportunities gone like spring in summer and for life diminished like Nature in its fall.

"Birches," another of Frost's best-known works, uses the image of the farm boy's sport of swinging upon flexible birch branches in order to contrast the heavenly reach with affection for earth. There is an urge within man to soar toward heaven, but when he is then returned to the mundane world, he realizes that earth is the secure basis for spiritual exaltation.

"Putting in the Seed" is a love sonnet, gathering human beings and Nature in the magic of love and birth, and finding such rich growth sufficient in itself.

"Range-finding" is a war sonnet indicating Nature's imperviousness to man's bloody destruction of his fellows. Man alone has the boon—and the curse—of awareness of life.

"The Hill Wife" is a miniature drama in five short poems alternating in lyric and ballad form. The intense loneliness of a remote farm grips a woman mentally, but her husband does not realize her plight. Once, straying so far that she scarcely hears his shout, she perversely hides and is never found.

"Out, out—" takes its title from Macbeth's famous reflection on life and death. A farm boy loses his hand while sawing wood; in spite of adequate medical attention for an injury seldom fatal, the boy dies. The boy here "saw all spoiled" and simply stopped struggling.

"Snow" comically reveals many facets of three New England characters. Brother Meserve, a fanatical and bombastic preacher, pauses briefly at the Cole farm during a blizzard. Mrs. Cole, although she cannot abide the man, urges him to spend the night. Meserve continues on his way. Mr. Cole takes everything calmly, but Mrs. Cole grows increasingly agitated as a phone call shows Meserve long overdue on his journey home. The preacher does reach home, to the Coles' relief.

New Hampshire: A Poem with Notes and Grace Notes (1923) centers about the title piece, with other poems as supplementary comment (the narratives as "notes," the lyrics as "grace notes").

"New Hampshire," although disarmingly humorous and discursive, is central to Frost's poetics.

Part 1 (to l. 60) condemns the materialism of other parts of the nation and sees in the spare, limited resources of New Hampshire the incentive to higher, spiritual values in its inhabitants.

Part 2 (ll. 61–214) carries the theme forward, showing that essences not vastnesses are the treasure of New Hampshire, which has given the nation one President, Daniel Webster, and "the Dartmouth needed to produce him."

Part 3 (ll. 215–357) states the major basis for Frost regional verse. The very spareness of New Hampshire makes it ideal as a poetic subject, for in this area of clear lines and meager "specimens" Frost finds the best opportunity for full scrutiny of "the world in general."

Part 4 (l. 357 to end) rejects theories such as poetry's arising from galvanizing experiences, mystic vision, or study of harmonious proportion. For Frost, it is immersion in living reality that permits the poet to reach for ultimate truths.

"A Star in a Stone-boat," in contemplating a meteorite used as a building stone, asks about cosmic order. The poet trusts that this object from space implies a larger scheme for the universe.

In "The Star-splitter," almost a companion poem, unsuccessful farmer Brad McLaughlin buys a telescope to seek answers from the riddle of the stars. "We've looked and looked, but after all where are we?" shrugs the poet, returning to the concrete human world about him.

"The Ax-helve" brings the poet together with a French-Canadian, Baptiste, who decries machine-made tools and favors hand-fashioned implements. Though they are from separate worlds, the two establish rapport on the basis of craftsmanship and farming lore.

"The Witch of Coös" (Coös is the northernmost county of New Hampshire) is filled with grotesque humor. The narrator listens in an old New England kitchen to an old woman whose lover was killed by her husband, Toffile (i.e., Theophile, "beloved of God") Lajway. The bones of the victim, hidden in the attic, pay a horrendous visit to the murderer. Few other narratives in English match the intensity of this tale of madness and guilt.

"I Will Sing You One-O" takes its title from an old Crusader's song. Punning upon the "one," it tells of the poet hearing the clock strike one o'clock during a snowy night. The "one" suggests a cosmic monism to the poet, a unified order prevailing in the universe. The variations upon a two-beat line are technically superb.

"Fire and Ice" is a lyric whose restrained, even casual, manner underlines the bitter paradoxes of life. Citing the geologic possibilities of terrestrial destruction, it actually applies to the warring elements within humans. Life is a perilous balance between love and hate, desire and reason.

"The Runaway" pictures the bewilderment of a Morgan colt with his first experience of snow. Like an errant child he would not accept the wisdom of parents but must encounter life for himself and make his own terms with it.

"Dust of Snow" in eight short lines fascinatingly conveys a man's change of mood.

"Stopping by Woods on a Snowy Evening" is one of the best-known of Frost's short lyrics and indeed one of the most notable poems of this century. The speaker is a farmer whose sleigh is drawn by his little horse through woods filling up with snow. Though pausing momentarily to enjoy the magic of the scene, the farmer is impelled to move on by "promises" he has to keep and the "miles to go" before he sleeps. The poem is built upon a series of contrasts: the physical ownership of the woods by a town dweller versus the aesthetic possession by the sensitive viewer; the animal world satisfied solely by creature comforts (symbolized by the horse) versus the human faculty of perceiving beauty; the call of duty versus the inclination to dream and contemplate. The repetition of the last line suggests an amplification beyond the immediate problem to the entire journey of life. Hypnotic as a work of art, the poem effectively employs an interlocking rhyme scheme.

"For Once, Then, Something" is Frost's wry defense of his poetry and his approach. Opponents, absolutists criticize him for concerning himself with the light of everyday instead of penetrating to ultimate certainties. Using the image of a gazer into a well, he humorously suggests that once this skeptical relativist glimpsed a truth, but Nature (or the scheme of things) intervened to thrust him back to the commonplace world that men truly inhabit.

"To Earthward" restates the Frost contention that while Nature is a heedless taskmaster to man, its very testing spurs him to effort and heroism.

"Two Look at Two" is another Frost portrayal of Nature's unexpected favors. A man and a woman see and are seen by a buck and a doe. The momentary spell of communication between them, with the catalyst of love, "made them certain earth returned their love."

West-running Brook (1928) received so little attention that Frost thereafter waited almost a decade to issue another volume of new verse. Here his familiar themes are repeated with even more expression of human loneliness and personal isolation.

"Acquainted with the Night" is Frost's indictment of man's city. Frost explained the poem as coming to him "after a visit from A.E. (George Edward Russell), the Irish mystic, who subtly murmured: 'The Time is not right!'" The wanderer through the dark city finds no personal, moral, or historical meaning. Symbolically it shows man's loneliness in a strange and obscure world.

"The Lovely Shall Be Choosers" is one of the rare examples of free verse in Frost (he remarked once that free verse was like playing tennis without the net). His mother is the subject of this allegorical dialogue between predestination and free will. Ironically, sorrow and pain intensify love, and from the difficulties of life is built its heroism.

"West-running Brook," the title piece, seems Frost's most explicit statement of his skeptical faith, a worship of the God proffered to modern man by science. The image is of a stream running contrary to the usual pattern, as most New England rivulets course eastward to the sea. A newly married couple contemplate the phenomenon, the wife in fantasy seeing the brook as personally speaking to them, the husband meditatively perceiving the analogy to cosmic conflict and renewal. Although the brook itself flows in a contrary direction, there is a current within the stream running oppositely. "It is us"—this resistance and countermotion of brook and humanity that mean eternal rebirth and creativity.

"Sitting by a Bush in Broad Sunlight" appears to refer to the burning bush of Moses. Now God no longer intervenes directly in the scheme of things. There was one creation and one revelation from which, states the poet in faith, all proceeds.

"The Bear" satirizes man's "metaphysical extremes" from Platonism to Aristotelianism. The poet compares man to a caged bear. Even though man thinks he is free, he is in reality hemmed in by the limits of his knowledge.

Collected Poems in the 1939 reissue of the 1930 text is prefaced by an important critical essay.

"The Figure a Poem Makes" argues that a poetic impulse arises from fresh recognition of either a powerful emotional experience or a focusing upon a thought. The tensions generated are resolved in the poem through an integrative process flowing from the first line. The poem, in a sense, "writes itself." "It begins in delight and ends in wisdom." A relativist, Frost refuses to construct a system or believe that it can be erected. The aim of poetry is "a momentary stay against confusion."

A Further Range (1936). As the title indicates, Frost here reaches beyond his regional area.

"Two Tramps in Mud Time," a familiar anthology piece, pictures the poet chopping wood as two hobo lumbermen approach him. They expect to do the job because it is their trade and they need the money. Frost justifies his own chopping "where love and need are one," a higher incentive of man to effort than the vagrants can imagine.

"A Blue Ribbon at Amesbury" has the owner of a prize hen meditate on "the breeder's art" and wonder if man's meddling with the pattern of organic life may be disrupting a greater plan.

"Departmental" is characteristic of growing ironic humor in Frost's verse. This devastating satire in three-beat lines with nonsense rhymes likens modern human behavior to the conduct of ants.

"Desert Places," in contemplating a snowy night, senses the loneliness of the landscape but recognizes a far more frightening desert within.

"The Master Speed," an epithalamion for the wedding of the poet's daughter, expresses faith in man and marriage in the form of a Shakespearean sonnet. Man has the power to freeze moments and to move in spirit through time and space backward and forward.

"Neither Out Far Nor In Deep," using the image of men watching the sea, celebrates the human capacity to look upon the cosmic mysteries and wonder.

"Design" is a sonnet employing ironic contrast to the "desert places" within the poet. Upon a white flower a white spider clasps a dead white moth. Is this combination of "death and blight" proof of a malevolent design of the universe? Or, even more horrifying in its ironic contrasts, is there no design at all?

A Witness Tree (1942) shows Frost's youthful vigor now tempered with aging wisdom. The title refers to the New England practice of marking boundaries by notches upon a tree, which henceforth bears witness to property lines.

"Beech" refers to the "witness tree" on the property line of Frost's farm. To arrive at some knowledge man must create such symbols, but by doing so he places limitations upon his capacity to fathom the world fully.

"The Silken Tent" is a sonnet employing a metaphysical conceit— likening a woman to a tent. All its flexibility is subordinate to fixed "ties of love and thought."

"Come In" pictures the poet hearing a night song of the thrush. He is tempted to sense a message. But Frost resists, for Nature does not speak directly to man.

"The Most of It" continues the theme as a man at a lake witnesses a buck swimming to shore. While Nature has strength and beauty, it is impersonal and unheeding.

"The Gift Outright" was read by Frost at the inauguration of President Kennedy. It is Frost's most forthright poem about America and the lonely sense of the American in a land not yet fully fashioned. It is built essentially upon the punning employment of "possession"—of the land by its inhabitants, and of the inhabitants by the land.

"The Lesson for Today" is addressed to Alcuin, the savant of Charlemagne's court. In contemplating the relative darkness of different eras, the aging Frost shrugs, "One age is like another for the soul."

A Masque of Reason (1945) is more a dramatic conversation piece than the closet drama the title suggests. The tone is mocking and facetious. The biblical Job seems a New England farmer, questioning why he has been unjustly subjected to manifold sufferings. Job's shrewd wife talks familiarly to God and finally obtains a group photograph of Job, God, and Satan. Without evil there would be no happiness. Man must accept the unreason of the cosmos, which thereby offers experience and subtlety impossible in a universe making total sense.

Steeple Bush (1947) in title refers to the flowering American shrub, the hardhack. The "steeple bush," whose flowers are shaped like a steeple, aptly applies to these poems on Nature and on man's spiritual quest.

"Directive" seems a summing up by the aged poet. In a brief saunter he scrutinizes the total past, geological as well as human, mankind's as well as the individual's.

"Too Anxious for Rivers" derides man's search for ultimates in science or in transcendence.

"A Steeple on the House," taken in conjunction with the volume's title, equates a steeple with eternity and suggests a striving for soul beyond the flesh.

A Masque of Mercy (1947), like the preceding masque, suggests a "wild old wicked man" resembling the later Yeats and Shaw. In a New York bookstore Jonah (of the Old Testament) converses in the liveliest fashion with Paul (St. Paul), the bookstore proprietor, Keeper (i.e., "My Brother's Keeper"), and Keeper's wife, Jesse Bel. Jonah laments the injustice of God in sparing immoral Ninevah. From the religious viewpoint of Paul and the humanistic position of Keeper, evil and injustice in the world are spurs to man's self-development. Jesse Bel (hardly the Jezebel indicated by her name) cynically suggests courage as the best, though saddest, element of life. Concerned with man solely in the human experience, Frost advocates the fullness of living, acceptance of failure and injustice in ourselves and in others, and recognition that "Nothing can make injustice just but mercy."

In the Clearing (1962) shows undiminished vigor in a man late in his eighties. Frost's "clearing" is the mortal boundary of life and the human struggle to comprehend. All around still remain the dark woods of impenetrable mystery, but in the clearing is ample scope for man to satisfy his needs.

Carl Sandburg (1878-1967). Of Swedish ancestry, Carl August Sandburg was born in Galesburg, Illinois. At thirteen he left school to work at a variety of small-town jobs such as huckstering fruit on street corners. At nineteen he wandered as far west as Denver, supporting himself by wheat harvesting and dishwashing. He returned to Galesburg just before the outbreak of the Spanish-American War. Sandburg enlisted and saw service in Puerto Rico. With his discharge money he spent four years at Lombard College but never received a degree. He left in 1902 to roam the East coast, his occupations including that of police reporter. Back in Galesburg he saw his first publication, *In Reckless Ecstasy* (1904), which was financed by one of his professors at Lombard College. In 1907 he embarked upon a journalistic career in Chicago and in the next year married the sister of Edward Steichen, the noted photographer. Continuing to write verse in his spare time, he submitted poems to Harriet Monroe, editor of *Poetry*. Their publication in 1914 aroused vehement protests from the devotees of conventional poetry but brought national recognition to Sandburg. By 1920 he was able to devote himself largely to his own writings (entirely after 1932) and to touring the nation as its master folksinger-poet. He lectured at many universities and received numerous honorary degrees that included a doctorate from the Swedish University of Uppsala. During World War II he was an active propagandist for democracy. In 1945 he took up residence at Flat Rock, North Carolina. Both his native state and his adopted state officially recognized his stature as a poet. As a greatly recognized authority on Lincoln, he delivered the Lincoln Day address in 1959 to the entire national legislature, Supreme Court, presidential Cabinet, and diplomatic corps.

Sandburg's intense love of twentieth-century America, his romantic exuberance, and his fervid optimism (only slightly modified by skepticism) ill accorded with the intellectual mood of our time. This limited his appeal for the critics, but won him a large audience.

Chicago Poems (1916) created quite a furor, eliciting bitter denunciations from the traditionalists but also calling forth support from many advocates of the new poetry. To capture the atmosphere of the strident Midwest, Sandburg totally departed from rhymed and metered verse; his cadenced free verse sought the brute vigor and sweep of Chicago. The diction was brashly colloquial. The subjects encompassed the raw violence and energy of Sandburg's adopted city. The *Review of Reviews* likened Sandburg's poetry to the roughhewn statues of Rodin. Many of the 150 pieces are short Imagistic poems, but the prevailing tone is vituperation against exploiters of the downtrodden.

"Chicago," probably the most famous Sandburg poem, is a sturdy tribute to the vitality of the city. It is a masculine city filled with explosive life, shouldering destiny with the joyous braggadocio of a "tall bold slugger."

"To a Contemporary Bunkshooter" derides a popular evangelist, Billy Sunday, in the gusty, informal jargon of the preacher himself. Sandburg sees Sunday as talking the people's lingo not for the avowed purpose of self-ennoblement but to blind the exploited to the injustice of their exploiters.

"Fog" is a delightfully straightforward impression of the harbor mist written in an Imagist style. Its purpose is to evoke a single clear image and to stand for nothing outside itself.

"Limited" ironically uses the proud label of a crack train to satirize the American worship of mechanical gadgets, which in time will all come to "scrap and rust." The poem can also be seen as an indictment of materialism, the rewards of which are as temporal as the train.

Cornhuskers (1918), as the title declares, moves from the Midwest metropolis to consider the wide countryside of Sandburg's early years. The tone is more meditative and lyrical.

"Prairie," introducing the volume, is profitably compared with William Cullen Bryant's "The Prairies," which expresses an expectancy a century before of creating upon the vast plains of the mid-continent a well-ordered imitation of Eastern and European society. Sandburg scornfully dismisses as "a bucket of ashes" the past revered by Bryant.

"Cool Tombs" states the age-old lyric lament for all men's efforts quenched by death, but asks the question whether while we live, is not love best?

"Grass" is a bitterly ironic commentary on war, whose horrors are all too soon forgotten. Nature quickly effaces the evidence of battle.

Smoke and Steel (1920), in a contrast with earlier volumes, shows an increasing tendency toward mysticism.

"Smoke and Steel" is a colorful and violent image of the raw power of a steel factory. An accident occurs in which five men fall irretrievably into a pot of molten steel. They achieve a strange transcendence, a true physical oneness with the product. The sense of terrible mystery is amplified in the red glow and sparks from the furnace and the female shapes that seem to dance from the smokestacks.

"Jazz Fantasia" utilizes Whitman's manner to describe Negro music in "jive talk," slang, and onomatopoeia.

"For You" is a powerfully optimistic incantation to the great works of Nature and of man. Sandburg reveals the great peace that can be found in embracing great works of art or the seas, the mountains, and the prairies.

Slabs of the Sunburnt West (1922) is misleading in name, for, outside of the title poem on the Grand Canyon, the subject area and style are Sandburg's familiar territory.

"The Windy City" is Sandburg's full-length portrayal of Chicago. Its brawny independence sets it apart from all other metropolises.

Abraham Lincoln: The Prairie Years (1926), a biographical work (in prose) started as a brief account for children but developed into a two-volume work for adults, carrying Lincoln up to his departure from Springfield for the presidency. This is a poet's biography, seeking in the man Lincoln the genesis of the Lincoln myth. Sandburg conceives of Lincoln as the product not so much of heredity as of environment. Amidst the rural atmosphere of the early nineteenth-century Midwest a man uniting human weaknesses and extraordinary capabilities was molded into greatness. The fantastic opposites of primordial earthiness and spiritual exaltation were the tensions that warred in Lincoln but also harmonized to make him simultaneously a representative of the people and their inspired leader.

The American Songbag (1927) is an anthology of almost three hundred folk songs assembled by Sandburg in his years of wandering in direct contact with farm hands, mill workers, hoboes, and other Americans. About a third of the collection was previously unpublished material.

Good Morning, America (1928) is Sandburg's most eloquent and optimistic celebration of his native land.

The People, Yes (1936) is a massive reassertion of the previous volume, partly through original Sandburg verse but largely from an accumulation of 107 sections of Americana—folk tales, anecdotes, proverbs, witticisms. Only a fraction of the work qualifies as poetry, but all is rich in the sound and sense of the American experience.

Abraham Lincoln: The War Years (4 vols., 1939) is for many Sandburg's masterwork. In prose, in Sandburg's characteristic style, it is the epic of America's most agonizing and crucial years. Hundreds of people and thousands of events are strung across a panorama of almost 2500 pages, but always, at the heart, stands Lincoln. At the outset Lincoln is the raw material of greatness, as demonstrated in *The Prairie Years*, but he is hesitant and confused. Sandburg shows how the giant challenge, however, summons the best from the President.

Complete Poems (1950) brought Sandburg belated wider recognition.

"The Long Shadow of Lincoln," the 1944 Phi Beta Kappa poem at William and Mary College, is generally considered the best of Sandburg's later verse. From a Lincoln speech of 1862 the poet takes as his text "We must disenthrall ourselves." Like Lincoln, man must face his most vexatious problems with calmness and charity.

Rootabaga Stories (1922) and its sequel *Rootabaga Pigeons* (1923) are charming folk inventions for children.

Hart Crane (1899–1932). Harold Hart Crane was born at Garrettsville, Ohio. His father, a wealthy candy manufacturer, had no sympathy for Crane's early interest in poetry. Crane attributed much of his later confusion and unhappiness to the unpleasant family life which resulted in his parents separating while he was a child. Never completing high school, he went to New York in 1915 and immersed himself in bohemian life, making the acquaintance of many of the literary figures of the period. From 1918 to 1925 he wrote poetry while working at such various tasks as riveter, candy packer, newspaper reporter, tearoom manager, and advertising copywriter. Crossing Brooklyn Bridge daily, he conceived of his major work, and after the publication of his first book in 1926, the patronage of Otto Kahn enabled him to give all his time to composition of *The Bridge*. Much of the writing was done in Cuba at a family-owned plantation on the Isle of Pines. A Guggenheim grant in 1931 permitted him to go to Mexico for a contemplated long poem based upon the Spanish conquest of that nation. Despondent over his addiction to alcohol and his homosexuality, and fearful that his poetic resources were drying up, he committed suicide by leaping from the ship on the return voyage.

Crane has been largely ignored by the general reading public, but widely hailed by intellectuals. His talent was never fully realized. Unlike most twentieth-century poets and because he was largely self-educated, he came to poetry through such moderns as T. S. Eliot before he absorbed traditional English verse from the Renaissance on. Though intrigued by the contemporary cult of the irrational in poetry, he nonetheless strained at ingenious cerebration. Attacking mechanized modern society, he was simultaneously fascinated by the machine as a symbol. The bewildering contradictions and complexities within the poet produced an incredibly convoluted verse, less successful in its totality than in its brilliantly arresting imagery and impressive bursts of lyricism.

White Buildings (1926) is one of the most remarkable first volumes from an American poet. Some pieces reveal Crane's early infatuation with the Imagists (e.g., "Garden Abstract") and his subsequent interest in Elizabethan verse (e.g., "Black Tambourine"). But included are poems in the undeniable personal idiom of Crane. Crane's works are musical but do not follow any rigid rhythm, preferring to let the subject or the lyricism determine the individual foot and line.

"Lachrymae Christi" (Tears of Christ) is typical of Crane's poetry in its abrupt transitions, tremendous compressions, and startling associations. Thus, examples of suffering are the personal torments of the poet, the struggle of spring from wintry bonds, and the passion of Christ. In contrast to the "one unyielding smile" of the modern industrial deity, Christ in his atonement is the earth's surge to new birth in His "Unmangled target smile."

"For the Marriage of Faustus and Helen" was Crane's retort to Eliot's *The Waste Land*. The ideal union of Faust and Helen in the second part of Goethe's drama is here translated into contemporary terms. In the first section of the Crane poem, Faustus (questing modern man), seeking ideal beauty today, finds Helen (modern urban civilization) in a streetcar. In the second part they achieve sensual fulfillment amidst the blaring jazz of a dance hall. In the concluding section, Faustus, flying with a combat pilot, recognizes the ghastly destruction of our era but urges recognition of this age as stimulus to the spirit to elevate itself through suffering. In spite of tawdry modern commercialism man can find and can create within today's world a synthesis of values and beauty.

"At Melville's Tomb," probably the best-known short Crane poem, utilizes his repeated symbol of the sea as apparent benevolence concealing the pain of life. Herman Melville is shown as refusing to console himself with illusions; although his body lies in earth, his soul reposes in that primordial symbol through whose terrors he dived resolutely to find (as in his great story *Billy Budd*) peaceful resolution.

The Bridge (1930) is an epic-like poem written in a sequential style that seeks to synthesize twentieth-century America. Crane termed the work "a symphony with an epic theme," and announced to his patron, "What I am really handling, you see, is the Myth of America." Critics have pointed out that *The Bridge* is not a narrative, and hence not an epic, and furthermore that its distinctly individual perception of America produces scattered though excellent lyrics rather than a unified, mythic whole. Crane's actual purpose was to find in the national past viable grounds for idealism and to exhort contemporary America to an idealistic faith in its present and its future.

"To Brooklyn Bridge" (Proem) establishes the dominant symbol, the bridge, which is to join the disparities of America in a historical and mystical unity. The meaning of the bridge consists of layered interpretations:

(1) The literal bridge joining islands and expediting the flow of men, goods, and ideas.

(2) Human triumph over the passivity of matter through vision and toil.

(3) Symbol of all links, as continents are unified by ship traffic or as years are joined together by human memory.

(4) Man's arching desire for the Infinite and the Eternal. Like Whitman's "Passage to India," nearest among all other poems to *The Bridge*, this work seeks to reconcile American materialism with idealistic faith.

The first three sections of the poem search the American past for idealistic questing, while the remaining sections try to find in the national present ample justification for an apocalyptic vision of the nation's future.

"I. Ave Maria" imagines Columbus contemplating his discovery of the New World. He feels a profound sense of wonder and of spiritual fulfillment. But these feelings are tempered by hints at the forces of ancient evil which the Old World will carry to the new land.

"II. Powhatan's Daughter" finds in Pocahontas the symbol of America's pristine innocence and beauty, a bridge launched from the New World. Flash-back or montage effects derived from moviemaking and the example of T. S. Eliot in "The Waste Land" merge the past and present. The "Harbor Dawn" section presents the waking port "400 years and more" from Columbus; even amidst the bedlam of today's New York, the virginal soil of America slumbers. "Van Winkle" makes the Irving character the symbol of memory that draws the poet to the past and westward. "The River" conceives of the Mississippi as the river of time itself; the Twentieth Century Limited in its precipitate haste blurs all America, but the hobos in slower wanderings across the land experience America's unifying spiritual power and beauty. "The Dance" portrays a Sachem Indian, Maquokeeta, lover of Pocahontas, whose ritual dance of love and fertility ends in his death and transfiguration; the union of Maquokeeta with the earth goddess Pocahontas revivifies her. "Indiana," not quite so intense as the two previous poems, marks the transition of the Indian spiritual relationship toward the earth to the white settlers; a pioneer woman in Indiana sends her son Larry to sea, recognizing in him the continuance of the adventurer.

"III. Cutty Sark" brings the poet to a bar in South Street to drink with a battered seaman. The background pianola suggests eternity while the sailor's voice speaks of time. About the drunkard still clings an aura of the grandeur when clipper ships, like the *Cutty Sark,* stirred men to the challenge of the ideal. This section acts as a journey through space and time (treated thus far in the poem) to the spaceless, timeless voyage ahead.

"IV. Cape Hatteras" captures the driving rhythms of a powerhouse, the symbol of the power that man is gaining over Nature. And nearby the Wright brothers made their flight, but this great symbol of man's aspirations is twisted by the making of war planes.

"V. Three Songs" demonstrates the downfall of the Pocahontas symbol in today's America. The "Southern Cross" section suggests this constellation as a symbol of spiritual fulfillment, but the pursuit of love has become purely sensual, represented by a prostitute. "National Winter Garden" sees the movements of a strip tease as debased burlesque of "The Dance" in Section II; frustration and vulgarity replace the primeval purity of Pocahontas. "Virginia" sees calculated coyness and standoffishness in Mary, a shrewd modern secretary, but there still reposes within her some vestiges of the virginal qualities of the land.

"VI. Quaker Hill" castigates modern American society for its failure to achieve its potential. The old Meeting House at Quaker Hill has been transformed into the "New Avalon Hotel" to lure tourist "high steppers," whose chief concerns are partying. Reality seems to eclipse the ideal altogether.

"VII. The Tunnel" explores the modern Hades in a subway ride. The most anthologized piece by Crane, it captures in a few lines the spirit of the mechanical jungle of the modern metropolis. As Whitman suggested the upper world to Crane, so Poe suggests the underworld, his specter appearing to the poet "Below the toothpaste and the dandruff ads." The poet's spirit reaches bottom as the subway train lurches to the lowest point in the tunnel. The lift of the train upward toward the surface, however, offers to Crane the hope of man's resurrection from the deathly existence of this era.

"VIII. Atlantis" was intended by Crane as "a mystic consummation toward which all other sections of the poem converge." All the themes and symbols of previous sections are summed up in Brooklyn Bridge. The epigraph from Plato is applied to the bridge, which is both a harp and the harmony of music and love played upon it. In the final metamorphosis, the bridge becomes the "whitest flower," rising radiantly like fabled Atlantis. "One Song, one Bridge of Fire" can revivify a misdirected nation to its mission of unbounded love and creativity.

Collected Poems (1933) includes poems from Crane's residence in Cuba and Mexico.

"Hurricane" arose from observing a gigantic storm at the Isle of Pines. The majestic might of God therein revealed is expressed in an ecstatic lyric indebted in metrics and breathless urgency to Gerard Manley Hopkins.

"The Broken Tower," the last significant Crane poem, was occasioned by his ringing of church bells in Taxco, Mexico. Like the ringing bells, Crane communicated faith and love, but the sheer intensity of poetic imagination seemed to destroy his physical body as the massive swinging bells threaten to break apart the tower in which they are housed. But the poet finds this destructive power paradoxically constructive as it bids him to encompass the whole arena of heaven and earth, building a spiritual tower of love.

Robinson Jeffers (1887–1962). In his native Pittsburgh, Pennsylvania, John Robinson Jeffers received his early education from his father, a Presbyterian clergyman, who introduced him early to classic Greek literature.

From 1889 to 1902 Jeffers traveled with his parents in Europe, and studied in Swiss and German boarding schools. When the family moved to Pasadena, California, in 1903, Jeffers entered Occidental College, graduating in 1905. In the next six years he studied at the University of Southern California, University of Zurich, Los Angeles Medical College, and the University of Washington; but, as he says in his condensed autobiography, "with faint interest. I wasn't deeply interested in anything but poetry." In 1912 he published his first volume of poetry, *Flagons and Apples,* the title derived from the *Song of Songs.* In the year following his 1913 marriage he moved to Carmel, California, thereafter his lifelong residence. The setting of most of Jeffers' narrative poems is California, especially the coast and often Point Sur. In 1919 he began construction of Tor House, a heavy rock structure largely built by his own hands, that for half a century has been a notable literary landmark. In the 1920s the reputation of Jeffers soared high, but during the Depression years and World War II his mounting vehemence in denouncing contemporary America caused many to lose interest. By 1958 he had regained respect and received the Academy of American Poets' Fellowship for "distinguished poetic achievement"; but at the time of his death a few years later, there was surprisingly little comment on one of the most explosive poets of American letters.

In the English language few writers are comparable to Jeffers in dark, brooding intensity and volcanic passion. Jeffers projects a bitter detestation of Anglo-American puritanism and a vehement insistence upon the virtues of deep unconscious instincts. He centers his assault upon the sexual inhibitions of this era, and proclaims his revolt against today's society with the religious exaltation of the great Hebrew prophets. In Jeffers' narrative poems, his characters are representative less of human attributes than of primeval forces kindred to the rugged scenery of the Monterey Peninsula that the poet loved. Violence, savage emotions, dark pains, and perversions give his verse a potent shock effect, but Jeffers claimed as his intention the revelation of the deep-buried, prehuman motivations of his characters. Intensely individualistic, he saw virtue in the personal relationships of men, but he scorned social groups as generating artificial conventions and restraints. The most vigorous denunciation of contemporary America by an American poet is couched in long Whitman-like lines of bursting poetic force, though tending toward more metrical regularity than the earlier poets.

Tamar and Other Poems (1924), primitively powerful, drew attention to Jeffers.

"Tamar" begins with the incestuous relations of Tamar Cauldwell with her brother Lee on their California ranch. Tamar tries to conceal her pregnancy by seducing the naïve Will Andrews. Through her aunt Stella, Tamar learns of the incest between her father, David, and her other aunt, Helen. On the tideline Tamar performs a dance in which she is symbolically ravaged by the ghosts of the Indians from whom her ancestors had wrested the soil. After Tamar's attempt to seduce her father, the whole clan is burnt to death as a moronic relative, Jinny, sets fire to the house.

The name Tamar is taken from a character in Genesis, but the fundamental basis of the poem is a rather naturalistic recounting of the classic Greek myth of the brother-sister union of Cronos (Saturn) and Rhea in a modern setting. Tamar is a woman in a world where "custom has created nature," and her conduct consequently appears highly unnatural. She is the arena of conflict between contemporary morality and inhuman forces. Jeffers is not advocating behavior stigmatized by society, but poses the question of the cosmic tragedy of mankind driven to violation and self-destruction by internal powers over which he holds no dominion.

"Continent's End," looking out on the Pacific, ponders on the ancient ocean far older than man, and on the even more primordial elemental cosmic forces.

Roan Stallion, and Other Poems (1925) is considered by many to be Jeffers' best collection of verse.

"Roan Stallion" details the intense sexual attraction exerted upon a woman named California by a horse won through gambling by her profligate husband, Johnny. Attacked by her drunken husband, California flees to the protection of the stallion. Johnny is trampled to death by the stallion, which California then kills.

The mythical underlay is the love of woman for beast, as Pasiphäe for the Cretan bull. It appears that Jeffers derived the idea of calling his heroine California from the account of Europa, apparently the personification of Europe, who was abducted by Zeus in the form of a bull. The roan stallion symbolizes the God-like power of Nature drawing to itself the worshiping female. In slaying the horse, California looks like one "who has killed God." Since California is a modern woman, the war within her between elemental powers and conventional conformity is resolved in favor of the latter. Yet it is there that for the first time Jeffers states his principle of "inhumanism": "Humanity is the mold to break away from."

"The Tower Beyond Tragedy" contains the legend of the fated House of Atreus, set in ancient Mycenae. Amidst a triumphant reception, Agamemnon, home from ravaging Troy, is secretly slain by Clytemnestra in the first scene. In the second scene Cassandra, the prophetess, reveals the crime and envisages the colossal futility of all empires of power. Clytemnestra effectively defies all except Orestes, her son, who slays her in revenge. In the third scene Orestes is freed from the burden of sin and guilt, not by the usual means of a formal trial but by a mystical identification with inhuman Nature, totally renouncing not only the human thirst for power but human involvement itself. In final explanation to Electra, his sister, Orestes announces his disengagement that makes him "like stone walking." The work was professionally staged in New York in 1950.

"Shine, Perishing Republic" may be compared with two later poems that begin their titles with the same word. Strongly influenced by the pessimistic theories of history advanced by Oswald Spengler, the German philosophic historian, this piece resignedly predicts the downfall of Western society.

"Night" states Jeffers' insistence that true peace emerges only from total immersion in the elemental violence of Nature. To man's fever, night stands as a symbol of "The primal and the latter silences."

The Women at Point Sur (1927) is Jeffers' longest narrative. Its theme is highly significant in the poet's philosophy.

Losing his faith because of his son's death in World War I, the Reverend Dr. Barclay quits his city church and comes to Point Sur where he proclaims a new religion based upon absolute freedom and natural instinct. Barclay encourages his followers to all forms of perversion, himself violating his own daughter, April. April commits suicide and Barclay wanders off to die of exposure in the hills.

By Jeffers' own statement the poem is a grave warning that the poet's inhumanism can result in horrible tragedy to those "breaking out of humanity" if they succumb to the lusts of power and self-gratification instead of being motivated solely by the pursuit of truth.

Cawdor and Other Poems (1928) treats more realistic human experience.

"Cawdor" details the marriage of young Fera Martial to a middle-aged widower, Cawdor. Frustrated, Fera attempts to seduce Cawdor's son Hood. Repulsed by the youth, Fera falsely accuses him of rape, and Cawdor slays his son. Learning of Hood's innocence, Cawdor gouges out his own eyes.

Legends of ancient Greece, especially those of Phaedra and Hippolytus and the self-maiming of Oedipus, are here transferred to modern Point Sur. The title, taken from *Macbeth*, suggests the mounting dominance of evil in a human heart. As in "Tamar" there are no villains, for man is the victim of basic drives beyond his rational control.

"Hurt Hawks" describes a wounded bird that the speaker is nursing. The hawk, one of Jeffers' most prominent images, is here represented as proud and savage, despite its incapacity. Although he would "sooner, except the penalties, kill a man than a hawk," the speaker feels compelled to end the hawk's misery. Even in death, however, the spirit of the hawk soars arrogantly from its limp body.

Dear Judas and Other Poems (1929) brought forth loud outcries against Jeffers.

"Dear Judas," a poetic drama, was banned in Boston upon its 1947 staging. In structure this is a Japanese Noh drama, enacted by ghosts recalling their past struggles.

Jesus is portrayed as an illegitimate child denying the truth of his origin by claims of being the son of God. He tries to dominate the minds of future men by intentionally seeking martyrdom.

In attempting to depict a "human" Jesus, Jeffers elicited vociferous protests from many. Jesus is interpreted as a tragic hero, but he has humanly failed to go "beyond tragedy" as did Orestes in the earlier Jeffers drama. Lazarus, freed of the taint of mortality, has purged himself of the defects still clinging to Jesus. Judas, pictured as dearest to Jesus of all the disciples, is viewed as antagonistic to the power drives of Jesus.

Give Your Heart to the Hawks and Other Poems (1933) marks the end of Jeffers' "realistic" narrative poems.

"Give Your Heart to the Hawks" centers about Fayne Fraser, whose husband, Lance, surprises her in the arms of his brother Michael and kills this rival. Fayne persuades Lance to disguise the slaying as an accident. Lance finds the burden of guilt increasingly onerous. He seduces Michael's fiancée, who then kills herself. Confessing to his puritanical father, Lance drives the old man mad. Fayne and Lance flee, but his mental unbalance causes him to leap over a cliff to destruction. Fayne remains to bear Lance's child.

This account treats of those who take the law into their own hands and of those who subscribe to society's laws. The conflict breaks everyone except Fayne, a woman of powerful will. Not evil herself, she triggers disaster among the people around her, who are not cast in her heroic mold. At the end sounds the suggestion that Fayne's offspring may portend a greater future of mankind rising toward inhumanism.

Solstice and Other Poems (1935) contains one more Jeffers narrative, in his retelling of a legend.

"At the Birth of an Age" recounts the *Nibelungenlied* story of the destruction of the Burgundians at the swords' points and flaming brands of Attila's hordes. Gudrun, instigator of the massacre, is the pivotal figure in the downfall of the old paganism and the emergence of the new religion that amalgamates the Mid-eastern Christ, the Greek Prometheus, and the Teutonic Wodin.

In a mystical experience Jeffers' mankind achieves a union with the inhumanist God; and the path of this goal leads through the darkest corners of the unconscious and the most savage paroxysms of violence.

"Shine, Republic" considers the fate of America with far more optimism than did the "Shine" poem of 1925. Paradoxically, the Depression era sparks Jeffers to hope that America will pin its future upon "love of freedom with contempt of luxury."

Be Angry at the Sun (1941) displays growing rancor over the course of American life, often expressed more vehemently than poetically. Jeffers' reputation began to fall off sharply, and for the 1948 volume (*The Double-Axe*) his publishers felt impelled to the rare expedient of prefacing that work with a statement of their disagreement with Jeffers' views.

"Shine, Empire" returns to the mood of the 1925 "Shine" poem. America became an empire seeking power and material welfare instead of spirituality and freedom.

Medea (1946) so freely adapts the Euripides original that it might best be deemed a new work by Jeffers. In his preface he states his conviction that the mixture of love and hate in Medea well accords with the modern spirit. Medea is sympathetically depicted as instinctive humanity stung to monstrous deeds by the unnatural conventions and repressions of a sophisticated materialistic society. Medea has proved one of Jeffers' most popular works, frequently re-enacted since its premiere in 1947.

Ezra Pound (1885–   ). Ezra Weston Loomis Pound was born at Hailey, Idaho, but was brought by his parents at an early age to suburban Philadelphia. An undergraduate at the University of Pennsylvania, he completed his bachelor's work (1905) at Hamilton College and took his M.A. at the University of Pennsylvania (1906). For a short time he taught French and Spanish at Wabash College, but was dismissed because of his unconventional personality. He left for Europe in 1908, dwelling thereafter in England until 1920. His first published volume was *A Lume Spento,* a slender book released in Venice, Italy. During his London residence Pound published several translations and was a leading figure in the Imagist movement. From 1921 to 1925 he lived in Paris, where he was at the center of literary circles as he had been in London. In 1925 he moved to Italy. In 1939 he made a brief return visit to the United States where he received an honorary degree from Hamilton College. In 1940 he began pro-Fascist broadcasts over the Italian radio and continued them until he was arrested by the U. S. Army in Genoa in 1944. He was jailed in Pisa for a time and then flown to Washington, D.C., where he was to be tried on charges of treason. But the court found him mentally unfit to stand trial and he was committed to St. Elizabeth's Hospital where he remained for twelve years. In 1958 fellow poets interceded for his release and he returned to Italy, where he established permanent residence.

A wild man in appearance and behavior, Pound's name is known to most Americans, although his verse is not widely read. Fellow poets and certain critics have generally been enthusiastic about his poetry, but some have vehemently denounced his work.

Pound is often referred to as the inaugurator of the revolt against traditional verse which resulted in modern poetry. The excitement, contemporaneousness, and compact energy of more recent verse in the English language owe a great deal to Pound's originality. Pound not infrequently alludes to many obscure works in many languages, and inserts into his poems quotations from European languages and Chinese. Elaborate concordances have been compiled to help the perplexed reader through the Pound wilderness. Despite this erudition, which often borders on obscurity, Pound has had a profound influence on modern letters. Pound was instrumental in the early publication of works by James Joyce and T. S. Eliot; and poets from Yeats onward admit literary debts to Ezra Pound.

In his study of ancient and modern cultures Pound has drawn freely from the reservoir of poetry and produced a richly allusive style.

Pound seeks to synthesize for his era the shared ideas and values of composite history. In his earlier writings he was quite intent upon the problem of individual freedom, while his later works are dominated by a savage disgust for "usury" (often appearing in the *Cantos* as the Latin *usura*), that is, modern finance capitalism, which Pound indicts as the underlying cause of all our woes and the symptom of a decadent and expiring society. The syndicalism of Mussolini appealed to Pound as a way out from what he deemed the economic morass of Western civilization.

Pound was strongly influenced by Laforgue and the other *symbolistes* early in his career although at times he claimed that he was strongly anti-symbolist. But Pound has never adhered to one style. He has been the leader in many major poetic movements.

THE IMAGIST (to 1916). Pound was largely instrumental in organizing the Imagist movement. He gave the movement its name, codified the Imagist tenets, and popularized the group by editing *Des Imagistes* (1915). Down to the present many anthologies represent Pound chiefly by his early Imagist pieces. As others became important in the movement, Pound moved away from what he was scornfully to call "Amygism" from the later dominance of Amy Lowell. The following volumes, though not all Imagist in technique, strongly reflect the influence of that form.

Personae (1909) in title means "masks," referring to the roles that a poet may adopt. The work should not be confused with subsequent collected editions of Pound verse bearing the same title.

"Sestina: Altaforte" is a dramatic monologue spoken by Bertran de Born, a twelfth-century knight and troubadour, relegated by Dante to the ring of the Inferno peopled by "sowers of discord" (Canto xxviii). The poem is itself a very free translation of "Praise of War," a ballade attributed to Bertran. The lusty warrior is wholly conditioned to kill and be killed: "I have no life save when the swords clash."

Ripostes (1912) moves largely toward free verse.

"The Sea Farer" is a translation from the Anglo-Saxon of one of the finest examples of Old English poetry in the language. The narrator is a sailor contemplating the exotic but lonely life at sea and the natural comforts of the land he left behind. But human civilization has become barbarous. There is no longer strong feeling, and there are no great-hearted men.

"A Girl" is one of Pound's most famous and most often quoted Imagistic pieces. The image is that of the loved one as a tree nymph but with the alternate suggestion of the tree as her lover interpenetrating her.

"In a Station of the Metro" is an often cited Imagist poem, an attempt in English to achieve the effect of the Japanese *haiku*. In a brilliant metaphor Pound likens the subway crowd on a rainy day to "petals on a wet, black bough."

THE VORTICIST (1916–25). With the British author-painter Wyndham Lewis, Pound joined in the movement termed "vorticism" and its short-lived polemic journal, *The Blast*. Pound notes his own change from static Imagism to dynamic vorticism: "The image is not an idea. It is a radiant node or cluster; it is what I can, and must perforce, call a vortex, from which, and through which, and into which, ideas are constantly rushing." In addition to presenting energetic motion instead of Imagism's frozen still life, vorticism emphasized the interrelationships of all the arts.

Quia Pauper Amavi (1918) contains the first version of three *Cantos*, later much revised.

"Homage to Sextus Propertius" may best be described not as a translation but as a "rendering," as Edward Fitzgerald described his *Rubáiyát*, of several poems into English from the Latin elegaic writer who lived in the first half century B.C. Like Fitzgerald, Pound uses the work of an ancient author to make a trenchant comment upon the contemporary world. Thus Pound is able to attack war and imperialism, and to assert that the lyric concerns of the poet with living and dying are more important than the political chauvinism of the moment. This work is particularly admired for its craftsmanship in a wide variety of rhythms.

Hugh Selwyn Mauberley (1920) consists of eighteen sections forming one extended poem upon the problem of the poet in today's world. Many critics deem it Pound's greatest single poem. The sequential form in which it was written strongly influenced the work of Hart Crane and T. S. Eliot, among others. The title character is an imaginary aesthete somewhat resembling Pound. Part One contains the first thirteen sections.

"Ode pour l'élection de son sépulchre" a parody of Ronsard's self-epitaph, describes Pound himself as "out of key with his own time."

II denounces the artistic lies which "the age demanded."

III describes the leveling of the noble concepts of antiquity by "a tawdry cheapness." Democracy is condemned as the source of mediocrity.

IV is a diatribe against the waste and the slaughter of World War I.

V regrets the mass slaying of the young men, "For a botched civilization."

"Yeux Glauques" attributes the origin of contemporary degeneration to the philistinism of the Victorian age.

"Siena mi fe', disfecemi Maremma" pictures the *fin de siècle* artist of the 1890s, a rather ridiculous poseur.

"Brennbaum," an expression of Pound's anti-Semitism, sees the Jew erasing his own tradition in order to join with others in outward conformity.

"Mr. Nixon" depicts the commercialized author for whom writings are no more than salable commodities.

X shows the dedicated artist, totally ignored in a run-down cottage.

XI ridicules the educated woman who superficially chatters about culture while actually concerning herself solely with status symbols.

XII is the wry self-confession of the poet of his unacceptability by today's crass standards.

"Envoi," incorporating the lyric references of seventeenth-century British poets, bids farewell to this crude age but expresses hope that some future time will again know how to appreciate art.

Part Two parallels the first part with more specific references to the imaginary Mauberley. Mauberley is a second-rater (I), realizing belatedly that active passion is more important than aesthetic attitudinizing (II). Amidst the artificialities of current culture he is the outsider ("The Age Demanded"), who proceeds futilely to his demise (IV). Mauberley leaves behind one poem ("Medallion"), coldly precise, the artifice of an artificial age.

THE IDEOGRAMMATIST (1925 to present). Early in the second decade of the twentieth century Pound became fascinated with the works of Ernest Fenollosa (1853–1908), the American Orientalist. Pound finally edited Fenollosa's essay, "The Chinese Written Character as a Medium for Poetry" in 1936; but long before this Pound had attempted to create in English a poetry achieving an effect similar to that of the Chinese ideogram. Thus, as Fenollosa would suggest, the Chinese ideogram meaning "strife" is an impressionistic picture of two women in one house; Fenollosa claimed that the efficacy of the Chinese written characters is to evoke from every reader not an abstract, bodiless idea but a concrete, sensuous visualization. Pound's later poetry attempts to emulate Chinese characters in this layering with many vivid examples and with allusions to men and to letters.

THE CANTOS. As early as 1912 Pound was apparently contemplating an extended poem trying to discover "what sort of things endure . . . what sort of things are transient . . . what sort of things recur." As early as 1918 he had made preliminary drafts which he continued to revise. In 1925 he first hit his stride with fifteen cantos, which steady publication has now built up to over one hundred cantos. Even the most informed of critics are quite divided about the value of the *Cantos* as well as about their form and organization. Detractors see only a heap of unrelated fragments. Supporters find here a modern epic, with endurance, transience, and recurrence as the unifying themes. Major influences on the *Cantos* include:

(1) Homer's *Odyssey* as the eternal quest, in which tribulations and testings often prove educating and purifying.

(2) Dante's *Divine Comedy*. Many of the *Cantos* suggest the Inferno of Dante, in their hell-like journey through this world; but the very last, more placid cantos suggest a sort of Paradiso.

(3) Ovid's *Metamorphoses* with its motif of constant transformation. Pound writes eloquently in scrutinizing the founders and the renewers of culture, and although he tends to avoid the poets of Renaissance and post-Renaissance Europe, he salutes the early Provençal and Italian lyricists. In religion he celebrates the natural myths of the ancient Greeks. In government he supports Confucius, Jefferson, and Adams. Simple and natural passion, direct and concrete perception, abundant creativity and perpetual renewal are his ideals.

1–30 (*Cantos I–XVI* in 1925, *A Draft of the Cantos 17–27* in 1928, and *A Draft of XXX Cantos* in 1930) are the most anthologized cantos and generally the most appealing to readers. The six initial poems establish the unifying themes: (1) the multiple hero, the quester for truth and revelation, (2) the veneration of artistic creativity in the life of action, (3) the search for tradition in social temperament and myth. After the transitional seventh canto, 8–11 ("Malatesta Cantos") picture the vigorous humanistic values of Sigismundo Malatesta of the early Italian Renaissance. Cantos 12 and 13 provide a center of sane order before the "Hell Cantos" (14–16) which stigmatize the modern world for the triumph of the anti-creative and the anti-artistic. The remaining cantos in this first group celebrate *virtu*, the spiritual resources by which men are able to transform matter to their own will and their fellow humans to creative activity.

31–41 (*Eleven Cantos: XXXI to XLI* in 1934) have become known as the "American History Cantos." Pound's heroes are Jefferson and Adams, whose economic, political, and social viewpoints Pound supported. Mussolini, appearing in the last canto of this group, is represented as carrying on the basic Jefferson-Adams principles before they were corrupted by banking and industrial interests.

42–51 (*The Fifth Decade of Cantos* in 1937) may be called the "Usury Cantos" because of their bitter doctrinaire attack upon finance capitalism, especially in number 45. References to what Pound deems a sounder economy range from prehistoric Western Europe to China.

52–72 (*Cantos LII–LXXI* in 1940) begin with the "Chinese History Cantos" (to 61). Confucianism is a practical idealism to Pound, an ordered intelligence in action. The Chinese ideogram, most especially, is to Pound the graphic image instead of the vague abstraction of Western alphabetical writing. Cantos 62–71 are the "John Adams Cantos," revolving about the second American President, the archetype of the virtuous ruler, who tried to establish the foundations of a good society. 72–84 (*The Pisan Cantos* in 1948) were largely written in the U. S. Army prison camp at Pisa, Italy, where Pound was incarcerated. When they were published, Pound was an inmate of St. Elizabeth's Hospital. The publication brought Pound the Bollingen Award and a storm of protests.

Pound writes while agonizingly expecting execution. The powerfully charged lyricism reaches its height in 81 where the poet recognizes his personal limitations but defiantly will not recant upon his principles or his actions. In 82, Pound identifies himself and his work with Whitman and Whitman's mission; the *Cantos* like *Leaves of Grass* will strive to depict the whole man and his total ethos. Adherents of Pound explain this section as a continuation of the quest and metamorphic themes.

85–95 (*Rock-Drill, 85–95 de los cantares* in 1955) takes its name from the piece of sculpture, "Rock Drill," by Jacob Epstein. These poems do not attain the heights of the "Pisan Cantos." The themes of the earlier cantos are recapitulated. Finance capitalism of the West is anathematized, while in contrast ancient Chinese history presents models of sanity, justice, and practicality. Especially clear is the emergence of an eighteenth-century mind in Pound. For all his celebrations of medievalism, it is evident that he is also at home in the Enlightenment.

96–109 (*Thrones: 96–109 de los cantares* in 1959) derive their title from the ascription of thrones in Dante's *Paradiso* to those responsible for good government. Pound asserted: "The thrones in the *Cantos* are an attempt to move out from egoism and to establish some definition of an order possible or at any rate conceivable on earth." Though probably intended as conclusion (for years Pound had predicted one hundred cantos) in analogy to the *Paradiso*, these late cantos continue many of Pound's querulous attacks. Byzantine culture presented in 96 may be Pound's ideal as it was Yeats's: a meeting of East and West, a sort of earthly Paradise. However, 107–109 open up stretches of English history without any clear resolution. Pound has constantly sought new ideas and techniques in his deep excursion into human history and civilization. His translations of Chinese, Egyptian, Hindi, Italian, Provençal, Japanese, Latin, and Greek poetry are some of the best in the language. He has written numerous essays on a wide range of subjects, and many of these are collections in the volume *Ezra Pound: Essays*. Another interesting book is his *ABC of Reading,* which explores several ways of approaching the great works of literature.

William Carlos Williams (1883–1963). William Carlos Williams was born at Rutherford, New Jersey, of mixed British and Puerto Rican heritage. After schooling in France and Switzerland he went on to take a medical degree at the University of Pennsylvania in 1906. Graduate work in pediatrics was taken at the University of Leipzig. In 1909 he demonstrated the dual role he would play throughout his life: he practiced medicine in northern New Jersey and published his first volume of poetry. Thereafter he combined the two personalities of a meticulous scientist and a determinedly modern poet.

Williams had by mid-century obtained high repute among the critics, but was virtually unknown to many of his countrymen. In total revolt against orthodox "literary" verse, Williams strives for a "pure poetry" of the immediate American experience. In the 1930s he headed the Objectivists, seeking "no ideas but in things," a direct, flat statement of the precise thing in itself. Allusions and moralizing are done away with in order to obtain "illumination in the environment." Meter and other traditional forms are largely discarded. The result is taut, bare, non-thesis making.

Al Que Quiere! ("To him who wants it," 1917) marks the first Williams verse in his distinctive style, although these poems are not as elliptical and compressed as later poems.

"Sub Terra" is the invitation to find the poetic experience not in reverie or transcendence but in the real world of life (and death), no matter how drab or vulgar it may be.

"Metric Figure" is an impressive Imagist piece in its sharp depiction of the rising sun seen through wind-blown poplar leaves.

"Pastoral" describes the weathered blue-green clutter of shantytown houses and, although "no one will believe this," the beauty that the poet finds in them. His attention to detail and to color enable him to find beauty where other men would find only ugliness.

"Gulls" employs the image of three gulls, spared by a circling eagle, to call for mutual tolerance and understanding between the "singer" and his "townspeople."

"The Young Housewife" is a vivid vignette of the unposed housewife calling to "the ice-man, fish-man." This is frequently quoted to reveal the astonishingly rich poetic overtones and implications that Williams can achieve in an unpretentious statement about apparently prosaic events.

"Good Night" demonstrates Williams' almost unchallenged position as the poet of domestic life, not of the usual sentimental kind but of the everyday routines. In the conflict between immediate reality ("a glass filled with parsley") and memory ("three girls in crimson satin"), the present wins out.

"Sympathetic Portrait of a Child" depicts the ten-year-old daughter of a murderer. Implicit is the guilt of society that wrongfully stigmatizes and isolates such an innocent.

"To a Solitary Disciple" is Williams' lesson in aesthetics and apparently a dedication to Imagism. Instead of color and decoration, the stuff of poetry is in the real object, the real experience.

Sour Grapes (1921) was born of Williams' disillusionment with World War I and the postwar era. Like T. S. Eliot's contemporaneous "The Waste Land" the prevailing note is the horror of spring as the challenge of life to an enfeebled society that would rather hibernate or die.

"Waiting" depicts an aging man who, having lost love and desire for his wife, is appalled by the vitality of his children and by his own sense of futility.

"The Widow's Lament in Springtime" expresses in a dramatic monologue the death wish of a widow whose drab emptiness seems mocked by the luxuriant life of returning spring.

"Portrait of the Author" is one of Williams' most impassioned poems, which rages at the thwarting of human energies.

Spring and All (1923) is Williams' affirmation of life, instead of the terror of the preceding volume. His "anti-poetry" hits full stride as he splashes his verses with such emblems of twentieth-century American life as elevators, telephones, Wrigley's gum, and appendicitis. The technique is montage, a surrealistic jerking of the reader from one vivid impression to another. To further the sense of relationship of all poems in the collection, titles, after the first edition, were discarded in favor of simple numbering from I to XXVIII.

"I" sets the tone for the entire series: "the stark dignity of / entrance." Similar in imagery to Eliot's "The Waste Land," it suggests, nevertheless, the cyclic rebirth of life in the "new world." Implicit is the acceptance of the American surrounding without demand that it conform to our dreams or our hopes. Frequently praised, it was one of Williams' own favorites.

"V," like other poems in the collection, records the difficulties of Williams' avowed purpose. As an Objectivist the poet determinedly will find only what is truly there: "There is nothing in the twist / of the wind but—dashes of cold rain."

"VII" while rejecting the hackneyed symbolisms of the rose constructs a memorable lyric out of perceiving the rose solely through the lenses of today's mind.

"X" asserts that "the universality of things" calls as much for poetic utterance about a garbage heap as about the nearby melon flowers.

"XVI" clinically describes the painful death pangs of an aged woman, shorn of dignity and all else but a wearisome inability to expire.

"XXI" is often anthologized as the epitome of Williams' Imagistic poetics. Resembling the Japanese *haiku*, it sharply etches a concrete wet red wheelbarrow beside white chickens.

Collected Poems (1934) bore a commendatory preface by Wallace Stevens, who saw in Williams' verse precise imagery, poetry in the anti-poetic, Spartan restraint, and a rigorous refusal to sentimentalize.

"Hemmed in Males" pictures the oppressive atmosphere of the times and the emasculating anti-creativity of the age in the grotesquely funny attempt of a man to cadge a drink during the Prohibition era.

"It Is a Living Coral" demonstrates the vulgar cheapening of American history in the manner of a side-show barker commenting on an incongruous mixture of scenes from the nation's past.

"The Winds," like many Williams poems of this period, uses the title as first line and in fact as the subject of all the verbs in the poem. The poet celebrates the cleansing sweep of March winds, blowing all things away in spring renovation.

An Early Martyr (1935) exemplifies the "social consciousness" of those bleak Depression years, during which Williams refused to identify himself with any proletarian movement.

"The Raper from Passenack" is perhaps Williams' strongest indictment of a brutal, dehumanized society. The woman's attacker was motivated solely by a desire to assert frustrated force and to have someone remember him, even though bitter disgust is the woman's response.

"The Yachts" is one of the best known of Williams' later poems, but it is atypical. Instead of his preferred short lines usually of two or three beats, this poem employs a line hovering about pentameter. The luxuriant imagery and the passionate intensity are again unusual for Williams. The essential basis is a contrast between the apparent fragility of the vessels in their first appearance and their concluding triumph over the forces that would thwart them.

Paterson (I, 1946; II, 1948; III, 1949; IV, 1951; V, 1958) is Williams' extended epic poem, considered by many critics as the most successful poem of this genre that has been produced in mid-twentieth-century America. Williams states the theme: "A man in himself is a city, beginning, seeking, achieving and concluding his life in ways which the various aspects of a city may embody—if imaginatively conceived—any city, all the details of which may be made to voice his most intimate convictions." Readers expecting the traditional structuring of the epic may be disappointed. Because dispersion is a reality of our times, the poem does not impose arbitrary unity. The hero is not the conventional molder of his own fate but the molded product of his time and place. Williams makes his central character what Paterson makes him. The diction of the poem designedly incorporates both lyric verse and common speech, sometimes in clashing juxtaposition, generally in the peculiar combination that is Williams' idiom.

Book I ("The Delineaments of the Giants") studies the city of Paterson in space and time, and establishes the central figure, Dr. Paterson, the city personified. The city is a giant lying in the valley under the Passaic Falls. The Falls are the dreams and thoughts of the giant, the substance of his life. The Passaic River is the ceaseless Life Force, apparently running out but constantly being renewed and recharged. Dr. Paterson is the poet, the product of Paterson, a man seeking to find himself amidst the welter. He considers the history of the community to discover a vigorous past shaping toward a decaying present. Escape, however, is no answer, for Dr. Paterson and the city must make and be made by what is their inevitable environment.

Book II ("Sunday in the Park") carries Dr. Paterson into the park where he perceives the present Paterson. All is disunity in this non-community, a huge mass of impressions and mankind held together neither by the weight of the past nor the friction of the present.

Book III ("The Library") is a denial of the salvations advocated by two notable poets of the era—T. S. Eliot and Ezra Pound. The title of this book implies a wry denunciation of academicism. Dr. Paterson refuses the withered leaves of academic writings in favor of plunging over the Falls and into life. The wellspring of life is not in any tradition or book but in the living of life itself.

Book IV ("Idyl") begins with the perversion of love in modern society in a sordid lesbian affair. The poet strives to overcome the failures of today's world, recognizing in dissonance the possibility of discovery and improvement. The conclusion employs the water imagery that began the entire poem. Dr. Paterson looks to the river's source for the ceaseless renewal and multitudinous possibilities of life.

Book V ("The Hunt of the Unicorn") has seemed to most critics a postscript to an essentially complete work. A Flemish tapestry depicting hunters amidst flowers in pursuit of a unicorn under the scrutiny of a queenly woman permits the poet to exploit the theme of life's quests. The supreme virtue is the unselfish struggle to create the greatest thing within one's capabilities. For most this good is outgoing love and altruism. For the comprehending it is art. Not the formal artist alone, but all perceptive humans can forge from their genuine, honestly observed experiences the substance of artistic reality.

Collected Later Poems (1963) includes most Williams verse of his last two decades, including *Pictures from Brueghel* (1962). Themes and attitudes remain essentially the same, though mellowed by added years and prosodic experience. Along with his perennial concern with the local environment and with the authentic American speech pattern, he increasingly displayed a concern with technique. Superficially this appeared in the triadic (three-unit) line in which most of his later poems are written. In "The Descent" (1955), for example, he terms Memory:

> an initiation, since the spaces it opens are new places
> inhabited by hordes
> heretofore unrealized.

More deeply, his sharpened poetic credo sought in each poem: concentration, to achieve the precise impression of the moment; interrelation, forming a complex unity from the parts; indirection, to avoid sentimentality or triviality and to permit richer overtones. In these final years he felt intensely that poetry "closes up the ranks of understanding," proffering truths beyond the range of science or logic.

"The Dance," one of the poems from *Pictures from Breughel*, describes a painting called "The Kermess." Following the rhythm of a dance in the poetic lines, this poem comes very close to being a rendering in words of both picture and music.

Life along the Passaic River (1938) is the most distinguished collection of Williams' short stories, naturalistic pieces exemplifying in prose his poetic principles. The best of these are based upon his medical experiences with the diseased and the downtrodden. Criticism of capitalism, seldom found in his verse, appears in such pieces as "Jean Bieoke," but the chief emphasis is upon the ability of one character's impact upon another character to force a reversal of personal and social values. In "A Face of Stone" the physician's prejudice against an immigrant family and their distrust of him are blunted by overtures of understanding from both sides. "The Girl with the Pimply Face" contrasts one physician's disgust at a worker family with another physician's amusement at the family's self-reliance and his partially successful attempt to help. "The Use of Force" spares no one in its depiction of an angry physician's violence in order to diagnose an obdurate child; like many of his stories, this is a starkly accurate detailing of human illness and human behavior.

Autobiography (1951) and *Selected Letters* (1957) are notably direct. Williams knew and discussed poetry with poets ranging from Ezra Pound to Allen Ginsberg, but most engaging is the straightforward, unpretentious account of the life he actually lived and the everyday people he encountered.

Wallace Stevens (1879–1955). A native of Reading, Pennsylvania, Wallace Stevens attended Harvard from 1897 to 1900. After a brief period as a newspaper reporter he entered the New York Law School from which he graduated in 1903. Admitted to the bar the next year, he practiced law in New York City until 1916. Although friendly with contemporary poets such as William Carlos Williams, e. e. cummings, Alfred Kreymborg, and Marianne Moore, Stevens maintained the aloofness of a smartly dressed, sober business attorney. In 1916 he moved to Hartford, Connecticut, as an executive with the Hartford Accident and Indemnity Company. Many of his associates never realized that this impressive insurance official (vice-president of the firm from 1934 until his death) was one of the major poets of American literature. Hesitant about his poetic avocation, he refused the Charles Eliot Norton professorship at Harvard, but in his later years did give occasional lectures about his concepts of poetry.

In the 1960s, with almost universal praise from fellow poets and from scholars, Stevens became a favorite poet of the intellectuals. As a very difficult poet, however, he is not widely read outside this circle. Even when his work is explained, he seems to baffle many twentieth-century readers. This pragmatic business executive is the most devoted poet's poet, the chief subject of his verses being poetry itself.

Art, Stevens repeatedly insisted, is the supreme means of finding reality. Poetic imagination alone possesses the faculty, first of animating the factual chaos of experience, second of transcending it. This transcendence is imaginative insight into the truth of oneself and simultaneously is the sole creator of actuality in the confused outer world. Art is to interpret and transform life, but not to flee from it. To Stevens the spirit (equated with imagination) resides wholly in the flesh. Poems to him are not *about* something but an attempt *to be* the thing. Stevens' verse exploits a dazzling array of symbols from modern living to compel the reader into the imaginative act. A meticulous craftsmanship of lines and a variety of moods from quiet meditation to bizarre ironic humor are characteristic Stevens poetic vehicles.

CERTAIN MAJOR IMAGES are important in Stevens' work. As a symbolist Stevens utilizes a series of personal symbols with remarkable consistency. Much of his startling effect arises from his unusual employment of familiar poetic symbols, while many other contemporary poets (except as noted) tend to use more obvious symbolism. The following is a simplified interpretation of the more recurrent images:

Images of *order* represent man's imaginative faculty of bringing pattern to the welter of experience. Clothes of all sorts, especially hats, symbolize imposed order. Likewise hair, beard, wig, parasols, and also hands and sculpture. Fruit, bouquets of flowers, leaves, and the songs, flights, and plumage of birds are metaphors of order from Nature.

Images of *disorder* are what the unimaginative mind accepts from the physical world. Rain, snow, mountain, volcano are such symbols from

Nature. The junk yard and the gangster are notable emblems of man-made disorder.

Images of *change* indicate the raw material which the imagination must bend to meaning: air, wind, clouds. The sea is the least manageable, representing the whole of chaos. The wheel, automobile, and moving machinery are such symbols taken from man's world. Images of *mind* are especially significant in the attempt of man to order existence. House and room stand for the mind itself. Reason is symbolized in straight lines, squares, angles. Curves, arcs, and circles represent the mind's turning inward upon itself to a rigid, closed pattern. Shadow is a favorable symbol, an imaginative projection necessary to give ordered meaning. A large body of terms for movements similarly celebrates the adaptive, fluid power of imagination: bending, dodging, turning, twisting. Color symbolism is especially prominent in Stevens—black conventionally for death and nullity, but white for the intellect devoid of imaginative scope, brown close to black, orange for falsified reality as red is unfalsified reality, blue and green as colors of life and imagination. The compass points seem to present the East as past cultures, the West as anarchy and extinction, the North as contemporary society, the South as more elemental primitivism. Summer is the period of imaginative construction, while Winter destroys such creations.

The following poems are discussed in the order of the *Collected Poems.* Although interpretations frequently reveal abstruse and esoteric meanings in Stevens, the following explanations espouse a moderate position.

Harmonium (1923) is a surprisingly late first volume from a poet, appearing when Stevens was in his mid-forties. Nonetheless, it is a work of scintillating youthfulness, celebrating in Stevens' own words "The freshness of a world . . . the freshness of ourselves." At the same time in its maturity it displays none of the groping imitations generally plaguing first books; for although he had published verses as early as his Harvard undergraduate days, Stevens refused to include anything he had written before 1913. The collection received scant attention initially, although it contains some of his best and now most anthologized poems.

"The Anecdote of the Jar," a poem typical of Stevens, seems to present a perfectly straightforward picture of a jar on a hill. What the poet asks us to do, however, is contemplate a more general truth represented by this object. By introducing a foreign object, however common it may be, Stevens transforms the wilderness for the reader into a new set of relations.

"The Ordinary Women" displays the power of commonplace people to rise from their dreary everydayness ("dry catarrhs") to imaginative engagement ("guitars"), but their timidity will often let them fall back into their mundane realm. The statement of the poem, as always with Stevens, is overshadowed by the splendor of image and language.

"Le Monocle de Mon Oncle" celebrates "The faith of forty," as the maturing man reassesses the enthusiasms of youth. Sensual experience (the apple) is contrasted with contemplation (Chinese philosophers) to appreciate nuances that earlier years deemed simple. All the rich meaning of life reposes solely within man, whose flickering imaginative creation alone gives truth. The poet seems ironically to ascribe this deepening of perceptivity and concomitant weakening of the sex drive to himself. *Opus Posthumous* contains a poem, "The Naked Eye of My Aunt," that looks like a companion piece. The aunt disastrously tries to see the world pragmatically. The aging man here employs an eyepiece giving a distortion of physical reality that twists it to imaginative truth.

"Metaphors of a Magnifico" is a poetic theory of knowledge. Physical reality is only meaningful to the imaginative response that builds beauty fortuitously, as a magnifico (man of creative sensibility) finds casual but deep significance in "twenty men crossing a bridge."

"Ploughing on Sunday" in wild exuberance proclaims the poetic mission to defy tradition (Sabbath day rest) and embrace change (wind) and formlessness (rain) in building a new creative aesthetic.

"The Comedian as the Letter C" was labeled "an anti-mythological poem," or mock heroic, by Stevens, who also stated, "The central figure is an everyday man who lives a life without the slightest adventure, except that he lives it in poetic atmosphere as we all do. This point makes it necessary for a translator to try to reproduce the everyday plainness of the central figure and the plush, so to speak, of the stage." The central character is Crispin, the buffoon of French comedy, whose pretentiousness to knowledge ill accords with his ludicrous blunderings. As a whole the poem explores the poetic quest of Western man in the modern world, in which a new land holds great potential for the imagination.

I, "The World Without Imagination," pictures the disinheritance of the modern spirit. Earlier man considered the world as made solely for his benefit, thereby creating false transcendencies and peopling Nature with conscious mythological beings. Modern man prides himself upon his realism and his elimination of the older consolations. However, just as desperately as his predecessors, he must "have a dream in face of the object" to bring order and meaning to the chaotic sea of phenomena. This section suggests the European imagination (Crispin) metamorphosed by the new land.

II, "Concerning the Thunderstorms of Yucatan," carries Crispin to his southernmost journeyings, the exotic Yucatan peninsula of Mexico.

Like Melville in *Typee*, he finds the lush tropical paradise ultimately unsatisfying.

III, "Approaching Carolina," compels Crispin to the plight (and glory) of the modern. In the more austere North he must find his poetry in the unpoetry of today's world. Discarded altogether is the notion of elevated man amidst a noble universe of ideas. The essential imaginative challenge to the poetic nature of our era reveals "that prose shall wear a poem's guise at last."

IV, "The Idea of a Colony," finds Crispin insisting that the poet write of naturalistic reality as only he experiences it ("in a colony"). But this is a half truth. While the human psyche truly possesses no supersensual or metaphysical knowledge, it cannot be content with the unimaginative life.

V, "A Nice Shady Home," abandons the "colony," as disenchanted Crispin settles for the commonplace environment. This apparent defeat, however, presages victory if within the frame of the mundane ("the quotidian") man will love his imagination ("prismy blonde").

VI, "And Daughters with Curls," brings Crispin to a poetic haven. A romantic at the outset of the poem, then a militant realist, he ends as an "indulgent fatalist." His daughters are the four types of poetry properly written, in descending order: (1) theorizing about the glory of the imagination, (2) imagining without understanding the vital role of the imagination, (3) valid perception of experience without the extraneous clutter of the outmoded traditions, (4) fresh and unblemished curiosity about the human lot. The deep truth remains fathomless, but the poet produces "curls" to impose fictive meaning upon life. By the creative imagination the poet stands as man's greatest prop and prophet.

"The Emperor of Ice-Cream," a favorite of the poet as well as of anthologists, states that the only human realities lie in the evidence of the senses. We cannot rejoice in the salvation of the poverty-stricken old woman, nor can we truthfully mourn her departure. Death is seen starkly in the cold light of the lamp, devoid of emotional coloring, the traditional evasive "sheet / On which she embroidered fantails." We must see things as they are, for life continually whipping up "concupiscent curds" overshadows a wake for an individual death. Ephemeral as it is, the one reality is the delicious confection of "the emperor of ice cream."

"Sunday Morning" deals with things which we can truly say are real, the question of faith in an era quite skeptical of orthodox religion. Sunday morning is the opportunity for sensual indulgence by the cultured, leisured class, here represented by a well-to-do woman sipping coffee on her patio. The traditional Christian meaning of Sunday makes her dissatisfied with the purely hedonistic life. Contemplating death she yearns for permanence amidst this transience, for some immortality in the face of the death of myth. In the two concluding stanzas Stevens proposes as the new faith a full recognition that the truth of life, as distinguished from any mythical "paradise," is the eternal death and rebirth of physical existence. Immortality or anything beyond the "wide water" of this life is denied to man in his "island solitude," but the eternal regenerative principle, worship of life itself, is amply sustaining.

"Peter Quince at the Clavier" takes as its title figure the bumbling stage manager of *A Midsummer Night's Dream,* whose inept desire to shape the music of life from that refined instrument, the clavier (the poetic process), symbolizes the average human condition. Gazing upon a lady in blue silk, the speaker thinks of the lovely Susanna and the prying elders in the biblical account. All art (music and painting are the major references here) is sensuous. But while "The body dies; the body's beauty lives."

"Thirteen Ways of Looking at a Blackbird" is a virtuoso performance parallel to Cubistic painting. The imaginative mind of the poet seeks to grasp the aesthetic meaning of the blackbird through thirteen brilliant explorations of its hidden significance. The intense concentration and variety of approaches find the sensual world in itself alone more than sufficient poetic stimulus and suggest that the reality is a sum of these separate angles of vision. (As the basis for a musical composition by Boris Blacher, this poem demonstrates the close relationship of Stevens' poetry to modern art in diverse media.)

"The Man Whose Pharynx Was Bad" deals with diminution of imagination under the relentless pressure of the "malady of the quotidian." Since, however, the myth of man must be imaginatively created from what he beholds, the very rigors of winter (the rational and mundane) may permit a cleansed and renewed vision beyond.

Ideas of Order (1936), in the poet's own words, "attempts to illustrate the role of the imagination in life, and particularly in life at present."

"The Idea of Order at Key West" stands, perhaps, as a late climax to the Romantic poetry of the previous century. Two men hear the singing of a woman upon a tropical beach and thereafter observe a harbor with lighted boats. Having heard the woman's song, they are now elevated to the heightened perceptivity of the artist. Reality is not the raw material of the physical world but what the imagination forms from it.

The Man with the Blue Guitar and Other Poems (1937) shows the incessant conjunctions between things as they are and things imagined. The blue guitar is the imagination and a reference to the individuality of the poet, the poet being any man of imagination.

"The Man with the Blue Guitar" adapts from one of Picasso's paintings the visual symbol of the blue guitar to discuss the poet's mission to man.

Men ask the poet to give them truth, but what they really wish is sentimental reassurance. Men may even be so hopelessly caught up in daily life as to dismiss poetry altogether. But the blue guitar persists as an imaginative force to nourish the human spirit by altering things as they are, thereby creating new reality.

Parts of a World (1942).

"The Man on the Dump" is a satiric parody about the outmoded lumber still cluttering the modern mind. The junk heap upon which the poet stands is the trash of the poetic, philosophic, and religious traditions above which the imaginative mind must soar to create new truths.

"Loneliness in Jersey City" indicts the city as one of today's vapid industrial infernos. With imagination interred, the city denizens flatten everything, equating the natural grace of the deer with the awkward domesticity of the dachshund.

Transport to Summer (1947) introduces Stevens' most prolific period. Although this and subsequent volumes include much of his best work, readers still seem to be intrigued most with the earlier *Harmonium*.

"Dutch Graves in Bucks County" explores the relation of the past to the present. The opening lines underscore the gap existing between war as fought at Gettysburg and war in the 1940s. The summary couplets after each stanza make more personal the general experiences of the previous lines. The paradox is that although each age repeats the past, nothing is learned from past mistakes.

"Chocorua to Its Neighbor" employs the New Hampshire mountain as man's concept of the deity. God is the most sublime of man's creations, the monarch of "human realizings." God is a product of man's highest imaginative faculty, "bare brother" rather than father to man.

"Esthétique du Mal" seeks to explain how imagination can transmute the anguish of existence into beauty. Denied the hope of finding a cosmic plan and poetic justice, man is nevertheless more at home on earth as he fully recognizes that pain and suffering are integral to life. Paradoxically, the very depths of despair and of the unpoetic stir the spirit to utterance.

"Credences of Summer" offers Stevens' most ecstatic paean to fruition and fulfillment in the world of the senses. He celebrates the rich completion of individuals, of family units, of man's institutions and nations.

"Notes Toward a Supreme Fiction" was written before the other poems of this volume but was made the concluding piece, since it sums up all the poet's central contentions. The "supreme fiction" is the representational human concept of the world. Reality is admittedly elusive and inchoate, while the imagination is the sole faculty to achieve creative union with actuality and give it meaning. Characteristic of Stevens' later poems, this one tends toward more incisive statement.

I ("It Must be Abstract") advises the "ephebe" (youthful poet) to strip experience clean of all man's past accretions. Finding the "thing-in-itself," he will possess an abstraction resembling the "minute particulars" of Blake, not a disembodied idea but the stark, unadorned truth. Upon this foundation he may erect his valid imaginings that in time will weaken through the "evasions of metaphor," but the cycle will recommence with a new abstraction. "Major man," the poetic imagination, will discover as the Supreme Fiction the ultimate knowable truths ascertained from the specific experience of individual men.

II ("It Must Change") denies heaven and hell, gods and immortality, all postulates of permanence. Growth and change are the only realities, and the Supreme Fiction of art makes sense only as it accepts these realities and itself partakes of them. From the "exhilarations of changes" emerge the rapture of poetry and life.

III ("It Must Give Pleasure") offers not conventional hedonism but a "purification" that enjoys total satisfaction from complete revelation of this worldly truth. This section versifies the contention of the essay "Imagination as Value"—"In the service of love and imagination nothing can be too lavish, too sublime or too festive."

The Auroras of Autumn (1950) furthered Stevens' reputation as one of the foremost poets of ideas of the century.

"The Auroras of Autumn" in the title refers to the northern lights, casting a brilliant aura upon the dying year. Stevens portrays the decline of the seasons, of man, and of society. The wise man, however, blames not the universe but himself for his misfortunes. Recognizing the tragic reality of life, he nonetheless finds within himself the resources to make life whole and satisfying.

"A Primitive Like an Orb" is a tribute to the poetic vision of the world. Below the rational life resides a compulsion for order that admits eternal change but asserts meaning, gives reality to phenomena, and sustains the human spirit.

"An Ordinary Evening in New Haven" fuses the actual New Haven with what imagination makes of it. Man must not flee to antiquated integrations (like Professor Eucalyptus, an idealistic philosopher), but must constantly repeat the process of imagination, by creating from what exists today. "The theory / Of poetry is the theory of life."

The Necessary Angel: Essays on Reality and the Imagination (1951) collects lectures given by Stevens between 1942 and 1951. The cryptic title is taken from a still life by Tal Coat to which Stevens arbitrarily assigned the title, "Angels Surrounded by Paysans" (the last poem in *Auroras of Autumn*). The title suggests art's essential stimulus to man. Later essays, along with a few last poems, appear in *Opus Posthumous* in 1957.

Collected Poems was published in 1954 when Stevens was seventy-five years old.

"To an Old Philosopher in Rome" praises Santayana as the reconciler of the real and the imagined. Comparing Roman architecture to the philosopher's mind, Stevens suggests that through imagination, Santayana completed the structure of his mind before dying.

"The World as Meditation" portrays Penelope waiting patiently for the return of Ulysses. An impossible hope for the perfection that we can conceive must yield to what we can achieve. Our lives may be composed with a joyous finality. The spring's return may be Ulysses himself. By imaginative construction upon the genuine substance of life we build ourselves and give a finished form to life.

"The Rock" continues the symbol of "Credences of Summer." The rock is the reconciler of opposites. Man clothes the rock of reality with "such mixed motion and such imagery" that it becomes multitudes of things, "the starting point of the human and the end."

OTHER IMPORTANT POETS OF THE PERIOD

Vachel Lindsay (1879–1931). In his native Springfield, Illinois, the parents of Nicholas Vachel Lindsay instilled in him the intense devotion of Campbellites (Disciples of Christ). Lindsay early intended to be a Christian missionary, but after schooling at Hiram College (1897–1900) he studied art in Chicago and New York (1900–5). He turned his religious evangelicalism into an apostleship of art. As a "vagabond poet" he tramped the country reciting poetry in exchange for food and lodging. *Rhymes to be Traded for Bread* (1912) literally meant what the title states. Finding inadequate response to his "gospel of beauty" (title for a lecture he often gave after 1912), he moved to the "higher vaudeville," a frank entertainment appeal to popular audiences. Eager crowds would join him in chanting his theatrical pieces. Lindsay became bored with his own recitals and produced little of note after 1920, although he continued to publish extensively. Disillusionment and a morbid religious conscience apparently combined to cause him to take his own life.

Lindsay wrote most enthusiastically about America. His perception of our history is a series of larger-than-life heroes, whether John L. Sullivan or William Jennings Bryan. Lindsay expressed his love of America in verse transparently clear to his fellow citizens.

General William Booth Enters into Heaven and Other Poems (1913), like Lindsay's other collections, includes verse of many types, but what he is remembered for is almost solely "verse to be chanted to a bass drum."

"General William Booth Enters into Heaven" is a stirring tribute to the then recently deceased founder of the Salvation Army, to be chanted against the background of the revivalist hymn, "The Blood of the Lamb" and Salvation Army banjos and tambourines. Booth is welcomed into the heavenly realm along with the motley throng of converts that he drew from the squalid slums and pestholes of all the world. The four-beat line, sporting any number of unaccented syllables, is hypnotically incantatory, achieving an almost primitive intensity.

"The Broncho That Would Not Be Broken" is the story of a colt "that would not be broken of dancing." The men come to break him and to destroy his free spirit. He is harnessed to a reaper, but instead of being malicious or slow like the mules that are shackled with him he strains and pulls the reaper until he collapses in death. Like Lindsay himself, the broncho is primitive and powerful, with a thirst for life and experience that cannot be broken by the constraints of civilization.

"The Eagle That Is Forgotten" pays tribute to the militantly liberal governor of Illinois, John Peter Altgeld, who died in 1902. It is at the same time a farewell to the Populist movement in American politics.

The Congo and Other Poems (1914).

"The Congo" and the Booth poem have always been the two best-known works of Lindsay. "The Congo" presents in three sections three clichés about the Negro character, "their basic savagery," "their irrepressible high spirits," "the hope of their religion." Lindsay creates a gripping, blood-surging rhythm largely with the paeon (i.e., a foot of four syllables, one long and three short). Subsequent generations have deemed its analysis of the Negro character stereotyped and lacking in understanding.

"Abraham Lincoln Walks at Midnight" is an eloquently simple and totally conventional interpretation of Lincoln, whose spirit roams Springfield in anguish at the outbreak of World War I.

The Chinese Nightingale and Other Poems (1917) contains poems which critics rate above Lindsay's earlier popular successes, but the poet became increasingly depressed by the less popular appeal of these pieces.

"The Chinese Nightingale" finds in Lindsay's Chinese laundryman Chang a treasury of oriental beauty and culture to sustain him amidst his drab, humble existence in America. Love inspires the song of the nightingale and makes spring "come on forever." The lyricism displays a delicacy not usually associated with Lindsay.

"The Ghosts of the Buffaloes" uses Lindsay's chanting style with more subtlety and variety than before. In a dream vision the poet witnesses a stampeding herd of buffaloes thundering west with Indians in pursuit. Even in the complacency of twentieth-century life the dream of the westward movement over the virgin wilderness still heartens Americans into giant creativity. "Life is the west-going dream-storm's breath" as reality is actually brought to birth only through the vision of the American myth.

Collected Poems (1923) contains all significant Lindsay verse, although he continued to write until his death.

"In Praise of Johnny Appleseed" celebrates the folk hero John Chapman who is credited with starting the apple orchards of western Pennsylvania and on through Illinois at the outset of the nineteenth century. The hero's close association with Nature and devotion to his fellowman are exultantly chanted in Lindsay's familiar leaping rhythms.

Edgar Lee Masters (1869–1950). Born in Garnett, Kansas, Edgar Lee Masters was taken at the age of one to his grandfather's farm near Petersburg, Illinois. His first work was as a printer, but eventually yielding to the wishes of his attorney father he read law in his father's office, and in 1891 was admitted to the bar. Largely self-taught, he attended Knox College for one year. In Chicago he became a highly successful lawyer, writing poetry as an avocation. Although he published many volumes, starting with 1898, only the *Spoon River Anthology* attracted wide critical approval. A strongly partisan Democrat, he shocked Americans with the iconoclastic *Lincoln the Man* (1931) which exalted Stephen Douglas and claimed that Lincoln destroyed many American freedoms with his wartime powers. In 1946 Masters was awarded the first fellowship granted by the Academy of American poets.

Spoon River Anthology (1915) was stimulated by a translation of the Greek Anthology given to Masters about 1911 by W. M. Reedy, editor of *Reedy's Mirror*. In 1914 *Reedy's Mirror* began publishing under pseudonyms the Masters "auto-epitaphs," supposed gravestone inscriptions in which the dead frankly evaluate themselves and their lives in short, unrhymed poems, sometimes in irregular four-beat lines and frequently in free verse. Many of the names actually appear on markers in the Petersburg cemetery, where Masters himself is buried. A few of the 250 characters, notably Lucinda Matlock and "Fiddler Jones," found life amply satisfying, but the majority decry existences of barren frustration in the drab small-town atmosphere of the Midwest. One of the best known and most moving of the epitaphs is uttered by Ann Rutledge, relating her thwarted love for Lincoln but taking consolation in the inspiration she imparted to him.

The deterministic naturalism of the poems, in revolt against the local-color school, paralleled naturalistic fiction of the era and evoked similar hostility. A judicious sampling of the collection can produce some sharply effective portraits, but the overall quality is repetitious. The chronicling of defeats and narrow-mindedness is largely without digging to the basic causes of inadequacy and bafflement. But Masters has sympathy for the vanished American pioneer (like Lucinda) and frustrated introverts (like Petit, the Poet, a wry self-portrait).

e. e. cummings (1894–1962). Edward Estlin Cummings was born in Cambridge, Massachusetts, son of a Harvard professor who later became a Unitarian clergyman. cummings graduated *magna cum laude* from Harvard in the class of 1915 and delivered the commencement address. The next year he received his M.A. from Harvard. In 1917 cummings became an ambulance driver in France, where his nonconformist attitudes caused him to be confined for several months in a French prison; the charges were later dismissed as wartime misunderstanding and overzealousness by the French authorities. cummings finished out the war in the U. S. Army. Throughout the 1920s he alternated his residence between New York and Paris, where he spent considerable time studying painting. From the 1930s on he exhibited his original paintings extensively. He received many poetic awards, including the Bollingen Prize in 1957. In 1952–53 he was the Norton lecturer at Harvard.

e. e. cummings is particularly delightful in his breaking of the traditional rules of typography very noticeably in always writing his name entirely in lower-case letters. But he also introduces more complex typographical twistings in his poetry. Librarians wonder at & and similarily uncataloguable titles by cummings, and readers are surprised by cummings' verses such as:

1   oo   k—
pigeons fly ingand

    whee (: are, SpRiN,k,LiNg an in-stant with sunLight
    t h e n)l-
    ing all go Black wh-eel-ing

To his publisher's plea for explanation of his verbal and typographical gymnastics, cummings replied in the foreword to *is 5:* "It is with roses and locomotives (not to mention acrobats Spring electricity Coney Island the 4th of July the eyes of mice and Niagara Falls) that my 'poems' are competing." In addition to the obvious showmanship to excite the reader, the typography of cummings attempts a maximum of communication. Believing that poetry is aimed primarily at the ear, cummings tries on the printed page to convey all the nuances of the spoken word: pause, running together, emphasis, tonality.

Perhaps the major difficulty in appreciating cummings is his incessant humor. The English-speaking public finds it difficult to believe that a really significant poet is satirizing or laughing at everything, including himself. The rampant individualism and unabashed sensuality in cummings are directed against culture consecrated to the acquisition of money. But at the heart of cummings is the conviction of a truth more real than the workaday world, a true vision obtainable solely through intuition. This is the truth of Nature, the eternal processes that modern man tries artificially to twist and thwart. One should note also that cummings is a great writer of lyric love poems.

The bibliography of cummings is sometimes quite tangled. Verses through 1954 are considered in the order of printing in *Poems* of that year.

Tulips and Chimneys (1923) is the first volume of cummings poetry and the only one to bear a conventional title. The contrast within the title suggests rural versus urban subjects, but the sections within the book itself indicate that "tulips" are poems chiefly in free verse ("natural"), while "chimneys" generally follow orthodox ("artificial") verse patterns.

"in Just—" was a favorite of the poet and of audiences. Spring takes on a delightful freshness through the wide eyes of children. Their imaginations transform the "balloonMan" into a creature with a strangely mythical quality.

"listen" recounts a man's dreams concerning his beloved. The desire to possess her is symbolized in spectacular visions capable of ready Freudian interpretation.

"consider O" appeals to every manifestation of Nature, from the human body to the vast cosmos, as the supreme beauty.

"O sweet spontaneous," one of his most famous poems, decries the artificialities and abstractions with which philosophy, theology, and science stifle life, and points to the eternal rhythms of earth.

"the hours rise up putting off stars and it is" sees the basic opposition between the laity and poets. The poet's dream is his reality while the daytime world "goes forth to murder dreams."

"Buffalo Bill's," an anthology pleaser, ironically smiles at the Wild West legend exploited by Cody and with him now defunct. Whether a fraud or an awesome hero, Buffalo Bill is claimed by all-conquering death.

"the Cambridge ladies who live in furnished souls" condemns as the living dead those who live stereotyped, uncreative lives.

& (1925) consists largely of poems written for the previous volume but omitted by the editor. Hence the title "and."

"raise the shade" is a dramatic monologue by a prostitute to a customer. She indicates sympathy for the pathetic slavery of average citizens to routine, but misses the irony of her own enslavement and futility.

"i will be" is a lover's anticipation of meeting his beloved. The swirl of passion is symbolized by the flight of pigeons (quoted above in the introduction to cummings). "SpRiN,k,LiNg" visually suggests the impact of the sun's rays upon the fluttering birds. The breaking of "whee" from its last letter indicates simultaneity with the parenthetical words. In conclusion the excited lover subsides into a calm expectancy.

"whereas by dark really released, the modern" contrasts the night and the day existence of a fashionable woman. By day (i.e., most of the time) she follows the accepted rituals and banal superficialities of society. Only privately at night is she truly herself.

"Dick Mid's large bluish face without eyebrows" is representative of cummings' manipulation of the sonnet, distorted to appear as unsonnet-like as possible. A 1920s hoodlum mulls over a gang slaying while awaiting the bribe-seeking police. The rhyme scheme is as unexpected as the subject, and the line arrangement would deceive the casual reader into believing this to be free verse.

"my naked lady framed" exalts natural beauty which surpasses even the most glorious examples of human art.

"i have found what you are like" is an exquisite love lyric describing the attributes of the beloved as akin to the eternal rhythms and gratifying sensations of Nature.

XLI Poems (1925).

"i will wade out" expresses the ecstatic immersion in the natural and the intuitive which gives imaginative transcendence to the fully alive and creative self.

"Picasso" pays tribute to the noted painter as achieving cummings' concept of imaginative art, freeing the world's truth and vision from the bonds of conventionally forged reality.

"the skinny voice" is spoken by a cynical observer in reference to a Salvation Army street service. The cynic notes how the ancient appeal to faith has degenerated to a sidewalk pitch. An innocent child alone among the onlookers is stirred to response. The cynic's "nix, kid" is simultaneously his desire to initiate the youngster into today's aloof negation and to save the youngster for more dignified consecration.

is 5 (1926) gives in the Foreword the meaning of the title. To the mundane mind two times two is four, but the transcendentalism of the poet reaches to more: two times two is five. Appropriately the volume contains five sections. Furthermore, cummings indicates that his technique seeks "that precision which creates movement." "Making" (i.e., process, the living dynamic) is to him far more significant than "made" (i.e., product, the static).

"Poem, or Beauty Hurts Mr. Vinal," in a wild parody of the hymn "America," lampoons the banality of modern advertising and the vacuous mass culture of today.

"voices to voices, lip to lip" is a typical cummings assertion of living over thinking, human concerns over scientific, but primarily it enunciates his perception of a world that has evil, but not sin. Man is totally free and has only to assert his will to live fully and creatively.

"since feeling is first" is a delicate praise to women. The lady has apparently deferred to the superior mentality of the male, who reassures her that womanly intuition and closeness to the wellsprings of life can surpass the masculine intellectual search for truth.

W (1931). The "W" signifies two interlocking Vs, which cummings interprets as "viva" (i.e., "live"). It contains some notable love poetry. This volume marks a decided increase in the transcendentalism of cummings and an emergence of his later style of syntax. Puzzling to many readers, this syntax tries to overcome the abstract nature of language largely by transforming other parts of speech into nouns. The poems become increasingly cryptic in their appearance upon the page.

"Space being (don't forget to remember) Curved" sarcastically denounces the pride of man in his scientific knowledge and his supposed mastery of Nature.

"n (o) w" proclaims the possibility, through the metaphor of a thundershower, of one world vanishing and another taking its place. The typography demonstrates the wildly unconventional experiments of the later cummings. The parenthesis in the first word indicates the breathless anticipation of the beginning of a new era.

"be unto love as rain is unto colour; create" calls for a poetic vision amid the pressures and hypocrisies of society.

"here is the ocean, this is moonlight; say" likens the lover to the sea, which is drawn by the pull of the moon even when daylight conceals the moon.

no thanks (1935) is so titled because fourteen publishers rejected the manuscript. Although eminently productive, cummings was too controversial a poet for most publishers to accept. The printing pattern of many verses in this collection becomes quite bizarre.

"sonnet entitled how to run the world)" urges the transcendental vision of the heart, which is closed to the meddling intellect.

"r-p-o-p-h-e-s-s-a-g-r" is one of the eye poppers of cummings frequently cited by appalled critics. It re-creates in the reader's mind the very effect of a leaping grasshopper.

"sh estiff" depicts a striptease not as a symbol of sexual desire and offering, but as an inhuman act, a hopeless symbol of sterility.

"love's function is to fabricate unknownness" tells of the ability to change and to discover, which is the special gift of lovers.

Collected Poems (1938) states in the Introduction that cummings' poetry is intended for human beings, not "mostpeople." Mostpeople accept as reality what science teaches and what advertising proclaims. Human beings see and respond for themselves, welcoming all genuine living.

50 Poems (1940) marks the climax of visual stanzas in cummings, ranging from rhythmic groupings of somewhat conventional lines to astounding combinations that wrench apart the individual words and syllables of the language.

"anyone lived in a pretty how town," one of his most popular pieces, is cummings' paean to those who love life and each other. The reader gradually realizes that "anyone" and "noone" are specific persons in a small town where all others ("isn't" people) think only of material things and social status. Children of the community intuitively perceive the truth about "anyone" and "noone." For the genuine lovers even death is a fulfillment.

1 × 1 (1944) in title ("one times one") signifies the oneness, the wholeness, of the transcendental vision.

"nonsun blob a" was termed a key to all of cummings by his enthusiastic friend, William Carlos Williams, but most readers are initially flabbergasted. It seems to be a picture of the birth-and-death cycle symbolized in an autumnal scene. Man is a fragile leaf but also a courageous experiment in living.

"ygUDuh" at first looks like gibberish, but cummings is reproducing the semiliterate speech of a fanatic ("ygUDuh" = "you GOT to") who wishes to impose so-called Western enlightenment upon the Orient.

"what if a much of a which of a wind" joyfully affirms a universal energy that will endure even though some force should "blow life to isn't."

"true lovers in each happening of their hearts" is a relatively regular Elizabethan sonnet, not only in structure but in its ecstatic praise of lovers.

XAIPE (1950) is an approximation in English letters of the word for "rejoice" or "greetings" in Greek.

"when serpents bargain for the right to squirm" laughs at the absurd unnaturalness of the actions of men.

"i thank You God for most this amazing" is a rhapsody to the glory of the world and the rapture in life itself.

95 Poems (1958), released when the poet was sixty-four, shows no diminution in lyric power or experimental zeal, but the poems essentially repeat his familiar subjects and techniques.

FICTION. *The Enormous Room* (1922) has been hailed as one of the great novels to come out of World War I; however, its subject is not war but totalitarianism and tyranny.

Chapters I–IV relate the French seizure of cummings from the ambulance corps and his eventual incarceration in the enormous room (80 feet by 40 feet) at La Ferté Macé along with sixty other inmates. Though surrounded by filth and exhaustion, cummings experiences mounting high spirits. He has been released from a bureaucratic monotony in the corps, and prophetic of the existentialists, feels joyous pleasure in having nothing either to lose or to gain.

Chapters V–VII describe a concentration camp. The experience (August 1917 to January 1918) made cummings a lifelong enemy of all forms of repression. It is hard to see how the French Republic could be imperiled by these nondescript, futile prisoners. The power structure created and wielded by the prison director is devastating; he is the god manipulating and controlling every one of his pathetic subjects.

Chapters VIII–XI concentrate upon the four "Delectable Mountains," four notable prisoners. The bestiality and meaninglessness of the enormous room reduce many inmates to animals, but these four clutch all the more resolutely their humanity amidst the squalor of Macé. Demestre, a gypsy, endures the especially refined cruelty of the director toward his wife and children. Zulu, actually a Pole, is the soul of generosity and brotherhood. Surplice is the clown, preferring the most brutal of curses to being ignored. Jean is a huge, good-natured Negro, stoically enduring the worst that life can bring and still finding life worth-while.

Chapters XII–XIII narrate the release of cummings and his return to America.

The phrase "Delectable Mountains" comes from *Pilgrim's Progress,* and suggests that cummings' novel is the quest of today's pilgrim through a society rendered dead by habit and conformity. "Mostpeople," as cummings was later to brand them, succumb. But the Delectable Mountains assert the principle of individuality and of life. *The Enormous Room* is not an anti-war or anti-prison novel, but a tribute to the power of human potentialities.

Stephen Vincent Benét (1898–1943). The son of an army colonel, Stephen Vincent Benét was born at Bethlehem, Pennsylvania, and spent his early years at military posts throughout the country. From Yale he received an A.B. in 1919 and an M.A. the next year. He studied at the Sorbonne in 1920–21, and through a Guggenheim Fellowship returned to Paris in 1926. After he came back to America in 1929, he wrote Hollywood scripts, edited, and reviewed. During World War II he threw all his talents into the war effort. *America* (1944), his propaganda thumbnail history of this country, was translated into every major language and was distributed throughout the world; in Hungary, Benét's *America* was the first book published after the expulsion of the Nazis. Benét's "Prayer" was read by Roosevelt at United Nations ceremonies in 1942. His indefatigable labors for the cause of democracy led to exhaustion and heart attack.

No one else has striven so zealously to fashion the poetic epic of American history and folklore. *John Brown's Body* in an inexpensive reprint was a favorite among American servicemen during World War II. It is perhaps a limitation in Benét that he employed Old World literary forms for the celebration of the New World. Unlike Whitman and his followers, Benét approached the American scene strictly from a literary point of view.

"The Ballad of William Sycamore" (1922) attempts to create an indigenous ballad myth. The title speaker, like Cooper's Pathfinder, is identified with freedom and the natural beauty of a vast, wild land. He is identified too with the nation's struggle, as Sycamore's eldest son fell at the Alamo, his youngest beside Custer. His name and career symbolize oneness with the wilderness frontier in contrast with the disparaging and constraining city.

"American Names" (1927), written in Paris as he yearned for his native soil, chants a litany of American place names, mounting to the final prayer for burial of the heart at Wounded Knee. The homey naming wrung from the American earth of the common man has, Benét feels, the smack of true life.

John Brown's Body (1928) was composed in Paris. Overall it consciously follows the traditional epic pattern while specific passages range from free verse to folk ballad to the Negro spiritual. Critics prefer to call it a historical novel in verse. Approximately fifteen thousand lines cover the Civil War conflict from Harpers Ferry to Appomattox. Its historical accuracy has been acclaimed by Northern and Southern historians alike. Benét interprets the Civil War as the climactic event of American history, an inevitable conflict between the feudal agrarian South and the egalitarian industrial North. There are portraits of historical personages such as Lincoln, Lee, Jefferson Davis, "Stonewall" Jackson, and Grant; and a description of the battle of Gettysburg. Like a historical novel, center stage is held by fictional characters, chiefly Jack Ellyat, an idealistic Connecticut law student who fights in the major battles as a Union infantryman, and Clay Wingate, a Southern plantation aristocrat who serves in the Confederate cavalry. Contrasting with these obvious opponents is the Vilas family which seeks neutrality but is unwillingly involved as the only Vilas son is drafted and dies in the Union army and daughter Melora bears Ellyat's child. The central symbol is the fanatic Kansan John Brown, rather bungling and ineffective in life, but in death a generative force compelling frightful sacrifice in order to eliminate human slavery. From the holocaust Benét sees a nation emerge, united once again to greater creative effort.

Western Star (1943). As *John Brown's Body* depicted the American drive toward unity and national fulfillment, this sequel was to unfold what Benét considered as the other crucial element in American life, the compulsion to movement and individual fulfillment. The published work of about two hundred pages was only the first of ten contemplated books that would trace the westward trek from its origins in England to the closing of the frontier about 1880. The colonial era from the initial British settlements at Jamestown and Plymouth to the eve of the Puritan witch hunts is here related in verse through historical characters such as John Smith and Thomas Morton and through fictional characters such as cockney Dickon Heron and stiffly pious Matthew Lanyard. The pervasive concept is Frederick Jackson Turner's thesis of the frontier as the real genesis of America. The dominant symbol is the star beckoning the adventurers westward with the lure of the American myth.

PROSE. "The Devil and Daniel Webster" (1936) is one of the best-known American short stories of this century. The Faust theme becomes a classic American fable set in early nineteenth-century New Hampshire, and its treatment is as poetic as any of Benét's verse. Jabez Stone, a farmer harassed by poor crops, sells his soul to Mr. Scratch (the devil) for a promise of ten years' prosperity. Daniel Webster, with consummate oratory, argues for the soul of Jabez before a ghastly jury of the damned souls of American traitors, and by appealing to their sense of having been at one time both men and Americans, triumphs over Mr. Scratch. With all their faults Americans are candidates for salvation because of their fundamental humanity, which seeks the greatest good for mankind.

In 1939 "The Devil and Daniel Webster" was produced as an opera with libretto by Benét and music by Douglas Moore. An excellent motion picture, *All That Money Can Buy*, following the story closely, appeared in 1941.

Conrad Aiken (1889–   ). Conrad Potter Aiken was the Savannah-born son of a New England physician practicing in Georgia. He started to write poetry at the age of nine. When Aiken was eleven tragedy struck the household. His father killed his mother and committed suicide. Their son was then sent to live with relatives in New Bedford, Massachusetts. He studied at Harvard, receiving his A.B. in 1912, married, and honeymooned for a year in Europe. Until 1926 he generally resided in England. In recent years he has lived in Massachusetts and New York City.

Aiken has been influenced by many aspects of twentieth-century liberal humanism: such movements as Imagism and Symbolism; such thinkers as Freud, Bergson, Havelock Ellis. From his early years, he was drawn to the work of Poe. Tending toward intense introspection stimulated by psychoanalysis, his persistent theme is the lonely plight of modern consciousness. His most ambitious experimentation in verse was a search during his earlier career for an "absolute" poetry with a clear musical quality. Consequently, he designated many of his pieces as symphonies.

His volumes of poetry include *The Charnel Rose, Senlin: A Biography* (1918), *Brownstone Eclogues* (1942), and *A Letter from Li Po* (1955).

Selected Poems (1961) brings together much of Aiken's best verse.

Senlin: A Biography is the story of an aging city dweller who "goes to work with thoughts of the universe." Senlin wonders about his origins and feels within himself primitive longings and a sense of relationship with an ancient past. There are giant undefined forces apparently working against him: Civilization has confused his basic instincts and left him without the ability to know himself or to communicate with others.

"And in the Hanging Gardens" is a romantic narrative set in oriental palace gardens. Amidst the rain a princess reads her lover's last letter telling of his impending death in a northern desert. While her royal father intoxicates himself with wine, the knave of diamonds, her lover's brother and envoy, stealthily approaches her room.

"The Room" portrays the struggle between creation and destruction. The agony of loss is essential to, in fact it generates, the marvel of creation.

"Changing Mind" states Aiken's abjuration to himself and other poets. In the search for meaning, the quarry lies within the individual psyche.

"The Coming Forth by Day of Osiris Jones" utilizes the structure of the Egyptian *Book of the Dead* as the grave book not of a monarch but of a very ordinary man. He was neither sinner nor saint; he was imperfectly understood; he was only partly self-comprehending: a commonplace being.

"Preludes for Memnon" was inspired by the colossal statue of Amenhotep III at Luxor, Egypt. Cut from a single massive rock, the statue is marred by an earthquake-induced fissure. Thus order is assailed by chaos, art by the vagaries of cosmic indifference. Aiken finds no transcendental meaning. The creative mind of man is the truth of the universe.

"Time in the Rock" states Aiken's strong conviction: In a godless world mankind is charged with enormous responsibilities. Exploration of the world's demands aids the human effort to create.

"Landscape West of Eden," narrated by God, interprets Adam as the yielder to the temptation of knowledge and experience. God and Eve would prefer "fixities," but Adam accepts the inevitability of death and disaster implicit in the challenging grandeur of change.

SHORT STORIES AND AUTOBIOGRAPHICAL PROSE. *The Short Stories of Conrad Aiken* (1950) brings together exceptionally poetic short fiction. Central to almost every one of these stories is man's discovery of evil, death, and love.

"Silent Snow, Secret Snow" studies a child's dream world in the transition from youthful imagination to psychosis. Paul Hasleman, a child of the Deep South who has never seen snow, dreams of snow while his schoolteacher, Miss Buell, talks about the tropics. Gradually Paul's preoccupation with his own secret snow takes him altogether away from the adult world. He flees from the attendant physician to refuge and death, with the snow hissing into his room.

"Mr. Arcularis" arose from Aiken's observation of a shabby, absent-minded little man upon a transatlantic steamer. Apparently recovering from a serious operation, the fictional character is advised by his physician to take a sea voyage. Not until the end does the reader realize that Mr. Arcularis has never left the operating table and that his imaginary sea voyage is a journey into death. The game of chess by a ridiculous parson symbolizes theology, useless to Mr. Arcularis (the soul leaving life) and to Clarice Dean (an angel suggested by a hospital attendant). Lonely and troubled by guilt, Mr. Arcularis passes into infinity.

Ushant: An Essay (1952) is an outstanding example of poetic autobiography. The central character D., actually Aiken himself, refers to Demerest in Aiken's novel *Blue Voyage* (1927). Ushant is a huge rock on the French coast at the opening to the Atlantic of the English Channel, a warning to mariners of dangerous shoals; symbolically it represents arrival and departure, a western limit but also a jumping-off place. This place name is also a pun on "you shan't," a reference both to the Ten Commandments and to the superego. One moment in a ship's bunk is expanded to a stream-of-consciousness review by D. of his life's struggle with art, sex, and self-comprehension. The great trauma of his life was the violent death of his parents. All his career is a vast circular course back to this event and out away from it again in ripples of guilt and compulsion. Against all obstacles D. attempts to live "as richly, and beautifully, as possible."

Edna St. Vincent Millay (1892–1950). Edna St. Vincent Millay was born in Rockland, Maine. Her father was superintendent of schools, and her mother was interested in writing. Miss Millay went to Vassar, and after graduation she lived in Greenwich Village among other artists. She was drawn to the theater and while writing sought to support herself by acting. For a time she performed with the Provincetown Players. In 1923 she married Eugen Boissevain, an importer, and they bought a farm near Austerlitz, New York, where she wrote many of her later poems.

Miss Millay's early volume *Renascence and Other Poems* (1917) won recognition for the lyric, almost jewel-like, quality of her verse.

A Few Figs from Thistles (1920) is closely keyed to the rebellious mood of the "jazz age," which was to characterize the early 1920s.

She turned then to other themes as in *The Harp-Weaver and Other Poems* (1923) which, in addition to the moving title poem, includes a number of sonnets. One of these, "Euclid Alone Has Looked on Beauty Bare," which praises abstract mathematical beauty above the imperfect beauty of all material things, strikingly illustrates a distinctiveness in Miss Millay's thought. In another vein especially in writing about people there are sonnets with an intimate, very personal note.

She wrote the libretto for Deems Taylor's opera *The King's Henchman* (1927) which was performed at the Metropolitan Opera House.

Later volumes are *The Buck in the Snow and Other Poems* (1928), *Fatal Interview*, a sonnet sequence (1931), and *Conversation at Midnight* (1937). After her death a collection of her *Letters* was published (1952).

THE IMAGISTS. When the Englishman T. E. Hulme gathered around him a group of dissatisfied young poets in London in 1909, he began a movement that would strongly affect most of the poetry of the twentieth century. The "School of Images" quickly dissolved but was reorganized in 1912 by Ezra Pound and H.D. (Hilda Doolittle) and included the Englishmen F. S. Flint and Richard Aldington. In 1914 a new magazine, *The Egoist*, published Imagist poems by these poets as well as by Amy Lowell, John Gould Fletcher, William Carlos Williams, and others. In the same year Pound edited the first Imagist anthology, *Des Imagistes*. In America, Alfred Kreymborg helped establish magazines which printed Imagist verse.

The Imagists set forth their principles as follows:

1. Direct treatment of the "thing" whether subjective or objective.
2. To use absolutely no word that does not contribute to the presentation.
3. As regarding rhythm: to compose in the sequence of the musical phrase, not in the sequence of a metronome.

The Imagist poems were characterized by their simple diction, classic brevity, and most of all by the hard, clear image which they presented. The Imagists believed that the image was at the very core of language and that traditional poetry had become weak because it used images not as the real substance of its poetry but rather as ornamentation to ideas. The direct presentation of a pure image, on the other hand, would offer, according to Pound, "an intellectual and emotional complex in an instant of time."

The Imagists drew upon similar forms in Western ancient and medieval poetry, notably the poems of Sappho, Catullus, and Villon. They also looked to the Orient and found inspiration in Chinese and Japanese poetry. Many Imagist poems are similar to the Japanese *haiku,* although the latter was more restricted in subject matter. An important modern influence upon the Imagists was the French *symbolistes* of the mid-nineteenth century. Their use of image was similar but while the *symbolistes* consciously looked for images that would contain symbolic properties, the Imagists tried to create images that would stand in and for themselves.

The most important contribution of the Imagists to twentieth-century poetry was their spreading of the use of free verse, that is, verse that is free of a regular metrical pattern. They believed that the rhythmical qualities of a poem should flow from the image rather than being fitted into a preestablished metrical pattern. While traditional blank verse sought to duplicate the rhythms of speech, free verse, according to the Imagists, was closer to the rhythms of music.

Amy Lowell took over the leadership of the movement from Pound in 1915 and published three annual anthologies entitled *Some Imagist Poems.* After 1917 many of the Imagists, as well as many poets who were influenced by the movement, began searching for other forms that would better express the more complex demands they were making on their poetry.

Amy Lowell (1874–1925). Amy Lawrence Lowell was born in Brookline, Massachusetts, of a distinguished family which had produced James Russell Lowell and other notable figures. Miss Lowell was educated in private schools and by foreign travel. It was not until she was twenty-eight years old that she decided to devote herself to poetry. She studied verse for the next eight years and in 1912 published her first volume, *A Dome of Many-Coloured Glass.* She soon became identified with the Imagist movement. Miss Lowell was a strong advocate of free verse and helped to spread its use among American poets. She devoted much of her later life to a notable and appreciative biography, *John Keats* (1925).

Complete Poetical Works (1955) brings together poems mostly written in her thirties and forties.

"Patterns" from *Men, Women, and Ghosts* (1916) is her best-known piece, illustrating her major theme. A free-verse interior monologue spoken by a lady presumably of the nineteenth century protests the rigid social patterns that compel her stylish restraint when her natural instincts urge her to live with unashamed passion.

A Critical Fable (1922) wittily imitates James Russell Lowell's *Fable for Critics* in an imaginary dialogue with the nineteenth-century poet. A score of poets of the 1920s are amusingly dissected.

"Lilacs" from *What's O'Clock* (1925) was her own favorite. It is an Imagistic evocation of the May-blooming lilacs of New England; and technically it is notable for its polyphonic style.

H.D. (1886–1961). Hilda Doolittle was born in Bethlehem, Pennsylvania, and was educated at private schools and at Bryn Mawr College. In 1911 she went to Europe for a projected summer vacation, but she never returned to this country except for brief visits. In 1913 she married the English novelist and poet, Richard Aldington, a fellow Imagist.

Collected Poems (1940) contains most of H.D.'s verse. She was an Imagist throughout her career. Untouched by two catastrophic wars, her poetry maintains always a delicate, flawless imagery, seeming to contain no message except the sensuous beauty of the world. She sought a classic Greek clarity, "sweet, bare, chill to the touch."

John Gould Fletcher (1886–1950). A native of Little Rock, Arkansas, and a Harvard graduate, John Gould Fletcher lived in England from 1908 until 1933. With his return to this country he became a leading figure among the Southern Agrarian poets. In his later works he attempted a lyric mysticism toward his native Arkansas and the American Southwest, in volumes including *South Star* (1941) and *Burning Mountain* (1946); but disappointment with the New World as well as the Old World caused him to take his own life.

Selected Poems (1938) consists almost entirely of his verse written as an expatriate. His poetry until the late 1920s was uniformly Imagistic, but thereafter gradually developed toward more traditional forms and themes. Fletcher was especially interested in the kindred arts of painting and music. Much of his verse sought the clear pictorial quality, while other poems imitated the contrapuntal effects of music.

Alfred Kreymborg (1883–   ). A native New Yorker, Alfred Kreymborg was active in the establishment of the little magazines so important in the literary life of the early twentieth century. In 1913 he started *The Glebe* as a vehicle for Imagist poetry, and he followed in 1914 with *Others* and in 1921 with *Broom.* He was an important critic and editor, particularly with *The American Caravan,* annuals of contemporary writing which he edited from 1927 to 1936. He was also active in the experimental theater and worked with the Provincetown Players and the Federal Theater Project.

Selected Poems, 1912–1944 (1945) includes many Imagist poems which dominated his verse until the late 1920s, when he began to move toward the sonnet and more conventional poetry.

THE AGRARIANS. The Southern renaissance of the twentieth century produced a remarkable group of poets at Vanderbilt University in Nashville, Tennessee. In 1922 several of these poets began the publication *The Fugitive*, and the poets of the group were henceforth known as the "Fugitives" or as the "Agrarians" because of their strong feelings about the traditional relationship of men and the land.

The Agrarians were strongly influenced by the ideas of T. S. Eliot; and they felt, like Eliot, the terrible loss of hope in the modern world and the need for tradition and a unified myth structure which men could look to as a guiding force for action. In the modern industrial world which had so abruptly cut itself off from traditional values, they sought to reaffirm the principles and the passions that existed in the antebellum South. Also they felt the need for re-establishing the ties between man and nature that had been broken by the rise of the industrial state.

The poetry of the group is often scholarly, but also makes use of regional material such as folk traditions, Civil War stories, and ballads. The poets were closely associated with the New Criticism, and John Crowe Ransom became a leading American spokesman for this movement (see Chapter 8).

John Crowe Ransom (1888–   ). A clergyman's son, born in Pulaski, Tennessee, John Crowe Ransom received his A.B. from Vanderbilt in 1909 and then proceeded to Oxford as a Rhodes scholar. Except for service with the field artillery in World War 1 and a year (1931–32) as a Guggenheim Fellow, he taught English at Vanderbilt from 1914 to 1937. In the latter year he became professor of poetry at Kenyon College, from which he retired in 1958. While a young instructor at Vanderbilt he was one of the founders of the Fugitives. Since then he has been acknowledged by the Agrarians as their leader. In 1939 he founded the *Kenyon Review*, one of the most distinguished of literary quarterlies. In 1951 Ransom received the Bollingen Prize for poetry. His first volume of verse, *Poems about God* (1919), was followed by several other volumes including *Chills and Fever* (1924) and *Two Gentlemen in Bonds* (1926).

Selected Poems (1945) includes forty-two of his poems from three previous volumes. "All my poems end inconclusively," Ransom has stated. He might have said "ironically," for his pervasive theme is the discrepancy between human hopes and human realizations. Technically, his poems are remarkable experiments avoiding familiar poetic expectancies in favor of muscular, surprising rhythms and a condensed, richly suggestive diction. He is often concerned with the loss of tradition in the modern world.

"Bells for John Whiteside's Daughter," probably his best-known poem, is a lament for the death of a little girl. The poem is built upon paradoxes: the child who is simultaneously a noisy youngster and a sweet young lady, the adults who were annoyed at her gaiety and now at her silence in death, the conundrum of the quick and the dead. Refusing to say the conventional things, the poet suggests a genuine flesh-and-blood child, and the true, though guilt-conscious, response of adults.

"Janet Waking" suggests a double vision partly by the use of two types of language. Beginning in a conversational tone, the poem seems to describe the early morning of a young girl who wakes to the thought of her pet hen. With the fourth stanza, however, the tone changes to a more comic one, almost mock epic, which progresses to the child's real sense of tragedy. The double vision occurs to readers who sympathize with the emotional experience of the child, but realize how small this event will be in her life.

"Conrad in Twilight" is an unsentimental picture of the aging of a Southerner. Decay and decline are mirrored in man and Nature.

"Armageddon" portrays the inconclusive struggle between the ascetic Christ and the hedonistic anti-Christ. The opposite pulls in man's nature can never be reconciled, nor can any but momentary happiness occur. Especially notable is the archaic vocabulary conferring strange brilliance upon a hopeless conflict.

"Blue Girls" begins as a charming picture of schoolgirls innocently reveling in their youth and loveliness, but the poem ends by contemplating how transitory that charm is.

"Piazza Piece," though brief, is a tragic irony of two lives. The aging gentleman yearns for the girl's beauty but is thwarted by his gray years. The girl, wistfully awaiting her "true love," is a victim of impossibly romantic sentimentalism.

"Dog" is a mock-heroic description of a dog attacking a bull and being driven off by Old Hodge, the owner of the dog. While the human is annoyed at the whole silly business, the dog glowers at this vulgar settling of a vigorous struggle.

"Survey of Literature" pokes fun at courses which survey literature by concentrating on biographical data. This poem expresses the essence of the New Criticism which concentrates on the literature itself and not the milieu in which it was written.

John Peale Bishop (1892–1944). A native of Charles Town, West Virginia, John Peale Bishop graduated from Princeton University and spent eleven years as an expatriate in Paris. Upon his return he displayed versatility as a critic, fictionalist, and poet. In 1943 he was Library of Congress consultant in comparative literature. The Bishop Prize contest, established after his death, led to the founding of the *Southern Vanguard* (1947), which was edited by Allen Tate.

Collected Poems (1948) reveals Bishop as the most thoroughgoing symbolist poet among the Agrarians. Although an outstanding lyricist, Bishop manifests a ceremonial formality and a cool precision that militate against wide popular recognition. Like his fellow Agrarians, he sees rootless urbanism, pervasive industrialism, and the triumph of capitalism as degrading man and vitiating his purposes.

Donald Davidson (1893–1968). Donald Grady Davidson was born at Campbellsville, Tennessee. He studied under John Crowe Ransom at Vanderbilt University, and from 1920 until his death was a professor at Vanderbilt.

Davidson has proved the most conservative and most defiantly regional of the Agrarians. He was the most vociferous in *I'll Take My Stand* (1930) and scathingly denounced the economy of the North in *The Attack on Leviathan* (1938). His most notable verse appears in *The Tall Men* (1927) and in *Lee in the Mountains* (1938), narrative and descriptive appraisals of the Southern past, with angry diatribes against the debased contemporary period. The first of these two volumes celebrates the pioneers who tamed the Southern wilderness with the plough and the long rifle. In the second volume, Lee, as president of the college in Lexington, Virginia, still believes implacably in the cause of the Confederacy but accepts God's will and pleads for a Southland united by bonds of history and blood, religiously attached to the fruitful soil.

Allen Tate (1899–   ). John Orley Allen Tate was born in Winchester, Kentucky. At Vanderbilt University he was active among the Fugitives. A Guggenheim fellowship made possible his stay in Paris, 1928–29. Since then he has shone as one of the most distinguished of American critics and poets. After teaching at various Southern institutions he was resident fellow in writing at Princeton, 1939–42; holder of the Library of Congress chair of poetry, 1943–44; editor of *Sewanee Review*, 1944–46. From 1947 to 1951 he taught at New York University, and since that date has been a professor at the University of Minnesota. In 1956 he received the Bollingen Prize for poetry.

Tate is an important disciple of T. S. Eliot, from whom he has accepted the metaphor of the "waste land" of twentieth-century existence. The same terse intellectuality, allusive force, ellipsis to the point of obscurity, and bold imagery of Eliot appear in Tate's verse. Eliot led Tate into an extensive study of Dante and eventually into Catholicism in 1950. Tate differs from his master in a much stronger emotional impact, and his deep commitment to the American South contrasts with Eliot's flight from America.

Poems, 1922–1947 (1948) shows perhaps less variety than is found in most major poets, but the repeated themes of loyalty to the past, detestation of the present, and the profound need for an informing faith are impressive and memorable.

"Aeneas at Washington" likens the Northern destruction of the Southern agrarian republic to the sack of Troy by the Greeks. Dispossessed, the loyal Southerner has no proper abode but, like Aeneas, is an outcast wanderer from his native land.

"Message from Abroad" tells of the Southerner in Europe who seeks the European past because his own American past has been destroyed.

"To the Lacedemonians" is spoken by a Confederate veteran on the eve of an old-soldiers' reunion. The modern Southerner is a total alien to the old Rebel. The veteran had fought for his land and his beliefs, but today's Southerners have succumbed to the Yankee technology and materialism.

"Ode to the Confederate Dead," Tate's best-known poem, presents a contemporary Southerner peering through a cemetery gate at the obliterated gravestones of the buried Confederates. These dead died for principles; they were the doers of heroic deeds. A skeptic, a scoffer against any and all absolutes and impossible ideals, the modern watcher turns away. He cannot understand these anonymous dead, and he has nothing to offer to or against their valorous belief.

"Seasons of the Soul," to the memory of John Peale Bishop, is the major long poem by Tate. Issued in 1944, during the war years, it scrutinizes the spiritual plight of Western man. The epigraph comes from Dante, and many of the allusions refer to *The Inferno*. The poem begins with summer and the capitulation of France to the Nazis. The tortured soul needs some protection against the world's monstrous forces. Autumn following is the time of ghosts, with the individual alive only for the moment and incapable of meaningful unity with his past. In winter the poet finds religion and love dead; all that remains is a sensual rapture of the body. With spring the speaker suffers a hopelessness that is reminiscent of the April mood at the outset of Eliot's *Waste Land*. He pleads with Santa Monica, Mother of Silences, to tell him if he is dying into absolute nothingness or into a rebirth in grace. By her silence, she leaves the outcome in doubt.

"Winter Mask," to the memory of W. B. Yeats, is a wartime poem that finds despair in the nature of man himself, that creature mysteriously compelled to self-frustration and self-destruction.

"Retroduction to American History" proclaims that man needs myth, but that modern life has reduced the old myths to tinselly decoration and has provided no new mythical concepts to give importance or continuity to man's existence. "The Meaning of Life" seeks to strike a balance between thought and action. Thought can stifle action but action without thought can become misdirected. These are dark growing powers within us that lust after experience and these powers must be willfully allowed to ripen.

Merrill Moore (1903–57). Son of John Trotwood Moore, noted for his writings on Tennessee life and legend, Merrill Moore took his medical degree (1928) from Vanderbilt, where he was an active member of the Fugitives. He later taught at Harvard, became a Harvard research fellow in psychiatry, and until his death was a well-known practicing psychiatrist in Boston.

Moore is included with this group because of his strong early identification with the Fugitives, but his poetry, always an avocation, quickly deviated from the Agrarian position. Moore wrote nothing but sonnets in his later years. He claimed to write at least one sonnet a day in his adult years and he learned shorthand so that he could dash them down between medical appointments. *M* (1938) actually prints one thousand sonnets. The psychiatrist-poet is frequently humorous, but every mood is manifested in his sonnets. He attempts an enormous number of experiments in rhyme, meter, and structure.

Robert Penn Warren (1905–   ). A native of Guthrie, Kentucky, Robert Penn Warren graduated in 1925 from Vanderbilt University, where he was an active member of the Fugitives. After graduate study at Yale and the University of California, he went to Oxford from 1928 to 1930 as a Rhodes scholar. From 1930 to 1942 he was a professor at Southwestern College (Memphis), Vanderbilt, Louisiana State University, and the University of Minnesota. In 1935 he helped found the *Southern Review*. In 1944 he was appointed to the Library of Congress chair in poetry. Subsequently he taught at Yale from 1950–56, and again since 1961.

Warren is an accomplished writer of fiction (see Chapter 5) as well as poetry, and is also known for his contributions to the "New Criticism" (see Chapter 8). His reputation as an important novelist has often obscured his achievements as a poet. Like his fellow Agrarians, Warren believes that the Old South created a balanced social system because it permitted "the traditional man to define himself as human by setting up codes, concepts of virtue, obligations, and by accepting the risks of his humanity." But he has a fuller realization than others of the Fugitive group of the shortcomings of the Old South. Most of his verse (unlike his fiction) is less regional than that of other Americans. The perennial concern of his poetry is the loneliness of the individual in a cosmos lacking in transcendental harmony.

Thirty-six Poems (1935), his first volume, omits most of his work from the Fugitive period.

"The Return: An Elegy" projects, in the fashion of modernist verse, the stream of consciousness of a man rushing by train to his dying mother. The mental conflict is between reality and unreality, the drive toward maturation against the wish for the protected status of childhood. Other themes are the guilt complex, rage against the transience of life and beauty, the burdens of responsibility to others and to oneself.

"Kentucky Mountain Farm" consists of seven eloquent lyrics upon the natural forces of Warren's home soil—the generations of men, the seasonal cycles, the achingly impersonal beauty of Nature.

"History" tells of an invader on the brink of victory before a fertile plain. At the moment of triumph he realizes his spiritual emptiness and takes refuge in the thought: "The act / Alone is pure."

"Letter from a Coward to a Hero" relates the attempt of a self-confessed "gun-shy" man to understand his boyhood friend who is now a vaunted hero. The writer praises the valiant but wonders if the unthinking hero by his simple devotion to an abstract virtue may not bring disaster.

Eleven Poems on the Same Theme (1942) plays remarkable variations upon one theme: the equation of love with innocence, disillusionment with knowledge.

"Monologue at Midnight" establishes the theme as a lover seeks to resolve his attitude toward his beloved in a mixed sense of joy and guilt.

"Original Sin" anatomizes the attempt of the protagonist to escape from guilt feelings about his past. At the end he becomes half reconciled to the assurance that "it" will continue to haunt him.

"Crime" depicts a sinner's successful attempt at escaping his guilty past, a murder, but the price is his sanity.

"Terror" arose from Warren's residence in Rome as World War II exploded. It attributes the self-imposed horrors of this age to man's present incapacity for genuine living. Without "an adequate definition of terror," they lack adequate definition of love and life.

Selected Poems, 1923–1943 (1944) contained one important new poem.

"The Ballad of Billie Potts" arises from the folklore of Warren's home country. Early in the nineteenth century Billie Potts maintained an inn in western Kentucky. After appraising his guests, he would steer them down the road to an accomplice who would rob and kill them. His son, Little Billie, bungles an attempted murder and flees west to make his fortune. Affluent, he returns ten years later but conceals his identity to "tease 'em and fun 'em." For the stranger's wealth Billie unknowingly and brutally murders his own son. The coarse folk ballad narrative is set off by an ironic commentary on the compulsion of guilt, flight, and return, and the search for the life source ending in death.

Brother to Dragons: A Tale in Verse and Voices (1953) is a poem of over two hundred pages in which eleven speakers, including "R.P.W.," discuss a shocking true-life crime of 1811. Critics have not yet come to an agreement on the value of this work. Some believe it to be one of the great long poems of our times, while others dismiss it as the sort of thing better treated in a Warren novel.

The brothers Lilburn and Isham Lewis, nephews of Thomas Jefferson and coproprietors of a Kentucky plantation, butcher a slave named George for a trivial offense. They make a pact to kill each other at their mother's grave, but Isham flees after slaying Lilburn. Later, Isham is reported dying in the Battle of New Orleans.

Warren was fascinated that Jefferson, believer in natural man and in human perfectability, was completely silent, as far as we know, about this monstrous criminality among his close relatives. The Jefferson of the poem is shaken to his depths and can take solace only in a resignation that pain and guilt are our mortal lot. "R.P.W." propounds that man is an inextricable mixture of good and evil. The truth is not the pure light of innocence or the unrelieved darkness of sin but "the shade of the human condition." Warren is supremely successful in a dialogue which captures the unique flavor of each character; the soaring idealism and abysmal horror of Jefferson; the earthy patois of Aunt Cat, Lilburn's Negro mammy; the girlish pleadings of Lilburn's wife, Laetitia; the gentle sorrow of Lucy, Lilburn's mother.

Promises: Poems 1954–1956 (1957) won numerous awards, including the Pulitzer Prize. As the title indicates, this volume envisions greater possibilities for the achievement of goodness and happiness than previous Warren verse. Warren here relates in easy colloquial speech his own personal and family experiences.

"To a Little Girl, One Year Old, in a Ruined Fortress" consists of five poems centered about his daughter Rosanna with her parents on the Italian seacoast north of Rome. The decaying fortification and the nearby hunchback with his deformed child symbolize the spent civilization of the Old World. Juxtaposed with these images is golden-haired, laughing Rosanna, emblem of renewal and promise.

"What Was the Promise That Smiled from the Maples at Evening?" is an older man's reminiscence of his boyhood retreat into the lonely darkness away from the love and security proffered by his parents. He assures his own son that the men of the past "died only that every promise might be fulfilled." Even if they failed and unaccountably withdrew from the world made for them, they gained peace and meaning in their struggles.

"Court Martial" examines a child's awakening to violence and guilt. Playing with his toy soldiers, he elicits from his grandfather an account of the summary lynching of bushwhackers during the Civil War. Suddenly he passes judgment upon the aged man, and his childhood innocence has vanished.

"Dark Night of" seems a Warren short story in verse. A twelve-year-old boy finds a dying old tramp in the woods, and the boy's strong curiosity compels the feeble tramp to slouch away. Not to the boy but to the tramp comes illumination: the "awfulness of joy" succeeding the "absolute and glacial purity of despair."

You, Emperors and Others: Poems 1957–1960 (1960) takes its title from two groups of poems, one set addressed to "you," the other set dealing with Roman emperors. Actually the entire series is concerned with the definition of the lonely self, an acceptance of what seems the pointless tragedy of human existence.

"The Letter about Money, Love, or Other Comfort, If Any" tells of a sinister stranger who gives the narrator a letter that he must deliver "by hand only." Fruitlessly pursuing the addressee throughout the world, he finally leaves the letter under a rock near the supposed hermitage of the addressee. The narrator is actually tracking his other self.

"A Vision: Circa 1880" scrutinizes the Kentucky boyhood of Warren's father. The poet yearns to speak to his father as a boy, but the unheeding youngster enters the shady wood confident of his future.

WRITERS OF LIGHT AND HUMOROUS VERSE

The thirties were a time of general decline in serious poetry, but light and humorous verse by exceptionally talented people became popular. It was aimed at the city dweller and was sophisticated and sharply polished. It is perhaps characteristic of the American experience that in times of great social distress, such as were these Depression days, humorists are at their best. This phenomenon illustrates Mark Van Doren's lines: "Wit is the only wall / Between us and the dark."

Louis Untermeyer (1885–   ). Disdain of geometry prevented Louis Untermeyer's graduating from high school in his native New York. In the family jewelry business he worked his way up to vice-president before resigning in 1923 to devote himself to writing. After two years abroad he began a career of writing and editing that would bring him a reputation as one of the most active and influential poetry anthologists of this century. He has lectured at many American universities and during 1961–63 was poetry consultant at the Library of Congress.

Collected Parodies (1926) represents only one phase of a voluminous and varied career in verse, but these superb burlesques of contemporary poets pinpoint many of the pretensions and absurdities of the explosive "new poetry" and are among Untermeyer's best-remembered works.

Dorothy Parker (1893–1968). Dorothy Rothschild was born at West End, New Jersey, and was educated in New York City at Blessed Sacrament Convent. In 1917 she married Edwin Parker and became drama critic of *Vanity Fair*. From its 1925 founding she was consistently a leading light of *The New Yorker* as both author and critic. Her caustic wit, the scourge of the literary world, is typified by her comment on a well-known actress: "She ran the whole gamut of emotion from A to B." After her divorce in 1928, she married Alan Campbell in 1933.

Her poems appear in several volumes including *Enough Rope* (1926) and *Death and Taxes* (1931), and her stories also have been collected.

Not So Deep As a Well (1936). Sparkling wit suffuses many pieces that toy with sentimentalism and then dash cold water over the romantic yearnings. Mercilessly and with a biting sardonic humor, Dorothy Parker dissects stupidity and pretense. Perhaps the most witty of all American women authors, she was scornful of the frailties and blunderings of a middle-class society. The title of this collection of poems is a quotation from the bitter dying speech of Mercutio in *Romeo and Juliet*.

Ogden Nash (1902–71). A native of Rye, New York, Ogden Nash studied for a time at Harvard, tried selling bonds, advertising, and other careers before finally settling on writing light verse, beginning with *Hard Lines* (1931). Nash's zany poetizing is seen in characteristic form, with its surprises in rhyme and in word usage, in *I'm a Stranger Here Myself* (1938). His verse became highly popular, especially in the society world of New York. Nash wrote the charming lyrics for the distinctive and beautiful Kurt Weill songs in the musical *One Touch of Venus* (1943).

Verses from 1929 on (1959) contains many extremely funny pieces. Nash makes his rules as he goes along. Very amusing is his habit of misspelling words or inventing new ones so that they will rhyme. He presents in this volume a wide variety of seemingly insignificant dilemmas and incidents of modern life and transforms them into humorous and human situations.

Phyllis McGinley (1905–   ). A native of Ontario, Oregon, Phyllis McGinley was educated at the universities of Utah and California. In 1937 she married Charles Hayden. Her first volume, *On the Contrary* (1934), exhibited her talent. She has been acclaimed as one of the major light-verse practitioners.

Times Three: Selected Verse from Three Decades (1960) is the only volume wholly devoted to light verse to earn a Pulitzer Prize. W. H. Auden and many other serious poets highly respect her poetic competence and her shrewd appraisal of everyday life. Recognizing the real pains and injustices of this era, Miss McGinley nonetheless views all with a smile and graciously affirms that living today can be tolerable, even pleasurable, for those maintaining a sense of humor.

VARIOUS DISTINCTIVE POETS OF THE PERIOD

Louise Bogan (1897–1970). Born at Livermore Falls, Maine, Louise Bogan briefly attended Boston University in 1915–16. She lectured both in this country and abroad, received many honorary degrees, and won the Bollingen Prize in 1955. In 1944 she was a fellow in American letters at the Library of Congress. *Selected Criticism* (1955) collects much of her significant prose. Her books of poetry include *Body of This Death, Dark Summer,* and *The Sleeping Fury.*

Collected Poems 1923–53 (1954) shows Louise Bogan using traditional verse forms and their variations to express restrained metaphysical poetry. Dealing less with broad contemporary issues than with personal perception of melancholy about the past, her poems have a delicate quality beneath their forceful diction.

"The Dream" delves into the mystery of the subconscious. With understanding for the suffering of man, she tames the poem with traditional structure, and finally tames the "terrible horse" of her dream, without destroying its emotional impact.

Kenneth Fearing (1902–61). Kenneth Flexner Fearing was the son of an Oak Park, Illinois, attorney. Leaving the University of Wisconsin in 1924, he tried many odd jobs in Chicago before going to New York as a free-lance writer. As a popular novelist he wrote extensively, triumphing with a murder mystery, *The Big Clock* (1946), later made into a movie. His first volume of poetry, *Angel Arms,* appeared in 1929.

New and Selected Poems (1956) with its strikingly ironic pieces seems a combination of e. e. cummings and the earlier John Dos Passos. The language is flavorfully colloquial, the typography can be as impish as that of cummings, and the technique is a montage of documentary impact. Fearing's two most popular poems are typical. "Dirge" in comic-strip patter is a mock lament for an obscure little office worker dazzled with impossible dreams of becoming an executive type. "Portrait (2)" derides a dead executive, a successful tycoon who is branded as wholly artificial like some mass production gadget.

Laura Riding (1901–   ). A native New Yorker, Laura Riding was long an expatriate in England and in Mallorca, where she collaborated with Robert Graves, the British poet, in *A Survey of Modernist Poetry* (1927).

Collected Poems (1938) and subsequent verse have shown her a strongly independent personality who demands that rhythms and verse forms fit her subject and thought. Although calling herself a "joke-less modern mind," Miss Riding is often wryly humorous. Her chief assertion, as in "One self," is the prime necessity of the integration of self into a creative wholeness.

Sara Teasdale (1884–1933). Educated privately in her native St. Louis, Missouri, Sara Teasdale displayed an early talent for highly sensitive verse. *Helen of Troy and Other Poems* (1911) won her fame in literary circles and involved her in love affairs with the poets John Hall Wheelock and Vachel Lindsay. In 1914 she married a St. Louis businessman, Ernst Filsinger, whom she divorced in 1929.

Like Lizette Reese, Miss Teasdale was a superb craftsman of delicate, perceptive verse that today is largely out of fashion. Her recurrent theme is the poignancy and impermanence of love, perhaps best illustrated in *Love Songs* (1917).

Elinor Wylie (1885–1928). Descendant of a family distinguished in Pennsylvania history and society, Elinor Hoyt was born in Somerville, New Jersey. She was educated at noted finishing schools in Philadelphia and Washington. In 1905 she began an unhappy first marriage from which she eloped with Horace Wylie, whom she married in 1912 after the suicide of her first husband. Her third marriage, in 1923, was to William Rose Benét, the poet and editor. Professionally she retained the name of her divorced second husband. She was an acknowledged leader of intellectual salons in New York and London.

The titles of Elinor Wylie's volumes of poetry suggest their moods: *Nets to Catch the Wind* (1921), *Black Armour* (1923), *Trivial Breath* (1928), and a collection of sonnets, *Angels and Earthly Creatures* (1929). She also wrote novels essentially in the manner of her poetry, the best known being *The Venetian Glass Nephew* (1925).

Elinor Wylie's verse is marked by precise craftsmanship and sharpness of image. She was inclined to sophisticated irony, yet she was capable of emotional intensity.

In "Unfinished Portrait," she talks about her feelings for someone, introducing color into the verse as though she was painting a portrait. In "Pretty Words," Miss Wylie writes, "I love words opalescent, cool, and pearly, / Like midsummer moths, and honied words like bees, / Gilded and sticky, with a little sting."

Her interest in words tended to favor the use of forms such as the ballad and sonnet. But she used more experimental forms also, as in "The Heart's Desire," which is on the borderline between poetry and prose.

Langston Hughes (1902–67). A native of Joplin, Missouri, James Langston Hughes attended Columbia University and graduated from Lincoln University in 1929. His early experiences as a seaman form the basis for his first autobiography, *The Big Sea* (1940). Residence in Italy, France, Russia, and Mexico provided material for a continuation of his life story, *I Wonder as I Wander* (1956). Vachel Lindsay was the first to read Hughes's verse publicly and to call it to national attention. In 1925 Hughes received the first poetry prize for a Negro poet from *Opportunity* magazine. Many subsequent awards and grants followed, including a Guggenheim fellowship in 1925 and the Ainsfield-Wolfe Award in 1954 for the best book on race relations. Public recognition was accorded to his lyrics for the musical version of Rice's *Street Scene* (1946). Among his most delightful works are collections of humorous prose pieces, *Simple Speaks His Mind* (1950) and *Simple Takes a Wife* (1953).

Selected Poems (1959) contains many of his pieces which are brusque depictions or protests of second-rate citizenship emphasized in the day-by-day buffetings of his race, especially in Harlem. Much of Hughes's work employs jazz rhythms, especially *Montage of a Dream Deferred* (1951) with its bebop and boogie-woogie effects. Always he lets the poetic mood, whether blues or sardonic humor, determine the cadence instead of conventional verse forms. The exciting and original rhythms of Hughes's poems have caused many to be set to music and to be translated into other languages.

Countee Cullen (1903–46). While in high school in his native New York City, Countee Cullen was already publishing significant poetry in *The Crisis,* organ of the National Association for the Advancement of Colored People. He received his A.B. from New York University in 1925 and his M.A. from Harvard the next year. From 1926 to 1928 he was assistant editor of *Opportunity,* a Negro journal. From 1934 until his death he taught French in New York junior high schools. For the early part of the twentieth century Cullen has been the outstanding American Negro poet employing traditional forms, although he has not been as well known as other less conventional poets. Many critics feel that Cullen was at his best in Keatsian lyrics totally free of racial concerns, but his own consuming theme was the racial question.

The Black Christ (1929), his ambitious long poem, moves from indignation and negation to acceptance and affirmation. Daily he has witnessed the crucifixion of the Negro in American life, but he comes to fair haven with the crucified white Christ. In suffering and atonement there is no color line.

John Neihardt (1881–). A native of Sharpsburg, Illinois, John Gneisenau Neihardt graduated from Nebraska Normal College in 1897. After teaching and farming, he lived with the Omaha Indians from 1901 to 1907, thereby obtaining the materials for most of his subsequent writings. In 1921 he was officially designated as poet laureate of Nebraska by the state legislature. Since 1923 he has taught poetry at the University of Nebraska and the University of Missouri, except for service with the Office of Indian Affairs (1944–48).

A Cycle of the West (1949) collects five epic narrative poems dealing with the conflicts between the Plains Indians and the encroaching white settlers. Best known is the first, *The Song of Hugh Glass* (1915), based upon a true episode of 1823 when this wounded trapper, left for dead by Jim Bridger, crawls many miles to safety. The cycle conceives of two cultures, both noble, crashing against each other by the vagaries of fate to create a heroic age but also a tragic downfall of the aborigines. Though occasionally drooping in prosaic passages, the cycle contains memorable, authentic pictures of historical personalities and impressive descriptions of the untamed landscape, Indian customs, and the vast herds of bison. Nothing else in American literature matches its broad sweep of that bygone era, but its elemental panorama and its epic attitude do not find extensive recognition in mid-twentieth century.

William Ellery Leonard (1876–1944). Born in Plainfield, New Jersey, William Ellery Leonard obtained a B.A. from Boston University in 1898, an M.A. from Harvard in 1899, and a Ph.D. from Columbia in 1904. In 1906 he began the teaching of English at the University of Wisconsin, continuing until his death. One of his most important contributions was his excellent translation of Lucretius in 1916.

Two Lives (1923) is a sonnet sequence. It explores all the nuances of Leonard's own tragic marriage. Two years after her wedding in 1909 his wife, fearing insanity, committed suicide. The passionate intensity, utter frankness, and Freudian overtones won the work wide recognition.

The Locomotive-God (1927) is an extraordinary and outstanding psychoanalytical autobiography. The title refers to a childhood fright that caused Leonard to identify a locomotive with God. His sensitive warped nature was further complicated by acute agoraphobia that after 1922 made him virtually a prisoner in his residence. The tensions affecting his entire career were his puritanical upbringing (as son of a New England cleric) and his vehement rebellion into free thought.

George Sterling (1868–1926). George Sterling was born in Sag Harbor, New York. From 1908 to 1915 he was a leading figure in the artists' colony in Carmel, California. His works, chiefly poetry, include *Testimony of the Suns* (1907), *The Evanescent City* (1915), *Lilith* (1919), *Sails and Mirage* (1921), and a biography, *Robinson Jeffers: the Man and the Artist* (1926).

The Testimony of the Suns and Other Poems (1907) contains characteristic shorter poems.

"The Summer of the Gods" is an exquisite sonnet in which the poet imagines that he sees Ulysses "Lured by strange music to the hidden West." He states his conviction that we have lost the days when there was a mystery "whose kindly veils / Fell as a radiance on sea and shore."

Lilith (1919) is a dramatic poem in four acts set in medieval Europe.

It tells of King Urlan and his son Tancred, and of Lilith who in her unearthly beauty appears suddenly to both of them. Alluring and enchanting, she casts her spell first upon Urlan and later upon Tancred. The story develops with many original details, and with an intensity comparable with that of the great romantic poetry of the early nineteenth century. Good and evil, pleasure and pain, the claims of the flesh and of the spirit are sharply contrasted, as the poetic drama's plot unfolds. There is much brilliance in the language, and the brightness and clarity of the images is striking. (Lilith in name and concept appears in ancient Hebraic legends, where she is sometimes referred to as the first wife of Adam.)

Like his friend Robinson Jeffers (of whom he wrote a biography covering the early years), Sterling questioned the trappings of modern civilization. He tended to find his inspiration in myths and magic, in moods and subjects more akin to the past; and this set him apart from the trend of most of his contemporaries. His work must be judged for its memorable lyric and imaginative quality.

John Hall Wheelock (1886–   ). A native of Far Rockaway, New York, John Hall Wheelock was educated at the universities of Harvard, Göttingen, and Berlin. While at Harvard he collaborated with Van Wyck Brooks in *Verses of Two Undergraduates* (1905). In 1911 he began a lifetime association with Charles Scribner's Sons, the publishers, that eventually elevated him to director and treasurer. His steady production over the years brought many poetry prizes, including the Bollingen in 1962.

Collected Poems (1936) and volumes as late as 1961 display one of the most consistent and prolific poetic talents of this century. Traditional in subject and technique, unheeding of fad and fashion, Wheelock has never gained a wide popular audience. Wheelock's main characteristic seems to be a joyful exuberance in confronting the paradoxes of man and nature.

Mark Van Doren (1894–   ). Brother of Carl Van Doren, Mark Van Doren was born in Hope, Illinois. He received the A.B. degree from the University of Illinois in 1914 and the Ph.D. from Columbia in 1920. His lifelong career has been the teaching of English at Columbia. For a time he was literary and film critic for *The Nation*.

Collected Poems (1939) shows Van Doren steeped in the rhythms and subjects of English poetry from the Renaissance and the Romantic era, yet concerned also with daily events of here and now. His poems are marked by superlative workmanship rather than by daring experiment.

Robert P. Tristram Coffin (1892–1955). Robert Peter Tristram Coffin was born in Brunswick, Maine, and New England was deeply present in his blood. After graduation from Bowdoin he went to Princeton and Oxford (as a Rhodes scholar) and saw World War I service in the Army. Afterward he taught English for a time at Wells College, New York, but returned to his native state as Pierce Professor at Bowdoin. His volumes range from the verse of *Golden Falcon* (1929) to the prose of *Maine Doings* (1950).

Strange Holiness (1955) brought popularity to Coffin. Lovingly he savors everything of Maine from its lobster fishermen to its potatoes, from its chilled mountain streams to its farmhouses redolent of fresh pie dough.

Robert Hillyer (1895–1961). A native of East Orange, New Jersey, Robert Silliman Hillyer graduated from Harvard in 1917. After service in World War I he began teaching English at Harvard in 1919. After 1945 he taught at Trinity and Kenyon.

Collected Poems (1961) suggests the traditional academic poet. Hillyer is essentially a neoclassicist. Especially felicitious is his handling of the eighteenth-century heroic couplet, appropriately in verse epistles such as "A Letter to Robert Frost" (1937). Humor, urbanity, and technical skill combine with a certain aloofness and disengagement from the modern world.

Maxwell Bodenheim (1893–1954). As a youth Maxwell Bodenheim left his native Hermanville, Mississippi, for Chicago and then New York. While in Chicago in the twenties, he became part of the literary revolt centered there.

Selected Poems 1914–1944 (1945) displays strong Imagistic tendencies in the earlier verse. During the 1920s Bodenheim proved quite a celebrity with his cynical, iconoclastic attacks upon conventionality and prudery. His mature poems register the plight of the sensitive artist in a brutalized mechanical era. Later poems become increasingly strident about social and political ills of the Depression and the war periods.

Horace Gregory (1898–   ). A native of Milwaukee, Wisconsin, Horace Gregory received his A.B. from the University of Wisconsin in 1923. As a free-lance writer in the 1920s, he was a mainstay of many little magazines and one of the best-known critics and poets of that era. Since 1934 he has taught poetry and criticism at Sarah Lawrence College. He received the Bollingen Prize in 1965. He has been assisted in some of his work by his wife, Marya Zaturenska, who is a gifted poet in her own right. Gregory has been especially adept as a translator, producing impressive renderings of Catullus (1931) and Ovid (1958). His volumes of poetry include *Chelsea Rooming House* (1930), *Poems 1930–1940* (1941), and *Medusa in Gramercy Park* (1961).

Collected Poems (1964) offers many early poems upon lower-class suffering, born of the poet's youthful difficulties and ill health. Later works fully expound the bitterness and destructiveness of existence in the twentieth century; but as in "Chorus for Survival" Gregory romantically insists upon human endurance and the possibility of a better society.

Babette Deutsch (1895–   ). A native New Yorker, Babette Deutsch received her A.B. from Barnard in 1917. She has lectured at Columbia since 1944 and received an honorary degree from that university in 1946. In 1961 she was a Library of Congress consultant in poetry. She has written many books for children and has translated extensively from German and Russian, often with her husband, Avrahm Yarmolinsky. She is a notable chronicler and critic of twentieth-century American poetry.

Collected Poems 1919–1962 (1963) includes poems which are intense impressions and also poems which make imaginative comment on the times through a verse that is highly intellectual but also emotional. Later poems are frequently concerned with social problems.

CHAPTER THREE

The Drama in the Early Twentieth Century

THE NEW THEATER

American drama was to find its true strength in the twentieth century. Few Americans had written for the theater in the nineteenth century, and the drama had not yet become an important part of American literature. There were no playwrights to compare with the great novelists and poets of those years. It was Eugene O'Neill, in a succession of great plays from 1916 on into the 1940s, who more than anyone else gave the American theater its rightful place not only in American literature but in World theater and World literature. At the same time a number of other writers of notable gifts became prominent, each making a distinctive contribution. And in mid-century a new group of outstanding playwrights brought powerful and refreshing points of view, and greatly enriched American drama.

In approaching the writers of the early twentieth century, it is important to have some knowledge of the development of the modern theater in Europe. The term "modern drama" by general consent applies first to the road-breaking works of Henrik Ibsen in nineteenth-century Norway, who—especially in his middle and later periods—explored the deeper motivations of his characters in everyday and also special social situations. The range of modern drama was extended by many other major dramatists. August Strindberg in Sweden started with a realistic emphasis, but later turned to a moving concern with dreamlike fantasies, which called for new stage techniques and gave rise to the school of "expressionists." Expressionism, as developed particularly by Frank Wedekind and Georg Kaiser in the German theater of the early part of the century, used ingenious methods of stagecraft such as bizarre lighting, often with rapid sequences of brief scenes shifting from place to place to convey their meaning. The world about the protagonist fades into symbols, and the subject is frequently the individual thwarted in his quest for self-fulfillment by the modern machine-like impersonality that surrounds him. Another major contributor to the direction of modern drama was Anton Chekov in Russia, whose plays are marked by a unique quality of mood, with a sensitive response to the relationships between individuals. All of these influences were felt, more often indirectly than directly, by American playwrights of the earlier part of the twentieth century.

Among the first American dramatists to sense the appropriateness of these new values for the American theater were William Vaughn Moody (1869–1910) in *The Great Divide* (1906) and especially Clyde Fitch (1865–1909) in his later plays *The Truth* (1907) and *The City* (1909). This new feeling in the theater was soon to be carried forward by the American dramatists to whom we devote this chapter. Another chapter later in the book (Chapter 7) will consider the dramatists of the middle of the twentieth century.

Before turning to individual writers, we want to call attention to the influence of the great course in playwriting conducted at Harvard between 1905 and 1925 by George Pierce Baker. Among those who attended Professor Baker's famous "47 Workshop" were Eugene O'Neill, Sidney Howard, Philip Barry, S. N. Behrman, and also several drama critics and stage designers, all of whom were to give great vitality and distinction to the American theater of the period.

Important in making these new playwrights well known was the "Little Theater" movement, which commenced during the early part of the century and had the enthusiastic support and active participation of groups in various parts of the country. Prominent among these were the Provincetown Players, who in 1916 were the first to produce a play by O'Neill; the Washington Square Players (later the Theatre Guild) in New York; and Chicago's Little Theatre. These and many others introduced the stimulating modern European plays and welcomed the new American dramatists with notable and creative performances.

EUGENE O'NEILL AND HIS WORKS

Eugene O'Neill (1888–1953). Eugene Gladstone O'Neill, the son of James O'Neill, a noted actor, was born in New York City. The family also had a home in New London, Connecticut. Educated at boarding schools and for one year at Princeton, Eugene O'Neill went to sea in 1909, and for a short time stayed in South America. When he came back to New York in 1911, he lived in the simplest lodgings over a saloon, with only odd jobs to support him. During the voyages and in New York he came to know the despairing world of outcasts, dreamers, and derelicts; these experiences are reflected in his early plays and in some written later.

In 1912 O'Neill spent several months in a sanatorium where he was cured of tuberculosis. It was at this time that he wrote his first plays, and it was then that he determined to devote himself to the theater. He studied with George Pierce Baker at Harvard in 1914–15, and in 1916 his short play *Bound East for Cardiff* was produced by the Provincetown Players. With *Beyond the Horizon,* a full-length play produced in 1920, his significance as a dramatist was clear, and later works enhanced this recognition. The Nobel Prize in literature in 1936 confirmed world-wide admiration for his deeply original plays. O'Neill was married three times and had children by his first two marriages, both of which ended in divorce. In his later years he suffered from Parkinson's disease, and wrote under severe handicap until in 1944 he could no longer do creative work. He died in 1953.

O'Neill is unquestionably America's greatest dramatist. He brought to the theater a tragic vision of life, which he expressed in many and varied forms, never repeating himself, always discovering powerful devices for revealing hidden depths of individual personality, and probing the meaning of relationships and situations. He turned almost always to the darker side of life: the pain of loneliness and rejection, the agony deriving from a sense of sin, the gnawing bleakness of frustration, the shattering greed and hypocrisy of the modern world's materialism, the escape into dreams, the perplexity and complexity of love.

In part O'Neill's vision of life was derived from his own tortured existence. There had been much alcoholism in his family, and he himself at various periods drank excessively. His mother had become addicted to narcotics but tried to conceal this from the family. O'Neill's temperament in his early adult years made it difficult for him to adjust to the daily ways of married life, yet in his later years home and marriage became truly right for him.

In studying O'Neill's plays the originality of his creativeness becomes increasingly apparent. He admired and was influenced by some of the leading European dramatists, but he approached his writing from within himself in a succession of plays which continuously reveal new, strong, inventive aspects of his profound individuality.

O'Neill's characters are strikingly alive, and their vitality fills the stage; they are meant for the theater. The language of the plays is vigorous and appropriate, ranging from sordid and violent to reflective and tender. The phrasing is not in itself outstanding, but it achieves its aim. And the plays, somber as almost all of them are, seem filled not with despair but with a struggle to find worthwhile meaning in life's puzzle.

THE EARLY YEARS (1913–20).

Bound East for Cardiff (1916). A short sea play. Yank, a seaman, dies while being consoled by Driscoll, his shipmate, with stories of riotous nights in port.

In the Zone (1916), *The Long Voyage Home* (1916), *Ile* (1917), *The Moon of the Caribbees* (1918). These four one-act sea plays already have many of the qualities which give O'Neill his special distinction. He was now more firmly in control of his material. *The Moon of the Caribbees* is a play of mood and character. In a West Indian port, sailors aboard the S.S. *Glencairn* anticipate shore leave and the pleasures of rum and women. A fatal stabbing darkens the atmosphere, and the liquor is confiscated by the ship's officers. *The Long Voyage Home* tells of the shanghaiing to a doomed ship of Olson, who had yearned for the supposed joys of a rural existence. *In the Zone* finds Smitty suspected of being a German spy because he jealously guards a metal box. Crewmen wrest his treasure from Smitty only to embarrass everyone by discovering the letters of a sentimental, broken love affair. All four plays portray average men sustained by dreams of unattainable and unrealistic happiness. A notable movie under the title *The Long Voyage Home* draws on these four short plays.

Beyond the Horizon (*1918*, 1920). O'Neill's first full-length play. The New York production in 1920 signaled a new era in the American theater.

Robert Mayo has always dreamed of leaving the family farm to sail "beyond the horizon," while his brother, Andrew, stolidly wishes to stay at home and farm. Ruth, loved by Andrew, is attracted to the adventuresome Robert; and the rejected Andrew unwillingly goes to sea. Practical Andrew makes and loses a fortune in wheat in Argentina, and returns to find the farm greatly deteriorated under the impractical Robert, while Ruth, bitterly disappointed, regrets marrying the wrong man. Succeeding again abroad, Andrew comes home to find Robert dying of tuberculosis. Robert will be "free to wander on and on—eternally."

Setting, characters, and tone substantiate the naturalistic denial of man's dreams. The structure is initially sharply defined: the soul of adventure in one brother, security in the other; the goddess of fortune willfully reversing the sought-for fates of both; each act symmetrically arranged with one scene atop a hill commanding a wide horizon, the other scene in the bleak farmhouse. But the subtlety of the drama rests upon the modulations of the dreamers and their delusions. Not understanding themselves, they deceive themselves; Robert believing that "love" has supplanted his earlier dream, Andrew taking refuge in business deals in the outer world that does not truly lure him. The O'Neill concept of tragedy, echoing through all subsequent works, asserts that salvation can be achieved only upon the other side of despair.

Other O'Neill plays of this period are: *The Rope* (1918); *The Dreamy Kid* (1918); *The Straw* (1921).

THE MIDDLE YEARS (1920–33).

The Emperor Jones (1920). The setting is a West Indies island. The central character was evidently suggested to some degree by Henri Christophe, ex-slave and emperor of Haiti early in the nineteenth century.

Using powerful naturalistic dialogue and an expressionistic technique, O'Neill made a sharp break with the traditional theater in *The Emperor Jones*. The play is in eight scenes, with extensive monologues. Brutus Jones, an ex-porter on U. S. Pullman cars, has fled to the island from an American prison where he had been confined as a murderer. The first scene between Jones and Smithers, a vulgar Limey trader, shows O'Neill's command of idiomatic language. Jones declares himself Emperor of the island. When the native subjects of the Emperor rebel against his tyrannous rule, he flees through the jungle toward the coast. Jones asserts that only a silver bullet can slay him. Tom-toms of revolt begin a steady beat that will gradually mount into a feverish pitch. In succeeding scenes, all of which are in the forest, Jones confronts visions of "little formless fears"—the fellow porter he murdered, the white prison guard he killed while escaping, a slave auction of the last century, the "Middle Passage" of a slave ship, and a frenzied Congo dance of human sacrifice. In the last scene Jones is slain offstage by a silver bullet and the drums finally fall silent.

Emperor Jones not only flees through the actual jungle, but also penetrates the forest of his own past. O'Neill draws upon psychological concepts of the deep-seated racial memory and primitive unconsciousness within man. Jones has deluded himself into believing that he can live without illusions. But he is actually destroying himself. As he tears through the jungle, he is gradually stripped of his magnificent military uniform and in the end is naked. At the same time his command of language drops until it is merely a primitive and fearful mumbling. Jones is the victim of his own nature, which in its very intensity gives him heroic stature.

Anna Christie (1921) is a revision of O'Neill's earlier *Chris Christopherson* (*1919*). To protect his daughter, Anna, from "dat ole devil sea," barge captain Chris Christopherson had entrusted her when she was five years old to the care and upbringing of relatives in Minnesota. It is now fifteen years later, and Anna has come to New York to meet her father. Through him she is introduced to Mat Burke, a young sailor; and they fall in love. Then Anna reveals to her father that she had been seduced by a cousin and had drifted into prostitution. Both men are horrified and seek to escape by signing up on the same outgoing boat. Seeing her once more that day, Mat is convinced of the depth and sincerity of Anna's love for him; and they marry on the eve of the sailing. Anna will await them, and have a home ready for them on their return.

O'Neill's main symbols here and ones which he often uses in his plays are the sea and the land. The land is the natural home of man, but life there has become dull and perverted and static. The sea is a symbol of the poetic imagination, of the spirit, and of a wild, lonely freedom.

The first meeting between Anna and Mat takes place on the deck of an offshore coal barge—in a sense between land and sea. Thus each of them can learn from the other; and this forecasts the happy ending, unusual for O'Neill.

The Hairy Ape (*1921*, 1922) is experimental in form, and once more a naturalistic-expressionistic drama.

Yank, a stoker on a transatlantic liner, takes pride in his mastery of his job, until Mildred Douglas, the frail and spoiled daughter of a millionaire, visits the stokehole and calls him a "filthy beast." Yank, who had felt himself part of the age of machines, is suddenly filled with a deep rage. Bent on revenge against the class that produced Mildred Douglas, he insults fashionable strollers on Fifth Avenue, and when they ignore him, he attacks one of them. He is thrown in jail. When he gets out he tries to join the I.W.W., but even they reject him. Finally he goes to the zoo and tries to befriend a gorilla; but Yank evidently does not even belong in the company of beasts, for the gorilla crushes him to death.

O'Neill explained that Yank represents man when he has lost his old harmony with nature. The old Irish stoker of the first scene remembers the days of sailing ships when there was a feeling and a unity between the sailors, their ships, and the sea. But Yank rejects this, for he sees his role as one who keeps the great ships moving.

He identifies himself with the men who make steel, the men who feed speed and power into the giant industrial machine. When he finds out that Mildred Douglas' father owns steel mills, he begins to resist machinery; and a gleam of human consciousness makes a man of him. Thus he is in effect an enemy of the gorilla.

Yank is an outsider to all life. Losing the security of the machine, he is rejected in every attempt to find himself.

Desire under the Elms (1924).

In 1850, dour seventy-five-year-old Ephraim Cabot brings his third wife, Abbie, to his flinty New England farm. His three sons by previous marriages hate him, and two sons run off to the California gold fields. Anxious for an heir that will ensure her grip on the property, Abbie seduces the remaining son, Eben. After the infant's birth, Eben denounces Abbie and she smothers the child to prove that her love for Eben is genuine. Eben is convinced of her sincerity and leaves with the law officers to share her punishment.

Old Ephraim emerges as the dominant character; while the others view him as a hypocritical tyrant, he conceives of himself as chosen by an Old Testament Jehovah. His puritanical certainty simultaneously embodies a granite-like strength and the *hubris* (excessive self-confidence) that precipitates tragedy. The conclusion with its exaltation of the lovers and with Ephraim scarred and shaken but still standing in jealous possession of his soil denies the sordid and produces a catharsis like that of ancient tragedy. Perhaps the truly central figure in the drama is Nature, as suggested by the elms in the title.

The Great God Brown (*1925*, 1926) was O'Neill's first use of symbolic devices and his first direct denunciation of American materialism.

Dion Anthony and William A. Brown both loved Margaret, but she chose the artist Dion over the business-minded Brown. As the means of supporting his family, Dion gives up painting and works as a draftsman in Brown's architectural office. To the world Dion presents the mask of a cynical sensualist to hide his real sensitive self. (The mask is used on the stage.) Only with the prostitute Cybel does he doff the mask to reveal his true nature. Dion finally drinks himself to death.

Brown now dons the mask of Dion, achieving artistic success in architecture and winning Margaret, who sees him as Dion. But with Dion's mask Brown also inherits Dion's perceptivity and recognition of truth. The warfare within Brown's self causes him to welcome death in Cybel's arms from a police bullet. Ironically he is sought as his own slayer. The confused police captain demands, "Well, what's his name?" Cybel answers, "Man."

O'Neill explains that Dion Anthony combines Dionysus and St. Anthony, "the creative pagan acceptance of life, fighting eternal war with the masochistic, life-denying spirit of Christianity." Margaret has some characteristics of Marguerite (Gretchen) of Goethe's *Faust*, though she is more mature than Goethe's virtuous but meagerly comprehending girl-woman. Cybel represents Cybele, the great Earth Mother of Asia Minor mythology. As Cybel's words indicate, Dion and Billy are the split personality of modern man, in whom the eternal artist and the eternal materialist destroy each other. Nowhere else in O'Neill is the language so lyrically effective, suggesting the ineluctable mystery and complexity of life.

Certainly the masks powerfully dramatize the conflicts between the public and private selves of the characters, between their outer and inner beings. In spite of the weight of symbolism, we have here genuine and engaging personalities.

Marco Millions (1924, 1927) is very different in mood and method. It uses fantasy and satire to make its point, yet it shares with the more experimental and more powerful *The Great God Brown* its denunciation of American materialism.

The Prologue depicts the carrying of the body of Princess Kuchakin from Persia to her native Cathay. The dead girl speaks of her death from unrequited love. But she is not bitter, for simply to love has been enough.

The play begins with young Marco Polo setting out from Venice for the court of Kubla Khan, accompanying his father and uncle in search of oriental riches. Before he leaves he promises Donata, his betrothed, that he will return to her. On the road to Cathay, Marco gradually learns the code of commerce and slowly trades away his youthful romantic spirit for a soulless materialism. At the court of the Kubla Khan, Marco secures lucrative trading privileges; and the Khan is initially amused but later repelled by the philosophy of occidental materialism shown by the Polo family. Kuchakin, granddaughter of the Khan, falls in love with Marco, but by this time his capacity for love has been destroyed by his obsession with money and power. Marco accompanies Kuchakin to Persia for her wedding with the Persian king and then leaves for Venice. There Donata, who has grown fat and dull, awaits him. Kuchakin, as shown in the Prologue, has died of a broken heart, for she deeply loved Marco. On hearing of her death, the mighty Kubla Khan can find no solace for his grief. In a brief Epilogue, Marco is spotlighted sitting in the audience "much as one of them."

The oriental scenes introduce a colorful lavishness rarely found in O'Neill's plays. And amidst this richness, the calmer traditional philosophy of the East is contrasted with the more impetuous goals of the West. Marco Polo is shown as courageous and able, but largely unresponsive to the beauty and mystery of the remote region which he has visited. The Khan is a man of far deeper feeling and far greater wisdom.

Lazarus Laughed (*1925*, 1927) has up to now not been performed on the professional stage, though given by some special theater groups. Those who read it are deeply impressed.

Risen from the dead, Lazarus, with "God's eternal laughter" on his lips, brings the message that "there is no death." His house in Bethany becomes the House of Laughter, and the whole Roman empire learns of his affirmative attitude toward life. Tiberius Caesar, hoping to find the secret of immortal youth, brings Lazarus to Rome. Pompeia, at the audience with Tiberius, poisons Miriam, wife of Lazarus, to see if Lazarus can restore her to life. Since Lazarus is unable to, Tiberius sentences him to death. The mad Caligula slays Tiberius and then stabs Lazarus, wildly proclaiming, "I have killed God. I am death. Death is Caesar." Lazarus dies this second time, but he exits laughing: "Fear not, Caligula. There is no death."

Lazarus possesses a strange life energy which casts an ecstatic spell over all with whom he comes into contact. And this energy transforms his own body back to a youthful and glowing vigor. He is totally opposed to the traditional concepts of denial of physical desire and of fear of heavenly wrath. He sees redeeming qualities in the debauched pagans who have indulged the senses. The point is emphasized by the half masks that Tiberius and Caligula wear and the full masks of all the others except Lazarus, who wears no mask. Lazarus brings them the message of ecstasy, but his words are soon forgotten. It is as if Lazarus must constantly be in the presence of men, constantly reminding them of his message of life, constantly laughing with them. For when they escape the power of his presence they fall back into their old ways and become bitter and vengeful. The last words of the play are spoken by Caligula, who has just killed Lazarus. He shouts: "Forgive me, Lazarus! Men forget."

Lazarus is the figure of the poet-priest, the man who has gone into areas of experience where others fear to go. He is the artist who reminds us of truths that we have forgotten.

Strange Interlude (*1926*, 1928), although its nine acts require five hours to perform, proved a remarkable success on the stage.

Nina Leeds, daughter of a New England college professor, hates her father whom she considers responsible for preventing her marriage. When her beloved is killed in the war in France, Nina becomes a nurse, and returns home only after her father's death. She is persuaded to marry good-natured Sam Evans, but learns after she is pregnant that insanity is rampant in the Evans line. She resorts to abortion, but to become pregnant again takes Dr. Edmund Darrell as a lover. The resultant son, Gordon, comes to love Sam and detest his actual father. Grown up, Gordon elopes with Madeline Arnold and repudiates his mother. After Sam's death, Nina marries Charles Marsden, a writer who had been once her childhood admirer.

The title derives from Nina's speech in the last act when Marsden urges philosophical calm as the only logical response to her troubled life. "Strange interlude!" she agrees. "Yes, our lives are merely strange dark interludes in the electrical display of God the father." In this play, O'Neill portrays essentially commonplace middle-class characters living fairly normal lives. The experiences of life prove to be quite different for these people from the simple ones they had learned to expect as children.

In *Strange Interlude* O'Neill introduces a striking alteration of the soliloquy as a theatrical device. In the midst of an ordinary conversation, the actors remain fixed in a tableau while each speaks aloud the thoughts going through his mind, the thoughts that social conventions often bar from speech. By this means O'Neill illuminates and explains motivations that are deeply hidden within the characters. The influence of Freudian psychology is clear throughout the play, and especially in the soliloquies. It may be said that the stream-of-consciousness technique of the novel is here translated to the stage.

Mourning Becomes Electra (*1929*, 1931) is a three-part play in thirteen acts. In a New England setting O'Neill places the classic Greek account of the fated House of Atreus.

"The Homecoming" shows Brigadier-General Ezra Mannon (Agamemnon) just back from the Civil War and murdered by his wife Christine (Clytemnestra) at the instigation of her lover, Captain Adam Brant (Aegisthus). Instead of stabbing her husband, as in the Greek original, Christine gives poison to the General in lieu of expected medicine. Daughter Lavinia (Electra) discovers the box of poison and vows revenge. Ezra is less the conquering hero than a tired and lonely old man whose crime in Christine's eyes was not the slaying of their daughter Iphigenia but Ezra's failure to give her sex fulfillment because of his puritanical nature. This modern treatment of a great legend substitutes neurotic hatred by a spiteful woman for the monstrous passions depicted in Clytemnestra by Aeschylus.

"The Hunted" brings back from the wars son Orin (Orestes) suffering from a head wound. Lavinia actually loves Adam Brant, but feeling guilty about the shift of affection from her father and jealous that Brant is her mother's paramour, she urges Orin to kill Brant. Confronted with this murder and with her own sins, Christine commits suicide. These variations from the classic original suggest the nonheroic stature of modern man. The Furies that attack Orin are not the ancient Erinyes but the war wounds that have injured his brain. Orin is a man of our times, sick in heart and mind because of the senseless bloodletting of war.

"The Haunted" is O'Neill's greatest departure from the Greek original. Lavinia and Orin flee to the South Seas by clipper ship (Brant and Christine had planned this voyage before Brant was slain). In his ravings, Orin suggests that he is now the Ezra figure and Lavinia the Christine figure. Orin rejects the Blessed Isles to return to his puritanical origins. Since he cannot be trusted to remain silent about his deeds, Lavinia does not prevent his suicide. For Lavinia, marriage with the drably normal Peter Niles is a possibility but she feels that she cannot live such a humdrum life, and equally she cannot contemplate killing herself. Last of her line, she decides to live alone in the guilt-stained house of the Mannons.

O'Neill, unlike Aeschylus, will not appeal to any outer source, human or divine, for final justice. The clear-eyed Vinnie (Lavinia) accepts and lives with her own Inferno, neither berating fate nor her fellows.

The dialogue is spare and direct, suggesting tragic intensity by action and emotion rather than by word. There is a strong contrast between the feverish Mannons and the ineffectual Niles family, Peter who loves Lavinia and Hazel who loves Orin. The place of the Greek chorus is taken by the quite commonplace townsfolk. One knowing, unintervening New Englander, Seth Beckwith, caretaker for the Mannons, bridges the gap between the hell-scarred Mannons and the light of everyday. The structure of the trilogy is a masterpiece of logic.

Ah, Wilderness! (1932, 1933), the only comedy among O'Neill's major works, is a thoroughly delightful play, easygoing in mood, but with O'Neill's feeling for characterizations and relationships.

Nat Miller, newspaper editor, lives in a small Connecticut town in 1906 with his wife, Essie, his son, Richard, his prim sister, Lily, and his alcoholic brother-in-law, Sid Davis. Richard, "going on seventeen," is intoxicated with poetry, socialism, and Muriel, daughter of a neighbor. The neighbor is infuriated at the poetry Richard addresses to Muriel (the play's title comes from *The Rubáiyát of Omar Khayyám,* a favorite of Richard's). Declaring his own independence on this Fourth of July, Richard dashes off to taste of forbidden fruits with a "college tart." He returns with his chastity but also with an ungovernable load of liquor. Nursed back to sobriety by knowledgeable Uncle Sid, Richard receives a lecture on the facts of life from his father, and all ends happily in his making up with Muriel.

O'Neill admitted that *Ah, Wilderness!* was "a sort of wishing out loud. That's the way I would have liked my boyhood to have been." Here is rebellious youth, funny and absurd as adolescence always can be.

O'Neill demonstrates the stability of middle-class conventions, but he also justifies Richard's revolt against mediocrity. Nat and Essie are good but ineffectual, willing perpetuators of shallow taste and thought. They do not interfere too much; adolescence runs its course, but they are happy when Richard and Muriel find each other again.

Other O'Neill plays of this period are *Gold, Diff'rent* (1920); *The First Man, The Fountain* (1921); *Welded* (1922); *All God's Chillun Got Wings* (1923); *Dynamo* (1928); *Days Without End* (1933).

THE LATER PERIOD (1935–44).

The Iceman Cometh (*1939,* 1946) is set in 1912, but its substance and significance reveal the mature O'Neill of the years when it was written.

In Harry Hope's West Side saloon in New York the down-and-outers remain drunk and self-deluded "with a few harmless pipe dreams about their yesterdays and tomorrows." In a spirit of maudlin sentimentality the proprietor has not ventured upon the street since his wife Bessie died twenty years before. Jimmy Tomorrow justifies his alcoholism by his wife's infidelity years ago. Larry Slade asserts that he is a dispassionate spectator of the silly business of life. He claims to have left the Syndicalist-Anarchist movement because of his disgust at human selfishness. Actually he was chagrined at the desertion by his mistress, a radical whose son, Don Parritt, now informs Larry that he has betrayed his own mother and sent her to jail. All the barflies await the annual visit of Theodore Hickman (Hickey), a hardware salesman, who always celebrates his birthday with them. Hickey's recurrent joke is that he has left his wife with the iceman (hence the title; Larry later equates the iceman with Death). Hickey has changed, however. He now demands that the men throw away their pipe dreams and face their pasts. Bessie was "a nagging old bitch." Tomorrow's wife was unfaithful as a result of his alcoholism, not the cause of it. Shattering of illusions does not give the beaten ones purgation; they are simply licked. Hickey tries to buck them up by his own life story. He had been faithless to his wife many times, and each time she wanted to believe in his reformation. Finally he admits that he killed her as an act of kindness. When the shocked listeners are told, however, by Hickey himself, that he must have been insane, they resume their revelry in relief. Only Slade and Parritt have been forced by Hickey to a realization of their self-delusion.

Throughout much of the drama, Hickey seems the voice of sanity, the reformed alcoholic who now faces the truth and seeks altruistically to lead other inebriates to reality. When he announces his wife's death, it appears that this tragedy has sobered him and at last effected his oft-promised reformation. Suddenly all is reversed as Hickey stands self-revealed as a mad killer. Larry declaims the moral: "To hell with the truth! As the history of the world proves, the truth has no bearing on anything. It's irrelevant and immaterial, as the lawyers say. The lie of a pipe dream is what gives life to the whole misbegotten mad lot of us, drunk or sober."

The play seems to question the value of the direct facing of reality and wonders whether it might be better to take refuge in illusions which will give life a personal meaning and consolation. Written in naturalistic guise, touching upon the grim and sordid, the play reaches out for the nature of truth, which may lie beyond man's wisdom. O'Neill points to the endless need for human understanding and compassion.

Long Day's Journey Into Night (1940, 1956) is O'Neill's masterpiece. Due to the intensely personal subject matter, O'Neill requested that it not be released until after his death. The four chief characters correspond in many details to O'Neill's father, mother, brother, and O'Neill himself on a single long day in 1912.

It is a summer morning and the Tyrone family have just finished breakfast in their country house (in New London, Connecticut). There is much small talk and many compliments by James Tyrone to his wife, Mary. But underneath their words there is a powerful undercurrent of nameless fear and guilt, which is made evident by the nervous mannerisms of Mary and self-contradictions of Tyrone. Tyrone and his sons, Jamie and Edmund, quarrel over small matters to cover up their mutual fears. Jamie and Edmund criticize Tyrone for his close-fisted avarice. Tyrone berates Jamie for his drunkenness and libertine ways and Edmund for his morbidly poetic nature and his "socialist anarchist sentiments." But their arguments never last long and always seem to be on the edge of the revelation of a truth when the subject is abruptly changed. It soon becomes clear that Mary is at the focus of their fears, and we gradually realize that she is addicted to morphine, a habit which took hold of her after giving birth to Edmund. Tyrone had hired a cheap doctor to care for her and the doctor's incompetent prescription was the cause of her habit. But Mary will not consciously acknowledge that she is an addict, and when the subject is insinuated she pretends that she didn't hear or that something else was said.

The family has also been avoiding the subject of Edmund's illness. It becomes obvious that he has tuberculosis, but Mary says that it is no more than a "summer cold." The three men begin drinking, and Mary goes to her room ostensibly to rest; but really, as the others know, to give herself an injection of morphine. Tyrone, Jamie and Edmund leave the house to learn the doctor's findings on Edmund's sickness. Mary is left alone in the house, and sinks deeper and deeper into a narcotic dream world and begins revealing her past life to the maid. Tyrone and Edmund return to the house in the evening. They are now quite drunk and their psychological battle of the morning continues, only now it is much more intense as they vacillate between the extremes of love and hate. Edmund's tuberculosis has been confirmed and he accuses Tyrone of trying to economize by having him sent to the cheaper state sanatorium. The guilt of the past rushes upon Tyrone and he seeks to explain himself and much that has happened. In this scene, father and son are alternately raging enemies and understanding and sympathetic friends. Jamie finally comes home and in a more drunken state than the others. When Jamie and Edmund are together without their parents, it is clear that Jamie in his disillusionment with life has sought to bring Edmund to a similarly negative view. But Edmund's strongly artistic and philosophic nature gives him the means of freeing himself. Despite the conflict between the brothers, they are bound together by a deep affection. (O'Neill showed understanding of his unhappy brother in a later play, *A Moon for the Misbegotten*.)

The family ties are strong among all four in *Long Day's Journey Into Night*. This sense of profound caring in the midst of almost endless problems gives the play a tremendously moving unity. Edmund clearly feels close to his mother. At one point, Jamie, in a moment of anger, calls Mary a "hophead," and Edmund defending her hits him. Mary, toward the end of the play, enters in a drugged trance dragging her wedding dress behind her. She has completely reverted to her childhood and speaks of those happy days when she wanted to be a nun and then fell in love with James Tyrone "and was so happy for a time."

O'Neill in his written version of the play includes unusually explicit directions dealing with tone of voice, gesture, and facial expression. Practically every piece of dialogue is preceded by a stage note telling how it should be spoken. These directions have been followed in the play's productions. Unconsciously the audience senses how completely the mind of O'Neill pervades this work.

In looking back over *Long Day's Journey Into Night*, one realizes increasingly the enormous power that the past has over the lives of the Tyrones. And it is Mary who puts this idea into words: "None of us can help the things life has done to us. They're done before you realize it and once they're done they make you do other things until at last everything comes between you and what you'd like to be, and you've lost your true self forever." And another time she says, "The past is the present, isn't it? It's the future too! We all try to lie out of that but life won't let us."

But though the Tyrones seem completely in the grip of the past, there are moments in the play which suggest that the family's great mutual love must carry with it some element of hope. To those who see or study O'Neill's plays, it may well seem that Eugene O'Neill's own life, darkened though it was at many points by tragic and disturbing events, in its rising to masterly creativity was the achievement for which the Tyrones of *Long Day's Journey Into Night* had been hoping.

Other plays of this period are: *A Touch of the Poet* (*1935–42*, 1958); *More Stately Mansions* (*1935–41*, unfinished, 1962 and 1967); *Hughie* (*1941–42*, 1964); *A Moon for the Misbegotten* (*1943*, 1957).

VARIOUS IMPORTANT DRAMATISTS OF THE EARLY TWENTIETH CENTURY

Maxwell Anderson (1888–1959). Son of a Baptist clergyman in Atlantic, Pennsylvania, Maxwell Anderson accompanied his family in moves to Ohio, Iowa, and North Dakota. In 1911 he received an A.B. from the University of North Dakota and in 1914 obtained an M.A. from Stanford. After teaching English at Stanford and Whittier, he went into journalism, which eventually took him to New York. His early interest in poetry resulted in a volume of lyrics, *You Who Have Dreams* (1925). His first drama, *White Desert* (1923), dealt with frustrated lives in North Dakota.

Anderson's basic theme is the purification that can be achieved through suffering. Through suffering, Anderson contends, man is illuminated by truth, and if man asserts ultimate goodness, he can rise to heroic stature. Most men, nonetheless, are selfish and narrow-minded and easy prey for tyrants. Fundamental also to Anderson is the theme of human liberty. Totalitarianism is of course the eternal enemy, but all government limitations upon individual freedom are suspect and dangerous. Under genuine freedom mankind may achieve its potentialities of happiness.

What Price Glory? (1924), written in collaboration with Laurence Stallings, was Anderson's first success.

Professional marines Sergeant Quirt and Captain Flagg renew an old enmity in World War I in France. Both seek the attractive Charmaine, daughter of the innkeeper, Cognac Pete. Quirt seduces her and Flagg nastily sees the chance to bind Quirt in marriage and garnish some of the sergeant's pay for this wife of a shotgun wedding. Orders to attack cancel these plans. In battle Quirt is wounded and the unit captures a German officer, a feat for which they are promised a month's rest. Arguing over Charmaine, the two marines draw cards for her. Flagg is the winner, but orders cancel their leave and return both to combat.

Wartime heroics are demolished in this raucous, irreverent drama. As the first resounding Broadway triumph of naturalism, *What Price Glory?* startled audiences with soldiers' obscenity and sex appetite instead of the time-honored sentimental grandiloquence long associated with war plays. Some groups loudly protested the debunking of war's glories in the savagely realistic trench scenes of the second act and were horrified at coarse fighting men to whom the splendid phrase "saving the world for democracy" had no meaning. Yet to a later era the swaggering, roistering pair of Quirt and Flagg seem quite romantic figures.

Elizabeth the Queen (1930) is a blank-verse drama.

Through the machinations of Sir Walter Raleigh and Lord Cecil, the Earl of Essex is precipitated into rebellion against Elizabeth, though he and the queen are actually in love. Essex captures Elizabeth but chivalrously releases her and restores her kingdom. She promptly imprisons him for treason. Torn between private love and public queenship, Elizabeth offers Essex pardon and even the kingdom itself. He prefers going to his execution, for he believes that she is best for England, and if he lived he would never tolerate secondary position. Elizabeth is left, as she states, to "be queen of emptiness and death."

The play is one of the most ambitious and successful attempts at romantic tragedy on the American stage. Anderson reveals faith in man's heroism, believing that even in weaving their own destruction human beings may be both enlightened and elevated by the transforming power of love. In this play, tragic flaws doom both heroic figures.

Both Your Houses (1933), its acid title taken from Mercutio's dying curse against both Montagues and Capulets in *Romeo and Juliet,* turns to a taut, hard-hitting prose.

Alan McClean, an idealistic ex-college teacher from Nevada, tries in Congress to represent both his constituents and the entire national interest. As he seeks support for his bill to provide for a dam in Nevada, he realizes with mounting horror the petty selfishness and despicable double-dealings of national legislators. In cynical disdain he concocts an omnibus bill incorporating every possible pork-barrel grab for public funds. To his agonized dismay, the bill sweeps Congress by so huge a margin that a presidential veto cannot stop it. Alan vehemently blasts both houses of Congress, asserting that this chicanery cannot go on and that the people will eventually cast out the unscrupulous politicos who defraud them.

The Jeffersonian concept of small and honest government is the ideal of Anderson and his appropriately named McClean.

Mary of Scotland (1933) returns to verse for another Renaissance romantic tragedy.

Because Catholic countries of Europe deem Mary of Scotland the rightful heir to the English throne, Elizabeth schemes with Protestant

Scots for Mary's downfall. Mary falls into their trap by refusing to marry Bothwell, a strong-minded Protestant, and by electing instead the weak Catholic candidate, Darnley. Bothwell supports Mary and marries her after the accidental death of Darnley. In civil war, Mary is captured and Bothwell agrees to disband his forces to obtain her release. The Scots lairds under Moray treacherously hold Mary and let Elizabeth capture her. Mary finally realizes in confrontation with Elizabeth that here is the malign force that plotted her fall. Hopeful that history will vindicate her and that her son will succeed to a united England and Scotland, Mary accepts the fate that will end in her execution.

Mary's tragedy is that of the idealist in a vicious world; her virtues of tolerance and mercy are ineffectual before the Machiavellian intrigues of Elizabeth. There are more developed characters and gripping dramatic scenes than in *Elizabeth the Queen*. The verse is frequently spare but rises to lyrical magnificence in the head-on encounter of the two queens at Carlisle Castle.

Winterset (1935) was stimulated by the Sacco-Vanzetti case and was one of Anderson's most successful plays.

Trock, a gangster, returns to his native New York slums after imprisonment for murder. For this same crime Romagna, an anarchist, had been electrocuted. Romagna's son, Mio, tries to clear his father's name by obtaining evidence from a witness, Garth, and in the process falls in love with Miriamne, Garth's sister. Trock warns Garth to be silent and orders his henchman, Shadow, to kill Judge Gaunt who, troubled by his role in Romagna's death, is also seeking Garth's evidence. When Shadow refuses to kill the judge, Trock commands his other hoodlums to slay Shadow. As Mio unsuccessfully questions Garth, Shadow staggers back from his East River tomb long enough to implicate Trock before he dies. Mio now goes out with assurance of his father's innocence, but he and Miriamne are shot down in the street by Trock's killers.

For most dramatists this account would seem to call for naturalistic treatment, but Anderson makes it a verse drama. The bitter snarling of Trock is immensely effective, and Mio speaks like a philosopher and poet caught up against his nature in merciless intrigue and violence. Mio and Miriamne die triumphant in their vital youth. The closing valedictory by Miriamne's father, Esdras, enunciates Anderson's stoic confidence in man's quest for freedom and spiritual fulfillment. *Winterset* is an amazing attempt to find in the gloom of the present the occasion for exalted poetic tragedy.

High Tor (1937) combines verse and prose in romantic fantasy. High Tor, owned by Van Dorn, is a lofty mountain peak on the

Hudson, frequented by John, last of the local Indians. Van Dorn's fiancée, Judith, wants him to sell the mountain and become a conventional town dweller; when the individualistic Van Dorn demurs, she breaks with him. Bank robbers flee to the area with their loot, two unscrupulous lawyers seek to buy the property, and the spectral Dutch crew of Henry Hudson's old ship eagerly expect a rescue vessel after centuries of waiting. The ghosts of DeWitt and others depart in relief, the robbers are captured, and Van Dorn finally sells the mountain for a handsome profit.

Vastly amusing hijinks cloak a bitter lament for the end of old-fashioned American independence and individualism. A mechanized era destroys the landscape and eventually forces conformity upon Van Dorn, last of the nonconformists, and he flees to a wilder mountain in the West. The last sorrowing words come from John, the Indian. "Nothing is made by men, but makes, in the end, good ruins."

Knickerbocker Holiday (1938) is a musical with a notable score by Kurt Weill. Ostensibly a rollicking skit of old New Amsterdam adapted from Washington Irving, the work lambastes the big government ideology of the New Deal administration. Stuyvesant plans to hang Brom Broeck, the rugged individualist who thwarts him. Brom's demand, "Let's keep the government small and funny," triumphs with the elders, especially with city-father Roosevelt, evidently a forebear of the incumbent President.

Key Largo (1939), like *Winterset*, asserts the heroic in contemporary life. King McCloud has deserted the Loyalist forces in Spain and taken refuge in the Florida Keys, where gangsters are terrorizing the inhabitants. Given a second chance, McCloud dies to support truth. Anderson is saying that man's advancement can come only through the altruistic.

Joan of Lorraine (1946) poetically reaffirms the heroic theme. Ingeniously linking the medieval account to the present situation, Anderson presents the play in rehearsal. The actress taking the title role declares that Joan is mystically inspired, uncompromising; Masters, the director, especially in light of the compromises with conscience that are necessary in order to stage this play, believes that Joan is opportunistic and vacillating. The actual dramatization of Joan's story proves her genuine nobility. The resolute Joan affirms that innocence and idealism can endure, though only by heroic self-sacrifice.

The Essence of Tragedy (1935), Anderson's essay on the nature of tragic drama, is a clear statement of the convictions which he illustrated dramatically in his plays.

Elmer Rice (1892–1967). Elmer Rice was born in New York City and graduated in 1912 from the New York Law School. In his first drama, *On Trial* (1914), he utilized his legal background for a murder mystery, and adapted for the stage the flashback technique of the movies to depict scenes described by witnesses on the stand. The most important of his later plays are *The Adding Machine* and *Street Scene*. His *Not for Children* (1935) satirizes critics and the contemporary stage and was not acted until 1951. Rice was a leading figure in the Playwrights' Company, the Dramatists Guild, and the American National Theatre and Academy.

The Adding Machine (1923) is an expressionistic play of notable originality and power.

Mr. Zero has worked for twenty-five years adding figures in a giant business firm and in the process he has become an automaton whose consciousness has all but worn away. His boss buys an adding machine and Mr. Zero is no longer needed. Mr. Zero kills the boss, is executed, and wakes up in an afterlife which he can no more cope with than he could his physical life. His soul is finally sent back to enter another body and begin again a life cycle working at the only job for which he has forever been fitted—his old monotonous job.

Mr. Zero and his wife and his friends are all the same. Their blank minds react only to Hollywood-inspired sexual fantasies, to hateful prejudices, and to feelings of petty revenge. For a moment in the Elysian fields Mr. Zero has a chance for ecstasy and for love, but he rejects this experience for a room with an adding machine where he can, through dull routine, escape the feeling of rapture which he fears so much.

Street Scene (1929), a Pulitzer Prize winner, is wholly realistic, set in a New York slum. Throughout the play actual recordings of New York sounds fill the audience's ears with the hum of traffic and the din of tightly packed humanity.

The entire community is the protagonist. We do not follow the threads of individual destiny but observe one demonstration after another of the spiritual destruction of a slum community. There are many familiar characters: the drunken father, the unfaithful mother, the Jewish radical, the Italian singing master, young lovers, the nosy gossip, the libidinous shop girl, the lawless youth. The humdrum routine is dramatically shattered when a coarse stagehand finds his wife hugging the milkman and kills both. But this showy violence is only a momentary ripple as the community rapidly returns to its implacable bustle. Somehow the area staggers on, but there is little hope.

A musical version of *Street Scene* in 1947 had lyrics by Langston Hughes and music by Kurt Weill.

Dream Girl (1945) is effective on the stage but less distinctive than Rice's other plays.

Before breakfast, bookstore clerk Georgina Allerton dreams that she stars on a radio program and then that she is a renowned novelist. At breakfast she daydreams that she is married to her dashing brother-in-law, Jim Lucas. At the bookstore her suitor Clark Redfield causes her to daydream as also does Mr. Hand with his proposal of a trip to Mexico. Clark takes her to a play and Georgina dreams that the actress drops out because of illness and Georgina histrionically leaps into the leading role. Clark whisks her off to be married by a justice of the peace, but even during the ceremony Georgina dreams that Jim Lucas sweeps in to rescue her.

Clark speaks with commendable practicality for the author in demanding a resolute facing of life's realities, but Georgina's sprightly imagination seems romantically to overpower such wisdom with the exciting escapism of dreamland.

Revolving stages and blackouts transport Georgina into her fantasy world with wild éclat. Perhaps such dreams shore up the spirit. Only by implication does Rice suggest that the false values of modern society compel this refuge in dreams.

Sidney Howard (1891–1939). Born in Oakland, California, Sidney Coe Howard graduated from the University of California in 1915. After study at Harvard in Baker's 47 Workshop, he served in France as an ambulance driver. Upon his return he combined a journalistic career with playwriting.

They Knew What They Wanted (1924) was Howard's first play to gain popular success.

Tony Patucci, a middle-aged winegrower in California's Napa Valley, deceives his mail-order bride, Amy, by sending her a picture of Joe, his handsome young hired man. On his wedding day Tony breaks both legs. Humiliated and shaken, Amy allows Joe to seduce and make her pregnant. Though the young folks are not in love, they decide to elope. Learning the truth, Tony is infuriated but persuades Amy to remain and give his name to the child.

Pride, passion, and theoretical loyalties yield to the more basic needs of the characters. Howard explained: "After all, the play is a little . . . treatise on the obsessions which make the world go round. The woman's obsession for security—the man's for a dynasty, on the one hand (Tony), and for rebellion on the other (Joe's)."

The Silver Cord (1926) in its title applies to the umbilical cord and metaphorically to emotional ties joining mother and child.

Overly protective Mrs. Phelps tries to hold on to her sons, David and Robert. David is married to Christina; they live in his mother's home. Robert is engaged to Hester, but Mrs. Phelps breaks up the affair in order to retain her son. Hester attempts suicide, and the aroused Christina forces a showdown. She compels David to choose between his mother and his wife; love causes him to leave with Christina. Robert, however, remains with his mother.

Mrs. Phelps is a domineering woman who uses every subtle device to chain her offspring to her. The profound tragedy is the helpless immaturity of Robert, who will never be able to free himself.

Yellow Jack (1934) is a documentary. This account of the fight against yellow fever is derived from a portion of *Microbe Hunters* by Paul de Kruif.

Three episodes in the battle against this tropical disease are depicted: Stackpoole in London, Stokes and Harkness in West Africa, Walter Reed and Carlos Finlay in Cuba, with the greatest emphasis placed upon the last. The researchers undergo harrowing dangers and bewildering problems (Dr. Lazear dies of the disease), but Reed conclusively establishes mosquitoes as the transmitters of the ailment, and Stackpoole produces an effective vaccine.

The de Kruif account highlights dramatic heroism, but Howard concentrates upon the realistic struggles of dedicated but human scientists. Contrasted with the hard-working, truth-seeking scientists is narrow-minded Colonel Tory who attempts with bureaucratic blockheadedness to thwart the forward march of research.

Robert E. Sherwood (1896–1955). Born in New Rochelle, New York, Robert Emmet Sherwood during his Harvard undergraduate years left to fight in World War I with the Canadian Black Watch regiment. Gassed at Vimy Ridge and wounded at Amiens, he returned with a passionate desire to prevent any future war. After receiving his A.B. from Harvard in 1918 he became a motion-picture critic for *Vanity Fair*. He served as president of the Dramatists Guild, and was a founding member of the Playwrights' Company. Strongly opposing totalitarianism, he was appointed special assistant to the Secretary of War in 1940 under President Franklin D. Roosevelt.

Sherwood was an ardent advocate of liberal democracy, with special emphasis on the dignity of the individual. As a playwright, he had a flair for light comedy, quite apart from his more serious interests.

The Road to Rome (1927) is a glorious, rollicking satire.

Fabius, the pompous and chauvinistic dictator of Rome, fearing the imminent fall of the city to Hannibal, lets his Greek-born wife Amytis leave ostensibly for Greece. Actually she goes to Hannibal and asks why he continues warfare. Hannibal dallies with Amytis and, convinced by her feminine common sense, eventually lifts the siege. In orotund fashion, Fabius solemnly asserts that Hannibal was defeated by the moral strength of Rome.

The brilliant dialogue has the nobles of classic antiquity chat in modern American slang. Fabius and the Romans represent American businessmen of the 1920s, self-righteous, hopelessly conservative, entrenched behind a barricade of platitudes. Fabius proclaims his credo of "respectability, modesty, economy, devotion to duty, reverence, chastity, and—and . . ." Amytis quickly supplies, "Mediocrity!" The extremely witty and intelligent Amytis, acting the empty-headed female, excuses her ignorance about Hannibal by citing Fabius' ignorance about Aristotle. Amytis cares little for Rome's fate, but she wishes for reason and good will to prevail over man's irrational habit of war. The romantic idealist Hannibal is led by Amytis to grasp "the human equation" and renounce war as the basest of human stupidities. Amytis returns calmly to Fabius bearing within her the child of Hannibal, the child that her impotent husband could not give to her. For the rest of her life she must patiently listen to Fabius' testimonial: "Hannibal, with all his elephants and all his men, could not subdue the high moral purpose of Rome."

Reunion in Vienna (1931) has its scene in the Vienna of 1930. Dr. Anton Krug, distinguished psychiatrist, is married to the lovely Elena, who before World War I was the mistress of Archduke Rudolf Maximilian. For the hundredth anniversary of the birth of Franz Josef, royalists are holding a clandestine celebration. When Rudolf appears in disguise, the clinical Krug urges his wife to see him, for thus, the psychiatrist reasons, the disillusionment of long-cherished romantic dreams will dispel her sentimental attachment to the deposed Hapsburg. Krug at his wife's request goes to the authorities to facilitate Rudolf's escape, leaving Elena with her former lover. Rudolf and Elena spend a night of reunion together, after which Krug civilly aids the ex-Archduke in his escape and Elena remains with her husband.

In 1930 Vienna, the extravagant splendor and gorgeous impudence of the Hapsburgs have been replaced by the wholly competent and wholly dull bureaucracy. For one insane moment Vienna flees from the drab present to relive the sumptuous past; then Rudolf flees back to driving a taxicab in Nice, and Vienna resumes its mundane course.

The Petrified Forest (1935) shows Sherwood in effect creating a microcosm for universal social comment. In this drama bizarrely different personalities are suddenly thrown together.

In 1934 old Gramp Maple, his middle-aged son, Jason, and his granddaughter, Gabby, operate the Black Mesa Filling Station and Bar-B-Q in eastern Arizona near the Petrified Forest. Gabby confides to Alan Squier, a defeated intellectual, her dreams of escaping to France and studying art. Squier gets a ride with rich Ohio banker Chisholm and the banker's wife, but their car is commandeered by Duke Mantee, an escaped murderer. Mantee holds all captive in the Bar-B-Q as he awaits his girl friend Doris and three of his henchmen. Squier makes over his life insurance to Gabby and persuades Mantee to kill him. The murderer flees amidst a crashing salvo of shots.

The title locale symbolizes timeless Nature against which ephemeral man plays out his drama and also suggests the petrifaction of our era. The theme of futility is carried out in the miserably sterile married life of the Chisholms and in the senile pioneer reminiscences of Gramp. Searching for a cause, Squier finds it in giving his life for Gabby's artistic future.

Idiot's Delight (1936) is Sherwood's denunciation of war.

On the eve of World War II (then still a few years in the offing) train passengers are herded into a small hotel near the closing Italian border. The group includes a German researcher who has almost solved the riddle of cancer, a honeymooning couple from England, a band of American peroxide-blond dancers managed by Harry Van, a French Communist, the munitions-maker Weber, and his mistress Irene (who poses as a White Russian). The sudden onslaught of war moves them all to action. Quillery, the Communist, denounces the Italians and is shot. The German scientist junks his humanitarian research to return to Germany to work on poison gas. Weber abandons Irene (left without a passport) to hasten to his bustling manufacture of death. Van, realizing that Irene is a dancer with whom he spent a night in Omaha in 1925, deserts his act and stays with her. The bombs start falling upon the hotel.

In the actual writing, comic entertainment almost dominates the play in the ludicrous predicament of a stranded troupe of American show girls, but the pacifist message, Sherwood's central purpose, is driven home in Irene's confrontation with Weber.

Abe Lincoln in Illinois (1938) has won a notable place for itself.

Twelve consecutive scenes cover thirty years of Lincoln's life from his postmastership in New Salem, Illinois, until his departure from Springfield to assume the presidency. The first act portrays a homespun frontiersman adept at getting along with his fellows. The second act scrutinizes his legal and legislative career in Illinois and his marriage to Mary Todd, ambitious to become the First Lady of the land. The third act details the debates with Douglas and the politicking that eventually sent Lincoln to the White House.

Sherwood's shift of ground from his previous work is apparent. The sacrifice of Lincoln is not for the benefit of any specific individual but for the entire national welfare. Most strikingly, Sherwood asserts that even war is justified when there is the threat of tyranny. Lincoln is interpreted as the common man sincerely anxious for a private life of peace. Mary aided him in becoming a national figure, but her political ambitions doomed both to a frustrated, quarrelsome married life. Not his own inclinations but the issues of human freedom compel Lincoln to take his stand even though civil war and his own death loom ahead. The loneliness of immense responsibility stalks through the spirit of Lincoln.

There Shall Be No Night (1940) is a play strongly endorsing the Finnish resistance to Russian invasion, which was then under way. Dr. Kaarlo Valkonen is a Nobel Prize winner in neurology. His entire family and circle are destroyed in fighting the Russian invaders, and only Valkonen's daughter-in-law, Kaatri, escapes. She will have her baby by Erik, ski-trooper son of Valkonen, in America.

Knowing the hopelessness of their resistance, the Valkonens nonetheless struggle to the end with confidence that the efforts of freedom fighters will eventually overcome totalitarianism.

The drama is interesting for its reflection of American attitudes at the time. Sherwood, like many of his fellow Americans, moved from a bitter detestation of war to a fervent support of the battle against totalitarianism.

S. N. Behrman (1893–   ). Samuel Nathaniel Behrman ran away from his native Worcester, Massachusetts, to attempt an acting career, but was persuaded to go to college at Clark University and Harvard (A.B. 1916). At Harvard he studied under Professor Baker in the 47 Workshop. Thereafter he continued training in playwriting at Columbia University.

Behrman is the American master of an essentially European theatrical genre—high comedy. He typically sets exquisitely urbane characters in ultrasophisticated settings. Talented artists and intellectuals generate verbal friction with wealthy businessmen or politicians. After very little action but after extremely witty dialogue, creativity and personal integrity are generally recognized.

The Second Man (1927) toys with the dual personality of Clark Storey, a second-rate novelist. Mrs. Frayne, an older woman, offers him financial security. Infatuated, youthful Monica Grey tries to snare him by an appeal to idealism, and, failing at this, attempts the time-honored gambit of claiming pregnancy. Storey elects Mrs. Frayne and trots Monica off to a patient admirer. The "second man" within Storey, his practical alter ego, triumphs over the impressionable artist within him and finds Frayne wealth preferable to Grey poverty.

Biography (1932) was tremendously successful on the stage.

Portrait painter Marion Froude has enjoyed Bohemian love affairs in her "laissez-faire" career. Financially strapped, she agrees to write her life story for Richard Kurt, editor of a popular magazine. Her first lover, Leander Nolan, now a dignified politician, tries to suppress or tone down her account, but the fiery editor urges the flaming truth. Although she falls in love with Kurt, she burns the manuscript and exits a free woman.

The real conflict of the drama is between tolerance, represented by Marion, and fanaticism, exemplified by Kurt, "Studying you," she informs him, "I can see why so many movements against injustice become such absolute—tyrannies." And although she loves him, she perceives that his ruling characteristic is hate for her most fundamental quality. Marion is Behrman's typical woman—independent, civilized, but warmly human.

End of Summer (1936), Behrman's own favorite, is set at the Frothingham summer estate in Maine.

Leona Frothingham's vast wealth has ruined her own marriage and now threatens to prevent her daughter Paula's marriage to an impecunious college graduate. Leona is bewildered by Paula's irreverent radicalism. Leona's wealth attracts a host of fortune seekers, but the psychiatrist Dr. Rice adroitly levers out the others. Paula lets him show his hand in making love to her. Broken, Leona is ready to accept a young radical, Dennis McCarthy, who plans a revolutionary journal.

The striking conflict is between the generations—Leona, a butterfly of the 1920s, versus Paula, the socially conscious youth of the Depression era. Paula comes to realize that her outmoded mother sincerely tries to make happy all those about her.

No Time for Comedy (1939) dramatically explores the playwright's own dilemma in a hell-bent age.

Gaylord Esterbrook is a successful comic dramatist, writing chiefly for his actress wife, Linda Paige. A banker's wife, Amanda Smith, persuades him to write serious drama, appropriate to these perilous times. Failing, Gaylord returns to his wife and plans to write a play entitled *No Time for Comedy*, based upon his own triangular affair.

The two women in Esterbrook's life implicitly ask which is better for the creative writer: the critical and questioning spirit of tragedy or the smiling affirmation of comedy. Behrman suggests that one's own talents should be followed, and he suspects that a culture which abandons its comic view of life has vitiated its humanity and has destroyed the very basis for its being.

George Kelly (1887–   ). A native of Philadelphia, George Edward Kelly began acting on the New York stage in 1912. His start as a playwright came through one-act plays for vaudeville. His first full-length play, *The Torchbearers* (1922), was a satire on the little theater movement, but his subsequent dramas showed the potent influence of the new naturalism.

The Show-off (1924) reveals Kelly's understanding of character, as well as his wit.

Although only a $32.50-a-week freight clerk for the Pennsylvania

Railroad, Aubrey Piper talks like a big tycoon. Amy Fisher marries him, but her family cannot endure the blatant show-off. Aubrey incurs large expenses in an automobile accident, and he and Amy are forced to move in with her family. Aubrey even persuades his mother-in-law to pay the costs of the accident with her dead husband's insurance money. Joe, Amy's brother, has an invention for which he is offered $50,000, but through Aubrey's big talk the offer is somehow raised to $100,000. Amy, always the loving wife, now has proof of just how wonderful her Aubrey really is.

The *Show-off* is an entertaining treatment of the business success story. Piper talks the part of the big executive, and then his cocky bluffing actually works. However, his own modest life is sharply contrasted with his inflated pretensions.

Craig's Wife (1925) is an unforgettable character study, and the title has won a place in the language.

Harriet Craig admits to her niece, Ethel Landreth, that she married Walter Craig solely for security. Guarantee of her home and her possessions is "control of the man upon which they are founded." She therefore tries to dissuade Ethel from mere romantic marriage to Fredericks, an impecunious college professor. Craig, seeking companionship that his wife has refused, visits the Fergus Passmore house and then comes under suspicion when both Passmores are found dead. Harriet conceals information that would aid her husband, for she doesn't want to be "involved." Craig is cleared, but he realizes his wife's disloyalty and leaves her. Ethel marries Fredericks, and Harriet is left alone with the house that she has so selfishly cherished.

Harriet Craig's greed for possessions finds her with them in the end, but with not much else. Ethel chooses love. Kelly masterfully depicts the Craigs' house as meticulously kept but devoid of affection.

Philip Barry (1896–1949). Philip Barry was born and raised in Rochester, New York. While an undergraduate at Yale, with the coming of World War I, Barry served in the State Department in Washington and with the American Embassy in London. After securing his A.B. from Yale in 1919, he studied at Harvard in the 47 Workshop until 1922. His earliest comedy, *You and I* (1923), won a warm welcome which was also accorded many of his other plays.

Like F. Scott Fitzgerald, Barry dissected the behavior of the rich, apparently with a light heart but constantly revealing a sad undercurrent of loneliness in people who live by illusions.

Paris Bound (1927) is a witty play with a serious theme.

With an eye to Jim's divorced parents, Mary and Jim resolve not to let their marriage break up because of a casual infidelity. Mary learns, however, that Jim has been faithless to her on his annual visits to Europe. Richard, with whom she has been working on a ballet, is attracted to her and she to him. Against the pleadings of her father-in-law, Mary asks Jim for a divorce. Finding him still strongly desirous of continuing their marriage, she is silent about his affairs. At dawn they set out for the country to celebrate their anniversary with their two children.

Jim's father, speaking from his own broken marriage, contends that sex is not the heart of marriage and that physical infidelity constitutes inadequate grounds for divorce. From her own experience with Richard, Mary realizes that physical attraction is not sufficient justification for breaking up a viable family.

Holiday (1928) is perhaps the most technically excellent of Barry dramas.

At Lake Placid, John Case meets and falls in love with Julia Seton. The wealthy elder Seton is astounded that Johnny intends to quit work and enjoy life when he receives a moderate windfall. Julia also becomes cool, but her nonconformist sister Linda is on Johnny's side. When the elder Seton attempts to plan his honeymoon and subsequent career, Johnny throws up everything and takes off for Europe. Linda dashes to the boat to accompany him.

Barry denounces the money-mad 1920s, especially in the hopelessly materialistic Mr. Seton. True to her breed, Julia is all for romantic love in courtship, but once married she expects a husband to buckle down to good solid money-making. Linda, one of Barry's most fascinating heroines, is the ideal young woman of the era—not pretty, but brilliantly witty and independent. She moves beyond her family to demand a life of freedom and creativity.

The Animal Kingdom (1932) takes a vigorous stand on the contrast between love and sex.

Rebelling against the staid conventions of his wealthy father, Tom Collier lives as he pleases. He heads the Bantam Press, which prints good writing that is unwanted elsewhere. Daisy Sage, an understanding artist, is his mistress. While Daisy is absent in Europe, Tom marries Cecilia Henry who quickly goes about altering his life. She decorates his country home in the fashion of respectable conventionality, steers him away from all his interesting friends, and engineers a deal to get Tom's press to print best-selling claptrap. Cecilia is affectionate when Tom gives in to her, but archly denies him when he dissents. Tom leaves her and returns to Daisy, who shares his ideals.

The Philadelphia Story (1939) is Barry's best-known comedy.

Seth Lord, head of a wealthy Main-Line Philadelphia family, has left his wife because of infatuation with a dancer. To counter the scandalmongering article planned by *Destiny Magazine*, the family brings reporters Mike and Liz from *Destiny* to cover the marriage of Tracy, Seth's daughter, to the coal mogul George Kittredge. Tracy's second marriage is imperiled by the appearance of her divorced husband, C. K. Dexter Havens. A champagne binge on the eve of Tracy's wedding, complicated by her midnight swim with Mike, appalls Kittredge. At the last moment Havens, recognizing Tracy's growth in sympathies and her new relaxed conduct, substitutes himself as bridegroom.

Barry here demonstrates his consummate proficiency as the playwright of America's aristocracy. Dexter appraises Tracy's greatest fault as a lack of "yare," a yachting term meaning "nimble maneuverability." Tracy is a hard, unyielding standard-setter who lacks tolerance, understanding, and outgoing love. Properly regenerated, she rightfully belongs to a man of her own class, her former husband Dexter.

In some of his other plays Barry turned from comedy to more philosophical themes, especially in *Hotel Universe* (1930) and *Here Come the Clowns* (1938).

Rachel Crothers (1878–1958). A native of Bloomington, Illinois, Rachel Crothers proved herself to be one of the most successful Broadway playwrights of the 1920s and 1930s, writing a series of witty plays that pleased and flattered the taste of the audience. Miss Crothers' plays intrigued viewers with attractive dialogue and apparent daringness of theme (her women were determinedly independent and intelligent). Then she resolved the problems of the plays by judicious sentiment and happy ending.

Susan and God (1937) is perhaps her best play. Susan returns from England infatuated with a new religious sect (resembling the Oxford movement) preaching love for all one's fellows. In practice Susan neglects her family, causing her husband to leave and to threaten divorce. But Susan realizes her errors in time and all is smoothed out.

William Saroyan (1908–   ). Of Armenian ancestry, William Saroyan was born in Fresno, California. Because of her numerous children, his widowed mother was forced to place him in an orphanage. Saroyan left school at twelve to be a telegraph messenger. He held no job for long but leaped to prominence in 1934 with the publication of several pieces of fiction, especially *The Daring Young Man on the Flying Trapeze*.

Saroyan's plays have a distinctive quality which won prompt recognition. His mixture of fantasy and realism, impertinence and breezy tenderness was a refreshing, almost intoxicating, change. Rejecting the 47 Workshop idea of the drama, Saroyan scorns the methods of traditional stagecraft, and attempts to create mood rather than plot or characterization.

My Heart's in the Highlands (1937), his first play, has no act divisions and on the stage uses a medieval device which simultaneously represents the Alexander residence and the Kosak grocery in Fresno in 1914.

Jasper MacGregor, an aged Scotsman and former Shakespearean actor, flees an old folks' home to play the bugle and take refuge with the Alexanders. A representative from the institution comes for Jasper, and the Alexanders are evicted for failure to pay their rent. Mr. Kosak cancels the grocery bills, but Mr. Alexander tries to pay by handing over his unsalable poems. Jasper flees again to the Alexanders and dies there. Nine-year-old Johnny and his penniless father hand over the house to the new tenants.

"There will always be poets in the world," insists Johnny's father as World War I breaks out. Alexander's plight is that of the poet in a materialistic world. The Alexanders and the old bugler bring music and beauty to their neighbors and in return receive food and love. Dispossessed, Johnny and his father go forth with only their hopes and dreams to sustain them.

The Time of Your Life (1939) received the New York Drama Critics' Circle Award and the Pulitzer Prize (which Saroyan refused because he deemed this work no more deserving than his previously ignored pieces).

Nick's Pacific Street Saloon in San Francisco harbors an astounding collection of hangers-on. The wealthy Joe sips champagne and listens interminably to "The Missouri Waltz" on the juke box. He dispatches his side-kick Tom on weird errands (kid's toys, an atlas, chewing gum of exotic flavors), conceivable only by a drunk. Kit Carson is an aged liar whose tall tales (he claims to have been married once to a thirty-nine-pound midget) are uproarious, while the routines of Harry, the hoofer-comedian, are old and stale. Blick, head of the vice squad, makes things hard for the Negro pianist Wesley and for the dreamy prostitute, Kitty Duval. Tom rescues Kitty, and Kit Carson shoots Blick.

Saroyan's down-and-outers are the wonderful little people of the world who ask only to live and let live. Refugees from a highly competitive, materialistic society, they love one another and applaud anyone's dreams or expressions that give happiness and hope. In righteous indignation Saroyan must destroy the discordant element, the zealous Blick, emissary of a rigorous morality that would impose its puritanical will upon the denizens of Nick's bar. Saroyan's sentimental whimsey and fertile imagination give color to his message.

Lillian Hellman (1905–   ). Born in New Orleans, Lillian Hellman was brought to New York City at the age of five. After attending

New York University and Columbia, she worked in book publishing and in a theatrical company.

Miss Hellman has been deeply concerned with the concept of personal integrity, and she portrays this strong moral sense in works in which the struggle of good and evil is clearly set forth. And though evil often triumphs at the end, the essence and the effects of evil are made frighteningly clear.

The Children's Hour (1934) was based upon a true happening in Edinburgh, Scotland.

Spoiled brat Mary Tilford is punished for misbehaving at the girls' school operated by Martha Dobie and Karen Wright. In revenge Mary distorts an overheard conversation to accuse Martha and Karen of lesbianism, and browbeats another girl, Rosalie Wells, into corroborating her story. Parents withdraw their children and force the closing of the school. Martha and Karen cannot convince an outraged community of their innocence, and Martha commits suicide. Mrs. Tilford then appears with Mary's confession that she lied. Although the harm cannot be undone, Karen may marry her fiancé, Dr. Joseph Cardin.

Lillian Hellman sees society as indecently hasty to believe any accusation and to increase its credulity if the scandal seems large enough. Miss Hellman's precise dramatic craftsmanship is matched by taut and intense dialogue.

The Little Foxes (1939) in title refers to "the little foxes that spoil the vines" from The Song of Solomon.

While Horace Giddens is being treated at Johns Hopkins, at home in the Deep South his wife, Regina, is approached by her brothers, Ben and Oscar Hubbard, who wish Giddens' backing to finance a cotton mill. Birdie, Oscar's wife, represents the traditional old Southern aristocracy. Horace returns and finds that the Hubbards want only his money, and refuses them. Regina cooperates in a theft from the Giddens' safe-deposit box, and tells Horace how she married him not for love but for security. Suffering from a stroke, Horace seeks his medicine but Regina coldly lets him die. In the end she forces from her brothers 75 per cent of their forthcoming profits.

The play is a model of structure and dramatic economy.

Another Part of the Forest (1946) treats again of the Hubbards of *The Little Foxes,* but its setting is twenty years before the time of that play.

Marcus Hubbard wants financially advantageous marriages for his sons, Ben and Oscar, and for his daughter, Regina. Regina's suitor, lacking the desired wealth, is discouraged by the family. Oscar is paired with Birdie Bagtry so that the Bagtry plantation can be secured by the Hubbards. Ben learns from his mother, Lavinia, that his father had informed to the Federal troops for a price during the Civil War and had thereby caused the massacre of twenty-seven Confederate soldiers. Ben uses this information to obtain the fortune of his own father by blackmail.

Marcus has instilled in his offspring a rapacious money ethic that denies all other values, and the younger Hubbards are destined for their avaricious roles in *The Little Foxes*.

The Autumn Garden (1951) is in a friendlier mood, although the problems of life are clearly presented.

Another season is drawing to a close at Constance Tuckerman's boarding house, and the aging guests, who for the most part have come there for years, are preparing to leave shortly. An old friend of Constance and Ned Tuckerman's, whom neither has seen in a long time, comes to visit. He is Nick, a painter. Nick quickly involves himself in the affairs of the guests Frederick and Sophie. Frederick and Sophie, who are younger, plan to be married, but decide to postpone their wedding; and Sophie senses that the wedding will never happen. Nick tries to seduce Sophie. Sophie, who seemed beyond the pettiness of others, extorts $5000 from Nick's wife in return for a promise not to spread the scandal.

There are several subtle reversals of outlook by the characters in the play. Some of the women seem wholly incapable of seeing beyond their provincial world. Some of the men have a realization of the trap that they have created and seem to have the will to escape it. But they do not escape; rather they fall more deeply into it. Yet all these people come to terms with themselves, and for a moment accept themselves as the limited people they are. The two young people, Frederick and Sophie, go off in different directions; Frederick settles for a boring life with his mother; but Sophie, whom everyone thought of as lacking in spirit, escapes to the life she really wants. Nick, the outsider, is the only one who has not changed at all, but he has changed the lives of all the others.

Sidney Kingsley (1906–   ). Born in New York City, Sidney Kingsley proved to be a competent playwright while still an undergraduate at Cornell. After graduation in 1928 he was an actor, play reader, and motion-picture script writer.

Men in White (1933) was the first Kingsley play to be presented on Broadway.

Dr. George Ferguson, while an intern, is engaged to the wealthy Laura Hudson. She is constantly piqued as he cancels dates with her because of the pressure of his work. Against the orders of callous Dr. Cunningham, Ferguson manages to save a patient's life. The attending student nurse, Barbara Dennin, admires Ferguson, and they have a brief affair. As Ferguson's marriage to Laura approaches, he is summoned to operate upon a woman critically injured by a clumsy abortionist. The woman turns out to be Barbara, and she dies. The disconsolate Ferguson plunges into more study, and Laura agrees to a postponement of their marriage.

The drama exemplifies the two noteworthy contributions of Kingsley: meticulous, photographic realism and a vigorously expounded social message. The drabness of the hospital is faithfully reproduced, and its tingling drama is encased in the actuality of busy routine. The duty to humanity is quietly and unheroically represented by Ferguson, whose personal wishes, regardless of the cost, must be sacrificed to a greater cause.

Dead End (1935) is Kingsley's best-known play.

The tenants of a plush New York East Side apartment house are annoyed that repairs compel them to use the back entrance which faces squalid tenements. Jack Hilton and Kay, his mistress, Mr. Griswald and his son Philip are all disgusted with the rowdy kids (Tommy, Dippy, T.B., Angel, and Spit) who play in the dead-end street and swim in the filthy East River. Planning vainly to remove the slum blight is Gimpty, trained in college as an architect, but cursed with rickety legs from his origin in the dead-end neighborhood. When an infamous gangster, Babyface Martin, returns to his old street, Gimpty informs on him, and Martin is gunned down by the F.B.I. Gimpty with his reward money asks Kay to marry him, but she prefers the security offered by Hilton. Tommy has been arrested for knifing Mr. Griswald in an attempted robbery. At the appeal of Drina, Tommy's sister, Gimpty permits his "blood money" to be used for Tommy's legal defense.

The play was born of the Depression years and Kingsley's memories of his own childhood. The drama is marked by robust, authentic dialogue and the tremendous vivacity of humanity within the most depressing surroundings.

The Patriots (1943) is a drama of American history. The democratic ideals of Jefferson are exalted over the aristocratic concepts of Hamilton. The play, written in the war years, stresses the necessity of national unity (illustrated by Hamilton's belated support of Jefferson) but especially Jefferson's unselfish devotion to his country against his personal inclination to rural retirement.

Detective Story (1949) is a reply to the conventional whodunit. Detective McLeod's precinct is preoccupied with avaricious and sordid criminals, not the glamorous characters of mystery stories. Kingsley long observed actual New York police stations in order to reproduce the genuine atmosphere of a grubby, overworked precinct headquarters.

The righteously indignant Detective James McLeod detests a man who is an abortionist. McLeod is the self-appointed protector of women because his father's brutality had forced his mother into an asylum. Learning from a lieutenant that his own wife, Mary, before their marriage had gone to the abortionist, McLeod beats up the man and calls Mary a whore. The angry McLeod wishes to prosecute a veteran who stole money for his needy girl friend. Mary leaves McLeod after making him realize that he has recast himself in the mold of his sadistic father. McLeod is killed by a criminal attempting escape. Dying, he repents and asks for a second chance for the veteran.

Paul Green (1894–   ). Born on a farm near Lillington, North Carolina, Paul Eliot Green worked on the soil, and received a desultory education. In 1916 he began collegiate study at the University of North Carolina, but left at the outbreak of World War I for extensive service in France with the A.E.F. Returning, he resumed dramatic studies under Frederick H. Koch and wrote for the Carolina Playmakers. After receiving his A.B., he did graduate work at Cornell University and from 1923 for a number of years he taught drama at the University of North Carolina. Later he was appointed to the United States National Commission for Peace and the executive board of UNESCO.

Green is the foremost folklorist among American dramatists, and his work is largely independent of the New York theater. His early one-act plays distilled the atmosphere and psychology of North Carolinians with especial sympathy for the Negro, as in *The Lord's Will and Other Carolina Plays* (1925) and *Lonesome Road: Six Plays for Negro Theater* (1926).

In Abraham's Bosom (1927) takes place in North Carolina in 1885.

Abraham McCranie is Colonel McCranie's mulatto son. Abraham's wish to teach school is furthered by his white father but vehemently opposed by his white half brother, Lonnie. After the Colonel's death, Abraham's meagerly attended school is closed. His attempts to resume teaching some years later are thwarted by whites, notably Lonnie. In a fight Abraham kills Lonnie and in turn is shot.

An episode of cruelty to a Negro school teacher witnessed by Green in his childhood is the basis for this tragedy.

The House of Connelly (1931) is concerned with the dissolution of the old Southern aristocracy.

The remnants of the old Connelly family live on their decaying plantation among the memories of a glorious and gracious past. Young Will, the last of the line, is suddenly inspired by Patsy, daughter of a tenant farmer, to rejuvenate the house and lands. Will's mother, his Uncle Bob, and his two sisters are dismayed by Will's actions and by his growing affection for the lower-class Patsy. The corruption which shrouds the Connelly name is brought out in a climactic scene in which Uncle Bob commits suicide. Mrs. Connelly dies shortly thereafter, the sisters leave for the city, and Will marries Patsy. But the last scene brings in a tragic new element as two elderly black women, Big Sue and Big Sis, strangle Patsy to death to revenge an old wrong by the house of Connelly, or perhaps to protest against all oppression.

Green then turned to "plays derived from the people's history, their legends, folk-customs and beliefs, their hopes and ideals." Green conceived for this presentation a new type of play which he terms "symphonic drama," extensively employing folk ballads, choruses, dancing, and singing, in which each character is treated as a musical instrument blending into the lyrical whole.

Green was very much interested in bringing good theater to audiences who ordinarily are not exposed to it. In 1937 he began a series of pageant plays celebrating historical events. *The Lost Colony* (1937), based on the pioneer settlement of North Carolina, is annually performed at Roanoke Island. Also annual is the production at Williamsburg, Virginia, of *The Common Glory* (1948), "a symphonic drama" of the American Revolution with emphasis upon the roles of the state of Virginia and of Thomas Jefferson in establishing democracy. In vivid contrast to Green's earlier tone, these "symphonic dramas" are among the most Whitmanesque writings of the twentieth century, extolling the energy and the idealism of Americans, finding in a glorious past sure promise of a vibrant present and future. Always impatient with formal dramatic structure, Green tends toward episodic construction, producing not so much mounting action as mounting lyrical intensity.

Clifford Odets (1906–63). Born in Philadelphia, Clifford Odets moved with his family to the Bronx at the age of six. Enraptured by the theater, Odets left high school in New York to act, though with only moderate success. He was one of the founders of the notable Group Theatre, and wrote several of his plays for it. In 1934, during the depths of the Depression, like many other creative people he was briefly interested in the tenets of communism. His meteoric success as a playwright took him to Hollywood, and thereafter he worked as both a playwright and a movie script writer. In 1943 he began to direct movies and stage plays, and direction became his major interest.

Waiting for Lefty (1935), in which Odets himself acted, is a strikingly explosive propaganda drama.

Taxi drivers, galled by starvation wages, await Lefty Costello whom they expect to lead them in a strike. Fatt, a union official under company control, seeks to dissuade them. Calling for the strike are the cabbies: Joe (in a flashback his wife, Edna, bitterly spurs him on because their children lack food and their furniture had been taken away), Miller (an idealistic chemical researcher who quit his job rather than work on poison gas), Sid (unable to marry Florrie because of his poverty), and Dr. Benjamin (a competent physician forced to drive a taxi when anti-Semitism caused his dismissal from a hospital staff). The news that Lefty has been murdered steels all to resolution, led by Agate, and immediately the curtain falls to frenzied cries: "Strike, Strike, Strike!"

Awake and Sing! (1935) was completed in 1933, but first produced after *Waiting for Lefty*. The characters are Jewish residents of the Bronx during the Depression, and the play is an intimate portrait.

Bessie Berger tries to keep a respectable, tidy home in spite of the meager income of Myron, her husband. Son Ralph contributes his small paycheck, while his grandfather, Jacob the Marxist, grumbles about the horrible state of the world. Their boarder, Moe Axelrod, has the security of a pension, due to the loss of a leg in World War I. Though daughter Hennie is cool to her suitor, Sam Feinschreiber, Bessie forces their marriage when Hennie becomes pregnant. Hennie lets Sam know that the child is not his, and she runs off with Moe. Jacob commits suicide, but his advice, "Awake and sing," impels Ralph to study and prepare himself to work for a better world.

Golden Boy (1937) has proved extraordinarily popular.

Joe Bonaparte, son of an Italian fruit peddler, becomes an accomplished violinist but realizes that art has insignificant cash value in a grossly materialistic society. Handy with his fists, Joe rises to wealth and fame in the prize ring. Always he intends to return to music, but he so injures his hands that he can never again play the violin. When he kills the former champion with a blow epitomizing "the fury of a lifetime," he cannot go on with boxing either. Death comes to Joe in an automobile accident.

The play is built upon the symbology of the violin (constructive, cultural) vs. the boxing gloves (destructive, materialistic). The destructive forces overwhelm the creative urge. The splendid automobile, which Joe drives so intemperately, is the trophy of his material success, an emblem of today's craze for speed, and the inevitable vehicle of his destruction.

Other characters are Fuseli, the racketeer who buys Joe like a commodity; Mr. Bonaparte, Joe's father, who seeks for his son self-fulfillment and personal happiness; Joe's brother Frank, who is a labor organizer and a fighter for social betterment.

The play is tightly constructed, with racy, lively dialogue.

The Country Girl (1950) draws somewhat upon Odets' years in Hollywood.

At fifty, Frank Elgin is an alcoholic actor hesitantly offered a starring role by director Bernie Dodd. Frank blames his wife, Georgie, for his failures, but Dodd soon learns that Frank is a spineless character trying to make a scapegoat of his wife. Dodd and Georgie are attracted to each other, but she elects to stay with Frank.

Frank is essentially an exhibitionist who desperately needs acclaim to bolster his ego. Georgie's decision to remain with him comes from her sensing the value of responsibility and family cohesiveness.

Thornton Wilder (1897–   ). A biographical sketch of Thornton Niven Wilder appears in Chapter 1, with the discussion of his novels. Because of his distinction both as a dramatist and a novelist, we divide his work between the two chapters.

Our Town (1938) is set in Grover's Corners, New Hampshire, between 1901 and 1913. No scenery is used. A stage manager, acting as narrator, appears from time to time, and discusses to some extent the events and characters. This device is drawn from the property manager of the Chinese stage and the chorus of ancient Greek drama.

George Gibbs, son of the town physician, marries Emily Webb, daughter of the local newspaper editor. The two lived next door and attended school together for many years. The second act shows the happiness of their marriage. But Emily dies in childbirth. George's grief is deep and inconsolable. The stage is filled with umbrellas of the mourners in the rain. When the umbrellas are removed, the dead are seen seated on their graves in chairs. Emily shyly joins them and learns that she may relive one day of her past life. She chooses her twelfth birthday. But living that day again brings her no joy as she is now aware of what lies ahead of her. She returns to her grave and joins the dead who eternally look up at the stars.

The central problem of the play is clearly expressed in the first act—the great difficulty in finding sense and meaning in the rushing continuum of life. The inhabitants of Grover's Corners are too caught up in the act of living to take a larger view. It is the function of the artist to do this.

The stage manager plays the part of the artist. He can look back into the past and forward into the future and separate the important moments from the mass of trivial events which surround them.

Wilder explained the purpose of the play: "It is an attempt to find a value above all price for the smallest events in our daily life. I have made the claim as preposterous as possible, for I have set the village against the largest dimensions of time and place." And Emily, taking a last look at the past, cries: "O Earth, you're too wonderful for anybody to realize you. Do any human beings ever realize life while they live it?"

The stage manager replies: "No. The saints and poets maybe—they do some."

The Skin of Our Teeth (1942) is likewise highly successful in its use of the expressionistic technique.

George Antrobus and his wife, Eva, experience human life through the millenia. At the outset, George is an Ice Age commuter from Excelsior, New Jersey, engrossed with the lawn and the pet dinosaur, but in his spare time inventing the wheel and the lever. By his wife he has sons Henry and Abel, and daughter Gladys. The eternal seductress Lily Sabrina, a family maid, lures George. Henry (Cain) kills Abel. As the ice approaches, Moses, Homer, and the Muses take refuge with the Antrobus family.

When the deluge threatens, George is elected President of the Ancient and Honorable Order of Mammals (Subdivision: Humans) meeting in convention at Atlantic City. On the beach he is seduced by Miss Lily-Sabrina Fairweather. He is about to leave his wife for Sabrina, but the floods induce him to unite his quarrelsome family and board the ark.

After a catastrophic war that destroys civilization the suburban New Jersey household displays normal turmoil. Sabrina drifts in from her wartime career as camp follower; Henry is busy with the newest youth movement; and Gladys is going to have a baby. Guided by the thoughts of great men and faithful in his fashion to family responsibilities, George vows to continue the search for a better human lot.

Wild farce and ludicrous anachronisms clothe a deeply serious message. Although specified as American, the Antrobus family represents all mankind for all time. In spite of Nature's impersonal catastrophes and man's own abysmal stupidity and cruelty, somehow humanity survives. And it even manages to inch forward. The destiny of man is largely his own to determine. Although the end of everything frequently threatens, we shall be able to squeeze through "by the skin of our teeth."

Some aspects of the play are suggested by sections of *Finnegans Wake* by James Joyce.

The Matchmaker (1954) is a rewriting of Wilder's earlier *The Merchant of Yonkers* (1938). The events are set in the 1880s.

Horace Vandergelder, a widower, owns a grocery store in Yonkers. He tries to break up the love affair between his niece Ermengarde and an artist, Ambrose Kemper. At the same time he is trying to secure a wife through Mrs. Dolly Levi, a marriage broker. Leaving clerk Cornelius Hackl in charge of the store, he proceeds to New York to see Mrs. Molloy. His clerks sneak off to enjoy New York and desperately try to evade the boss. In a farcical melée all works out. Ermengarde and her artist are married, Cornelius becomes Vandergelder's partner and the spouse of Mrs. Molloy, and Vandergelder is cleverly maneuvered into proposing to and wedding the vivacious Dolly.

The play is a very free adaptation of *Einen Jux will er sich Machen* (1842) by the Viennese Johann Nestroy. Wilder frankly intended it as a zany burlesque of familiar stage comedy. Conventionality is represented by Vandergelder. All the other characters are in revolt against his drab, unimaginative world. Madcap Dolly in conquering Vandergelder imposes upon him her own philosophy. "Money," she postulates, "should circulate like rain water." The play was transformed into a popular musical, *Hello, Dolly*, in 1964.

"Thoughts on Playwriting" (1941), written for inclusion in *The Intent of the Artist*, enunciates Wilder's dramatic theory. Wilder insists on imaginative suggestion in the theater, which will compel the audience to creation within itself. Thus drama may demonstrate the human experience and man's interplay with his fellow man, with Nature, and with the cosmos.

CHAPTER FOUR

Prose of the Early Twentieth Century

PROSE AS A MEDIUM FOR THOUGHT, STYLE, AND CRITICISM

Prose in the sense in which we use the term here applies primarily to writings other than fiction or the drama (or poetry, of course) which are a part of literature, and does not to any large extent include other works in such fields as history, biography, or the sciences, even though these are of course also prose in its larger meaning.

A few works beyond the central area of literature are discussed here, however, when they seem to have a close relation to the literature of the period. Thus our opening discussion deals with George Santayana, who although primarily considered a philosopher is more broadly a man of letters. This section may be looked upon as a twentieth-century continuation of the discussion of William James, Josiah Royce, and other great thinkers of the nineteenth century, who are considered in our companion volume, *History of American Literature From the Beginning to 1910.* Following Santayana, we take up John Dewey, whose writings in both philosophy and education have been so widely influential as the expression of ideas leading to application.

After this first group of thinkers in various fields, we turn to writers who are noted as distinctive prose stylists, some of them following traditional standards and others establishing criteria of their own. This latter approach to style is well demonstrated in the work of Gertrude Stein, with her conception of language as conveying mood through the sound of words rather than through their meaning. The section on

Gertrude Stein covers the whole range of her work, and references to her in other chapters of the book are to this section.

Many of the writers who follow offer fresh approaches to traditional prose style, and several bring an intriguingly humorous quality to their work.

Toward the end of the chapter we turn to the subject of literary criticism, and consider a number of important critics whose writings have a valued place in American literature of the earlier part of the twentieth century, and who won for literary criticism the recognition which was to be extended further by the more recent critics, who are discussed in Chapter 8.

MAJOR PHILOSOPHERS, POLITICAL THINKERS, AND ECONOMISTS OF THE PERIOD

George Santayana (1863–1952). Born in Madrid, George Santayana never relinquished Spanish citizenship, but, brought to the United States in 1872, he used the anglicized form of his name instead of Jorge Ruiz de Santayana y Borrais as originally in Spanish. He received an A.B. in 1886 and a Ph.D. in 1889 from Harvard, where he studied under William James and Josiah Royce. From 1889 to 1912 he was a professor of philosophy at his alma mater, adding a new dimension to the great strength and distinction of that famous department at Harvard. After 1912 Santayana resided in Europe, chiefly England and France. At the outset of World War II he entered a nursing home in Rome conducted by Roman Catholic sisters of an English order. He is buried in the Spanish cemetery in Rome.

Although he gave forty of his choicest years to America and this country gave him the language in which he wrote and spoke, Santayana was always, by his own admission as well as the consensus of those who knew him, an alien in our midst. He was an aristocrat in a democracy, a mellow humanist among the eminently practical, a poet in a very prosaic land, a Catholic—as he stated, in everything but faith—amidst Protestantism. His subtlety of thought was a challenge to the minds he came into contact with, and he expressed himself in richly cadenced and gently melodious English.

THE POET. Until about 1905 Santayana was chiefly interested in the writing of poetry. His first publication, *Sonnets and Other Verses* (1894), began a verse output that continued until *Poems* (1923), his selection of what he deemed his best. His achievement of poetic excellence is unique among formal philosophers of modern times. His verse notably displays one quality absent from his prose: Platonism; and omits a quality omnipresent in his prose: ironic humor. Santayana is outstanding as a sonneteer. His most ambitious attempt in verse was *Lucifer: A Theological Tragedy* (1899, rev. 1924), a search for "natural religion" when Santayana found Christianity unacceptable. Greek and Christian deities confront each other to no avail. Lucifer concludes by invoking Truth.

THE PHILOSOPHER. *The Sense of Beauty* (1896) was based upon Harvard lectures "under the inspiration of a naturalistic psychology." Beauty, he asserts, is "pleasure objectified." The aesthetic response arises from sensuous and ideal experiences of pleasure. "Beauty is a pledge of the possible conformity between the soul and nature, and consequently a ground of faith in the supremacy of the good."

Interpretations of Poetry and Religion (1900) contains brilliant literary criticism. "The Elements and Functions of Poetry" offers Santayana's four poetic elements: euphony ("sensuous beauty of words and their utterance in measure"), euphuism ("the choice of colored words and rare and elliptical phrases"), experiential immediacy ("the volume of experience as well as its form"), rational imagination ("out of that living but indefinite material to build new structures, richer, finer, fitter to the primary tendencies of our nature, truer to the ultimate possibilities of the soul"). At their ultimate imaginative development, Santayana finds poetry and religion are identical. "The Poetry of Barbarism" is critical of some of Santayana's contemporaries and some earlier poets, who "have no total vision, no grasp of the whole reality, and consequently no capacity for a sane and steady idealization."

Three Philosophical Poets (1910) is a uniquely perceptive study of Lucretius, Dante, and Goethe by a philosopher-poet. Santayana here contrasts three approaches to man's sensing of the meaning of his world. Lucretius, accurately appraising much of Nature and aware of human limitations, fails to comprehend fully the potentialities of experience. Dante surpasses these potentialities with an ordered vision of the entire universe and of ultimate human good, but his universe is imaginary, not true. Goethe responds to immediacy, valuing experience for its own sake. While the spadework of philosophy is not poetic, poetry can fuse with the philosophical vision: "focus all experience within it, make it a philosopher's vision of the world."

The Life of Reason (5 vols., 1905–06) is the basic statement of "philosophical naturalism." It is simultaneously a historical study of the application of human intelligence to every aspect of life and a moral treatise. Santayana opens with his naturalistic credo that all forces governing human life "must betray themselves in human experience." For James's "stream of consciousness" he substitutes "flux." From an initial life of impulse, man's flux moves toward the life of reason. Santayana distinguishes three stages: prerational (directed solely by impulse, habit, and desire), rational (conscious, deliberate planning), and postrational (reaching for the ideal as "imagination clothes a rational and humane reason"). "Everything ideal has a natural basis and everything natural an ideal development." The naturalistic ideal provides a yardstick to measure man's past accomplishments and the incentive to strive toward the future life of reason.

Scepticism and Animal Faith (1923) forms with *The Realms of Being* (4 vols., 1927–40) another five-volume philosophical study. These works are still fundamentally naturalistic. Santayana pictures the world as consisting of four fundamental manifestations: matter (the primary real substance of nature, even if unknowable), essence (mental reflections or intuitions), spirit (the dynamic flow of experience), truth ("frozen history," the accumulated wisdom of civilization, for there is no other ultimate truth). Although the areas of speculation and imagination intrigue the philosopher, he resolutely insists that "immaterial things" are only true as "qualities, products, or ideal implications of the physical world."

THE CRITIC. *Soliloquies in England* (1922) is a detached, urbane appraisal of England, or rather of the cultivated English gentleman. The book contains some notable prose lyrics on the English countryside.

Character and Opinion in the United States (1920) analyzes the American mind-set in its strength and in its weaknesses. Santayana is particularly struck by the vast gulf between academic values and everyday viewpoints in America, the contrast between professed devotion to ideals and culture and the emphasis on mercenary pursuits.

THE NOVELIST. *The Last Puritan* (1936), Santayana's only novel, brought him fame among many unacquainted with his philosophy and gracefully introduced them to that philosophy.

Oliver Alden (the last puritan) feels the inadequacy of his New England background but cannot shake it off. His wealthy father, finding nothing to substitute for the puritanism he has repudiated, commits suicide. Oliver's cousin Mario Van de Weyer, a cheerful European sophisticate, is attractive but baffling to the Brahmins. Oliver proposes to Rose Darnley but is refused because she loves Mario. Oliver departs with the World War I expeditionary force and is killed in France.

Mario is obviously Santayana's preference and his own idealized self— the gay, natural, untroubled Continental in love with life, the intellectual and aesthetic hedonist. Nonetheless he lacks the sharp reality of Oliver, the troubled puritan. Oliver seeks perfection through a sense of duty, while Santayana cautions that perfection can only be reached through love. Oliver is neither a fanatic nor a hypocrite; he is in conflict between his inclinations and the bonds of his heritage.

John Dewey (1859–1952). A native of Burlington, Vermont, John

Dewey received his A.B. from the University of Vermont in 1879 and his Ph.D. from Johns Hopkins University in 1884. After teaching at the universities of Minnesota, Michigan, and Chicago, he commenced his long association with Columbia University in 1904. World fame caused him to lecture as far afield as China and Japan. He was one of the most fearless champions of free speech and thought in American life, and for the early twentieth century stood as a major philosophical and educational force in this country.

Dewey declared that "Philosophy is of account only if it affords guidance to action." Often grouped with the pragmatists, Dewey preferred to call his viewpoint "instrumentalism"; it is also termed "experimental naturalism." Dewey's writings are not distinguished as literature, and are important rather for the points they make.

Outlines of a Critical Theory of Ethics (1891) advances an experimental approach in evaluating morality. Ethical behavior is not conformity to fixed standards; it must show regard for others and must lead to beneficial usefulness. Freedom of inquiry is essential, and newly discovered facts as well as newly created institutions can well operate to supersede the most time-honored moral concepts.

The School and Society (1899) is his most widely read and influential work. It derives from talks that he gave to raise funds for the University of Chicago Laboratory School which Dewey established as an experiment in progressive education. To Dewey, true education is the very antithesis of conventional training, which is largely devoted to indoctrination in traditional beliefs and to the stimulation of mechanical reflexes. Education, Dewey proclaimed, should be the liberation and growth of individual intelligence. He particularly sought an active community life within a school and a vital interaction of the school with the social and natural environment.

How We Think (1909), as the title indicates, is not concerned with distinguishing between the world of things and the world of mind. As an instrumentalist Dewey sees ideas as meaningful only as they are plans of action. "The having of ideas is not so much something we do, as it is something that happens to us." When some conflict in experience presents a problem, an obstacle to activity, thought is the generation of responses seeking to restore activity. Thought and action are therefore continuous and interrelated processes.

Experience and Nature (1925) linked Dewey with Alfred Whitehead as a leading philosopher for much of modern science, particularly experimental physics. Denying the mechanistic concept of nature, Dewey posits nature as essentially interrelated events. "Structure" is no rigid principle but simply a term for a more slowly changing "process." In Dewey's naturalistic universe, all is Becoming. "Qualities have defects as necessary conditions of their excellencies; the instrumentalities of truth are the cause of error; change gives meaning to permanence and recurrence makes novelty possible; . . . only a living world can include death."

A Common Faith (1934) is Dewey's contribution to religious thought. His primary position is a denial of the traditional assumption that religion consists of set beliefs and practices, tied to supernaturalism and institutionalized in a church. Religious experience is not a separate facet of human experience but "faith in the continued disclosing of truth through directed cooperative human endeavor."

Art as Experience (1934) belied critics who felt Dewey to be little interested in art. Dewey here insists that the imaginative activity engendered by art produces the greatest intensity and meaning of experience. Art is pure experience, without distraction or distortion, with balanced incorporation of tension and resolution.

Freedom and Culture (1939) is a classic expression of modern liberal democracy. Dewey examines other political theories, notably Marxism, and concludes that a free democracy is the most satisfactory system for today's society. Democratic development through experiment and education can best realize the potential of the individual and the social group. The guiding principle of liberal democracy is the democratic employment of the state's total resources for the well-being of all. Unlike the Jeffersonian concept that the best government is the least government, Dewey's contention is that the democratic state should enter any and every field where it can assist in social betterment.

Felix Adler (1851–1933). Felix Adler was born at Alzey, Germany. His father, a Jewish rabbi, brought the family to America in 1857. After graduating from Columbia University, Adler completed his studies at Berlin and Heidelberg. From 1874 to 1876 he taught Hebrew and oriental literature at Cornell. In 1876 he founded the Society for Ethical Culture in New York, as the cornerstone of a movement toward liberal religion. From 1902 for a number of years he was professor of social ethics at Columbia University. Adler was one of the most noted reformers of his time, a pioneer seeking improved methods in education and housing, especially for the underprivileged, and encouraging continuing work in child study and other fields concerned with bettering human relations and human life.

An Ethical Philosophy of Life (1918), his major work, expounds Adler's Ethical Culture. An agnostic about any orthodox deity, Adler was nonetheless a philosophical idealist: "The divine ideal is to be represented not as One but as a manifold, not as an individual however supereminent, but as an infinite holy community—every person being in his essential nature a member of that community." Adler calls for faith not in any past revelation but in the vision of a better mankind as humanity purposefully directs the evolutionary process.

Morris Raphael Cohen (1880–1947). Born in Minsk, Russia, Morris Raphael Cohen was brought to this country at the age of twelve. After taking degrees at the College of the City of New York and Harvard he taught at C.C.N.Y. from 1906 to 1942. He was one of the group instrumental in the founding of the American Association of University Professors and the New School for Social Research, and was widely recognized as a penetrating and creative thinker.

Reason and Nature (1931) was Cohen's first book, although his essays and articles had made him famous for almost three decades. The "rationalistic naturalism" of Cohen seeks intelligibility of the universe within its own terms of experience, denying any explanation from outside principles. But individual experience and individual insight are useful only to another truth seeker as they are universalized by the rational techniques of logic. To an age that tended toward the extremes of absolutism and relativism he proposed "the principle of polarity." Truth involves both the specific and the universal; from particular instances ceaseless testing and refinement reach toward the end, which is the genuine condition of the successive stages in self-corrective reason.

The Faith of a Liberal (1946) collects the best short pieces of Cohen from 1915 on. Whether examining ethics or literature, religion or politics, Cohen is urbane and forward-looking, eschewing extremes and demanding constant naturalistic reappraisal and revaluation.

Woodrow Wilson (1856–1924). The twenty-eighth President of the United States, Thomas Woodrow Wilson was born at Staunton, Virginia, the son of a Presbyterian cleric. He studied at the universities of Princeton, Virginia, and Johns Hopkins. After teaching, he returned to Princeton, rising to its presidency in 1902. A Democrat in politics, in 1910 he became governor of New Jersey and in 1912 the nation's President. Although he hated war, events forced him to commit the country to World War I. The League of Nations, Wilson's own project and the first real attempt at a global congress of nations, failed of its objectives to a considerable degree because political opposition in the United States kept the country out of the League.

Quite apart from his role as President, Woodrow Wilson was a man of distinguished scholarly qualifications.

A History of the American People (1902), one of the most felicitously written of American histories, is less important for any novelty of interpretation than for the cool fervency of its conviction. The lesson of American history, which Wilson tried subsequently to apply to the whole world with history-making consequences, is that "self-determination" for all peoples is the only justifiable basis for government, and that "social progress" is the preeminent responsibility of any political administration.

The New Freedom (1913) has as its title a phrase closely associated with Wilson's aims. The book brings together many of Wilson's views as expressed during his campaign for the presidency. Headings under which these topics are discussed include: "Free Men Need No Guardians," "Life Comes from the Soil," "The Emancipation of Business," and "What Is Progress."

Wilson's important speeches during World War I both before and after American participation are major documents, including his proposal of the Fourteen Points for Peace and the indications of his conception of the League of Nations.

Oliver Wendell Holmes (1841–1935). Justice Oliver Wendell Holmes was the son of one of the leading literary figures of nineteenth-century America, for whom he was named. Justice Holmes, like his father, studied at Harvard. He interrupted his education to enlist in the Union Army where he was three times wounded, twice severely. "My Hunt after 'The Captain' " (1862) is his father's famous account of locating young Holmes in a Union hospital. Completing his Harvard studies, Holmes started law practice in Boston in 1867, and in 1870 began teaching at Harvard Law School. In 1882 he was appointed to the Supreme Court of Massachusetts, rising to its chief justice in 1899. President Theodore Roosevelt appointed him a justice of the United States Supreme Court in 1902, a post he held until his retirement in 1932. "The great dissenter" became world famous for his legal opinions, which established Holmes as one of the outstanding exponents of Anglo-American law.

Proud of his background, Holmes nevertheless for years struggled to escape from "the shadow of his father." The two strong wills were often opposed to one another. The elder Holmes eloquently resisted the extension of evolutionary principles to moral freedom and the human spirit, while the younger Holmes strongly favored this very extension.

The Common Law (1881), one of the major pieces of American legal theorizing, is the enunciator of sociological jurisprudence, an application of pragmatism to law. "The life of the law has not been logic: it has been experience." Law is made for society, not society for the law. Never an absolute, law "must found itself on actual forces." Law must constantly adapt itself to a changing social environment.

Often called a great liberal, Holmes was in some ways rather conservative; his liberal decisions arose largely from his pragmatic philosophy. Even when he personally disliked a social development, he felt bound to direct the law upon the path of indicated social change. His most notable contribution while on the Supreme Court bench was his defense of free speech.

Thorstein Veblen (1857–1929). Born on a farm in Cato Township, Wisconsin, Thorstein Bunde Veblen was brought up in Minnesota, with Norwegian, his parents' language, as his earliest tongue. After graduation from Carleton College, he did graduate work at Johns Hopkins and Yale. He taught at the universities of Chicago, Stanford, and Missouri. In 1918 he became one of a famous group constituting the editorial board of the magazine *The Dial* in New York; he also lectured at the New School for Social Research. His private as well as academic life was stormy, but brilliant minds found him one of the most stimulating thinkers of the age.

The Theory of the Leisure Class (1899) was a retort to classical economists who held the economic struggle to be simply rational self-interest. With devastating irony Veblen attacks this sober edifice, asserting that civilized society is merely savage society evolved into more complex patterns but driven by equally irrational forces. The two contrasting human drives are "productive," in industry, and "predatory," in business. (The words and phrases in quotation marks in this and the following sentences are keys in Veblen's writings.) Primitive societies like that of Odysseus, "sacker of cities," praise as strong and valiant the predators who seize possessions by force. Modern societies (like that of the late nineteenth-century American "robber barons") similarly extol the predators who now win money by shrewdness and guile; and they deprecate nonpredatory means of livelihood—as in productive work—as lacking dignity. The successful predators of today, like the shoguns of feudal Japan, publicly parade their position by "conspicuous waste" and "conspicuous consumption."

Veblen increased interest in a "technocracy," a proposed economic system under which the processes of production and distribution would be the responsibility of specially trained engineers. He came to the conclusion that as society advances financially men use surplus wealth to impress others rather than as a means of achieving more leisure. Veblen's views gained wide popularity among sophisticated readers and thinkers who found his essentially iconoclastic approach to economics timely and refreshing.

The titles of some of Veblen's other works indicate the areas which especially interested him: *The Theory of Business Enterprise* (1904), *The Instinct of Workmanship* (1914), *The Engineers and the Price System* (1921). It is not his manner of writing which impresses, for his style is often difficult; it is rather the incisiveness of his ideas.

ESSAYISTS AND VARIOUS DISTINCTIVE PROSE STYLISTS

Edmund Wilson (1895–   ). A native of Red Bank, New Jersey, Edmund Wilson was educated at Hill School and Princeton, receiving the A.B. in 1916. At Princeton he edited the *Nassau Literary Magazine* with John Peale Bishop as his associate. World War I broke off his reportorial work with the New York *Evening Sun;* he saw service in France at a base hospital and with military intelligence. During 1920–21 he was managing editor of *Vanity Fair,* and during 1926–31 an associate editor of *The New Republic.* In 1944 he began reviewing for *The New Yorker,* to which he has contributed extensively for more than two decades.

The range of Edmund Wilson's writings includes many fields, but he is best known as a critic and interpreter of literature.

Axel's Castle: A Study in the Imaginative Literature of 1870 to 1930 (1931) is the most influential of Wilson's critical works. Yeats, Valéry, T. S. Eliot, Proust, Joyce, and Gertrude Stein are examined as exemplars of the modern symbolist movement, a revolt against the naturalistic and rationalistic trends of nineteenth-century art and thought. Hewing to his sociological approach, Wilson carefully analyzes the intellectual and cultural influences that evoked the intensely personal communication of the symbolists. The title is derived from the hero of the poem "Axel" by Villiers de l'Isle-Adam, Wilson interpreting this work as the definitive image of the symbolists' withdrawal from the public world. Wilson finds in symbolism "a new flexibility and freedom" which he wants to "wake us to the hope and exaltation of the untried, unsuspected possibilities of human thought and art."

The Triple Thinkers (1938) consists of ten essays in the original edition and twelve in the revised edition of 1948. One of the later essays, "The Historical Interpretation of Literature," especially supports the sociological approach, which Wilson states was originated by the early eighteenth-century Italian philosopher Vico. The most controversial piece in the collection, "The Ambiguity of Henry James," proposes a Freudian interpretation of *The Turn of the Screw,* claiming that the ghosts are projections by the narrator-governess from her own neurotic consciousness. The title of the volume derives from Flaubert's concept of the artist as a God-like creator, manifesting three times the average man's perceptivity of life.

The Wound and the Bow (1941) takes its title from Sophocles' *Philoctetes,* in which a Greek warrior is exiled from his fellows because of the foul odor of his wound, but is nonetheless sought out because his magic bow is essential to the winning of the Trojan War. To Wilson this episode suggests the nature of the artist, in whom beneficial aid to society is often bound up with personal disability. The very society that rejects the artist as a sick soul desperately needs the restorative power of his art. In separate essays this theory is applied to Dickens, Kipling, Joyce, Edith Wharton, and Hemingway.

Notable among Wilson's books in other areas are: *Memoirs of Hecate County* (1946), a work of fiction which consists of related episodes, beautifully written; it was banned for a time because of its physiological frankness. *Travels in Two Democracies* (1936) recounts experiences in Russia and in this country. *To the Finland Station* (1940), following the revolutionary movement of Europe from its eighteenth-century forerunners down to Lenin and Trotsky, began in enthusiasm for and ended in disillusionment with communism. *The Dead Sea Scrolls* (1955; revised and expanded, with this title, in 1969) introduced many to the great recent discovery and the significance of these exciting ancient biblical materials. (The title of the original book was *Scrolls from the Dead Sea.*)

Lewis Mumford (1895–   ). A native of Flushing, New York, Lewis Mumford earned no academic degree, but studied at C.C.N.Y., Columbia, New York University, and the New School for Social Research. He made himself one of the foremost scholars and writers on architecture and city planning, receiving numerous awards and teaching at the universities of Stanford, Pennsylvania, M.I.T., and Wesleyan. He became president of the American Academy of Arts and Letters in 1962.

Sticks and Stones (1924) is a most stimulating examination of American architecture. From early colonial times to the present, Mumford considers our buildings as demonstrations of the spirit of American civilization, imparting in his accounts many unusual viewpoints and insights.

The Renewal of Life is the collective term for a four-volume study of the emergence of modern science and technology, beginning with *Technics and Civilization* (1934) and continuing with *The Culture of Cities* (1938), *The Condition of Man* (1944), and *The Conduct of Life* (1951). Mumford is concerned with the interrelations between man's changing view of the world and of himself and the techniques he employs for human welfare. Insistent is a plea that man carefully plan to utilize all possible resources to create a better, more human surrounding. *The City in History* (1961) maintains the same felicitous style in an extensive study of man in history as an urban creature.

A more recent work is *The Myth of the Machine*. The first volume (1967), subtitled, like his earlier work, *Technics and Civilization*, deals with the effect of the introduction of the machine on society from prehistoric times through the Middle Ages. The second volume (1971), subtitled *The Pentagon of Power*, continues the account to the present.

Gertrude Stein (1874–1946). Born to a wealthy family in Allegheny, Pennsylvania, Gertrude Stein was educated abroad in her earlier years. At Radcliffe College, from which she graduated in 1897, she was especially influenced by William James. For the next four years she studied medicine at Johns Hopkins University but took no degree; examinations bored her, she declared. In 1902 she went to Europe with her brother Leo, and in 1903 she settled in Paris with her friend Alice Toklas. She quickly became the guiding spirit of the avant-garde and in the 1920s was the acknowledged doyenne and mentor of American expatriate writers in Paris. Her home became a gathering place for artists and writers. Her only return to this country was for a notable lecture tour in 1934–35. At all times, however, she considered herself wholly American.

Gertrude Stein is virtually unclassifiable. She was a central figure of new, experimental literature; yet her works presented baffling eccentricities.

She fulfilled at least three major roles:

1. She was guide and spokesman for many modern American writers. It was she who described those of the twenties as "the lost generation." Ernest Hemingway, F. Scott Fitzgerald, and Ezra Pound were encouraged by her. Over the years she was a correspondent and friend of Sherwood Anderson, T. S. Eliot, Thornton Wilder, Richard Wright, and many others. She also recognized early the great gifts of many modern painters in Paris, among them Picasso and Matisse.

2. She was a theorist of language and literature. Her first published work was "Normal Motor Automatism" in *Psychological Review* (1896). Her subsequent theory and practice developed to a large extent from this study of automatic writing. Especially indebted to *Principles of Psychology* (1890) by William James, she originally intended to be a "scientist of the mind," but her temperament propelled her to belles lettres. She felt that she must jettison tradition ("the past did not matter," she declared) and advocate a determinedly accurate reproduction of the spirit and rhythms of actual, immediate experience. This experience, she asserted, impresses itself upon the subconscious mind, which in turn throws up groups of words not in logical order but as the experience is meaningful deep within. *Composition as Explanation* (1926) proposes that all proper expression is not of a general, universal idea but of a highly individualized recording of experience. *How to Write* (1931) does not discuss but demonstrates her concept to the fullest (and, say many, to the most puzzling). Here language is completely divorced from public sense to provide the maximum of private sense, the unique consciousness of the author. Subject is virtually ignored in her concentration upon a state of mind. Consequently in writing she indulges in many deliberate simplicities, repetitions, apparent non sequiturs. Her insistence upon stripping away all the superfluities has been immensely potent in stimulating the twentieth-century experiments in exploring both the inner life and the immediately present external life. In a sense her approach to language was not unlike that of the cubist painters who drew a new view of objects by depicting them from all sides at once.

3. She was an original, creative writer. *Three Lives* (1909), three novellas upon three women who are pictured as servants in Bridgeport, Connecticut, shows her earlier, less experimental, style. Though imperfectly comprehending themselves and their milieu, all three are engaged upon extracting meaning from their lives and constructing inner characteristics of strength and nobility.

Tender Buttons (1914), brief statements set as verse, interested a limited number of people on publication, and more attention was given to it on its reprinting in 1928. Three sections, "Objects," "Food," "Rooms," consist of aphoristic impressions divorced from dictionary logic into free association. These are independent moments of consciousness. Celery, for example, is described: "Celery tastes tastes where in curled lashes and little bits and mostly in remains." The most famous Steinism, "A rose is a rose is a rose," appears in *Sacred Emily* (1922).

Four Saints in Three Acts (1934), an "opera libretto," with music by Virgil Thomson, contains the famous phrase, "Pigeons on the grass alas." There is no objective meaning to the drama, for Miss Stein purposely clears literature of logical content in favor of pleasurable sensual stimulus. Even so, the opera as produced was a thoroughly interesting experience.

Somewhat more conventional writing is *The Autobiography of Alice B. Toklas* (1933) which actually is Gertrude Stein's own account masquerading as the narrative of her confidante. This is an invaluable record, with many insights into the lives and achievements of American expatriates and Continental artists. *Wars I Have Seen* (1945) uses an essentially straightforward style. Most of the book details her World War II exile from Paris to the Rhone Valley, rising to a dramatic and moving final section, "The Coming of the Americans."

H. L. Mencken (1880–1956). Henry Louis Mencken tells of his early years in his native Baltimore in three autobiographical works: *Happy Days* (1940), *Newspaper Days, 1899–1906* (1941), and *Heathen Days* (1943). Few writers have been able to make so much of so little; the material is quite slender, even superficial, in content, but it reads with a beguiling delight. Mencken ended his formal education at Baltimore Polytechnic Institute (a high school) in 1896 and ever thereafter was scornful of academicians. He began his journalistic career with the Baltimore *Morning Herald* in 1899. By 1903 he had risen to city editorship and by 1905 to general editorship. In 1906 he moved to the Baltimore *Sun,* where he continued until his death. In 1908 he became literary critic of the *Smart Set* magazine, and from 1914 until the publication was suspended in 1923 he coedited it with George Jean Nathan. He and Nathan also joined in editing the *American*

Mercury upon its founding in 1924; Mencken continued as editor in chief until resigning in 1933.

No one could out-invective Mencken, one of the greatest masters of vituperation in the language. Liberals often, but mistakenly, thought him one of their number because of his denunciation of the "booboisie," the Ku Klux Klan, puritanism, censorship, Prohibition, the Monkey Trial, and kindred phenomena of the times, but Mencken spattered his venom over F.D.R. as freely as over Hoover. Actually, Mencken was a conservative iconoclast, a belated representative in Baltimore of the eighteenth-century German *Aufklärung* (Enlightenment). Scornful of democracy and its weird aberrations, he yearned for a cultural elite who would cultivate life and art without heed of the "mob." His bludgeoning of the conventions and caprices of the 1920s made him the idol of the rebellious.

In the 1940s it was customary to dismiss Mencken as a period piece of the 1920s but more recently he has regained repute as a master of language and a truly significant social critic.

The American Language (1919) was revised in 1921, 1923, 1936; huge additions are housed in *Supplement One* (1945) and *Supplement Two* (1948). Mencken had started short discussions of the national tongue in 1910 in the Baltimore *Sun*. His antipathy to England caused him to emphasize the differences between British and American English to the point of claiming a New World evolution of a quite different language. From the 1923 edition onward, however, he acknowledged many similarities, ascribing them, of course, to American influence upon British English, the offspring now overpowering the parent tongue. Surprisingly, from a constant disparager of many of the ways of this nation came a labor of love about its language: vocabulary, pronunciation, spelling, slang, and practically everything else about American English are given a remarkably detailed scrutiny.

Prejudices collected Mencken's short pieces in six volumes (1919, 1920, 1922, 1924, 1926, 1927). Most of these originally appeared in *Smart Set, American Mercury,* or the Baltimore *Sun.* Strongly influenced by Nietzsche, Mencken excoriated the American democracy of his day as a means to consecrate mediocrity and reduce superior men to the average level. National law, politics, religion, morality, *et al.* were wittily reviled as the ludicrous but dangerous devices of narrow minds to aggrandize their own selfish little egos, keep secure their own little realms of material possession, and thwart larger spirits in their attempts to live individual and creative lives.

Gamaliel Bradford (1863–1932). Gamaliel Bradford was born in Boston, and lived a great part of his life in Wellesley Hills, Massachusetts.

Bradford dedicated himself to developing biography as an art form. From Sainte-Beuve, a French critic and biographer whom he deeply admired, Bradford took for himself the label, "naturalist of souls." He assembled over a hundred "psychographs" (only five in full-length books), perhaps most notably in the collections of shorter studies, *American Portraits, 1815–1900* (1922) and *Bare Souls* (1924). Although Bradford labored assiduously in primary sources, he worked essentially by intuition, striving to penetrate to the inner essence of his subject. The result is engrossing, constantly spotlighting a character not statically but in vivid, revealing movement. Historians of literature assign Bradford not to factual biography but to imaginative belles lettres.

Clarence Day (1874–1935). Clarence Shepard Day, Jr., a native New Yorker and long a resident of New York and nearby Westchester, was troubled over many years by very serious arthritis. But his sparkling humor rose above pain to create works of endless delight.

Day is best known for *Life with Father* (1935), a collection of refreshingly entertaining sketches recalling episodes in Day's early life in Manhattan and in nearby Westchester, with emphasis upon his father's overwhelming, yet well-meaning domination of the family, his mother's pleasant role, and the development of Day and his three brothers, all little redheads. The life of New York at the time is abundantly reflected in Day's pages.

Actually these recollections were published as three volumes, *God and My Father* (1932), *Life with Father* (1935), and *Life with Mother* (1937). The tremendously popular play which Howard Lindsay and Russel Crouse developed so skillfully in 1939 from Clarence Day's sketches had the title *Life with Father,* but it included episodes from all of the volumes.

Clarence Day's distinctive quality, however, is not represented solely by his entertaining reminiscences.

This Simian World (1920) is a work of memorable originality. The title is immediately challenging. Day takes it upon himself to consider what characteristics man has as a result of his belonging to the simian branch of the animal world; and he finds many traits which are also found in apes. From these observations, he proceeds to consider what the human race would be like if it had an altogether different animal background. He turns to the cat family and pictures a feline world in which the human descendants reveal many traits which are quite different from those which they now have. He does not overwork this intriguing idea by applying it except very briefly to other groups, but he does point out that dogs are so faithful to man that they would always be companions rather than ancestors. All of this truly inventive short book is written in an appropriately light, distinctive style. It is illustrated at points by Clarence Day's very individual and amusing pen-and-ink drawings.

Don Marquis (1878–1937). Donald Robert Perry Marquis was born at Walnut, Illinois. At eighteen he left his native small town to wander through a maze of miscellaneous jobs from farm hand to actor. In 1907 Joel Chandler Harris hired him as assistant editor of *Uncle Remus' Magazine.* After the death of Harris, he proceeded to New York as a newspaper journalist. In 1912 he began the column "The Sun Dial" for the *Sun,* and although this was the heyday of the most successful New York personal columnists (Christopher Morley, Heywood Broun, F.P.A.), Marquis quickly became a favorite. In 1922 he moved to the *Herald Tribune,* but after two and a half years quit in favor of freelance writing. His last two decades were clouded by the deaths in his family and his own poor health.

The Old Soak (1921), derived from Marquis' newspaper columns, creates an old-fashioned crackerbox philosopher in Clem Hawley, supposedly of Baycliff, Long Island (suburban New York), but actually of nineteenth-century rustic vintage. Retired, Hawley devotes himself to contemplating life and obtaining illegal liquor. The "Old Soak" is the wise fool, expressing his distaste for modern idiocies in mangled diction and wild malapropisms. Although E. B. White termed Marquis a "citydweller" in temperament, here he essentially yearns for an earlier, simpler America where the individual had greater freedom and less congestion.

archy and mehitabel (1927) and *The Lives and Times of archy and mehitabel* (1940) will undoubtedly be the chief sustainers of Marquis' reputation. Casually in 1916 Marquis, as padding for his column, wryly concocted the idea of two inhabitants of the *Sun* office, archy the cockroach and mehitabel the alley cat. Initial pieces were intended as burlesque of the *vers libre* movement, but over the years his two characters ranged the whole gamut of human experience from garbage cans to cosmic destiny. Everything came from archy, who never used capitals because obviously he was too small to hold the shift key while typing. The character of mehitabel was relatively simple—the frowsy flapper, an engaging sinner who with a shrug of her whiskers blames others for her predicament and nonchalantly yields to tomcats and abandons her kittens. "Toujours gai" expressed her easy hedonism. But archy was the convenient guise for Marquis to express one of the most complex and profound personalities of this century. Marquis was simultaneously rationalistically skeptical and deeply religious (Morley, a close friend, called him a "divinity student"). Through archy he was free to criticize contemporary American life as scathingly as Mencken. Both men were basically old-fashioned individualists. Archy, after deploring man's folly, observes:

> dear boss i relay this information
> without any fear that humanity
> will take warning and reform.

Christopher Morley (1890–1957). Christopher Darlington Morley attended Haverford College in his native Haverford, Pennsylvania. After graduation in 1910 he attended Oxford from 1910 to 1913 as a Rhodes scholar. Editorial work for New York and Philadelphia newspapers and magazines was combined with the writing of numerous books. Morley's novel *Kitty Foyle* (1939) was recognized as an impressively realistic work about a lower middle-class working girl in the Philadelphia of the time.

Essay collections from *Shandygaff* (1918) to *The Ironing Board* (1949) reveal Morley as a gifted practitioner of the traditional personal essay. His relaxed style permitted him to range with wit and erudition from the loftiest realms of literature to the lowly realms of dogs and tobacco. He was an aloof, gentlemanly spectator of life, refusing to commit himself intensely to any philosophy of life or art.

Elliot Paul (1891–1958). Elliot Harold Paul was born at Malden, Massachusetts. After less than a year at the University of Maine, he joined his brother on irrigation projects in Idaho and Wyoming. He served in France during World War I, and afterward stayed on in Paris to write for American newspapers and also to engage in avant-garde literature. He was a founder in 1927 of the famous magazine *transition*, in which much important experimental writing of the period first appeared. In the early 1930s Elliot Paul lived on Ibiza, one of the smaller of Spain's Balearic Islands. The story of the small community there is movingly told in *The Life and Death of a Spanish Town* (1937). In his later years he wrote highly popular crime and mystery novels.

The Last Time I Saw Paris (1942) takes its title from a popular song. Paul's volume is the epitome of nostalgia for the Paris between wars. With novelistic skill he evokes the exciting cultural atmosphere of those days and a host of extraordinary, sometimes eccentric, denizens of Paris, whether natives or aliens.

Robert Benchley (1889–1945). Robert Charles Benchley came from a family of modest means in Worcester, Massachusetts, and was aided by family friends to attend Harvard. There, as president of the *Lampoon*, he worked with Gluyas Williams, later the illustrator of all Benchley books. After graduation in 1912 he worked in New York, chiefly on the *Tribune Graphic* and *World*, and on *Vanity Fair* in the days of that magazine's great influence. From the start of *The New Yorker* in 1925 until 1940 he was an active contributor.

From *Of All Things!* (1921) to *Benchley Beside Himself* (1943), more than anyone else Benchley created the archetype of the Normal Little Man Bewildered by Modern Life. The best known of his books is *My Ten Years in a Quandary and How They Grew* (1936). Benchley presents himself as the average New York resident with good intentions and innate decency who is baffled by gadgets, overawed by imperious doormen, thwarted by traffic jams and subway turnstiles, reduced to appalled confusion by an income-tax form. Lighter in tone, more insouciant in manner than Marquis, Benchley just as fully satirizes the madness of contemporary life.

James Thurber (1894–1961). While still a boy in his native Columbus, Ohio, James Grover Thurber suffered an injury that impaired his eyesight throughout his life and in the 1950s brought total blindness. His disability prevented military service; and while he was editor of the campus magazine, *Sun Dial*, at Ohio State University, wartime scarcity of manpower caused him to illustrate as well as write for the publication. A college friend was Elliot Nugent, who later collaborated with Thurber on the highly successful drama *The Male Animal* (1940). After graduation in 1919 Thurber worked for various newspapers until *The New Yorker* became his happy haven from 1927 on.

Thurber brought a rare gift of distinctive literary style to his writings, whether humorous, satiric, or serious.

Beginning with *Is Sex Necessary?* (1929), written in collaboration with E. B. White, Thurber is preoccupied with "the battle of the sexes." The furor about sex generated by psychoanalysis and the art of the 1920s stimulated a reaction in Thurber, not toward puritanism but toward moderation. The males of his cartoons and literary pieces are repressed, generally cowed individuals whose only refuge from an intractable world and nagging females is psychosis or withdrawal.

My Life and Hard Times (1933) in its depiction of the bizarre Thurber household of his Columbus youth shows the world as too much for this family that must thereby indulge in daydreaming or occasional rebellious and unsatisfactory violence.

"The Secret Life of Walter Mitty" (1939) is one of the outstanding short stories of this era. The stream of consciousness of this pathetic, commonplace man seeks refuge from the miasma of facial tissues and balky auto engines in a vivid dream world where heroic Walter Mitty is a fearless airplane pilot, a superlative surgeon, a daredevil who flips away his last cigarette and nonchalantly faces a firing squad. So adequately does Thurber epitomize the sense of utter inadequacy in modern man and his pitiful flight to fantasy that the sober medical journal *The Lancet* diagnosed "The Mitty complex."

The Last Flower (1939) reaches the depth of Thurber's pessimism as it contemplates civilization lifting from one cycle of destruction only to plummet into another.

E. B. White (1899–   ). Elwyn Brooks White was born in Mt. Vernon, New York. He received an A.B. from Cornell University (1921), and honorary doctorates from Harvard, Yale, Dartmouth, and other institutions. After World War I military service, he worked for an advertising agency and for newspapers. Soon after the 1925 founding of *The New Yorker* he became one of its mainstays. He also conducted "One Man's Meat" for *Harper's* from 1938 to 1943. In 1963 he was awarded the presidential Medal of Freedom.

Where Christopher Morley is mellow, White is astringent. Where Morley is the detached observer of the human pageant, White is in there pitching for a world of sanity and immediate humanity. From *Is Sex Necessary?* (1929), in collaboration with James Thurber, to *The Points of My Compass* (1962) he has proved one of the wittiest and most incisive commentators upon life as it is lived in contemporary America. His honors are not solely for literary competence but in recognition of one of the great humanistic voices of our time. His felicitous style has made his essays favorites of the anthologists.

GIFTED WRITERS IN SPECIAL FIELDS

William Beebe (1877–1962). Brooklyn-born Charles William Beebe received his B.S. from Columbia in 1898. From 1899 until his death he was curator of ornithology for the New York Zoological Society. His study of plant and animal life took him to many parts of the world. In 1934 he gained world renown for a record-breaking research descent in a bathysphere off Bermuda into the ocean depths.

Jungle Days (1925), detailing his nature studies in British Guiana, is the best known of his works for the lay reader. To impeccable scientific knowledge he added a remarkable poetic imagination that in the flashing arc of a fish could epitomize the beauty of nature and in the persistent plodding of the ant could encompass the relentless cycle of life and death in the tropical jungle.

Richard E. Byrd (1888–1957). A direct descendant of colonial William Byrd, the explorer Richard Evelyn Byrd was born in Winchester, Virginia. He graduated from the Naval Academy in 1912. In 1917 he entered the aviation service of the Navy. In 1939 and 1946 he was commander of U.S. antarctic expeditions. From 1930 he held the rank of rear admiral. In addition to his antarctic explorations, he made flights over both the North Pole and the South Pole.

Little America (1930) and Byrd's other books on antarctic exploration depict the new mechanized era of man's probing into the inhospitable corners of the globe. No longer is man pitted against brute Nature with only his muscle and raw courage, as in the days of Shackleton. But the new problems, while less elemental, are now far more complicated. The Byrd volumes are enthralling for their record of the world's last wild, empty continent, with geography no human ever gazed upon before. It is Byrd the man, however, who remains the most memorable revelation, especially in *Alone* (1938), relating his long voluntary solitude at an advanced observation post close to the South Pole. He was truly an aristocrat, not solely in his distinguished family, but as a patient and tolerant gentleman and as a leader who faced the greatest perils himself before asking any of his associates to brave them. In *Alone* Byrd plumbs introspective depths seldom associated with so bold a man of action.

W. E. B. Du Bois (1868–1963). William Edward Burghardt Du Bois was born in Great Barrington, Massachusetts. He was educated at Fisk University, at Harvard, and at the University of Berlin. From 1894 to 1910 he taught at Wilberforce University, the University of Pennsylvania, and Atlanta University. With others he founded the National Association for the Advancement of Colored People and edited its magazine, *The Crisis,* from 1910 to 1933. Du Bois did pioneering studies of the American Negro in several fields including anthropology, sociology, and history. Throughout his life he was an activist in the fight for social equality for the Negro. Among his works are: *The Souls of Black Folk* (1903); *John Brown* (1909); a novel, *The Dark Princess* (1928); *Black Reconstruction in America, 1860–1880* (1935); *Dusk of Dawn* (1940); *In Battle For Peace* (1952).

The Souls of Black Folk (1903) is a collection of essays ranging from a study of the Negro population in a county in the Black Belt of Georgia to observations on Negro folk music. There is much historical information and also much autobiographical data. And through these pieces there is a strong feeling for the destiny of the black man in America.

Dusk of Dawn (1940) with subtitle, "An Essay Toward an Autobiography of a Race Concept," traces the evolution of Du Bois' thought from his childhood in a primarily white New England community in the later nineteenth century up to 1940 when the book was written.

The book reflects the scientific honesty which Du Bois valued so highly. During his university years he had developed the belief that if the truth about Negro character could be brought before the public, then ignorance and its by-product, racism, would lose the firm hold they had on American life.

But the book also shows that Du Bois' thought later changed considerably. He came to feel that while ignorance was an important contributing factor, a more fundamental cause was perhaps to be found in the irrational drives of men, forces which could not be explained away by science, but must be combated with propaganda and with activism.

In the first three decades of the twentieth century Du Bois did much traveling throughout the world, seeing increasingly that the great cultural tradition of the West included a long history of colonial exploitation and suppression of many peoples.

In 1921 Du Bois organized the first Pan-African Congress, which was followed by others in 1922, 1923, 1927. During the twenties and thirties, he developed a program of economic separatism for American Negroes, and he was instrumental in organizing Negro consumer unions as a step toward this goal. While his program was by no means extreme, it created strong opposition within the ranks of his more conservative black and white supporters and forced him to resign from the NAACP.

In his later years, Du Bois stressed his conviction that the Negro had particular contributions to give to the world, contributions which the twentieth century was in great need of. Until his death he worked tirelessly to achieve the racial equality in which his vision could be realized.

Bernard Berenson (1865–1959). A native of Lithuania, Bernard Berenson was brought to this country as a child. He graduated from Harvard in 1887 and thereafter devoted his life to the study of art. From 1900 until death he resided in Italy, but visited this country frequently to lecture on art and examine art objects. He was the chief adviser to Mrs. Jack Gardner in locating and assembling the renowned collection for her house, Fenway Court, in Boston, which is now the Gardner Museum.

Venetian Painters of the Renaissance (1894) was the first of many studies upon Renaissance Italian art that established Berenson as the undisputed world expert of his day in that field. Unlike John Ruskin, Berenson avoids impressionistic criticism for the most meticulous and painstaking knowledge, presented in a calm and elegant prose. Van Wyck Brooks marveled at the ability of Berenson to reconstruct unknown artists from their paintings as paleontologists reconstruct primordial animals from a few fragmentary remains.

The Passionate Sightseer (1960), Berenson's concluding work, consists of excerpts from his diary from 1947 to 1956. Except for a 1955 excursion to northern Africa, the entries trace his roamings around Italy and Sicily, savoring to the utmost the art heritage of the centuries and the vivacity of life today in the quietest Italian hill town or amidst the mighty ruins of Leptis Magna. Art and life conferred great happiness upon him and richly endowed him with wisdom.

Waldo Frank (1889–1967). Waldo David Frank became especially noted for his interpretation of Latin American culture in *America Hispana: A Portrait and a Prospect* (1931) and in many other works. *The Rediscovery of Man* (1958), broad in scope and philosophic in point of view, surveys all modern life, hopeful that humanism will assert itself to make men socially responsible and individually well-rounded and creative.

Irwin Edman (1896–1954). In his native New York, Irwin Edman virtually spent his lifetime at Columbia University as student and subsequently as professor of philosophy. He might be described as a pragmatist with a touch of Platonism. *Philosopher's Holiday* (1938) and *Philosopher's Quest* (1947) attracted the larger reading public. They are written with a flair that belies Edman's firmly grounded erudition. His major concern is the uncovering of individual resources that can surmount the confusion and standardization of the machine age.

SOME IMPORTANT LITERARY CRITICS

Van Wyck Brooks (1886–1963). Born in Plainfield, New Jersey, Van Wyck Brooks graduated from Harvard in 1907. His first book was published in England in 1908 during his residence there. Back in this country he was associate editor of *Seven Arts* (1917–18) and of the *Freeman* (1920–24).

Most of Brooks's career was devoted to an appraisal of our national literature from its inception to the present. The term "usable past" was his coinage to describe what he considered the genuine American tradition as distinguished from the lesser qualities of the Brahmins. *The Wine of the Puritans* (1908), establishing his critical reputation, blamed the New England heritage for the doldrums into which American literature had then fallen. *America's Coming of Age* (1915) heralded the new attitude. Brooks saw puritanism as bequeathing to American culture the equally inadequate traditions of gross materialism and vacuous gentility. The significant strain of Americanism he interpreted as the liberal democratic tradition, with Whitman as its greatest exemplar.

Brooks then turned to individual American writers to substantiate his thesis. *The Ordeal of Mark Twain* (1920) asserted that Clemens was the victim-hero of nineteenth-century American letters because his Calvinistic upbringing and his own susceptibility to Gilded Age money-making warred with his creative genius. *The Pilgrimage of Henry James* (1925) interpreted the great novelist as an American who felt that in order to salvage his creativity he must flee the bitter conflict of art and life in this country. *The Life of Emerson* (1932) provided Brooks with the opportunity to praise a New Englander who had transformed and transcended his puritan background.

Finders and Makers is the collective title for a five-volume scrutiny of American literary culture from 1800 to 1915, which brings vividly alive the major nineteenth-century American writers. In this volume Brooks does not overemphasize his earlier thesis. He achieves a notable feat in portraying these authors as emerging from their cultural milieu, reacting to it and modifying it. *The Flowering of New England, 1815–1865* (1936), first of the series to be published, centers on Boston and Concord, with Emerson and Thoreau the dominant personalities, but Brooks presents so much of the men and movements of the era as to make it appear the most exciting and creative period of American letters. *New England: Indian Summer, 1865–1915* (1940) carries on to Frost and O'Neill, with extensive discussion of Henry Adams, Henry James, and William Dean Howells. New England gradually loses its intellectual monopoly and merges with the larger national literature. *The World of Washington Irving* (1944) considers the earliest literary period of the series, the early nineteenth century in New York. *The Times of Melville and Whitman* (1947) treats of mid-nineteenth-century American letters outside of New England. *The Confident Years: 1885–1915* (1952) ranges over the entire national literary scene, again outside of New England.

Henry Seidel Canby (1878–1961). A native of Wilmington, Delaware, Henry Seidel Canby received his Bachelor's (1899) and Doctor's (1905) degrees from Yale. He taught at Yale from 1911 to 1941. With Wilbur L. Cross he was a founder of *The Yale Review* in 1911; and he was the founder, with William Rose Benét and Christopher Morley, of the *Saturday Review of Literature* in 1924.

Canby remarkably combined academic sholarship with practical journalism. His *Saturday Review* articles collected in *Definitions* (first series, 1922; second series, 1924) and *American Estimates* (1929) stand high among critical-review pieces. Mild and balanced, he sought understanding of the changing values in successive eras of national life as reflected in literature. Among his books are notable evaluations of authors who especially interested and appealed to him: *Walt Whitman: An American* (1943), and *Turn West, Turn East* (1951) which contrasts Mark Twain's concern for the West with Henry James's attraction toward England. Recording his recollections of the earlier years of his life, he called these reminiscences *The Age of Confidence* (1934).

Bernard De Voto (1897–1955). His father of Catholic-Italian origin and his mother of pioneer Mormon stock, Bernard Augustine De Voto was born at Ogden, Utah. After two years at the University of Utah he went to Harvard, graduating in 1920. After teaching English from 1922 to 1927 at Northwestern University he returned to Cambridge to join the Harvard faculty. In 1936 he succeeded Canby as editor of the *Saturday Review,* but went back to Harvard in 1938. From 1935 to 1955 he wrote "The Editor's Chair" for *Harper's Magazine.*

De Voto was inclined to be at the center of controversy. Though a powerful scholar, he prided himself upon hard-boiled realism. He constantly preached that present urban existence obscures the actualities of the American past. *Mark Twain's America* (1932) asserts that Clemens had an inner life as does any man but was primarily a mirror of lusty, untamed America. *The Literary Fallacy* (1944) energetically assailed literature as self-contained art, demanding that it be a vital revelation of the American experience. De Voto took greatest pride in his historical studies, especially *Across the Wide Missouri* (1947), about the "mountain men" who in the 1830s in their quest for furs unknowingly bound together the East and the West coasts into one nation.

Carl Van Doren (1885–1950). The elder brother of Mark Van Doren, Carl Clinton Van Doren was born in Hope, Illinois. After graduating from the University of Illinois in 1907 he proceeded to Columbia University, receiving the Ph.D. in 1911 and teaching there from 1911 to 1930. He was associated with John Erskine and Stuart Sherman in editing the *Cambridge History of American Literature* (1917–21). He served on the staffs of *The Nation* (1919–22) and *The Century Magazine* (1922–26).

Van Doren is one of the distinguished academicians who did much to establish American literature as a worthy and integral part of university study. His early critical evaluation is seen in *The American Novel* (1921, revised in 1940).

Benjamin Franklin (1938) successfully delineates the many facets of Franklin's personality, describing him as "more than any single man: a harmonious human multitude." The eighteenth century was Van Doren's favorite. *The Great Rehearsal* (1948) presents a masterful analysis of the drafting and ratifying of the national Constitution.

Joseph Wood Krutch (1893–1970). A native of Knoxville, Tennessee, Joseph Wood Krutch graduated from the University of Tennessee in 1915. The next year he received the M.A. from Columbia, where he taught for many years. From Columbia he received the Ph.D. in 1923 and the Litt.D. in 1955. He wrote for *The Nation* from 1924 to 1952, chiefly drama criticism.

Edgar Allan Poe: A Study of Genius (1926) is the first full-scale psychoanalytic examination of a literary figure by an American writer. Krutch predicates the entire artistic career of Poe upon the early traumatic experiences of the author. "The forces that wrecked his life were those that wrote his works." Poe's childhood attachment to his mother affected later sexual adjustment, resulting in brotherly rather than husbandly relations with his child-wife, Virginia, and in his recurrent idealized dead beauties. The quest for a father figure brought bitter hostility toward John Allan, who had taken him in as a child, and resulted in Poe's ceaseless inner warring. Literary fame was Poe's compensation for his lack of status and for his psychic disharmony.

Krutch in his later writings turned to broad themes, and achieved some of the most sane and balanced scrutinies of the predicament of modern man. *The Modern Temper* (1929), *The Measure of Man* (1954), and *Human Nature and the Human Condition* (1959) analyze the conflicting philosophies of our age and suggest the necessity for humanistic as well as scientific values.

V. L. Parrington (1871–1929). Born in Aurora, Illinois, Vernon Louis Parrington was brought up under the influence of Kansas Populism. Beginning at the College of Emporia (Kansas), he did his last two years of undergraduate work at Harvard. He taught at the College of Emporia, at the University of Oklahoma, and later at the University of Washington (1908–29).

Main Currents in American Thought is the collective title for three volumes tracing the cultural atmosphere of American literature from the beginnings to 1920. *The Colonial Mind* (1927) covers 1620–1800, and *The Romantic Revolution in America* (1927) deals with 1800–60. *The Beginnings of Critical Realism in America* (1930) scans 1860–1920 but remained unfinished at his death. Parrington frankly admits in his introduction that he chooses "the broad path of our political, economic, and social development, rather than the narrower belletristic." Thereby Parrington was largely responsible for a tremendous vitalization of American literature study, relating American letters to every major trend in the national history. Furthermore, his integrated approach has inspired the serious academic consideration of much Americana (e.g., folklore, folksy philosophers, tall tales, frontier literature) previously dismissed rather lightly. Parrington also firmly stated his viewpoint as that of a liberal democrat in the Jeffersonian tradition. He ws influenced by the belief of Hippolyte Taine, nineteenth-century French literary critic, that the writings of peoples are the inevitable outgrowth of their time, place, and national characteristics. In the tradition of Charles A. Beard's *Economic Interpretation of the Constitution* (1913), Parrington sought to explain the national literature as a result of economic determinism. His bias caused Parrington to minimize authors such as Poe and Henry James who refuse to conform to his thesis, but the illumination of much of our literature as the unique expression of the American experience has yet to lose its exhilaration. He is highly successful with the noted liberals: Franklin, Paine, Jefferson, Emerson, Thoreau, Whitman. Critics often feel that his preoccupation with the twofold approach of economic determinism and liberal democracy blights aesthetic considerations. His unfinished final notes, surveying the 1920s, display disillusioned concern; for Parrington is less an architect of the present and the future than a voice of the American past, a valiant spokesman for democratic idealism.

F. O. Matthiessen (1902–50). Born in Pasadena, California, Francis Otto Matthiessen graduated from Yale in 1923, spent two years in England as a Rhodes scholar, and returned to take a Harvard Ph.D. in 1927. Thereafter he taught English at Harvard until his death. Two important books of his are studies of individual literary figures: *The Achievement of T. S. Eliot* (1935) and *Henry James: The Major Phase* (1944).

American Renaissance: Art and Expression in the Age of Emerson and Whitman (1941) is outstanding among works dealing with a specific period of American literature. Though a stanch liberal, Matthiessen reacted against Parrington to assert the artistry of Emerson, Thoreau, Hawthorne, Melville, and Whitman, as well as their social conscience. Vigorous exponents of democratic ideals, these nineteenth-century authors were also Renaissance giants in their concepts of literature, their far-reaching interests, their total concern for mankind, their equation of the poet and the seer. Matthiessen particularly exalts Melville and Hawthorne for their tragic sense, arising from a mature comprehension of "the mixed nature of life." No other single work has proved as influential as Matthiessen's in its reinterpretation of classic American literature, combining a strong historical viewpoint with a sensitive aesthetic appraisal of the American author as artistic genius.

PART TWO

American Literature in Mid-Century

CHAPTER FIVE

Important Novelists of the Mid-Twentieth Century

RECENT DIRECTIONS IN THE NOVEL

In mid-century the American novel has been marked by great diversity. Some novelists have written with exceptional stylistic skill, some have stressed their individualism with unusually frank self-expression, some have continued the realistic approach to social and personal problems, while others have dealt with these topics in a new way.

Among the authors of fiction noted for their gift of style, special mention should be made of Katherine Anne Porter, who wrote some of her most famous short stories earlier in the century, but whose influence has been greatest in mid-century with additional powerful short stories and the publication of her first novel. Likewise the extraordinary Vladimir Nabokov, born in Russia in Czarist days, an American by naturalization since 1945, and a master of the English language, has written his most widely-known novels in mid-century. And with the authors whose style is important we place J. D. Salinger, a writer wholly of mid-century, who has captured a mood that characterized many of the young people of his generation, especially those in the academic world.

There has been a true renaissance in novels by Southern writers. Even though set frequently in Southern locales, these novels are not regional in their powerful themes; they are universally meaningful. In our discussion, Robert Penn Warren, Eudora Welty, Carson McCullers, and others are grouped together merely because their use of Southern backgrounds suggests this arrangement rather than placing them in categories corresponding to subject matter.

Soon after the Second World War there were powerful novels dealing with experiences in the war, notably the first novels of Norman Mailer, James Jones, and Irwin Shaw. And another expression of violence, the world of poverty and narcotics addiction in the urban jungle, was vividly portrayed in the novels and stories of Nelson Algren. At about the same time, a number of Negro novelists became widely known for the vigor and distinction of their writings.

Certain writers have come to be grouped together because of their point of view or emphasis. Thus we have the "hard-boiled" novelists, the "beat" novelists, the writers of science fiction, and the sardonically ironic and pessimistic writers whose work is referred to as "black humor."

Toward the end of the chapter we have a number of novelists whose best-known works are quite recent.

NOVELISTS DISTINCTIVE IN STYLE AND THEME

Katherine Anne Porter (1894–   ). Much of the early life of Katherine Anne Porter remains undocumented through her own wish. She was born in Indian Creek, Texas, and educated locally. At sixteen she ran away from school to get married; each of her three marriages has ended in divorce. Much of her life has been peripatetic. Until achieving fame with "Flowering Judas" (1930), she worked at journalism, ghost writing, and acting, and lived in Denver, New York, Chicago, Paris, and Mexico. In 1931 she received a Guggenheim fellowship. Since 1949 she has been a guest lecturer at many American universities and at the University of Liège, and has had her home chiefly in New York. Her collected stories won the Pulitzer Prize in 1966.

Unquestionably Miss Porter is one of the great artists of American fiction, a rigorous stylist and examiner of the secret wellsprings of human behavior. Her persistent theme is the sense of isolation of intelligent and perceptive spirits. Weaker natures drift into relationships with other persons that produce frustration and unhappiness. The more courageous beings in the search for truth and beauty are predestined for even greater suffering, but achieve a sense of noble, tragic endurance. Though Miss Porter's output has been slender, it has maintained an extraordinary level of distinctive quality.

Flowering Judas and Other Stories (1935) collects ten short stories written after 1922. (The title story and five of the others first appeared in 1930.) Most of the stories are concerned with expatriate Americans in Mexico.

"María Concepción," Miss Porter's first published story, tells of a

Mexican Indian woman who loses her child at birth, kills her husband's mistress, and takes his child by that mistress as her own. In her instinctive actions María is following the dictates of a primitive code; by so conforming to her natural promptings she is rewarded with a life of severity and dignity.

"He," a favorite anthology piece, concerns the Whipples, poor whites who have never even given a name to their feeble-minded son. The affection they pointedly confer on "Him" is for the benefit of their neighbors. A physician persuades the Whipples to take "Him" to the County Home. Their relief at being rid of "Him" displaces their hypocritical piety.

"Flowering Judas" is one of Miss Porter's best and most representative stories. Laura, an American schoolteacher, because of her humanitarian sensibilities has become interested in Xochimilco, Mexico, a small town that is experiencing a revolutionary ferment. Laura soon becomes the recipient of the unwelcome attentions of Braggioni, the chief revolutionary, who has used his political influence to obtain a comfortable sinecure with the proletariat. Braggioni considers himself a realist and holds the general welfare above the good of the individual. He is therefore willing to sacrifice the rights of Eugenio, one of his young subordinates who has been imprisoned, to the cause of temporary stability. As an act of mercy, Laura succeeds in getting drugs to Eugenio, which he uses to kill himself. That evening Laura sees him in a dream, in which he offers her the blossoms of the Judas tree, as a sacrament. Laura realizes that both Eugenio and she were betrayed and that she can no longer follow the lead of her own firmly held principles and beliefs.

The Leaning Tower and Other Stories (1944) contains nine stories written after the previous collection. Most deal with the early Texas years of the author.

"The Source" depicts Sophia Jean Rhea as a matriarchal grandmother of the post-bellum South. Sophia in Greek means "knowledge," Jean derives from the Hebrew "God is gracious," and Rhea was the ancient mother of the gods. Her annual visit to the farm is a rather awesome event; Grandmother Rhea rules her descendants in the manner of a strong-willed aristocrat. Miranda, the central character of this series of stories, is here an impressionable child.

"The Witness" has Uncle Jimbilly, a slave of Grandmother Rhea before Emancipation, recount to the children some of the actualities of the slavery period. His honest account differs considerably from the sentimental legend which the white youngsters had received from their parents.

"The Last Leaf" tells of the retreat of Nannie, the Rhea servant, after

Grandmother Rhea's death. The aged Negro had no real affection for her husband, Uncle Jimbilly; she had married him simply because they were both owned by Grandmother Rhea. Now she goes off to live and die alone, as the world that gave meaning to her is gone.

"The Circus" is an initiation story of the girlhood of Miranda, granddaughter of old Sophia. The circus that she attends is a microcosm of the world, and Miranda senses the falsity, pandering, and animality of the experience.

"The Grave" relates another revelation to the child Miranda as she and her brother play in the empty grave of their grandfather, whose coffin is moved to the family graveyard. Paul kills a rabbit that is gravid with unborn leverets. The youngsters conceal their knowledge from their elders: the knowledge of life, death, corruption, and the ceaseless building of new life from the destruction of the old.

"The Leaning Tower" is a novella about the residence in Berlin during 1931 of Charles Upton, a young artist from Texas. The title is a symbol of German culture of the period, precarious and ready to crash down before the stridency of Nazism.

Pale Horse, Pale Rider: Three Short Novels (1939) contains three novellas of exceptional merit.

"Old Mortality" takes its title from a novel by Sir Walter Scott. Young Miranda, Miss Porter's autobiographical persona, has been nurtured throughout childhood on the myth of her aunt Amy, the heroine in a drama of Southern chivalric glory and poetically early death. In her teens Miranda has an uncomfortable encounter with Amy's surviving husband, Gabriel, a debauched and degraded casualty of that myth. Finally the idyll crumbles at the hands of Cousin Eva, a spinsterish progressive educator, who recalls her role as supporting actor to Amy with scathing bitterness. Miranda resolves to break free of the past's associations and find a more rational and spiritually satisfying existence.

"Noon Wine" begins in 1896. Olaf Helton, a remarkably taciturn drifter of mysterious origin, is hired as a hand by Royal Earle Thompson to help him run his small, somewhat dilapidated Texas farm. Nine years later, when Helton's unstinting labor has put the farm on its feet, an unctuous bounty hunter, Homer T. Hatch, calls on Thompson to return Helton to an asylum from which he purportedly escaped. In a brief scuffle Thompson kills Hatch to protect Helton. Although the courts accept his plea of self-defense, the confusion of the episode leaves in Thompson an intimation of unspecified guilt which colors his protestations of innocence. Friends and family recoil in a semi-superstitious horror of bloodshed until Thompson is driven to take his own life. The story's title is that of a Scandanavian song—Helton's one diversion—

about field hands who consume their daily ration of wine before the appointed time.

"Pale Horse, Pale Rider," a vision of death, is Miss Porter's own favorite. Roughly autobiographical, it deals again with Miranda, who is now twenty-four, and a Denver newspaper columnist during World War I. Amidst a city teeming with fierce patriotism and dedicated to sacrifice, she and Adam Barclay, an army officer from Texas, commence a love affair clouded by the realization of their imminent separation and Adam's possible death at the front. Miranda is laid low by the raging influenza epidemic. As the disease runs its course prophetic dreams of symbolic death come to her. Finally, there is delirium in which death itself appears in progressive stages of horror, loss, oblivion, and ultimately a vista of consummate beauty and serenity. When at last she recovers, she learns that Adam has succumbed to the epidemic and died; but her sense of bereavement is identified more with the paradise of the fever dream than with reality. As her strength returns she becomes convinced that life will take on new value, although its full meaning for her has been irreparably darkened.

Ship of Fools (1962), Miss Porter's first novel, was begun in 1940. Readers and critics had awaited this promised work with the greatest interest.

The ship is the S.S. *Vera,* a German ship voyaging from Veracruz, Mexico, to Bremerhaven, Germany, late in the year 1931. In the steerage are almost a thousand Spanish workers returning home after the failure of the Cuban sugar crop. Most of the cabin passengers are well-to-do Germans, clannishly banded together as representatives of "the master race." Excluded from the group is Julius Löwenthal, who is Jewish, and later, Wilhelm Freytag, whose wife is revealed as Jewish. Among the few Americans are the recently divorced Mrs. Mary Treadwell and William Denny, a chemical engineer from Texas. A sinister Spanish zarzuela troupe precipitates a riot on fiesta night (Mrs. Treadwell has to fight off Denny with her spiked slippers), but all regain their composure and disembark to resume their wonted careers.

The story ignores conventional plotting and purposely avoids resolution. As Miss Porter states in her preface, this novel utilizes the "simple, almost universal image of the ship of this world on its voyage to eternity." The ship's name *Vera* means "truth." Happiness and wholeness are impossible for any of the forty-some major characters as they are trapped in their own selfish egos, incapable of full engagement in love but eminently capable of oppressing their fellows, whether in desire for material gain, lust, or anti-Semitism. The moment of illumination comes to Mary Treadwell: "What they were saying to each other was only, '*Love me, love me in spite of all! Whether or not I love you, whether I am fit for love, whether you are able to love, even if there is no such thing as love, love me!* " But in isolation, in lack of comprehension, and in cruel selfishness all are drifting into the monstrosity of Nazism and a catastrophic war. The supreme Porter criterion is truth vs. falsehood, rather than good vs. evil. Lack of awareness and lack of self-cognition lead to delusion and pain; all of modern humanity voyages onward as fools.

The title of the book is a translation of the title of an early German satire by Sebastian Brant, *Das Narrenschiff*, published in 1494.

Vladimir Nabokov (1899–   ). Vladimir Vladimirovich Nabokov (pronounced with the accent on "bo") was born in St. Petersburg, Russia, to a noble Russian family. He received his A.B. in 1922 from Cambridge University, England, and thereafter resided in France and Germany until coming to this country in 1940. He was naturalized in 1945. He has taught Russian literature and creative writing at Stanford, Wellesley, and Cornell. Quite apart from his writing and teaching he is an internationally recognized authority on butterflies and moths.

Nabokov has graced his adopted tongue with an individual style and several significant works. Until settling in this country he wrote verse and prose in Russian (banned in his native land) under the pen name of "V. Sirin." Beginning with *The Real Life of Sebastian Knight* (1941), the life of a Russian novelist as seen by his secretary, he has become increasingly notable as a novelist in English.

Lolita (1955) created quite a stir because of its seemingly shocking subject, the relations of a middle-aged roué, Humbert Humbert, with a teen-age girl, Dolores Haze, known to him as Lolita. He kills Clare Quilty, with whom Lolita was eloping, and recounts his adventures from the cell in which he is confined. Despite the central situation the book is not in any sense pornographic. This is an intellectual farce, a comic game played with the reader—false scents, uproarious parodies, plays on words, jokes, astounding allusions. With Continental suavity, Nabokov satirizes much of the vulgarity and hypocrisy of today's America. The central character Hum, possessed by a desire for art, loses any moral vision of life in his aesthetic vision. Beneath the coruscating laughter is a terrible tragedy of man in a world he did not make and cannot understand, but which he tries to shape as his own nature demands.

Nabokov's Dozen (1958) is a collection of thirteen stories which deal with the different worlds in which Nabokov has lived during this century —his early days in Czarist Russia, various cities in Central Europe between the World Wars, and the United States from the mid-forties up to recent years.

"A Forgotten Poet" is set in St. Petersburg in 1899. A cultural organization rediscovers the work of a mid-nineteenth-century poet, Konstantin Perov, whom they believe to have died many years before at the age of twenty-four. At a conference attended by many notable intellectuals, Perov, who is now well along in years, appears and asks for the money which has been collected to build a statue of him. He is finally ejected from the meeting, but as it appears that they will be made fools of, the poetry committee promises Perov a monthly pension for the rest of his life on condition that he will stay away from St. Petersburg. Perov accepts and goes back to his farm. Twenty years later Perov appears again. He is running a small museum containing his own works and several artifacts from his time. He dies in a back room of the museum and his works once more slip into obscurity.

"Cloud, Castle, Lake" takes place in Germany in the late thirties. Vasili, an unfortunate petty official in Berlin, wins a lottery and his prize is a train excursion to the countryside. Throughout the journey he is constantly tormented by his traveling companions because of his lack of companionable spirit and his hesitancy to join in their songs. When the group arrive in a beautiful forest with a clear lake reflecting a great cloud and a black castle on a hill overlooking it, Vasili decides that he will remain there for the rest of his life. When he mentions to his companions his plan, he is told that he must return to Berlin because that is what the itinerary says. He is dragged away and on the return trip is beaten. The last we hear of him he has resigned his position and lost his faith in the human race. Nabokov tells the story with such sparkling wit that it completely avoids the disturbing reflections which its subject matter would seem to imply.

Pale Fire (1962) is a novel with the unusual form of a scholarly study of a long poem, complete with a Foreword, the poem itself in four Cantos, a Commentary (which forms the bulk of the work), and an Index.

Charles Kinbote, exiled king of Zembla and now an American scholar, takes up a teaching post at Wordsmith University in New Wye, Appalachia. He is surprised to find that he has moved in next door to John Shade, a poet whom he has long admired. They become close friends and Kinbote reveals his dream of putting into verse the story of himself and of his kingdom. He recounts the legends and stories of Zembla to Shade and is confident that Shade will make them the subject of his next epic poem. But this is not to be; and Shade's masterpiece, entitled "Pale Fire," turns out to be strictly autobiographical. Shortly after he finishes the work, Shade is killed by a Zemblan assassin who was attempting to kill Kinbote. Kinbote gets possession of the manuscript of "Pale Fire" and receives permission to publish it, and in so doing, manages to accomplish his original purpose—that of telling the story of Zembla. By crafty digressions he traces the course of Gradus,

John Shade's killer, from Zembla to New Wye, and, in the process, tells not only of Zembla but also of himself. The above account, however, is only one way of looking at the novel. The poem "Pale Fire," it should be noted, takes up only a fraction of the whole book yet is good enough to stand on its own. It is typical of Nabokov's sense of humor that he would write an excellent poem and then place it in the most difficult and ludicrous of environments. He constantly plays such tricks on the reader and one soon realizes that the main conflict of this work is not between the characters in the fictional situation but between the reader and Nabokov.

Ada (1969) shows Nabokov further increasing his command of his unique style, and clearly confirms his distinctiveness and his importance among modern American novelists.

Anaïs Nin (1914–   ). Born in Paris, France, of a Spanish father and a Cuban mother, Anaïs Nin was brought to this country at the age of ten. At fifteen she ran away from school and has subsequently been self-educated. After marrying Ian Hugo, she returned to France until World War II when she came back to the United States. Finding publishers unreceptive to her writings, she bought a printing press, set type, and for four years published her own works.

The House of Incest (1936) and subsequent novels have been studies in psychiatry written in poetic prose. Miss Nin gives a key to her technique in likening it to the attempts of modern painting. She is not interested in the conventionalities of plot and character but in the vivid impact of powerful and subtle emotions. Publishers and critics have come to appreciate her as a superb stylist and experimenter.

J. D. Salinger (1919–   ). Jerome David Salinger was born in New York City. In 1936 he graduated from the Valley Forge Military Academy. He attended New York University, Ursinus College, and Columbia University, but took no degree. His first published short stories in 1940 began an extensive writing career. During World War II he saw considerable service in France. Though traveling widely in recent years, he has maintained residence in New England.

Salinger's favorite subject is children—particularly children with a spark of precocity. He customarily focuses upon them in adolescence. They perceive that their elders have unlearned the simple mechanisms of joy and fellowship that children employ daily, are unconscious of the loss, and have proceeded on to cultivate spurious gratifications. This view from the threshold of maturity usually precipitates a crisis. But the very violence of their reaction is indicative of their potential worth.

Salinger's young characters conduct the search for themselves in a vigorous flow of speech that is largely inventive slang with the incongruous intrusion of bits of technical jargon. The effect is always charming, whether it connotes innocence or mocking disdain, and it aptly depicts the grappling of a perceptive youthful mind with the inexpressibilities of emotional truth.

The Catcher in the Rye (1951) has been an unusually popular book with those who are of its young hero's generation. It is the story—told by himself—of Holden Caulfield, who is in an institution recovering from the effects of a severe identity crisis.

The story begins soon after Holden learns he has been expelled from his school, Pensey Prep, for poor grades. Depressed and ashamed for his parents' sake, he finds the company of his schoolmates—an unappealing assortment of grotesques and insensitives—even more exasperating than usual, and elects to leave early for Christmas vacation. Once back in New York, he avoids an immediate confrontation with his family by putting up at a cheap hotel. In the evening he roams the streets and bistros of Manhattan, meeting people who further discourage him by their "phoniness," a quality that frustrates his need for genuine human contact. Back in his hotel he arranges an assignation with a prostitute, backs out at the last minute, but is coerced into paying her fee regardless. The next few days are nightmarish. Holden's old friends when he seeks them peer out at him with contemptuous curiosity from behind their newly erected façades. A trusted former teacher appears to be a homosexual. The one respite is a brief, clandestine meeting with his young sister, Phoebe. Holden revels in Phoebe's unfeigned affection and delightful candor; he confides that he wants to be a "catcher in the rye," a guardian of childhood innocence. But Holden's grip on reality and on his defensive shell of stoicism is slipping. Abruptly he decides to run away to the West after seeing Phoebe for a last time. She has guessed his intention, however, and means to join him. Moved by her loyalty, he accompanies her back to their parents instead.

The Catcher in the Rye is one of the great initiation novels of America literature. In telling his story, Holden is sufficiently objective and analytical to persuade the reader that balance has been restored. Holden's sensitivity cannot be curtailed by an act of will, and he is too forthright to predict a ready accommodation to the world for himself. Salinger's tone seems clearly to suggest, however, that Holden's adventures to come will be productive ones; that the alternative to participation has been found wanting, while the ordeal has confirmed the strength of a sensitive youth who will soon grow into an effective manhood.

Nine Stories (1953). Along with some masterful studies of children ("For Esmé—with Love and Squalor" and "Teddy") and pathetic adults ("Uncle Wiggily in Connecticut"), this collection introduces the very sensitive and precocious offspring of Les and Bessie Glass, a former vaudeville team. Their daughter Boo Boo appears unforgettably as a housewife in "Down at the Dinghy." "A Perfect Day for Bananafish" deals with the suicide of the eldest, Seymour, at Miami Beach in 1948. *Franny and Zooey* (1961) consists of two longer Glass stories. The first story, "Franny," introduces the youngest of the Glass children. Franny is a college coed visiting a male campus on the weekend of the big game. Her escort is an ordinary undergraduate—callow, socially conscious, a trifle conceited—with whom she has been trying to persuade herself she is in love. As he rehearses his minor academic triumphs it becomes obvious that Franny is strangely agitated. She is pale and distracted; at one point she excuses herself for the ladies' lounge where she weeps uninhibitedly for several minutes. Her enigmatic behavior arouses the impatience of her date, but the necessity of being apologetic seems to unhinge her even more. They are about to leave when Franny suddenly faints, to awaken in the manager's office. The story ends on a discordant note: relieved at her recovery, Franny's escort suggests they dispense with the afternoon's scheduled activities and retire to make love.

"Zooey," the second story, actually concerns Franny and her brother Buddy, a television actor. Franny has returned to the Glass apartment in New York and withdrawn entirely into herself. It is discovered that having become obsessed with an obscure book on religious mysticism that teaches how to pray perpetually she has lapsed into a semi-trance. Mrs. Glass appeals to Buddy, the next oldest, to intercede, and his efforts throw some light on the family history.

The Glass children are numerous and brilliant. At one time or another they have all appeared on the radio quiz show "It's a Wise Child." But what was exhilarating in their nonage has changed complexion over the years, so that both Buddy and Franny tend to see themselves as intellectual monsters who cannot adjust to the mediocrity of their fellow creatures. Buddy has learned to cope with the world by maintaining an exterior of testy truculence, but Franny's hopes for an acting career have come up against her inability to compromise with the second-rate. Her recent unsuccessful love affair is further evidence of her unreasonable insistence upon perfection, she believes; and she has now chosen the path of the religious ascetic to humble her spirit. As the two siblings thrash out these matters they speak increasingly of Seymour and Zooey (Zachary), the eldest of the Glasses, who had anticipated their conflict and seen to it that Buddy and Franny had an early introduction to the great spiritual prophets of the world's history. In his attempts to reason with his sister, Buddy discovers for himself the true intent of his older brothers' plan, and is able to make Franny recognize her extraordinary talents as gifts to be bestowed on mankind.

Zooey's place in the story that bears his name is purportedly that of narrator. He also prefaces the scene in the Glass apartment with some archly whimsical introductory remarks and a transcription of a letter he has written to Buddy that testifies to the eccentric but special relationship the children share. Otherwise the substance of *Franny and Zooey* is two extended conversations.

"Raise High the Roof Beam, Carpenters" and "Seymour: An Introduction" (1963) published in one volume, continue Salinger's treatment of the Glass family.

NOVELISTS RESPONSIVE TO THE INTERNATIONAL SCENE

John Hersey (1914–   ). Son of American parents, John Richard Hersey was born in Tientsin, China, where he secured his early education. He received his A.B. from Yale in 1936 and later studied at Cambridge University in England. During 1937 he was secretary to Sinclair Lewis. Subsequently as editor and writer for *Time, Life,* and *The New Yorker* he covered many of the Pacific campaigns of World War II. After the war, Hersey devoted himself primarily to the writing of novels, usually drawing upon events which had moved him deeply. Some of these accounts use imaginary characters as a means of conveying the full impact of the happenings, thus achieving through narrative a more immediate effect than would be possible by means of direct reporting. In 1965 Hersey became master of Pierson College at Yale, remaining for five years as he had planned, then turning again to writing.

Men on Bataan (1942), about American fighting in the Philippines, and *Into the Valley* (1943), dealing with the Guadalcanal struggle, were at once recognized as notable accounts of the events. Hersey's first novel, the Pulitzer Prize-winning *A Bell for Adano* (1944), depicts an Italo-American major who reconstitutes a war-shattered Sicilian village, and shares with the inhabitants the concepts of democracy. *Hiroshima* (1946), read by people throughout the world, is a rigorously factual account of the first atomic destruction, an overwhelmingly eloquent report of the human suffering which resulted, and an indictment of war. *The Wall* (1950) deals with the Warsaw ghetto and the heroic attempt by the Jews within this walled area to defend themselves against the Nazis, who in great numbers and with powerful military equipment had been sent to destroy them during World War II and who relentlessly carried out the destruction.

A Single Pebble (1956), a short novel, is a work of broad philosophical implications.

The narrator is an American engineer who recalls his voyage up the Yangtze in China in the 1920s to examine possible sites for a hydro-electric dam. The title comes from the name of the chief tracker, Old Pebble, who heads the gang of coolies pulling the river junk upstream.

Old Pebble falls from a ledge and is swept to his death in the river. The narrator returns without fulfilling his mission.

The story is an enlightened and effective contrasting of the East and the West. The ebullient American youth initially brushes aside the Chinese way of life as backward in comparison to Western efficiency and science. Gradually he becomes aware of the age-old harmonies that the Chinese, epitomized in Old Pebble, have established between man and Nature, man and man, and the individual and himself. The tracker is horrified at the American's impious plans for the alteration of the sacred river (and, by implication, of all oriental society). Old Pebble is swept away, as is most of an immemorial way of life; with the later disquietudes of China in the offing.

Some of Hersey's more recent novels deal with problems of individuals in a suburban setting, with his deep social concern and concern for the individual always evident.

James A. Michener (1907–   ). James Albert Michener was born in New York City but later moved to Doylestown, Pennsylvania, where he spent most of his early years. He graduated from Swarthmore College and spent a two-year period of study in Europe. He taught for a while, and in 1941 enlisted in the Navy.

Tales of the South Pacific (1947) is a group of stories derived from Michener's experiences as a naval officer on various islands of the South Pacific in World War II. The characters are drawn from the American sailors and marines, the French colonists, and the Tonkinese and Polynesian islanders that he encountered on his tour of duty in the early part of the war against the Japanese. Some of the stories relate the bloody battles that were waged on the small coral islands, while others describe the everyday life of the Americans who were stationed on the islands and how they dealt with the alien environment, the tropical disease, and the lack of women. The stories are tied together by the imminent American invasion of the island of Kuralei. Episodes from the book form the basis for the musical *South Pacific* with music by Richard Rodgers and lyrics by Oscar Hammerstein II.

Sayonara (1954) is set in Japan during the American military occupation of the early fifties. Major Lloyd Gruver, a West Pointer, Korean flying ace, and the son of a four-star general, is transferred to Japan so that he can marry Eileen Webster, the daughter of his commanding officer and an old friend of the family. Gruver and the Websters are at first condescending toward the Japanese and think that the love affairs between American soldiers and Japanese women are a disgrace. However when Gruver meets and falls in love with Hana-ogi, a beautiful Japanese actress, he joins in defiance of the barriers that have been set up to discourage such unions. He has the backing of his friend

Private Joe Kelly who has married a Japanese girl. But when Kelly is suddenly told that he is to be transferred to the States and will not be allowed to take his wife, the couple commit suicide. General Webster talks to Hana-ogi and convinces her that she should go away. She leaves; and Gruver, accepting General Webster's advice, does not follow her. The Japanese word "sayonara" means farewell.

Other novels by Michener include: *Hawaii* (1959), in which the author combines fictional characters with actual historical and anthropological data; and *The Source* (1965), in which he turns to Israel where an archeological team burrows deep into the past of the storied land.

NOVELISTS OF INDIVIDUALISM AND SELF-EXPRESSION

Henry Miller (1891–   ). Henry Valentine Miller was born in Manhattan but the family moved to Brooklyn when he was one year old. His father was a tailor, and Miller was an only son. Miller's formal education ended after two months at City College of New York in 1909. From 1910 to 1928 he worked at an incredible melange of jobs ranging from door-to-door salesman and Western Union messenger to "speak-easy" operator and panhandler. From 1928 to 1940 he resided mostly in Europe, where his works were first published (circulation in this country was long prohibited). In 1942 he moved to California, living for a time at Big Sur, the artists' colony made famous by Robinson Jeffers. His home more recently is Los Angeles.

Miller is a most controversial novelist. To his devotees he is a literary giant, a fully liberated Whitman. To his detractors he is the nadir of obscenity and pornography. Perhaps he is best classified as a rebel-buffoon and an early exponent of "black humor." The Millerian comedy is a wild, amoral nihilism. Miller has dabbled extensively in many occult thinkers, but his guiding principle has really been American individualism defiantly asserted against all the conventionalities of our time.

Tropic of Cancer, first published in Paris in 1934, was banned in America until 1961. The "tropic" of the title Miller defines as "the meridian that separates the hemisphere of life and death"; "cancer" is one of the recurrent images of disease and decay plaguing the contemporary world. The book consists of fifteen anecdotal chapters about Miller's experiences in France during the early 1930s. On the opening page he asserts that the book is a prolonged insult to Art, and to God, Man, Destiny, Time, Love, Beauty. Destitute, even starving, he falls into degradation, savage sexuality, and scatophilia, descriptions of which have few if any counterparts in English. From the abyss he eventually emerges. Pervading the book is the image of flow—fluids of all sorts. To the mechanical rigidity of modern nonlife he opposes the process of eternal becoming, of total self-expression and total experience. Miller felt this work to be a colossal purgative, a grappling with the problem of self-liberation.

Tropic of Capricorn, initially published in Paris in 1939, appeared in print in this country in 1962. This largely autobiographical work sought to find in Miller's American experiences before 1930 what had made a novelist out of him. The "capricorn" of the title clearly refers to the sign of the zodiac under which Miller was himself born (December 26) and is also highly suggestive in its component parts (*caper*, "goat," and *cornu*, "horn"). The "tropic" is the personal hell encountered by Miller in Brooklyn, especially during his tenure as employment manager for a large telegraph company in 1920–25. Miller vacillates from prophetic rage to sentimentalized self-pity, and intersperses these outbursts with great numbers of sexual encounters and dreams. In leaving his job, Miller feels that he has found freedom, and expresses his conviction that no man must do this or that to earn a living.

Other works by Miller include *Big Sur and the Oranges of Hieronymus Bosch* (1957), *Stand Still Like the Hummingbird* (1962), and *Black Spring* (1963).

J. P. Donleavy (1926–   ). James Patrick Donleavy was born in Brooklyn, New York. He served in the Navy in World War II, after which he attended Trinity College in Dublin where he studied science. He tried painting, but later decided to devote himself to writing.

The Ginger Man (1958) refers in title to the Gingerbread Man of the nursery rhyme, who escapes all pursuers until swallowed by the fox. Most of the novel is an interior view of Sebastian Dangerfield, a young American in Ireland who, under the pretense of studying law, carouses through Dublin while awaiting an inheritance to be settled on him by his father.

When Dangerfield's English bride, Marion, disappoints his expectation of a generous dowry, the two of them and their infant daughter barricade themselves in squalid lodgings and resist the siege of landlord and creditors. Marion's patience is rapidly exhausted by Sebastian's imperturbable irresponsibility, drunken revels, and infidelities. She deserts him, but not before prompting his father to further delay his legacy. A new mistress, Mary, supports Sebastian and makes possible his removal to London, only to leave him after he lashes out against her persistent amorousness. A comrade from Dublin who has blundered into wealthy circumstances rescues Dangerfield from the streets, and he soon manages a reconciliation with his mistress. Incorrigible as he is basically, this refuge becomes only a transient phenomenon.

Dangerfield is an ardent sensualist of freakish if beguiling tastes; a conglomerate of sloth, profligacy, idealism, irresponsibility, pride, vivacity, and charm. His merits derive from the exuberance of his appetites, his failings from his slavery to them.

Some of Donleavy's other works are *A Singular Man* (1963), *The Saddest Summer of Samuel S.* (1966), and *The Beastly Beatitudes of Dalthuzar B.* (1968).

NOVELISTS CONCERNED WITH SOCIAL AND PERSONAL PROBLEMS

James Gould Cozzens (1903–   ). A native of Chicago, James Gould Cozzens was brought up in the East. His first novel appeared when he was nineteen and a sophomore at Harvard. In 1924, after two years at Harvard, he left to work and travel in Canada, Cuba, and Europe. Since 1933 he has resided on the East coast except for service with the Army Air Corps from 1942 to 1945.

Cozzens displays a solid, polished competence in his works. In subject he can range from a Cuban sugar plantation in *The Son of Perdition* (1929) to the sinking of a passenger liner in *S.S. San Pedro* (1931) or a physician's dominance of a Connecticut village in *The Last Adam* (1933); in mood he can range from a macabre, Poe-like fantasy in *Castaway* (1934) to the factual problems of an Episcopal parish in *Ask Me Tomorrow* (1940).

Cozzens is somewhat of a traditional realist who accepts things as they are and wishes somehow to maintain the order we have rather than risk chaos by regression or change.

Guard of Honor (1948) is an outstanding novel of World War II.

Ocanara Air Base, Florida, in 1943 is commanded by General Ira ("Bus") Beal, hero of air battles in the Pacific earlier in the war. Colonel Ross, a judge in peacetime, is his right-hand man. A Negro pilot, Lieutenant Willis, blunderingly almost wrecks the general's plane and is beaten up by Colonel Carricker. A racial flare-up by Negro airmen and nearby townsfolk is narrowly averted. In a military parade, paratroopers accidentally fall into a lake, but General Beal ably directs rescue operations.

The central interest of the novel rests in its characters, most of whom are officers. They are decent human beings, fallible and far less effective than they should be, but doing their honest best in the face of almost insurmountable obstacles. Colonel Woodman, commanding Sellers Field, is a failure and, after long diatribes against the mysterious clique he blames for his botched career, a suicide. General Nichols, visiting from the Pentagon, holds the highest rank and is deservedly in the councils of Churchill and Roosevelt. General Beal stands at his crossroads; the complexity and ambiguity of his problems, especially the race issue, produce an irresolution from which at last he emerges successfully. Colonel Ross, the shrewd observer for much of the novel, realizes the validity of the Nichols creed: Do your best, and things will generally maintain their wobbly but essentially dependable course. While other novelists have concentrated on combat situations, *Guard of Honor* is a scrutiny of the behind-the-scenes Army—an improvisation of such vast dimensions as to dwarf and baffle even General Nichols.

By Love Possessed (1957) was greeted with critical praise.

Brocton, a small city in the Delaware Valley, deeply respects Noah Tuttle, a lawyer who some years ago saved the Brocton Rapid Transit Company from bankruptcy. Tuttle's partner Julius Penrose is crippled by polio. The other partner, fifty-four-year-old Arthur Winner, is the novel's central character. Between three o'clock of a midsummer Friday and four o'clock two days later Winner's whole world is overturned. Ralph Detweiler, ne'er-do-well brother of Helen Detweiler, secretary of the law firm, is charged with rape, and Helen commits suicide. Marjorie Penrose, Winner's partner's wife with whom he has conducted an affair, threatens an exposure. The amazed Winner discovers that Penrose has known of the liaison and has also been aware of Tuttle's years of embezzling to straighten out the transit-company tangle. Though badly shaken, Winner decides to keep going, trying to make things work and avoid a scandalous revelation.

Cozzens surveys in depth an American provincial city and all its population strata. All the characters are "possessed." Much of the "possession" is sexual love, all varieties of which, natural and unnatural, legal and illegal, are explored. But in larger scope the "love" is the imaginary vision of life cherished by each character. Thus Penrose's is unqualified pursuit of reason, and Ralph's is unbridled pursuit of women. Winner steps outside himself and his hopes to conduct a forced self-appraisal, and discovers himself quite otherwise than his personal or public image—pillar of church and community, perfect husband and father, member of an eminently respectable and honest law firm— would suggest. He concludes that he must compromise between his dreams and the intruding reality in order to maintain his course, and must make do with uncertainties.

John O'Hara (1905–70). John Henry O'Hara was born in Pottsville, Pennsylvania. After graduating in 1924 from Niagara Preparatory School, he worked at a variety of jobs from boat steward to steel-mill laborer, with journalism and motion-picture writing along the way.

O'Hara employed detail in a manner not unlike that of many nineteenth-century English novelists. His characters are upper middle class, whose motivations, as sexuality in *A Rage to Live* (1949), and surround-

ings, as Manhattan's Upper East Side in *Butterfield 8* (1935), are presented with unusual completeness.

Appointment in Samarra (1934), O'Hara's first novel, shows many of
his best qualities. The title is taken from an old Arabian story of a man's
unsuccessful attempt to avoid a meeting with Death by fleeing from
Baghdad to Samarra.

At a Christmas Eve party at the country club of Gibbsville, Pennsylvania, Julian English, scion of one of the important families of the
community, impulsively throws a highball into the face of Harry Reilly,
a wealthy nouveau riche to whom he owes money. His subsequent
humiliation precipitates English's suicide.

English, a snob and an alcoholic, is not fully characterized, but the
anatomizing of Gibbsville is thorough and revealing. O'Hara knows his
Gibbsville (Pottsville) to the last nuance of social position, which, of
course, is derivative from the supreme arbiter, Dun and Bradstreet.
Status is the polestar of existence to these people, and every person is
irrevocably assigned his precise niche. With no other goals or standards,
O'Hara's business and professional people are inwardly dirty, selfish,
immoral beings.

Pal Joey (1940) is a famous short-story collection by O'Hara. All the
stories concern a night-club entertainer, Joey, whose tawdry, raffish existence and surroundings make him a heel, a thoroughly selfish and
unscrupulous opportunist. However, his incredible resilience and almost
Runyonesque expressions reveal him as a fascinating scoundrel. O'Hara
wrote the libretto for the 1940 musical comedy *Pal Joey*, with music by
Richard Rodgers and lyrics by Lorenz Hart.

Ten North Frederick (1955) is one of O'Hara's most representative
novels.

The book is a retrospective examination of the life of Joseph B.
Chapin, the most prominent citizen of Gibbsville. He is born with money
and position, attends Yale University, marries within his class, and forms
a prestigious law partnership with a Yale classmate. Casting about for
greater worlds to conquer, he conceives the idea of becoming President
of the United States, and even goes so far as to bribe a local party
organization to sponsor him. This group, however, which is headed by
Mike Slattery, feels that Chapin's credentials are inadequate for success
in any sort of election. Disappointed in his hopes, Chapin loses interest
in life beyond the maintaining of appearances, and spends his remaining
years lulling his frustration with alcohol.

There is little that is admirable about Chapin. His unruffled self-
esteem is largely unjustified, and his intolerance toward shortcomings in
others is the ruination of his son and daughter and the aggravation of
his wife, Edith.

The matrix from which Chapin emerges is minutely scanned, and Gibbsville's history is analyzed from the Civil War to the present. Although not attractive, the community is impressive and real in all the ramifications of economic and social interrelationships.

From the Terrace (1958) traces the life of Alfred Eaton through his boyhood, his years at Princeton, his service as a naval officer in World War I, and the various careers that he worked at through the Second World War. The novel is a long one and describes in detail Eaton's jobs in the aviation business, on Wall Street, and as a government official. An example of O'Hara's documentation is his inclusion of the full syllabus of the Princeton entrance examination taken by Eaton.

Wright Morris (1910–   ). From birth until 1924, Wright Morris lived in his native Central City, Nebraska, or in other towns along the Platte River. In 1924 he began wanderings that have since taken him through all of this country and much of Europe. He attended Pomona College, California, from 1930 to 1933. His first novel, *My Uncle Dudley* (1942), helped him to secure the first of three Guggenheim fellowships. In 1944 he began lectureships at Haverford College, which won wide attention. Since 1962 he has been a professor at San Francisco State College.

In *The Territory Ahead* (1958), a critical study, Morris keynotes the position of the new generation of realists. Thomas Wolfe, as Morris diagnoses him, was a magnificent failure because he rashly attempted to encompass the total American experience. For himself and his compeers, Morris asserts, "the fragmentary approach seems almost compulsory to me." Morris' manner, unlike that of most fellow realists, is lightly ironic. Critics and fellow fictionists have consistently praised him as a "novelist's novelist."

The Home Place (1948) is probably the best known of over a dozen Morris novels. There is no traditional plot continuity but rather a series of impressions as Clyde Muncy brings his wife and two children from New York to his birthplace in Lone Tree, Nebraska. Nostalgia has prompted Muncy to return to his old community, but farming or any of the other available jobs are impossible occupations for this city dweller. Few novels so sensitively perceive the subtle and unbridgeable differences between the surviving ruralists and the contemporary urbanites.

Departing from Lone Tree, the Muncys in *The World in the Attic* (1949) pause in nearby Junction, where Clyde had lived in his youth; and there even more intensely Muncy feels the contrast of the past and the present.

Norman Mailer (1923–   ). Born in Long Branch, New Jersey,

Norman Mailer grew up in Brooklyn. He went to Harvard in 1939 intent upon becoming an aeronautical engineer, but soon revealed talent as a writer of fiction. Shortly after his graduation in 1943, he entered the Army and saw extensive war service in the western Pacific. After the war he traveled widely in both Europe and America. By his own statement Mailer is determined to "serve as the gadfly to complacency, institution, and the dead weight of public taste." His first novel, dealing with the war, won him immediate recognition. In his later books he has turned to other subjects.

The Naked and the Dead (1948) is a major novel of World War II. The overall pattern is not unlike the structure of the best World War I novels. Men representing every important racial, geographic, and social unit in the United States are thrown together as a small group in a common war effort.

Lieutenant Hearn, aide to General Cummings, rebels against his superior's pettiness, and as punishment is given command of a reconnaissance platoon assigned a virtually impossible mission against the Japanese on Anopopei Island. Sergeant Croft, who resents the lieutenant, maneuvers Hearn into a position where he is killed. Croft leads the survivors upon a backbreaking stint, only to find their efforts unnecessary. During the general's absence enemy resistance had simply evaporated.

Through flash-back techniques Mailer explores the America from whence his motley platoon came. His enlisted men find that war gives a charged meaning to their impoverished lives only to substitute a more monstrous meaninglessness.

The issue of individualism versus collective action is lengthily debated by the intellectualized officers. General Cummings is the extreme conservative, seeing all life as a power struggle, with the palm going to the strongest and cleverest. Lieutenant Hearn is a liberal, seeking for each man that fundamental security that will permit his self-fulfillment without regimentation. The ultimate horror of war is that Cummings seems right when the chips of battle are down. Croft, a bully, can drive forward, as Hearn cannot, against the physical and psychic obstacles confronting him. The outcome, blood and effort needlessly spent, is in keeping with Mailer's theme of war's senselessness.

The Deer Park (1955) is a satire on the lives of the wealthy film personalities who live in southern California.

Sergius O'Shaugnessy, just discharged from the Air Force, has won $14,000 in a poker game in Tokyo and comes to Desert D'Or, a resort town near Hollywood, to spend it. Through the eyes of Sergius we see a succession of movie types and the wealthy who cling to them. The lives of these aging celebrities, starlets, producers, and oil millionaires are spent in endless nights of drinking, neurotic love affairs, and boring conversation. Mailer portrays them with a cynical humor.

An American Dream (1965) is an occasionally incoherent but enormously energetic, pseudonaturalistic tale of modern life.

Stephen Rojack, a television celebrity, ex-congressman, and professor of existential philosophy, believes that "magic, dread, and the perception of death" are the basis for human behavior, and suspects that his separated wife, Deborah, is using these phenomena as active forces to enslave his spirit and drive him to suicide. Late one night he visits her in her New York duplex, strangles her, thrusts her body out the bedroom window, and violently seduces the German maid. Thus begins a period of several days during which Rojack is awake and peripatetic throughout the city, operating on alcohol and nervous tension, trying to locate the malevolent influences and exorcize them. He asserts himself and his identity, regardless of moral considerations. A chaotic series of fantastic events and revelations leads to his being exonerated by the police for his crime and rendered "something like sane again."

James Jones (1921–   ). A native of Robinson, Illinois, James Jones enlisted in the United States Army and served from 1939–44. He had brief collegiate training at the University of Hawaii in 1942 and at New York University in 1945. His recent residence has been in Paris.

From Here to Eternity (1951) is one of the most notable novels to come out of World War II. The title comes from a poem by Kipling, whose "Gentleman Rankers" are "Damned from here to Eternity."

The time is late 1940, and the place the Schofield Barracks in Hawaii. The principal character Robert E. Lee Prewitt ("Prew") is a hardened young soldier from a small Kentucky town. Prew's most admirable trait is his reluctance to exploit his talents as a pugilist; this moral uprightness exposes him as a target for Colonel Delbert, the company commander, who fancies the prestige a prize athlete will confer upon his outfit, and for the lesser officers, who are always on the watch for the irregular and culpable. Prew is persecuted until he strikes back and then punished until he kills his tormentor. As a fugitive he takes refuge with Alma Schmidt, a prostitute of his acquaintance. The attack on Pearl Harbor rallies him, however. He leaves Alma's house and is making his way to his company amidst the falling bombs when he is shot by a suspicious sentry.

This is a novel of professional soldiers. The "thirty-year" enlisted men are the unruly underprivileged who are likely to be failures in civilian life. The most animalistic of these savage young males are often chosen as NCOs, which allows them to play the sadistic tyrant. Jones knows these "regulars" to the marrow, and captures them with stunning authenticity. But his view as an enlisted man limits his portrayal of the officers. The infantryman's life is the last refuge of raw maleness. Its challenge and relative freedom are menaced partly by the military hierarchy and partly by women, who represent an annoyance except when they satisfy bodily lust. Prew is a tough-luck Joe sporting a quixotic principle untenable in the brutal society of the Pineapple Army. Ridden to the breaking point, he lashes back in the only way possible for him.

Some Came Running (1957) is set in the Wabash Valley of southern Illinois.

The town is Parkman and the time is the years of peace between the end of World War II and the outbreak of the Korean War. The central conflict is between the Hirsh brothers—Dave, a drifter who once wanted to be a writer, and his brother, Frank, a successful and ambitious businessman. There are many other important characters and conflicts in this long novel and Jones develops them all quite fully.

The Thin Red Line (1962) is Jones's newer novel about the war. The plot is straightforward. C-for-Charlie Company fights through the jungles of Guadalcanal until half its complement are casualties. The holes are plugged up, and the company starts training for the impending attack upon New Georgia. The account is almost unpalatably naturalistic; it is virtually a textbook of battle. For the purposes of war, an individual is meaningful only as a unit of matériel; the individual as an individual is meaningless, except to himself.

Irwin Shaw (1913–). A native New Yorker, Irwin Shaw left Brooklyn College because of the rigors of freshman mathematics to work in a cosmetics factory, a department store, and a furniture company. He returned to write college dramas and graduate in 1934. *Bury the Dead* (1936) was a notable pacifist play that opened off Broadway but won later fame on Broadway itself. From 1942 to 1945 Shaw served in the United States Army in North Africa, Europe, and the Near East. He has written screenplays for Hollywood and prize-winning short stories. In recent years he has resided in Switzerland.

Shaw's short-story collection, *Welcome to the City* (1942), showed his acute social awareness. Of his longer works only the first, *The Young Lions*, has won wide recognition.

The Young Lions (1948) is one of the notable novels based on World War II. There are three main characters, and the discontinuous narrative focuses on each separately until all three are brought together at the conclusion. Michael Whitacre, an American soldier whose civilian career was associated with the Broadway theater, is a disaffiliated freethinker who hopes the war will bring some kind of commitment into his life. Noah Ackerman, another American, is manfully struggling to overcome the prejudice against him as a Jew. Christian Diestl, a rabid Austrian Nazi, has given himself entirely to the German cause. The careers of all three involve parallel incidents from which ironic commentaries can be extracted. In the symbolic finale, which takes place in a Bavarian concentration camp, Diestl kills Ackerman and is in turn slain by Whitacre.

The novel seeks to understand the nature of the enemy in Diestl. Groping for relief from his personal mediocrity, Diestl had espoused ideologies that promised glory and success. As hate seemed the most powerful of human emotions, he found an outlet in anti-Semitism. Ackerman, the most sympathetic character, is the scapegoat. Whitacre is a well-meaning man who has been only moderately successful in private life. It takes the visual demonstration of injustice and cruelty to incite him to action.

Nelson Algren (1909–   ). Born in Detroit, Michigan, Nelson Algren was brought up in the tough Northwest Side of Chicago. After high school he tried numerous jobs ranging from door-to-door salesman to stud-poker dealer. His first novel, *Somebody in Boots* (1935), ignored at the time, now seems a terrifyingly accurate portrayal of rootless youth in the Depression era. Critical attention came to *Never Come Morning* (1942), about Polish immigrants in Chicago; Bruce Bicek, who pathetically dreamed of becoming the world's heavyweight boxing champion, has his hopes dashed at the age of eighteen when he is indicted for murder.

The Neon Wilderness (1947) is a group of short-story portraits of blighted lives. These are urbanites, denizens of Chicago's Skid Row. Some are failures because of low mentality, but most are victims of their immigrant background and confinement to the slums. The bitter ironic humor often characteristic of the downtrodden is prominent. "Poor Man's Pennies" relates the abortive and incompetently planned attempt at a department store holdup.

The Man with the Golden Arm (1949), Algren's best-known book, deals with a problem and setting that Algren had seen at close range.

Frankie Machine (Francis Majcinek) is accredited with possessing a "golden arm" because of his proficiency with cards, dice, and pool cue. That arm becomes scarred with the heroin needle as Frankie seeks escape from the dreary Polish slums of Chicago. A complication is his love for Molly Novotny, a stripper. Frankie's wife, Sophie, crippled in an automobile accident when Frankie was driving while drunk, does her best to afflict him with consciousness of his guilt. Frankie finally escapes through suicide.

The novel is a devastating evocation of the urban jungle. Here clusters the backwash of an abundant society, the misfits. As Frankie roams the squalid back streets, his drugged mind creates a phantasmagoria of unspeakable hideousness and horror. Frankie has the capacity for love, for self-discovery, but he is a moral coward shackled by his time and his place. Algren's profound sympathy for his characters is apparent. A notable movie was made from this novel.

Charles Jackson (1903–68). Charles Jackson was born in Summit, New Jersey. When he was three years old his family moved to Newark, New York, a small town in Wayne County, where he grew up. Later he lived in Boston and Chicago and for a while in Switzerland, France, and Italy. More recently his home was in New York City; he was active for a time in writing for radio.

The Lost Weekend (1944) was Jackson's first novel and it was immediately recognized as an amazingly original and powerful work. It tells in detail the events of five days in the life of Don Birnam, who has become an alcoholic and cannot control his need for drink despite the loyal and devoted efforts of his brother Nick and his friend Helen, both of whom understood his moods and his difficulty. The five days which constitute the "lost weekend" are an almost continuous succession of opened bottles, visits to bars, hangovers, brief hospitalization with attempt at cure, and eventually safe return to his home but with no certainty as to the future.

The novel is written in awareness of alcoholism as an illness and essentially a psychiatric disturbance, but it is not in any sense a tract. The narrative moves rapidly with the characters understandingly portrayed. *The Lost Weekend* was the basis for a memorable movie.

Later works by Charles Jackson include the novel *The Fall of Valor* (1946) and a volume of short stories *The Sunnier Side* (1950).

Gore Vidal (1925–). Grandson of Oklahoma Senator Gore, for whom he is named, Gore Vidal was born at West Point, New York. A month after his graduation from Phillips Exeter Academy he enlisted in the Army and served from 1943 to 1946. His initial novel, *Williwaw* (1946), was based upon his experiences as first mate on an army freighter in the Aleutians. He gained prominence as a television writer, notably in *Visit to a Small Planet* (1956), produced as a Broadway drama in 1957, cleverly satirizing the Earth as seen by a visitor from space. He has written several novels with present-day settings. *The City and the Pillar* (1948) deals with alienation of individuals in a modern city, with the theme of homosexuality dominant in several episodes.

Gore Vidal is one of the few modern American novelists to choose as a theme a period of early European history marked by serious philosophical and religious doubt. In selecting for *Julian* (1964) the life and times of Julian the Apostate, Vidal evidently felt that the subject has definite present-day meaningfulness.

Julian is presented as the fictional memoirs of the fourth-century Roman emperor Julian. Additional perspective is provided by the hypothetical Priscus and Libanius, who undertake to edit Julian's journal thirty years after his death.

As nephew of the great Constantine, Julian grows up amidst continuous peril, for in the fourth century potential heirs to the imperial throne were frequently assassinated. Julian concentrates upon his studies and remains inconspicuous. Regretfully, the ruling Constantius, a cousin, proclaims Julian as his successor, having no sons himself. During his brief reign (361–63) Julian ("The Apostate") tries to revive the old paganism, but Callistus, a fanatical Christian, stabs him to death during a battle against the Persians.

In this seriously conceived historical novel, Vidal is concerned with the side of the coin seldom considered—the case for paganism against rising Christianity. Highly educated and critical, Julian detests the Christians for their bigotry, their interminable hair-splitting debates over theology, their haste to slay heretics in the name of a loving Lord. In his anxiety to preserve the great tradition of Hellenism, Julian becomes as fanatical as his Christian opponents and does not truly merit the rank of philosopher-king that he aspires to. It is a painful and inevitable tragedy that an ancient heritage must largely perish and that its well-intentioned supporters should blacken that heritage in their very attempts to maintain it. Too human and too little of the genius he yearned to be, Julian was trapped by history. Vidal so immersed himself in study as to produce a convincing and detailed picture of what life must have been like in that distant era.

Saul Bellow (1915–   ). Born in Lachine, Quebec, of Russian immigrant parents, Saul Bellow moved with his family to Chicago in 1924. In 1937 he graduated with honors in anthropology and sociology from Northwestern University. He began graduate studies at the University of Wisconsin but married and did not continue for a degree. Anthropological studies have taken him to Mexico and to Indian areas in this country. During World War II he served in the merchant marine. He has mixed free-lance writing with extensive teaching at the universities of Minnesota, Princeton, New York, and Chicago.

Bellow seems an extraordinarily protean figure in our contemporary fiction, attempting a scope and variety otherwise rare today. Informing all of his varied works, however, is the quest of the unlucky but struggling character. Bellow's Russian and Jewish backgrounds have had the effect of directing his novels counter to his professional training in sociology. His characters are the lonely men of our age, unable to make effective contacts with others; but their vigorous reaching for truth and understanding produces a most zestful affirmation of life and personality.

Dangling Man (1944) is the wartime diary of Joseph, unemployed and unemployable because he is eligible for the draft. While awaiting induction he tries to find himself in his scribblings. His encounters with the outside world become increasingly sordid and violent, so he finally volunteers, dominated by a death wish and feeling guilty that others are dying in his stead. Without any faith or any plan, he can make no use of his "freedom," a freedom that itself is illusory.

The Adventures of Augie March (1953) brought Bellow wide national recognition. In this novel he discards the tight Flaubert-like construction of his previous novels in favor of a Fielding-like picaresque pattern.

Simon March, eldest of the illegitimate children of a Jewish woman, marries into the wealthy Magnus family during the Depression years and urges his younger brother, Augie, to court Lucy Magnus, his sister-in-law. But Augie enjoys his freedom and is glad to be rejected. Augie helps to rob a store and pals around with hoodlums. At the University of Chicago he supports himself by stealing books. The remainder of his career is multifarious. He is a demonstrator at a sports goods shop. He sells shoes, organizes for a union, smuggles aliens. He is side-kick for a mad scientist and ghost writer for an eccentric millionaire. At last he marries Stella, a rich young woman who hunts iguanas with eagles in Mexico.

The compelling characteristic of the novel is its enormous vitality. Augie is the adventurer in life, zestfully exploring every type of job, social stratum, idea, and event. With a rare and heady vivacity, Bellow maintains that the present world, as compromised as it is, can offer ample fulfillment to the human spirit that wills for true self-identity.

Herzog (1964) was greeted with wide popular approval.

Moses Herzog is a middle-aged Jewish intellectual whose stream of consciousness largely constitutes the volume. Few present events occur as he relives his past: the immigrant area of Montreal, a modest academic career, gradual breaking away from orthodox faith, unproductive friendships, two broken marriages, and unsatisfying extramarital affairs. Terribly disturbed at the outset, he returns toward the end to the Berkshire farmhouse where his second marriage fell apart, but he has attained a degree of serenity.

A series of imaginary letters, almost certainly never mailed, to every conceivable person from Adlai Stevenson to God—to the living and the dead, the great and the unknown, upon every conceivable topic —represent a kaleidoscopic outpouring of all Herzog's "unemployed consciousness." And a lambent irony plays throughout in that Herzog is able to view himself objectively or even with wry amusement. Herzog (whose name comes from a minor character in Joyce's *Ulysses*) rejects the contemporary pessimism about Western civilization. He emerges from confusion to discover a reverence for life as it is lived at the moment.

A more recent novel by Bellow is *Mr. Sammler's Planet* (1970).

Bernard Malamud (1914–   ). Born in Brooklyn, Bernard Malamud received an A.B. in 1936 from City College of New York and an M.A. from Columbia University in 1942. From 1940 to 1944 he taught English in New York high schools. From 1949 to 1961 he taught English at Oregon State University. Since 1961 he has been on the staff of Bennington College.

Malamud's subject most often has been New Yorkers of Jewish descent, but the implications of his work are as wide as humanity. A constantly recurrent theme is the Jew as sufferer, and by implication, in this world all men may be considered Jews. The downtrodden characters of Malamud exemplify the condition of man— never winning but also never wholly losing. In failure or even debasement there can be found an affirmation of love, brotherhood, and life. These affirmations are bought at a high price and are possibilities rather than full consummations.

The Assistant (1957) established Malamud's reputation and his main subsequent area of concentration. Critics immediately likened this work to that of Dostoevski.

Frank Alpine, a penniless Italian, is Ward Minogue's accomplice in the beating and robbing of Morris Bober, a poor Jewish grocer. Conscience-stricken, Frank eventually becomes Bober's assistant. Though he helps the poor grocer, Frank takes the curse off his kindness by petty thefts from Bober's till. After the grocer's death he operates the store largely out of love for Helen, Bober's daughter. Frank saves Helen from an attempted rape by Ward, but his romantic overtures to her are repulsed. In the end he has himself circumcised and continues to run the store, hoping that Helen will reconsider.

Bober is an unwitting saint, laboring without any of this world's benefits in a run-down subsection of urban New York. Frank, a fascinating creation, is an incongruous mixture of good and guilt who purposely punishes himself by stealing from Bober's till while also working at another job to pump money into Bober's wretched little store. Sometimes he lusts for Helen, while at other times he struggles like a father to provide money for her education. Ultimately, the young Italian thief is spiritually reborn the son of the aging Jewish grocer.

The Fixer (1966) of the title means merely the "handyman." The scene is Russia at the time of anti-Semitic persecutions following the revolution of 1905.

Half-starving Yakov Bok, a Jewish odd-job man, has been abandoned by his wife because they are childless. He rejects orthodox Hebraism and goes to the city of Kiev to work. Venturing out illegally from the ghetto, he saves the life of a drunken Russian who, ironically, is a noted anti-Semite. Bok conceals his origins and works as foreman of the brick works of the man he saved. As part of his job he must prevent the stealing of bricks by driving way pilfering children. A boy he had pointedly ejected is found savagely murdered and entirely drained of blood by his long exposure. Bok's Jewish origin is discovered, he is accused of ritual murder, and the circumstantial evidence and ingrained bigotry seem certain to convict and execute him.

The Fixer is written very much in the manner of the Russian novelists. Bok is the victim and martyr of a heartless society, merely an ineffectual peasant without deep awareness of himself or of life as the novel opens. He is aided in understanding himself by reading a book by Spinoza, which convinces him that the true test is not what is done to or thought of him but by what he does and thinks.

Edwin O'Connor (1918–68). A native of Providence, Rhode Island, Edwin O'Connor graduated from the University of Notre Dame in 1939 and became a radio announcer and producer. After 1946 he devoted himself to writing. *The Edge of Sadness* (1961), about Father Hugh Kennedy and his parishioners in a run-down section of Boston, won a Pulitzer Prize.

The Last Hurrah (1956) is O'Connor's skillful presentation of the Irish-Catholic world of Boston (although the city is never specifically named).

Scarred by the political tussles of half a century, seventy-two-year-old Frank Skeffington announces his candidacy for a fifth term as mayor. Skeffington has been long entrenched as an Irish, Catholic, and Democrat boss (Mayor James M. Curley of Boston was convinced that this was a portrait of him) by a combination of personal charm, political shrewdness, and absolute ruthlessness. Because he is disappointed in his café society son, Skeffington invites his nephew, Adam Caulfield, to take part in the inner councils of the campaign. In the end Kevin McCluskey, his telegenic opponent, defeats Skeffington.

The Last Hurrah chronicles the passing of an age. Skeffington is not defeated by his adversaries so much as by change and time. His flamboyance renders Skeffington a most engaging character, and he is supported by a zesty guard of politicos.

J. F. Powers (1917–   ). James Farl Powers was born in Jacksonville, Illinois, and was educated at Northwestern University. He has taught at St. John's University, Marquette University, University of Michigan, and Smith College.

Prince of Darkness and Other Stories (1947) and subsequent short story collections establish Powers as an outstanding fictionist dealing primarily with Roman Catholic subjects. Powers is not anti-clerical, nor does he treat of the self-created hell of an intransigent Catholic. He is concerned with the inferior priests who are mired in the everyday trivialities, or at worst engrossed in the materialism of the world and unable to realize their own spiritual shortcomings. Often they shunt aside the eager, unconventional priests who are sincerely motivated by love of God and man. But Powers maintains an unobtrusive conviction that the Church is infinitely stronger than its weak links and vigorously reponsive to forceful stimuli. The authenic realism and meticulous art of Powers have made "The Lord's Day," "The Forks," "Prince of Darkness," and other stories favorite anthology pieces.

THE SOUTHERN RENAISSANCE AS SEEN IN NOVELISTS CONCERNED WITH SOCIAL AND PERSONAL PROBLEMS

Robert Penn Warren (1905–   ). For the biographical sketch of Warren, see the discussion of his poetry in Chapter 2. See also the discussion of his role in the "New Criticism" in Chapter 8.

Robert Penn Warren looks upon the goal of fiction as "the stimulation of a powerful image of human nature trying to fulfill itself." His own fiction, like his verse, is preoccupied with this problem of identity. The struggle within the self to discard all accretions leads eventually to an outer source of strength in the community of men. This process of self-analysis and quest in Warren's novels arises from Southern agrarianism. The tradition and myth of the past, Warren believes, provide man with a sense of belonging.

Night Rider (1939) is based upon the actual Kentucky Tobacco War of 1904–05.

Attorney Percy Munn is caught up in the formation of the Association of Growers of Dark Fired Tobacco, a group of farmers seeking higher prices from the giant tobacco corporations. As the monopolistic companies resist, Munn goes further in helping found the Free Farmers' Brotherhood of Protection and Control. This euphemistic label conceals a fascistic terrorist band of night riders who force hesitant farmers into the Association by destroying their crops. As rage and frustration mount, the night riders dynamite the warehouses of the tobacco trust. Munn murders a reluctant terrorist, Buck Trevelyan, and is himself shot down.

A dominant Warren theme is how a drive for social justice can eventuate in gross injustice. Contrasted with Munn is Captain Todd who astutely withdraws from the Association as he observes its sinister turn. Todd has his own mind and well-perceived standards, while Munn as a divided man descends into oblivion.

At Heaven's Gate (1943) takes its title, employed ironically, from the well-known song in Shakespeare's *Cymbeline*, but by Warren's own admission, the structure of the novel arises from Dante's Seventh Circle of the *Inferno*, which is peopled by violators of nature who direct their destruction against God, themselves, or their neighbors.

The scion of a distinguished Southern family, Bogan Murdock is the financial power of the community (Nashville?) and the local university (Vanderbilt?). He makes a protégé of Jerry Calhoun, a simple country boy and an All-American football player at the university, who under Murdock's tutelage becomes a bond salesman. Murdock's daughter Sue breaks her engagement to Jerry and becomes the mistress of Slim Sarrett, a boxer, poet, and graduate student. Later she turns to Jason Sweetwater, a union official bucking the rule of her father. Sue has an abortion to rid herself of Jason's child, and while recovering, is strangled by Sarrett. When Murdock's corrupt financial empire collapses, Jerry is made the scapegoat and is sentenced to prison.

The characters are actually representatives of Dante's sinners, headed by Murdock the usurer, who uses the money complex to enslave others. Sue is a potential suicide, destroying herself in desperate attempts to escape parental tyranny. Sarrett is a homosexual. Jerry Calhoun despises his humble origins and repudiates his duties to his family. These people are all not merely at hell's gate but already within.

All the King's Men (1946) brought Warren wide public recognition. Much of this popularity arose from interpreting the novel as a *roman à clef*. The central figure seems to suggest Huey Long, prominent Louisiana political figure and in effect a demagogue.

Willie Stark began as a naïve country lawyer sincerely interested in aiding the common man. Cynical newspaperman Jack Burden and factotum Sadie Burke guide Stark's rise to the governorship of an unnamed Southern state. Entrenched, Stark does accomplish some good for his constituents, but revels in graft and unscrupulously attempts to crush all opposition. His son Tom is a spoiled wastrel, who while drunk kills himself playing football. Stark's wife, Lucy, formerly a rural schoolteacher, becomes bitterly disillusioned and leaves him. Stark takes as a mistress Anne Stanton, the daughter of an aristocratic Southern family. Her brother Adam, director of Stark's medical center, kills Stark, and in turn is cut down by Stark's bodyguards. At the end Jack Burden tries with Anne to reconstruct a viable life from their shattered fragments.

The title is from "Humpty-Dumpty," the nursery rhyme. This novel of broad philosophical ramifications owes much of its original popularity to its sensational fictionalizing of the politics of its day. Stark is a powerfully conceived character. He deeply senses the mystery of life. He believes that out of man's natural depravity can emerge, like the phoenix, the image of good. In this fallen world he pragmatically plays the game of corruption. The only successful synthesis is that of Burden. Stark's career is elaborately scrutinized chiefly because of its impact upon Burden, who is initially an idealist, hoping to remain aloof from the political morass. Gradually the pressure of events compels Burden to resort to the philosophy of the Great Twitch, the "dream of our age" that life is solely the "dark heave of the blood and the twitch of the nerve." This naturalistic viewpoint absolves him of blame for his actions. Later Burden comes to experience human isolation and simultaneously to recognize that guilt knits together all mankind. Only by recognition of this dilemma and by the assertion of love can modern man reintegrate himself.

The Circus in the Attic and Other Stories (1948) collects fourteen short stories by Warren. Most of the stories (and especially "The Circus in the Attic") in their superabundant wealth and diversity of plot and character suggest that Warren's best fictional home is the novel. But one story is a classic upon the theme of a youth's initiation into the adult world.

"Blackberry Winter" in the title means an unnaturally cold and damp spring day. A nine-year-old boy, Seth, on this raw June day encounters "jags and injustices" from Nature and man. The disturbing events that wrench Seth from the green paradise of Nature and the snug security of his household deeply puzzle the youngster, but as recounted by the grown man thirty-five years later the meaning of the episodes becomes clear. Warren explained the lesson as "human communion," the necessity of brotherhood and responsibility in spite of the inexplicable rampages of Nature and of our fellows.

World Enough and Time: A Romantic Novel (1950) is Warren's longest and most ambitious novel; a conscious attempt to block out in full his total vision of the world. The basis for the plot is the actual "Kentucky Tragedy" of 1824–25 in which Jeroboam O. Beauchamp was incited by his bride, Ann Cook, to kill her seducer, Solomon P. Sharp. The real-life tragedy has been a subject of other American authors, notably in *Politian* (1837), a drama by Poe, and *Beauchampe* (1942), a novel by Simms.

A young Kentucky lawyer, Jeremiah Beaumont, is about to marry Rachel Jordan, but she demands as a betrothal commitment that he kill her seducer and Jeremiah's friend, Colonel Cassius Fort. Fort refuses to meet Beaumont in a duel, and Beaumont is compelled to murder him. Although his trial is marked by all manner of corruption, Beaumont is finally convicted and sentenced to death. He and Rachel escape to the Western wilderness. Later she commits suicide and he is slain by a bounty hunter.

The title quotation from Andrew Marvell's "To His Coy Mistress" suggests that reality is more important than an impossible ideal. Jeremiah, in the fashion of many sensitive young men of his era, gleans from Plato and Shelley a thoroughgoing idealistic romanticism. The inner world of Jeremiah must find reconciliation with the outer world. Still another clash of two worlds occurs in the westward rovings of Rachel and Jeremiah. To Warren the West of those years represents chaos and lawlessness confronting the order that puny man tries to impose.

Eudora Welty (1909–   ). Eudora Alice Welty was born in Jackson, Mississippi. After studying at Mississippi State College for Women from 1925–27, she attended the University of Wisconsin, graduating in 1929. After studying advertising at Columbia University she returned to Jackson. Her short stories won increasing recognition. In 1962 she became Neilson Professor of English at Smith College.

Miss Welty's native Mississippi Delta country has won a place upon the literary map. The historical South and its social structure, omnipresent in William Faulkner, occupy Eudora Welty far less than the problem of human isolation. Though often termed "Southern gothic," her stories are primarily based upon the tensions in separation and in communication. She loves to dwell upon the nuances of feeling that masculine authors generally summarize brusquely. Her decadents are scrutinized with poetic humor. Her work combines clarity and subtlety.

A Curtain of Green and Other Stories (1941) collects seventeen Welty stories all essentially upon the theme of the defenseless individual who often resorts to fantasy for sustenance in bleak isolation.

"Petrified Man" appears in a number of anthologies. The denizens of a Delta beauty parlor discuss their private lives and public sensationalism. The story is told of Mrs. Pike's recognizing a "petrified man" in a traveling side show as a certain Mr. Petrie, who is wanted for raping women in California. She informs on him and collects the $500 reward. The inimitable chatter of the women is unalloyed vulgarity. All the males of the community are actually "petrified" by female domination.

"A Worn Path" is a paean to life. An aged Negro woman, Phoenix Jackson, trudges through a frosty countryside at Christmastime to get the medicine from a Natchez hospital that will prolong the life of her ailing grandson. The woman's name is properly symbolic of the rebirth theme of the season. Her difficult journey is her own odyssey. Whether encountering jibes or condescension, Phoenix unshakably maintains her dignity and her determination to save the boy.

"Why I Live at the P.O." is told by "Sister" (the postmistress of China Grove, Mississippi) to explain why she has decamped from her family to reside at the post office. Properly enraged, Sister has no realization of the humor of this account that stigmatizes herself and her family as hopeless vulgarians. The delicious comedy conceals a dark undercurrent of loneliness and estrangement.

The Robber Bridegroom (1942), Miss Welty's first novel, is a wondrous wedding of European fairy tale and the tall tale of the American frontier.

Clement Musgrove is an innocent soul who narrowly escapes destruction through the perils of the early Natchez Trace: Indians, Mike Fink, and the terrifying Harpe brothers. Musgrove's second wife, Salome, plays the wicked stepmother and compels his daughter Rosamund to appear in the role of a kitchen slave to gentleman Jamie Lockhart. But Lockhart has an alter ego as a highwayman who steals Rosamund (both are startled to recognize each other in the daylight). Jamie quells his enemies, reforms, marries Rosamund, and both live happily ever after.

The Wide Net and Other Stories (1943) ventures into the special world of dreams and fantasy, the legendary Natchez Trace. This is a realm of pastoral poetry in which lonely souls strain for illumination of life's mysteries or take refuge in illusions.

"Livvie," the most popular story, concerns the young wife of Solomon, an elderly Negro who owns a sizable tract of land. As Solomon sinks into a comatose state, Livvie flees to Cash McCord, a vigorous tenant farmer of Solomon's. Solomon gives the couple his blessing before he dies. The old man's name is well chosen.

"A Still Moment" is Miss Welty's most metaphysical story. Three historical characters of the early nineteenth century meet upon the Natchez Trace: Lorenzo Dow, a fanatical evangelist; James Murrell, a demoniacal criminal; and James Audubon, the distinguished naturalist. Each man is consumed by his monomania, but Audubon's killing of a heron shakes them all out of the rigidity of their previous convictions. Audubon now realizes that life is infinitely more complex than his scientific dogma had presumed, Murrell is anxious for reassessment of his vicious existence, and Dow senses the unknowableness of God.

Delta Wedding (1946) is an idyllic, gently amused account of nuptial preparations within an ancestral plantation family of the Deep South. The narration is from the viewpoint of the bride, Dabney Fairchild, her mother, Ellen, and sister, Shelley, and especially through the perceptions of nine-year-old Laura McRaven, a visiting niece.

The numerous Fairchilds compose the principal family of their rural community in the Mississippi Delta. Pride in the traditions of their line has brought about a cohesiveness that resists wholehearted acceptance of outsiders. Dabney's choice of Troy Flavin, the northern Mississippian who oversees the plantation, is consequently the cause of some uneasiness in the Fairchild clan.

The pivotal event of the novel occurs somewhat before the narrative commences; Dabney's visiting uncle, George, whose warm, quiet manner has placed him at the center of the Fairchild intrafamilial affection, risks death attempting to remove his mentally retarded niece Maureen from the path of a train. George's wife, Robbie, as yet a partial outsider, feels both jealous and injured by George's rash behavior. A painful rift develops between them that is healed only gradually by George's patience and a new understanding on Robbie's part. At the same time the process of throwing open the hospitality of the Fairchild house to the people of the countryside promotes the acceptance of new in-laws by blood members of the family. At the novel's end both George and Troy have decided to settle with their wives on the Fairchild lands, and all the main characters have an augmented sense of enrichment and belonging.

The Ponder Heart (1954) is a novel imbued with the comic spirit.

Miss Edna Earle Ponder, proprietress of the small hotel in Clay, Mississippi, garrulously details the career of her uncle Daniel Ponder, the town's eccentric man of wealth. Daniel has a mania for giving things away: the hotel to his niece, banana ice-cream cones to all the girls of the burlesque show at the county fair, and so on. His first marriage to the strong-voiced and strong-minded widow Magee doesn't work out. His second marriage—beneath him, says Edna—is to Bonnie Dee Peacock. Bonnie Dee runs away but returns to die of heart failure during a thunderstorm; in a childish game by which he hopes to distract her, Daniel literally tickles her to death. At the murder trial, Daniel eagerly hands out his money to everyone in the courtroom. The jury, "hating to miss anything," quickly returns a verdict of not guilty.

The prosecutor Gladney represents the stiff-necked attempt of society to maintain absolutes, and portray everything as completely wrong or right. But Uncle Daniel and life refuse these easy generalities and conformities. Uncle Daniel's final isolation is tragic.

The Bride of Innisfallen (1955) consists of seven stories differing from Eudora Welty's earlier works in that, except for "Ladies in Spring," they venture beyond the usual Welty country as far as Cork, Ireland, and the Mediterranean. Plot is secondary in these experimental pieces, which seek the moment of illumination for isolated individuals.

Carson McCullers (1917–64). Lula Carson Smith was born in

Columbus, Georgia. She early felt a dislike for her first name and dropped it. In 1935 she went to New York to study at Columbia University and the Juilliard School of Music. She had to abandon her prospective career in music when she lost the money which she had set aside for tuition. In 1937 she married Reeves McCullers. During much of her life she was weighed down by severe illness.

Carson McCullers' work is often marked by gothicism, which produces a tragic subjectivism instead of comedy. Especially, Mrs. McCullers finds that love paradoxically intensifies loneliness and inevitably induces suffering. Her bizarre characters are alienated from both society and self.

The Heart Is a Lonely Hunter (1940), her first novel, is the remarkable achievement of a woman only twenty-three years old.

The pivotal character is a Mr. Singer, a deaf mute boarding in the Kelly household in a small Georgia mill town. Singer is an unassuming man of regular habits whose quiet smile and perpetual silence give the impression of wisdom and compassion. Consequently he becomes the object of several symbiotic relationships with townspeople who lack an audience for their views.

The most frequent visitors to Singer's room are Jake Blount, a drifter and disseminator of socialist-revolutionary propaganda; Dr. Copeland, a Negro burdened by his sense of the injustice done his race; and Mick Kelly, an adolescent daughter of the household whose youthful fancies and enthusiasms are in need of a discreet confessor. Because he never replies or volunteers information, Singer is for all these three a product of their separate imaginations. He listens out of civility and with little comprehension, but his doing so endows him with sympathetic understanding in the sight of those to whom he listens.

Singer in his turn has a confidant to whom he mistakenly attributes the identical powers. This is Spiros Antonapoulos, another deaf mute who shared Singer's home until he was declared socially irresponsible and incarcerated in a state asylum. Singer is occasionally able to visit the institution, and at those times by their means of communication he eagerly unburdens himself of all the events and minutiae of the interim to the listless, uncomprehending, and thoroughly indifferent Antonapoulos. At last Singer learns his friend has died, and the news precipitates him into suicide. For his three intimates Singer's act is inexplicable. Although their relationships with the mute were illusory and one-sided, the importance of the relations is illustrated by the changes and terminations that affect the lives of each at Singer's death. Actually these come not from the man Singer but from the images of him the three have manufactured for their own purposes.

The Member of the Wedding (1946) is probably the best-known

McCullers work, particularly because of the highly successful dramatic version.

Gawky twelve-year-old Frankie Addams is an outsider in her Georgia home town. Her one real confidante is Berenice, the Negro cook, who has remained unmarried because she is the only true mother for Frankie. Frankie's soldier brother Jarvis is going to marry Janice Evans in August, and Frankie decides that she wants to accompany them after the wedding. She has to be dragged away from the honeymooners' car. By November, however, things have changed. Frankie and her father move to a new suburb, she develops new friends and new interests, and now she wishes to be called Frances.

Frankie initially suffers from insecurity, a loathing for her drab surroundings, and a profound need to belong. Berenice quietly instructs her in the meaning of love and prepares her for the inevitable changes of life. All is conceived in a mood of appropriate lyricism.

The Ballad of the Sad Café (1951) has the quality of sadness characteristic of much of Carson McCullers' work.

Cross-eyed, amazonian Amelia Evans, from a dreary Southern town, marries a man with a criminal record, Marvin Macy, whom she drives away from an unconsummated union. Macy falls back on crime and is sent to prison. Lymon, a hunchback, claims a dubious cousinship with Amelia and intrudes himself as an object for her love. Together they open a café. Macy returns and Lymon obsequiously attaches himself to the criminal. Amelia and Macy engage in a battle that wrecks the café; Lymon intervenes to defeat the almost victorious Amelia, and the two men go off. Amelia and the town sink back into their wonted dreariness.

These three unlovable characters form a weird love triangle. Macy displays the only normal sexual love in his affection for Amelia, but she loves Lymon, who in turn loves Macy. Each of the three wants to be a lover, but no one wants to be the beloved. The café is a bulwark against chaos and loneliness, but proves an inadequate one.

The Ballad of the Sad Café was made into a play by Edward Albee in 1963.

Truman Capote (1924–   ). A native of New Orleans, Truman Capote formally obtained only a secondary education, but his varied experience includes entertaining on a river boat, writing speeches for a politician, studying fortune-telling, and working on *The New Yorker*.

Capote asserts that he is a Southerner only by accident, but he is drawn to the themes and atmosphere of the South. Capote characters are often crippled in mind and/or body and condemned to an existence of lonely terror and defeat. Society and man himself thwart the quest for affection and communion. For his dark settings Capote writes in a richly textured prose surcharged with the mysterious and foreboding. But his harp has another, different string for daylight effects: a zany anecdotal chatter. This daytime narration specializes in rather bizarre humor and treats of harmless eccentrics.

Other Voices, Other Rooms (1948) has a Southern gothic feeling. Joel Harrison Knox, a child of divorced parents, bears his mother's surname. He comes to Skully's Landing, a decaying plantation near somnolent Noon City, to find his father, Edward Sansom, who turns out to be a thoroughly incapacitated invalid. Idabel Tompkins, a tomboy, assumes the male role toward Joel; and the only female encouraging his growth to normal manhood is Miss Wisteria, a tiny circus midget. By the end of the story Joe is succumbing to a homosexual attraction to Cousin Randolph, a male transvestite.

This initiation story involves Joe in a search for the father, a quest for sustaining love, a groping for identity, and a maturation from childhood into adulthood. Joel is so frustrated in his normal outlets and so encompassed by decadent evil that he apparently is drawn to perversion. At the end Joe has unquestionably gained in perceptivity, but the overpowering impression is of a modern fallen world in which the individual is thwarted and deformed by other humans and by himself.

A Tree of Night and Other Stories (1949) collects Capote short stories, all deeply disturbing, that display his almost diametrically opposed styles. All involve freakish characters with maimed, disintegrating psyches. The title story and "The Headless Hawk" well illustrate the nighttime horrors of Capote, where evil and insanity triumph. The daytime style produces in "Children on Their Birthdays" one of Capote's best and best-known short stories. The incredible Miss Bobbit, with her childish dreams of Hollywood grandeur, momentarily arouses the spirit of vivacious life in a small, drab Southern town.

The Grass Harp (1951), Capote's second novel, is in his daylight style.

At the age of eleven, orphaned Collin Fenwick comes to live with his father's cousins, Verena and Dolly Talbo. Verena is shrewdly practical, while Dolly is the shy innocent. Verena hounds them all; thus Dolly, Collin (now sixteen), and the Negro Catherine take refuge in a tree house in an old chinaberry tree. The community ludicrously tries to reason with the bizarre refugees, but the death of Dolly really ends the idyll. Collin goes north to study law.

The story is told by the adult Collin in the form of reminiscences. The theme sees the world as a bad place, but the private realm of the individual as good. The values of childhood are set above those of maturity. Dolly seems to be creating her own universe—and a better one. Verena acknowledges this after being robbed and deserted in the matter-of-fact world she inhabited. The account is sung by a field of Indian grass, "a grass harp, gathering, telling, a harp of voices remembering a story."

Breakfast at Tiffany's (1958) takes its title from the dream of Capote's picaresque heroine, Holly Golightly, of reveling in the luxuries of New York City. She had been a child bride in Tulip, Texas, at the age of fourteen, and this initiation has had its aspects of seamy squalor and outrage. Now in New York at nineteen she throws herself into living, exemplifying the Capote contention that living intensely and naturally, while producing pain, will lead to the fullest joy and completion of self. Holly is a naïve artist of life but commendable in Capote's eyes; but he shows her agent as considering her a *"real* phony," employing every artifice to transform life from its dreary routine into the stuff of her imagination.

In Cold Blood (1966) was frankly intended by Capote as a "nonfiction novel," which might also be called parajournalism. It holds closely to the established facts of the 1959 murder of Herbert Clutter, a well-to-do Kansas farmer, and of his wife and two children by Richard Hickock and Perry Smith. Here in the cold light of everyday Capote introduces probably his most provocative questioning about the nature of and the reason for evil in the human psyche. He indicates that emotional deprivation and refusal to scrutinize one's own selfhood may in part explain these horrendous acts of violence.

Harper Lee (1926–   ). Monroeville, Alabama, was the birthplace of Nelle Harper Lee. She attended Huntingdon College in 1944–45, and the University of Alabama in 1945–49.

To Kill a Mockingbird (1960) is set in an Alabama county seat in the 1930s, and concerns itself principally with the childhood idylls and adventures of Jean Louise ("Scout") Finch. Her lawyer father, Atticus Finch, is appointed as defense counsel for Tom Robinson, a Negro accused of rape by Meyella Ewell, a part of the town's less reputable white element. Atticus is unsuccessful in his vigorous pleadings, but points out to Scout that the long deliberation of the jury portends a day of more equitable justice ahead. Recognizing Atticus as their conscience, his fellow citizens reelect him to the legislature.

The title comes from a lesson learned by Scout and her older brother Jeremy ("Jem") when they receive air rifles as presents. To kill a mockingbird or any guiltless creature is a sin. Scout sees in her few years several symbolic mockingbirds (Tom, not least of all) whom it is sinful to slay. Although the trial is the dramatic peak, this is not a mere "courtroom" novel but a remarkable evocation of a Deep South community and preteen girlhood. The South is seen as moving by its own inward nature toward a brighter future.

William Styron (1925–   ). William Clark Styron, Jr., is a native of Newport News, Virginia, who received his A.B. from Duke University in 1947. In 1953 he was a fellow at the American Academy of Arts and Letters in Rome, and in the same year he became an editor of the *Paris Review*. Since 1964 he has taught at Yale.

Lie Down in Darkness (1951) was recognized as a most remarkable first novel. Styron's Port Warwick, the locale of the story, recurs in most of his subsequent work.

The coffin bearing Peyton Loftis, a suicide, is followed from its arrival at Port Warwick, in tidewater Virginia, to the burial. During this process the whole past of the Loftis family is scrutinized. Peyton's father, Milton, is a failure as husband and father, taking up with Dolly, another man's wife. Helen, Peyton's mother, showers love upon her crippled daughter, Maudie, and hates her other daughter, Peyton. This hatred, plus Peyton's quasi-incestuous relations with her father, has led to the failure of her marriage, her promiscuity and alcoholism, and eventually her self-destruction.

The novel is a tragedy of love in which there is no villain, unless it be the community. Heredity and environment force incompatibility and frustration upon all the characters. Corruption is rampant in the domestic life of the Loftises because the props—spiritual and personal—are gone, and nothingness remains.

Set This House on Fire (1960) takes its title from a sermon by John Donne calling for the purification of the soul.

While in a Virginia prep school, Peter Leverett had been both fascinated and repelled by Mason Flagg, the spoiled and utterly dissolute son of a wealthy Hollywood producer. Some years later, working at an overseas relief agency in Italy, Leverett finds Flagg on location with an American film company. Flagg corrupts Cass Kinsolving, an American painter, rapes and presumably kills an Italian girl, and in turn is slain by Kinsolving. Leverett finds out the full truth in a subsequent conversation with Kinsolving, who has successfully returned to painting in Charleston, South Carolina. The theme reverses the traditional pattern of the American innocent and Old World corruption. Here the New World, in the person of Flagg, is the corrupter, and the Old World is the innocent. Flagg would have himself considered the Virginia gentleman, but he is working with decayed remains of a dead tradition. Leverett and Kinsolving succumb for a time to Flagg's spell, as indeed does Italy. But Leverett and Kinsolving, freed of Flagg's influence, are once more able to establish their own identities.

Styron's mastery of style is evident throughout.

The Confessions of Nat Turner (1967) is a novel based upon an actual pamphlet by Nat Turner, who led a Negro revolt against slavery in 1831 in southeastern Virginia. Styron had long hoped to present this very significant episode to modern readers, and he has aimed for fidelity to the basic facts.

Shirley Ann Grau (1929–). Born in New Orleans, Shirley Ann Grau lived most of her early life in Alabama, the locale for many of her stories. She received her A.B. from Tulane University in 1950 and in 1955 married James K. Feibleman.

The Keepers of the House (1964), a Pulitzer Prize winner, in certain elements suggests Faulkner. In an unnamed Southern state the house built in 1815 by William Howland is effectively defended, even against mob violence, by his descendant, Abigail Mason Tolliver. The segregationism of her politician husband, John, and the anti-segregationism of Robert Carmichael, her distant Negro cousin, Abigail finds, are both less than central concerns of the real South. Civilization and its traditions, she concludes, must be built from the challenge and the opportunity of environment. Abigail strives to understand the heritage —both inspiring and burdensome—of her dynasty and learns that the task of keeping it is difficult but rewarding.

Flannery O'Connor (1925–64). A native of Savannah, Georgia, Flannery O'Connor received her A.B. in 1945 from the Women's College of Georgia and her M.F.A. in 1947 from Iowa State University. Except for brief forays that included a trip to Lourdes, she resided in her native Georgia. Her premature death seems a very great loss to American letters.

Miss O'Connor was a Roman Catholic from birth, and her background was thus counter to the dominant ethos of the South. Her theme is the spiritual distortions that can arise from primitivistic Southern Protestantism. To the objections that her work was a grotesquerie, she replied that what she wrote was intended as literal representation. "I am interested," she insisted, "in the lines that create spiritual motion."

Wise Blood (1952) was her first novel and first published volume, although her reputation had been established in 1946 as a short-story writer.

As a result of his war experiences, Hazel Motes, a descendant of a fundamentalist preacher, proclaims a new religion, the Church of Christ Without Christ. He proceeds from his native Eastrod, Tennessee, to Taulkinham, Georgia, to begin his "ministry." A succession of conventional and hypocritical religionists conflict with Hazel. Eventually he blinds himself with quicklime, wears barbed wire next to his skin, and walks with glass fragments in his shoes. His broken body is brought back to die in the presence of his landlady.

Flannery O'Connor termed Hazel "a Christian *malgré lui*," an anti-saint obsessed with sin and suffering. He follows the pattern of removal-prophecy-immolation, a sequence frequent in Miss O'Connor's works. Bizarre as his course and his end seem, Hazel does represent the naïve search for spiritual reality in a society otherwise capitulating to Mammon and conventionality.

The title comes from the claim of Enoch Emery to have "wise blood"; when he steals a mummy from the museum and gives it to Hazel as a new "Jesus," he unwittingly demonstrates what man presumably is if God and redemption do not exist—meaningless dust.

A Good Man Is Hard to Find and Other Stories (1955) collects ten O'Connor short stories. All the characters are trapped little people with a painful realization of the futility of their lives. In their spiritual struggles these characters to some degree resemble certain characters of Hawthorne (with whom O'Connor felt a special kinship). Through selfish materialism, stupidity, or pride these people vainly seek their own salvation. All the stories are told in a heady compound of the tragic and the comic.

The Violent Bear It Away (1960), her second and last novel, takes its title from Matthew 11:12.

Mason Tarwater, a religious fanatic, has balefully influenced his young grandnephew, Francis Marion Tarwater, with his rigid preachments. George F. Rayber, an atheistic schoolteacher and uncle of the boy, tries to counter Mason's indoctrination. Rayber has refused to baptize his own idiot son, Bishop, but Mason had charged Francis to undertake this ritual. On a boat ride Francis baptizes Bishop and then drowns him. Returning to his granduncle's grave, Francis becomes aware of a compulsion to continue spreading the fundamentalist beliefs of the dead man.

As the name Motes in *Wise Blood* suggests a clouded vision, so does Tarwater here. The perversion of the spirit is so strong that Francis is trapped into becoming a reincarnation of his great-uncle. The structure of the novel suggests an initiation pattern, but the tragedy is Francis' incapacity to transcend the limitations of his background. As in *Wise Blood* the sequence is removal-prophecy-immolation, but the final self-anointing of the boy's head with earth from Mason's grave is a horrible consecration to a living death. In the earlier novel only Hazel's landlady effectively suggested the world of "normal" people; in this second novel there are extensive counterpoints and contrasts provided by the introduction of reasonable characters. In spiritual intensity, as well as in brilliant depictions of eccentrics, this is a novel of extraordinary power.

Everything That Rises Must Converge (1965) is a posthumous collection of nine O'Connor short stories. The subjects and themes are essentially those of Miss O'Connor's earlier writings, but there is a heightening of tension and a greater metaphysical awareness in these later stories. "The Lame Shall Enter First," a novella, largely follows the scheme of *The Violent Bear It Away.* Here again is an agonizing dilemma between the old-time Protestantism inflicted upon Rufus Johnson by his grandfather and the secular knowledge proffered by his mentor, Sheppard. The implications in the story are perhaps broader than in the novel.

NEGRO NOVELISTS

Among the most powerful American novels of this century are protests from Negro authors. Their driving desire is twofold: to obtain for their race a position in national life wholly comparable to that of whites, and to have the Negro appraised as an individual not as a racial stereotype.

Richard Wright (1908–60). Richard Nathaniel Wright was the son of a plantation farm hand near Natchez, Mississippi. His father deserted the family when Wright was five, and young Wright was shuttled back and forth between relatives. While working at odd jobs in Memphis, Tennessee, at the age of fifteen, Wright read Mencken's *Book of Prefaces* and determined to be a writer. In 1934 he settled in Chicago, associating himself with the Federal Writers' Project, which took him to New York in 1937. His sympathies with communism during the Depression were followed by disillusionment. His later years were spent in Paris.

Native Son (1940), essentially naturalistic, is an outstanding literary achievement.

Bigger Thomas is a young tough from the rat-infested slums of Chicago's South Side. The Daltons, known for their philanthropy toward Negroes, hire him as a chauffeur. While driving the drunken Dalton daughter Mary home, he tries to conceal her condition from her blind mother and unintentionally smothers Mary to death. Panicked, Bigger hastily burns the corpse in a furnace and is captured while attempting to shoot it out with the police. Although he is ably defended, Bigger is convicted and electrocuted.

Much of the novel's effectiveness arises from Wright's avoidance of the obvious clichés. The Daltons are well-intentioned humanitarians. Bigger is not a sentimentalized character; he stumbles into violence unwittingly. The prosecuting attorney Buckley is perhaps too obviously a manipulator of race prejudice. The defense attorney seeks to make Bigger, as he faces death, realize that his persecutors are themselves fear ridden. Until his capture, Bigger is conceived so intensely by Wright that the reader enters into his panic, his flight, and his desperation.

Willard Motley (1912–65). Chicago-born Willard Motley spent years wandering across the nation as waiter, short-order cook, ranch hand, photographer, and so on before writing *Knock on Any Door* (1947). This is a naturalistic account of the gradual criminal hardening of a boy from the Chicago slums. His personality warped by his shanty-town environment, Nick Romans is destined inescapably for the penitentiary death row. Perhaps the greatest significance of the novel lies in its all-white cast of characters. Identifying with the underprivileged regardless of race, Motley sounds the plea of the Negro novelist to be considered not by the qualifying adjective of skin color but simply and fully by his literary credentials.

Ralph Ellison (1914–   ). Ralph Waldo Ellison is a native of Oklahoma City, Oklahoma. He studied at Tuskegee Institute from 1933–36. He has lectured on Negro culture at Columbia, New York University, Princeton, Fisk University, Bennington College, Antioch, and at other collegiate institutions. Since 1957 he has been on the faculty of Bard College. By his own statement it was the reading of T. S. Eliot in 1935 that caused him to determine upon a writing career.

The Invisible Man (1952) is certanly the most subtly analytic novel ever to deal with the problem of a sense of race.

The unnamed central character's story begins at his graduation from a small Southern high school. As valedictorian he delivers a speech on the proper humility of his race, and is rewarded with a scholarship to a Negro college. The town's white gentry take a patronizing attitude toward him. At college he discovers that his color imposes certain unwritten rules upon him. He inadvertently violates one of these— by allowing a white benefactor from the North to see too much behind the scenes of the college town. The school's president Dr. Bledsoe, who is cynically pragmatic, craftily ships him north where he finally finds work in a paint factory. But he is denounced as a scab by the white workers and hospitalized by a boiler explosion. Now unemployed, he reveals a talent for public declamation and is taken into a Harlem brotherhood. Through his appearances at various rallies he becomes something of a public figure; he works vigorously to guide his movement away from the white exploiters and consolidate it in Harlem. But there his organization collides with the followers of Ras the Destroyer, who espouses violence and anarchy as a racial solution. Ras threatens the hero with physical violence, and in his haste to escape he falls through an open manhole into a coal cellar. At the end of the novel he has elected to remain underground and visible only to himself. But he is confident he will someday emerge.

Ellison's nameless hero is, as a man, invisible. His essential humanity, his desired oneness with the whole human race, is obscured by the many symbols thrust upon him because he is black. The anonymous hero is constantly seeking his own identity in this world that will not permit him to be neutral, to be truly and solely a human being. While much of the work displays vivid naturalism, the dominant effect is nightmarish, a struggle not of economic or other measurable forces but of extended arrangements of symbols.

James Baldwin (1924–   ). A native New Yorker, James Baldwin did not attend college. His literary talents were recognized early. He lived in Europe for a time after being awarded a Guggenheim fellowship. His numerous essays and lectures have established him as a chief spokesman for Negro intellectuals.

Go Tell It on the Mountain (1953) is an outstanding lyric novel. Much of the book is written with the feeling of the Old Testament, which permeates the lives of the characters. The novel considers a Saturday and the following Sunday in the lives of the Grimes family in Harlem.

Gabriel Grimes is a preacher at the Temple of the Fire Baptized. His stepson Johnny, who celebrates his fourteenth birthday on Saturday, returns from a movie to find his younger half brother Roy stabbed in a gang fight with white boys. In the ensuing family quarrel, both boys identify themselves with their mother. At the church service, which begins Saturday night and continues into the wee hours of Sunday, Johnny undergoes a torment of the soul from which he emerges as "converted." With a sense of peace he goes out to meet the dawn as screaming ambulances lug away the dead from a wild Harlem night.

Racial tensions are implicit rather than explicit. Baldwin is less concerned with the black man vis-à-vis the white man than he is with the condition of being a Negro. The church service at the Temple of the Fire Baptized is a scene of immense power. Amidst the frenzied hymn singing of the faithful and of Gabriel's demoniacal, sin-scourging exhortations, flashbacks evoke the entire racial history of the Negro and his present bitter frustration. Intellectuality and sexuality, the compulsions to rebellion and to submission, love and hate, all war in Johnny's heart. God as a substitute for and a superior to his stepfather is his haven. Baldwin's book is a penetrating analysis of what religion means to the Negro.

The Fire Next Time (1963) was written on the one hundredth anniversary of the Emancipation Proclamation. Baldwin here turns from
fiction, and in terms of his own life and experience writes powerfully about the bitter racial conflict in the United States.
Baldwin tells of his early days on the streets of Harlem and his
attempts to escape the temptations of the pimps and racketeers who
constantly tried to win him over. Many of his friends turned to crime,
and at a critical point in his life, Baldwin turned to religion. After
a time he became disenchanted with the church and decided to devote
himself wholly to writing. Some years later he met Elijah Muhammed,
the leader of the Black Muslims, who tried to interest him in the concept of black separatism. Baldwin rejected this idea, and for the rest of
the book, describes how he feels about the position of the American
Negro at this point in history. The American Negro does not belong
to Africa or to Islam but to America; and before he can raise himself, he must accept the reality of his own past. Baldwin communicates
a strong sense of urgency and predicts that if racial inequality in
America is not soon ended "the fulfillment of that prophecy, re-
created from the Bible in a song by a slave, is upon us: 'God
gave Noah the rainbow sign; No more water, the fire next time!' "

"HARD-BOILED" NOVELISTS

The term "hard-boiled fiction" has been applied to writers whose
stories feature vulgar dialogue, swift-paced action amidst seamy surroundings, brutal violence, and lust. The "hard-boiled" authors concentrate upon melodrama instead of emphasizing the shaping environ-
mental influences stressed by the naturalists. Especially, they differ from
the naturalists in ignoring determinism. Hard-boiled fiction apparently
originated in *Black Mask Magazine* (1919–53), and its most famous
practitioner was Dashiell Hammett, writer of detective stories. It seems
to have been derived at least in part from the lawlessness of the
Prohibition era.

Dashiell Hammett (1894–1961). Samuel Dashiell Hammett inaugurated
the hard-boiled detective story, discarding the genteel kid gloves that
lent an air of dignity to most previous fictional sleuths. *The Maltese
Falcon* (1930) featured his most famous detective, Sam Spade. Hard-
drinking Nick Charles of *The Thin Man* (1934) has proved almost
equally well known. Critics have generally considered the realistic Hammett mystery novels as outstanding.

James M. Cain (1892–   ). James Mallahan Cain was born at Annapolis, Maryland. After graduation from Washington College in Chester-
town, Maryland, he was a reporter for Baltimore newspapers. H. L.

Mencken encouraged him to write and published some of his short stories in *The American Mercury.* After World War I service in France and a year as professor of journalism at St. John's College, Annapolis, he concentrated upon journalistic and scenario writing. *The Postman Always Rings Twice* (1934), about hobo Frank Chambers' attempts to murder the Greek proprietor of a California roadside sandwich shop and seduce the Greek's wife, made Cain's name for a time synonymous with hard-boiled fiction. Disclaiming the label, Cain has insisted, "I merely try to write as the character would write, and I never forget that the average man . . . has acquired . . . a vividness of speech that goes beyond anything I could invent."

Other novels by Cain are *Serenade* (1937) and *Mildred Pierce* (1941).

Mickey Spillane (1918–). Frank Morrison Spillane was born in Brooklyn and educated at Fort Hays State College, Kansas. While an undergraduate he wrote for pulp magazines so successfully that he abandoned early plans for a legal career. During World War II he served in the Army Air Corps.

Although Spillane dismisses himself as a writer rather than an author, his popularity has been such as to afford him a literary influence beyond the scope of his intent. His "private eye" hero, Mike Hammer, has been the model for the modern, amoral detective who employs the methods of the criminal underworld to combat it.

"BEAT" NOVELISTS

Apparently a brief, passing phenomenon, the Beats seemed the major subject of literary discussion in the second half of the 1950s. The term was first popularized in the novel *Go* (1952) by **John Clellon Holmes** (1926–), which depicted "this beat generation, this underground life." In a *New York Times Magazine* article of the same year Holmes defined "beatness" as: "More than mere weariness, it implies the feeling of having been used, of being raw. It involves a nakedness of mind, and, ultimately, of soul; a feeling of being reduced to the bedrock of consciousness." The Beats were in a sense intellectual refugees of the postwar era. Their rebellion took the form of a complete withdrawal from the middle-class society about them. Their testament was Zen Buddhism, which urges its followers, since finally there is nothing to sustain them, to love one another and to create for themselves an existence of true being instead of the reliance upon the material things of Western civilization.

Jack Kerouac (1922–69). Jean-Louis Kerouac, a native of Lowell, Massachusetts, studied at Columbia University from 1940 to 1942, and

at the New School for Social Research from 1948 to 1949. From
1942 to 1944 he served in the merchant marine. In the latter half
of the 1940s he was a leading figure among the New York Beats,
the group which included John Clellon Holmes, Allen Ginsberg, and
William Burroughs.

On the Road (1957), which dramatically achieved wide critical
and popular attention for the Beats, centers about Dean Moriarty
(actually Neal Cassady, one of the New York Beats). Sal Paradise
(a narrator-surrogate for Kerouac) despairs of the emptiness and futility of his collegiate studies, and drops them to embark upon frantic
auto trips back and forth across the country with Dean, the "new
kind of American saint." Sal discovers that Dean has jettisoned all
"bitterness, recriminations, advice, morality" and plunged unreservedly
into "the ragged and ecstatic joy of pure being." The book conveys
the exhilaration of new scenes, new people, and new experiences
always around the turn or over the hill. The overall effect is of innocence and naïveté in the paean to life and of the insane speed
of the road that brings forgetfulness of the contemporary malaise.
Dean's adventures continue in *Excerpts from Visions of Cody* (1960).

The Dharma Bums (1958) means "The Truth Bums," *dharma,*
or "truth," being a term from Zen Buddhism. The character Japhy
is modeled after the Beat poet Gary Snyder (1930–   ), who lived
for some time in the Orient and has a scholarly knowledge of Chinese
and Japanese. Under his highly informal tutelage the Beats of this
novel strive for Tao, "the way." But these are determinedly raffish
Truth Bums and their discussions and visions do not aim at pro-
fundity.

William Burroughs (1914–   ). A native of St. Louis, Missouri,
and a Harvard graduate, William S. Burroughs was a narcotic addict
for fifteen years. Using the pseudonym "William Lee," he reported
in *Junkie* (1953) his experiences with drugs in many parts of the
world.

Naked Lunch (Paris, 1959) vividly relates Burroughs' drug-induced
hallucinations in a series of "episodes." The nihilistic pessimism of
this volume is its only coherent connective; the episodes consist of the
wildest conceivable nightmares of the unbalanced mind. The fantasies
are a demoniacal extension of the evils of the modern world. Written
in various styles, the book's greatest effectiveness is in its staccato
incisiveness.

WRITERS OF SCIENCE FICTION AND FANTASY

It is only relatively recently that works referred to as science fiction
have taken their place as a part of modern literature. Of course

there are many notable writers of the past whose work includes great imaginative stories about worlds beyond the earth or experiments beyond the ordinary human range. But the increasing achievements in human space travel and experimentation undoubtedly have stimulated many recent writers to embark on flights of fantasy, which qualify as science fiction only if they are infused with a basic fidelity to the data and indications of science.

A notable example of fidelity to science combined with engrossingly interesting exposition is found in the writings of **Arthur C. Clarke** (1917–   ). British by birth, and a scientist of distinction, he has been editor of *Science Abstracts,* conducted important underwater researches in the Great Barrier Reef of Australia, and has spent considerable time in the United States. Among Clarke's works are *Interplanetary Flight* (1950), *Islands in the Sky* (1952), and the more recent *2001: A Space Odyssey* (1968). Clarke is associated with Britain and Australia, but American writers have also approached these and other themes with comparable grounding in science and with great inventiveness.

It should be stressed that science fiction does not limit itself to space as a theme or to the physical sciences as a basis; the variations stemming from biological and psychological concepts are also often central in these stories. And associated with science fiction, perhaps supplementing it, are tales of sheer fantasy in which the imagination is permitted to develop its own bases and boundaries.

H. P. Lovecraft (1890–1937). Howard Phillips Lovecraft, born in Providence, Rhode Island, is the acknowledged twentieth-century master of the Poe-like tale of cosmic perturbation. He was an only child. His father died when he was very young; he grew up mostly in the company of the adults of his mother's family, and was often very much alone. He read a great deal, delving into many fields; and in his teens he contributed articles on astronomy to the Providence *Tribune.* He wrote at one point that time, space, and natural law represented to him an intolerable bondage; and in his stories he escaped into the supernatural and the macabre.

During Lovecraft's life his only published works were *The Shunned House* (1928) and *The Shadow over Innsmouth* (1936), but disciples have since zealously searched through periodicals to reprint most of his work. His extraordinary imagination about unknown worlds is often expressed in highly poetized style.

The Dunwich Horror and Others (1963) is a collection of some of Lovecraft's best stories, selected by August Derleth.

"The Shadow out of Time" was one of Lovecraft's later stories and demonstrates certain aspects of the weird mythology which formed the basis of so many of his works.

A professor of economics, Nathaniel Wingate Peaslee, is suddenly physically possessed by a being from another time. Peaslee's own mind is catapulted back 150 million years to a vast city in a steaming prehistoric jungle where he inhabits the fantastic body of the creature who replaced him in his own time. After more than five years Peaslee returns to his former state, but subconscious memories of that ancient world plague his dreams. He attempts to explain them by psychology, thinking them to be part of deep-seated race memories or phantasms arising from myths that he had read. He dreams of a great stone cavern and a "Great Race" of highly intelligent creatures who travel in time in order to collect information for their libraries. Peaslee himself had written for them the history of his own age. When he was to be returned to his own time they subjected him to hypnosis which would drive from his mind the conscious reality of those years. One thing that he remembers was that these creatures of the Great Race had an overwhelming dread of the "elder things" which had inhabited the earth before them and which were now held captive in caverns below the earth. While Peaslee is investigating the source of his dreams, he is suddenly called to Australia to examine some ruins which seem to be from the city he had dreamed about. To his horror the ruins are quite familiar to him and he finds the book that he had written for the Great Race. On his way out of the ruins, however, he is pursued by the elder things and drops the book which was the only proof that he actually experienced what he had been dreaming. He manages to escape and tries to dissuade others from exploring the ruins any further.

Robert A. Heinlein (1907–   ). While the Manhattan Project was secretly operating, Robert A. Heinlein wrote an imaginary story about nuclear fission so incredibly close to the actual researches that it had to be suppressed. In *The Green Hills of Earth* (1951) and later works, Heinlein ably develops the H. G. Wells technique of the one bizarre element introduced into an otherwise reassuringly commonplace world. An impressive science-fiction movie, *Destination Moon* (1950), was adapted from his *Rocket Ship Galileo* (1947).

Stranger in a Strange Land (1961) has proved Heinlein's most widely acclaimed novel.

Valentine Michael Smith is a human by ancestry (his parents were on the first space ship to visit Mars) but has been raised by the Martians and considers himself to be one of them. The book traces the course of his life after he is brought back from Mars. He creates a sensation on Earth but soon becomes alienated to all but a close circle of friends to whom he teaches the wonderful powers that he possesses. They learn telepathy and teleportation from him, and form themselves into a dedicated communal society. However, the government and the mass of the people hate and dread Smith and his group; and in the end, he goes out to meet a furious crowd and is stoned to death by them. His disciples carry on without remorse, for Smith has convinced them that there is only physical death.

August Derleth (1909–71). August William Derleth is an immensely versatile novelist in various genres. Sinclair Lewis termed him "a champion and a justification of 'regionalism'" on the basis of his *Sac Prairie Saga,* a series of novels on the Midwest. Derleth has been an active anthologist of science fiction, the biographer and outstanding follower of Lovecraft, and the head of Arkham House, a publishing firm in his native Sauk City, Wisconsin, that specializes in science fiction and kindred writings.

Isaac Asimov (1920–   ). A professor of biochemistry at Boston University, Isaac Asimov won the Edison Foundation Award in 1957 for *Building Blocks of the Universe,* the Blakeslee Award of the American Heart Association in 1960 for *The Living River,* and the Grady Award for science writing from the American Chemical Society in 1965. With all his distinguished scientific works, Asimov is best known to the public by science fiction such as *I, Robot* (1950), which presents some of the most stimulating and provocative ideas about man's relations to machines, space, and himself.

Ray Bradbury (1920–   ). Perhaps because his writings tend more to gripping fantasy than to conventional space travel, Ray Bradbury appears more often in "best short story" collections than do his peers. *Punch* asserted that his tales in *The Illustrated Man* (1951) "raise Bradbury to a secure place among the imaginative writers of today."

Shirley Jackson (1919–65). Shirley Jackson left her native San Francisco at the age of sixteen. After graduating from Syracuse University in 1940 she married the noted critic Stanley Edgar Hyman.

Amidst overtly ordinary people and ordinary surroundings Miss Jackson finds terrifying mental aberrations and twisted, morbid behavior. The title work from *The Lottery* (1949) has become a favorite anthology piece. In a seemingly normal American village a drawing of lots is enacted in a festive mood, although the meaning of the ritual appears forgotten. The woman who receives the marked lot is stoned to death as if she were a "scapegoat" in a primitive society. Jackson's macabre talents are seen to best advantage in her plunging through the veneer of commonplace, avowedly civilized people to discover horrifying depths.

Walter Michael Miller, Jr. (1923–   ). Walter Michael Miller, Jr., has won numerous awards both here and abroad for *A Canticle for Leibowitz* (1960), perhaps the outstanding science-fiction novel of this century. Amidst the destructive cycles of man's civilization, Miller depicts a monastic order that alone will preserve our cultural heritage and eventually will send it rocketing toward the stars from man-doomed earth.

NOVELISTS OF BLACK HUMOR

Though recent in general parlance, perhaps reaching widest publicity with the B. J. Friedman anthology *Black Humor* (1965), black humor seems to have an ancestry at least as far back as Voltaire and Dr. Samuel Johnson at his most sardonic. Black humor stems from a revulsion against the entire homogenized, cholesterolized, polyethylenized, supersaturated era. Where optimists point out that the airplane can whisk you in a few hours to Hong Kong, the black humorists point out that the airplane can obliterate mankind; where those who believe in progress note that atomic power may cure cancer, black humorists note that radiation may hopelessly pollute everything. The absurdists such as Beckett and Ionesco in similar revulsion see the cosmos as meaningless. The black humorists see it as a ghastly joke. Where romantic humorists offer a resounding yea to the scheme of things, black humorists stem from the realistic tradition in proclaiming that the whole business is vile. Nonetheless, to perceive all as a bizarre joke permits us to face the darkest aspects of existence with human solidarity. By the laughter of black humor we can will ourselves to endure what must be endured.

Nathanael West (1909–40). Born in New York City, Nathanael West attended Tufts University and graduated in 1924 from Brown University where a close friend was the humorist S. J. Perelman, who later married West's sister. West's name at birth was Nathan Weinstein. As a hotel manager in New York, West provided free lodging for indigent authors including Erskine Caldwell, James T. Farrell, and Dashiell Hammett (who while a guest there finished *The Maltese Falcon*). From 1933 on, West found lucrative employment as a scenario writer for Hollywood. He was killed in an automobile accident.

During much of his lifetime Nathanael West was virtually an unknown writer; his four short novels received favorable critical attention but won few general readers. Since World War II, however, the applause of numerous articles in scholarly journals has elevated him to a major rank, and the popularity of black humor has afforded him wider dissemination. His *Complete Works* were published in 1957.

Miss Lonelyhearts (1933), the newspaper-column label for the nameless hero of West's most celebrated novel, is a journalist who writes an advice-to-readers column for a metropolitan newspaper. A neurotically repressed individual whose only emotional outlet is a passion for Christ,

"Miss Lonelyhearts" is tormented by the mockery of his frustrated, sadistically inclined managing editor, William Shrike, and the preposterously pathetic letters of anonymous subscribers which he must answer in his column. When these pressures become intolerable he escapes to his small lodgings to brood for days at a time.

The novel proceeds to its crisis through episodes as Miss Lonelyhearts seeks either relief or revelation. There is a series of ludicrous and unsatisfactory adventures with sex and alcohol, culminating in a catastrophic attempt to console an obese nymphomaniac and her impotent, crippled husband. Miss Lonelyhearts again goes into retreat in search of detachment and spiritual calm. He is about to emerge with new confidence in his compassion and sublime imperturbability when he is shot down in a confused tussle with the irate cripple, who believes himself cuckolded.

The book's other characters are also benighted and tortured, but have all made some sort of stable adjustment on the margin of sufferability. It is Miss Lonelyhearts who struggles, and his resistance renders him dangerous. In every case his zealous interference in another life precipitates a minor or major crisis for them and for him. Even those who seek his advice find themselves struggling to preserve their status quo from his ministrations. When Miss Lonelyheart's final revelation endows him with his greatest potential (for good or evil), the exasperated gods find means to dispose of him through a chain of bizarre accidents.

The Day of the Locust (1939) is a surrealistic novel set in Hollywood and deriving its title from the plague of locusts investing Pharoah's Egypt in the Book of Exodus.

The central figure is Tod Hackett, a movie costume-and-set designer and the book's most reflective character. Tod, both repulsed and fascinated by the sham culture of Hollywood, becomes infatuated with Faye Greener, a would-be starlet he feels so unthinkingly artificial as to be genuine (she quarrels in song, dances provocatively when she fears sexual assault). Faye, however, is instinctively suspicious of Tod's intellect and reserves her intimacies for Earl Shoop, a displaced cowboy with no intellect at all, and his friend Miguel, a Mexican of purely sensual predilections. Upon the death of her father, Harry, a destitute vaudevillian, Faye goes to share a house rented by Homer Simpson, a timorous, neurotic Midwesterner visiting California for his health.

Homer is a personality so stricken and querulous that he is unable even to assert control over his own body. His shy solicitude, at first gratifying to Faye, soon provokes her contempt. Unabashedly she carries on with Earl and Miguel until she leaves secretly in chagrin. Homer, although almost insensible to her infidelity, has become so dependent upon her that her departure unhinges him. Tod finds him running distracted through the streets and tries to reason with him, but both are caught up in a self-destructive orgy of celebrity worshippers at a movie premiere.

A proposed painting of Tod's, "The Burning of Los Angeles," serves as a gloss upon the novel's thesis. Jaded by Hollywood's superficial novelties, hungering for new titillations, the disenchanted, embittered masses have created this inferno as a climactic entertainment and ultimate revenge for their unsatisfactory existence. By West's implication, the specious glitter of the California pleasure dome is paralleled throughout modern civilization, where surface show and activity overlay an absence of meaning and purpose.

Kurt Vonnegut, Jr. (1922–   ). A native of Indianapolis, Indiana, Kurt Vonnegut, Jr., studied biochemistry at Cornell University, mechanical engineering at Carnegie Institute of Technology, and anthropology at the University of Chicago. During World War II he was captured at the Battle of the Bulge and spent five months in a German POW camp. From 1947 to 1950 he was a public-relations officer for General Electric. Since 1950 he has been a free-lance writer, residing in New England.

Cat's Cradle (1963) takes its name from the ancient pastime of forming patterns with a loop of string upon the fingers.

The narrator is a professional writer and his story is a retrospective account of the end of the world. The indirect agent of this cataclysm is the nuclear physicist Felix Hoenikker, more machine than man, who before his death created "ice-nine" as an intellectual exercise. Ice-nine is explained as a heretofore unknown form of frozen water with a high melting point. When introduced to moisture it instantaneously spreads itself in a sort of molecular chain reaction. Ice-nine has the consequent potential of freezing the entire world solid, as it will do eventually in the irresponsible hands of Hoenikker's three strange children.

Events ultimately take some of the characters to San Lorenzo, an island dictatorship in the Caribbean, which is both a parody of tropical paradises and a microcosm of the modern police state. The popular religion of San Lorenzo is Bokononism (whose priest is Bokonon). It contains a humanistic fatalism that hoots at man's self-effected estrangement from himself. A bizarre accident during an aerial display by the tiny San Lorenzan air force unleashes ice-nine. The few survivors include Bokonon himself, who contemplates but discards the idea of a flippant suicidal gesture and elects to expire with a whimper.

The book's physical configuration is unusual; the continuous narrative is divided into chapters hardly more than a page in length, each preceded by a nonsense title of only superficial relevance to the content. Such solemn methodology is the supreme farcical device in this breezy tale of man's deliberate and systematic self-destruction.

Joseph Heller (1923–   ). Brooklyn-born Joseph Heller, after World War II service, received his bachelor's degree in 1948 from New York University and his master's degree in 1949 from Columbia University. From 1950 to 1952 he taught at Pennsylvania State University. More recently he has worked on various magazines.

Catch-22 (1961), Heller's first novel, is a pulverizing tour de force on the theme of the military mind. The title refers to a mythical army regulation that is cited whenever logical explanations fail; since they always do so in Heller's book, Catch-22 is the true operational basis of the armed forces during World War II.

The 256th Squadron of the U. S. Army Air Force is based on the Mediterranean island of Pianosa after the liberation of Rome, fighting a war of attrition. The horrors of repetitive battle and the responsibilities of command have had the result of driving everyone utterly but comfortably mad, each in his own peculiar fashion. The one sane man is Captain John Yossarian, and being sane he is desperately frightened. Throughout the novel Yossarian pleads, rages, and plots to get himself grounded, encountering at every turn bemused or sadistic commanders and various manifestations of Catch-22. At the conclusion it appears he will succeed in escaping to neutral Sweden.

All the personnel of the Pianosa base have developed their compulsive neuroses into army institutions that permit them to take the war pretty much on their own terms. Major Major's office is open to visitors only when he is absent therefrom. Lieutenant Milo Minderbinder, the megalomaniac mess officer, has expanded his black-market operations into a colossus that controls the economic fate of whole nations. The entire Mediterranean theater of war is apparently under the command of ex-Pfc. Wintergreen, who through his assigned duties as mail clerk has begun to issue command directives. The city of Rome exists for the Pianosa base only as an enormous brothel to which the men periodically repair.

Heller reinforces the book's pervasive atmosphere of unreason by the masterful use of circular exposition. An absurd situation often waits several chapters for an explanation that is preposterously intricate and brilliantly disorganized. The humor in *Catch-22* is strong and relishable without obscuring the horror and anguish that gave it birth.

MORE RECENT NOVELISTS CONCERNED WITH SOCIAL AND PERSONAL PROBLEMS

John Cheever (1912–   ). A native of Quincy, Massachusetts, John Cheever was educated at Thayer Academy.

The Enormous Radio and Other Stories (1953) collects Cheever short stories, many of which first appeared in *The New Yorker*. Cheever concentrates on the apparently favored members of an affluent society, the denizens of fashionable New York apartments or the commuters from Westchester, whose real lives belie appearances. He digs in his knife to reveal the terrible psychic disturbances plaguing the upper middle class. Wealth and leisure only compel them to feverish activity and spending to conceal from themselves the vacuity of their existence.

Other notable collections of Cheever short stories are in *The Housebreaker of Shady Hill* (1958) and *The Brigadier and the Golf Widow* (1964). It is his novels, however, that are most widely known.

The Wapshot Chronicle (1957) brought Cheever a wide audience. St. Botolphs, once a bustling Massachusetts port, has been left behind by the fevered pace of modern society. The town's inhabitants, however, are quite satisfied with their quaint existence; none more so than the Wapshot family, the last survivors of St. Botophs' elite society. Now in their declining years, Leander and his wife, Sarah, subsist on the generosity of the wealthy and eccentric old matriarch, Cousin Honora. Leander fills his days by operating the *Topaze,* a battered tourist launch; Sarah is deeply involved in club work. In opposition to this pastoral community stands the teeming outside world, with which the Wapshot males must periodically sally forth to do battle. In their turn Moses and Coverley, the sons of Leander and Sarah, go out to try their tactics in furtive skirmishes with modern urban society. Moses is fired from a government post and comes to rest in a New York fiduciary house. Coverley finds a niche at a missile base. Both marry wives that complement their natures (Moses' wife is Melissa, and Coverley's is Betsey) and both have sons who continue the Wapshot line.

A consummate stylist, Cheever is both whimsically lyrical and deliciously satiric. The heroic days of the clipper ships are contrasted with a painfully empty present. Surviving, however, are the sturdy character of Cousin Honora, and love and the instinct for life.

The Wapshot Scandal (1964) continues the account of the Wapshots with a more scathing denunciation of today's supermarket, superhighway, supermotel mélange. The ambiguous title ostensibly refers to stiff-necked Honora's refusal to pay income tax; before a horrified Internal Revenue agent in Italy she gives away her entire fortune to charity. Actually the scandal is the degenerate era in which the Wapshots and all of us are living. St. Botolphs, where Cousin Honora dies, is a pathetic and isolated little island of the past. Moses and Melissa Wapshot inhabit Proxmire Manor, a Westchester suburb depicted as cheerless and tasteless. Coverley and Betsey Wapshot live in secretive Talifer, a missile-research base; although trained as a technician, Coverley has been irrevocably assigned to public relations because of a computer error.

Perhaps the most symbolic character is Gertrude Lockhart, a neighbor of Moses in Proxmire Manor. When her household appliances break down *en masse,* she commits suicide, because the prop of life for her and others is the unbroken flow of material euphoria. But against this, Cheever suggests man's incredible power of continuance. *Bullet Park* (1969) is an important recent novel by Cheever.

Louis Auchincloss (1917–). Louis Stanton Auchincloss was born in Lawrence, Long Island, New York. After Groton and Yale he took his law degree from the University of Virginia in 1941 and in the same year was admitted to the New York Bar. An eminent attorney, he practices in New York. He is a noted leader in many New York cultural organizations.

The Indifferent Children (1947) and later novels reveal Auchincloss as a consummate craftsman. Like Henry James and Edith Wharton, he belongs to the highest and wealthiest social circles of New York. He describes this social milieu superlatively well, and shows that these aristocrats encounter disappointments in their private lives.

The Rector of Justin (1964), Auchincloss' most widely acclaimed novel, is about the founder and headmaster of a New England Episcopal preparatory school, told through a series of sympathetic sketches extracted from the journal of one of his associates.

The esteem in which the Reverend Dr. Francis Prescott is held by graduates and colleagues has made him the most respected name in secondary-school education. On the eve of his retirement and subsequent death this chronicle of his origins, triumphs, and failures reveals him to have been the dominant influence in many lives. Diplomatic but inflexible, Dr. Prescott has made of his school, Justin Martyr, a reflection of himself and his ideals. But the very strength of his personality has overwhelmed some who have sought to defend their individualities. In the end he reconciles himself to the entirety of his past and the necessity of relinquishing the future to others.

Mary McCarthy (1912–). A native of Seattle, Washington, Mary McCarthy was orphaned at six and brought up by various relatives of Protestant, Catholic, and Jewish backgrounds. *Memories of a Catholic Girlhood* (1957) revealingly studies this confusing but stimulating upbringing. She graduated from Vassar in 1933 and has taught at Bard College and at Sarah Lawrence College. Her first husband was Edmund Wilson, and her second, James R. West.

It is likely that the McCarthy wit is the most trenchant to be found in a recent writer. She has made the intellectuals her special subject, dissecting by surgically stripping away all pretense and hypocrisy. With monumental detachment Mary McCarthy probes frailties and futilities in the contemporary jousts of mind and sex.

The Company She Keeps (1942) consists of short stories that are frequently autobiographical. Miss McCarthy is represented in these stories by the character Margaret Sargent, who works in various art establishments and associates with avant-gardists. She proceeds to Nevada for a divorce and upon her return undergoes psychoanalysis.

"The Man in the Brooks Brothers Shirt" portrays a conventional middle-class businessman from Cleveland who believes he has contracted a grand passion for Margaret Sargent. Her intellectual and behavioral differences from his norm excite him, but in the end their obvious incompatability prevails.

"Portrait of the Intellectual as a Yale Man" cynically traces the progress of a conscientious young man from a struggling left-wing publication to a news weekly.

The Oasis (1949), Miss McCarthy's first novel, sarcastically demolishes utopians. A band of idealistic liberals attempts a sort of modern Brook Farm experimental community. Stubborn realities intrude, especially in the form of difficult traits of human nature. When outsiders invade the community to pick the utopians' strawberries, the resulting crisis brings the whole project crashing down.

The Groves of Academe (1952) is a notable novel upon the academic life, as distinguished from student life. It is essential to remember that this McCarthy book is set during the "witch-hunt" period of Senator Joseph McCarthy (no relation to the novelist in blood or politics).

Henry Mulcahy is a clever, unscrupulous, and inadequate professor at Jocelyn College, a progressive liberal-arts college in Pennsylvania. The liberal president fires Mulcahy, who claims that his discharge is a breach of academic freedom resulting from Mulcahy's earlier affiliation with communism. Mulcahy elicits the support of his colleagues, and in the end is rehired and forces the resignation of the president.

Although greatly perturbed by the novel's purport, academicians have been irresistibly fascinated by this delineation of aspects of their behavior. Mary McCarthy has wickedly caught every intonation of academic jargon, pose, internecine warfare, and genteel superficiality.

The Group (1963) gained wide attention, in part because of the candor of its sexual portrayals. The novel deals with the lives of eight Vassar graduates of the 1933 class (her own class) from 1933 to 1940.

Seven of the dormitory mates of Kay Strong attend her wedding soon after commencement. Seven years later they gather again for her funeral following her suicide. In the intervening years all but one of the alumnae have battled away at marriages, babies, husbands, lovers, and careers without conspicuous success. The exception is Elinor Eastlake ("Lakey") who has lived in Europe in a lesbian arrangement with the Baroness d'Estienne, perhaps achieving some self-knowledge.

Although these years span the Great Depression, economic and financial problems are virtually nonexistent for "the group." They are scions of wealth who came out of the college scornful of their strait-laced parents and confident that with their greater wisdom they would make a far better showing. But as Miss McCarthy herself stated, the novel's theme is "the loss of faith in progress." These younger women manage their affairs no better than did their predecessors.

Jean Stafford (1915–   ). Born in Covina, California, Jean Stafford received her A.B. and A.M. from the University of Colorado in 1936 and studied at the University of Heidelberg during the following year. Her first husband was the poet Robert Lowell. She has been married twice since.

Miss Stafford, an admirer of the Jamesian tradition, is concerned, as she has said, with "emotional motivations and their intellectual resolutions."

The Mountain Lion (1947) pits brother and sister, Ralph and Molly, against their parents. Their togetherness breaks down as sexual maturing forces Ralph toward independence and outwardness. Molly tries to hold him, even by disfiguring herself with acid, but he kills her while supposedly shooting at a mountain lion. Thus he tragically resolves the conflict between the closed, static world they tried to create and the open world of freedom and growth.

The Catherine Wheel (1952) takes its title from the wheel upon which Catherine of Alexandria was a Christian martyr in the fourth century; today the term is commonly used to describe a revolving, circular firework.

Young Andrew Shipley spends the summer at Congreve House, the lovely old home of his cousin Katharine in Hawthorne, New England. He meets and seeks the companionship of Victor Smithwick, but Victor's sickly brother is an impediment. Accordingly, Andrew conceives a guilty desire for this brother's death. On her part, Katharine experiences guilt because she desires John Shipley, Andrew's father, and had wished Andrew's mother dead. Now she feels that Andrew senses her sin, and so she wishes him dead. At a party Katharine catches fire from a catherine wheel and dies.

The wheel symbol whirls through all of this intense study of sin and guilt. Outward action is negligible; Miss Stafford is preoccupied with the inner wars in puritanical natures.

John Updike (1932–   ). John Hoyer Updike was born at Shillington, Pennsylvania, and graduated from Harvard in 1954. During the next year he studied at the Ruskin School of Drawing and Fine Art. From 1955 to 1957 he was with *The New Yorker*, which published several of his short stories. His novels have continued the strong interest in his work.

Rabbit, Run (1960) is set in a small city in southeastern Pennsylvania in the spring in 1959.

Harry Angstrom, known to his friends as Rabbit, is twenty-six years old, married, with one child and another expected soon. He works as a demonstrator of a kitchen gadget in a five-and-dime store. Dissatisfied with his listless wife, he runs away and begins living with a prostitute, Ruth. He goes back to his wife when she is giving birth, but leaves her once more. He goes to Ruth's apartment, but finds that she is pregnant and won't accept him back unless he gets a divorce and marries her. The complications involved in doing this seem to Rabbit to be overwhelming; so once more he runs away.

The Centaur (1963) treats of three days in 1947 in the high school in Olinger, Pennsylvania. The events of these days are presented realistically and then at many points a comparable happening or situation in Greek myth is related. Updike provides an index to associate even the most obscure of his characters with personages of ancient mythology.

The principal of the Olinger High School, Louis Zimmerman (Zeus), is notoriously promiscuous. George Caldwell (Chiron, the centaur) is a general-science teacher at the school; his son Peter Caldwell (Prometheus) is fifteen at the time and a student at the school. Bedeviled by his students and by colitis, George almost abandons his work, but rallies to return to the job and subsequently aid his son toward an art career in New York.

Looking back upon these difficult days, Peter asks, "Was it worth it?" His father was an extremely conscientious and overworked teacher, trying desperately to provide properly for his family out of a small income. George was under no illusions about his students, who were far more interested in diversion than wisdom. On a realistic level the novel is a portrait of a modern man in a limited world but with a noble spirit; and the events at Olinger High are photographically convincing. But the pattern of the novel is to see today's ordinary mortals as recapitulations of ancient myths. This mythic structure implants within modern Olinger the struggle for endurance and the care of one generation for its successor. It is worth it. George is defeated but he does not quit, and he extends to Peter a chance for victory. Updike's stylistic skill and his inventiveness are notable.

Couples (1968), a more recent Updike novel, deals intimately with the relations between husbands and wives, all members of a small group of couples in a New England town called Tarbox. The account is marked by extraordinary frankness.

CHAPTER SIX

Poetry of the Mid-Twentieth Century

CHARACTERISTICS OF THE NEW POETRY

The period since World War II has been a time of intense experimentation in American poetry. The war itself produced some powerful poetry, and the specter of the horrors of Nazi Germany has haunted many poets from the end of the war through the sixties. But the newer poets have been confronted directly by the inhumanities of the present—the Cold War, the threat of the Bomb, and a growing power structure and technology that seem remote from the individual human needs of man.

Many modern poets feel that these vast forces are somehow beyond their reach. And many of them have despaired of infusing a sense of humanity into what seems an increasingly inhuman civilization. The postwar poets for the most part rejected the role of social commentators and instead plunged into an intensely subjective examination of their own lives. They rejected T. S. Eliot's idea of the "objective correlative," which held that a poet must not put himself directly into his poetry but find some device, some correlative to experience, that would express the emotion that he wanted to convey. Instead many of the newer poets have placed themselves directly within their poems and told of their own personal lives, their feelings of guilt, and their fears. This type of poetry has been called "confessional" and its chief practitioners have been Robert Lowell, John Berryman, Theodore Roethke, Sylvia Plath, Anne Sexton, and W. D. Snodgrass. These poets recount their lives and tell of their neuroses with an openness that is perhaps embarrassing in its detail.

In the early fifties there was also much experimentation with form. Perhaps the best example of this was in the projectivist verse of the Black Mountain group of poets. Other poets, notably the Beats, often made use of obscenity within a confessional style to shock the sensibilities of what they believed to be a repressed society. Wallace Stevens and William Carlos Williams served as major influences upon the newer poets of the fifties and sixties.

The sixties' poets have continued the experimentation with form, and many of them have shown a greater involvement with society. There is also a popular poetry of social protest written by popular singers and folksingers, as well as by poets. Many poets have been concerned with the civil-rights movement and the Vietnam war. But no single movement is dominant in the poetry of the sixties. The poets, like many others in the arts, seem to be in the midst of a search for new moral and spiritual values.

MAJOR POETS OF THE MID-TWENTIETH CENTURY

Robert Lowell (1917–   ). Robert Trail Spence Lowell, Jr., was born in Boston to the well-known family that has included James Russell Lowell and Amy Lowell. In 1937, Robert Lowell left Harvard to study under John Crowe Ransom at Kenyon College, graduating from there *summa cum laude* in 1940. During 1941 and 1942 he was an editorial assistant for a New York publishing house. A conscientious objector during World War II, Lowell consequently served a prison term in 1943–44. He has taught at several colleges including Kenyon College, Harvard University, and Boston University.

The basis of Lowell's life and poetry seems to be rebellion. His conscientious objection in wartime was a protest against war and the profiteers whom he held responsible for the catastrophe. Much of his early life and poetry portray Lowell's rebellion against his own Puritan New England heritage. Although espousing Roman Catholicism initially as the answer to his dilemma, he has since begun to strike out in an essentially humanistic direction. Always, however, his verse has been a search for some means of faith amidst the materialism and skepticism of the mid-twentieth century.

Land of Unlikeness (1944). The title is a translation of *regio dissimilitudinis*, a phrase from St. Bernard. The poem castigates the modern world for its unlikeness to God and to its former, truer soul. Repeatedly through the volume St. Bernard is exalted as the saved Christian in contrast with Faust, the lapsed Christian, and Cain, the damned soul. These concepts are expressed in verse of power and fervent conviction. "The Bomber" protests the all-out Allied aerial bombardment instituted in 1942. The bombardiers themselves are Cain-like figures, exerting a force they cannot control, forfeiting their own salvation as they shatter the bodies of others and deny them burial in consecrated ground.

"In Memory of Arthur Winslow," which has gone through considerable changes since its 1939 appearance in *The Kenyon Review*, concerns his grandfather who died of cancer in 1938. Lowell denounces the whole materialistic culture of his mining-executive grandfather and the New England background that fostered him. In exorcism of his own origins the poet asserts that the measure of a man is not his worldly achievements but his spiritual likeness to God. Lowell's intense personal involvement calls particularly for his densely packed lines, striking figures of speech, rich weaving together of classical and Christian allusions, and potent symbols of life and death.

Lord Weary's Castle (1946) takes its title from a Scottish ballad in which injustice excites bloodshed and produces still more slaying in retaliation. The conflict is between custom and change. Continuing the prophetic denunciation of the previous volume, this collection proclaims the necessity of the Christian ethos in a godless era. Generally the poems move toward some type of liberation.

"At the Indian Killer's Grave" is occasioned by the burial place of Major Thomas Savage, a colonial slayer of Indians. The bloodshed in the name of religion and culture parallels the slaughter of World War II. The failure of both the American past and the American present impels Lowell to demand a course of spiritual contemplation as found in the Catholic tradition.

"Mr. Edwards and the Spider" is derived from the sermons and writings of Jonathan Edwards, the zealous Calvinist preacher. Many of Edwards' own phrases in his sermon "Sinners in the Hands of an Angry God" are used to characterize the man and the tradition he represented. What emerges from the fiery images is a vision of hell awaiting the sinner. Predestined man can do nothing to escape this fate unless God has chosen him to be saved. The poem is directed particularly to Josiah Hawley, a Revolutionary patriot who opposed Edwards' preaching.

The Mills of the Kavanaughs (1951) concentrates upon longer descriptive and narrative poems, previously less evident in Lowell's work.

"Falling Asleep over the Aeneid" consists largely of an old man's dream about the Vergilian poem as bird sounds lull him to sleep when he should be in church. The sleeper identifies himself with Aeneas, the hero and the lover, but church bells awaken him and suggest that he is totally deficient in heroism, love, and faith.

"The Mills of the Kavanaughs" depicts the decline of a wealthy New England industrialist family through Anne, widow of Harry, last of the line. They had vowed to protect and restore the family property for their children, but they were childless. She contemplates their apparent total failure, even to Harry's death outside the Church, but finds consolation in a life dedicated to love. The possibility of other solutions than Lowell's previous passionate Catholicism suggests a major turning point in the poet's attitude.

Life Studies (1959) indicates a trend away from essentially religious poetry toward more humanistically oriented poetry. Still contemplative, the poems in this volume are increasingly concerned with aesthetic and cultural quests. Brooding over his family's part in the Puritan tradition, Lowell tries to find an escape from this heritage. Although the imagery, structure, and approach are as precise as before, here this precision often seems heartbreaking because the subjects are so intensely personal.

"Beyond the Alps" keynotes a modified Lowell in its more conversational style. A train trip between Paris and Rome conducts the poet on a survey of history revealing recurrent cycles of civilization.

"91 Revere Street," a prose piece, details Lowell's youth spent at this address on Boston's Beacon Hill. Hemmed in by Victorian furniture which "looked nervous and disproportioned" and seemed to "wince, touch elbows, shift from foot to foot," the boy projects his feelings about his ancestors onto his inanimate surroundings.

Part Three of this volume consists of portraits and tributes to other writers, some of whom were Lowell's personal friends. Among those included: Ford Madox Ford, Hart Crane, and Delmore Schwartz.

Part Four of *Life Studies,* perhaps the most innovative and influential portion of the book, consists of portraits from Lowell's personal life.

"My Last Afternoon with Uncle Devereaux Winslow" details a young boy's coming to terms with death. Presenting a portrait of the sterility surrounding his youth, Lowell then introduces his uncle who was dying at age twenty-nine. The final lines of the poem suggest acceptance of the human condition without a frenzied search for consolation.

"Waking in the Blue," a type of poem Lowell has become noted for, presents intense pictures of his bouts with mental illness. Trying to order his universe from inside a hospital where things seem less than orderly, the poet portrays both the change and the stasis within human life. He recognizes the potential illness in all humans.

Imitations (1961) translates a selection of poems from writers ranging from Homer to Boris Pasternak. Rather than trying to translate literally, Lowell "imitates" the original poem, which is to say that he takes the essential meaning of a whole poem and tries to render it in verse as close to the original form as possible.

The Old Glory (1965) is a collection of plays which Lowell adapted for the stage from well-known American short stories, including "Benito

Cereno," by Herman Melville, and Nathaniel Hawthorne's "My Kinsman, Major Molineux" and "Endicott and the Red Cross."

For the Union Dead (1964), a continuation of the direction of *Life Studies*, reveals man, hopeless, helpless, loveless, the victim of a repressed era. The religious elements are considerably muted, and the style is one of impressionistic virtuosity.

"For the Union Dead" is obviously indebted to Allen Tate's famous ode. A modern observer gazes first into a fish tank in the South Boston Aquarium, likening himself to a snail. He moves to the statue on Boston Common of Colonel Robert Shaw, Civil War commander of the 54th Massachusetts Infantry, the first Negro regiment in the United States Army. Many of the details of the poem are taken from the speech of William James, dedicating the statue.

Theodore Roethke (1908–63). The Roethke family long conducted a famous floral business in Saginaw, Michigan, the poet's birthplace. After education at the universities of Michigan and Harvard, Theodore Roethke taught at Lafayette College, Pennsylvania State University, Bennington College (where he also coached tennis), and, until his death, at the University of Washington.

Many critics call Roethke's verse "pure poetry," since his principal concern is the individual inner life, the struggle of the self to establish harmony within itself and with its relation to other men and to nature. He tends to write in two fashions. His verse in conventional meter and stanzas is usually a witty, rational exploration of everyday experiences. He uses free verse as a vehicle for meditative poems, sometimes surrealistic in expression, which show kinship with the subconscious utterances of the young Dylan Thomas or with the mystic visions of Blake, one of Roethke's favorites.

Open House (1941), his first volume, already demonstrates with a finished craftsmanship most of the poet's persistent themes.

"Open House," the title poem, announces the search for self-identity, for being itself, in deepened consciousness.

"The Light Comes Brighter" seeks the correspondences between the psychic life and the life processes of Nature.

The Lost Son and Other Poems (1948) marks his fully mature style. Roethke examines his childhood attempts in the family greenhouses to grasp the essence of the life of the flower and its relation to his own growth. Plants are scrutinized with almost microscopic care in the quest for psychic identity and spiritual evolution.

"The Lost Son" presents the mature Roethke surrounded by a strangely menacing Nature. He recalls his youth and its "lively understandable spirit."

"Orchids" hauntingly evokes the living presence of these exotic flowers, their mysterious yearning for being and for fulfillment.

"The Minimal" minutely observes the tiny world of small insects and microörganisms. With the lesser forms of creation man shares primordial levels of existence.

"Big Wind" transforms the greenhouse into a ship. Here the poet is intent upon capturing sense images of all kinds. By juxtaposing the tensions and changes of his feelings when writing with his past experience, he synthesizes a new reality. The moment when lived must be transient, and can only become real through later associations. *Praise to the End!* (1951) takes its title from *The Prelude* by Wordsworth. Most notable is a sequence (rearranged in his last volume) of poems which Roethke termed a "history of the psyche." The youthful association with growing things is the background for a remarkable series of questing poems descending into the psychic underworld, undergoing ordeals of the spirit, and ascending toward "unity of being," that is, back to the phenomenal world now transformed by the spiritual odyssey.

The Waking (1953).

"The Waking," a villanelle, powerfully affirms the comprehension of life through a natural and intuitive perception of the surrounding world. "I learn by going where I have to go."

"Four for Sir John Davies" is dedicated to the sixteenth-century British poet whose *Orchestra* (1596) is a long philosophical poem upon cosmic order. Roethke's moderately long sequence uses the symbol of the dance to assert transcendental harmony.

Words for the Wind (1958), essentially Roethke's collected poems, earned the Bollingen Prize.

"Words for the Wind" is an epithalamion written for his bride during their honeymoon visit to Auden's residence. In the person of his wife, love "wakes the ends of life." Roethke finds all the ecstatic fulfillment that Edmund Spenser in his *Epithalamion* found in the physical and spiritual harmonies of union, but Roethke further finds in the Jungian *anima* the means to psychic balance and imaginative creativity.

John Berryman (1914–   ). Born in McAlester, Oklahoma, John Berryman studied at Columbia University. He continued his studies in Cambridge, England. He has taught at Brown, Harvard, and Princeton, and more recently at the University of Minnesota. His first notable book of poems was *The Dispossessed* (1948). Another important work was the book-length poem *Homage to Mistress Bradstreet* (1956), which concerns the first poet of colonial America.

77 Dream Songs (1964), which won a Pulitzer Prize, brought Berryman into the public eye. Strikingly original, these poems concern an imaginary character called Henry, whose identity shifts back and forth from a black-faced minstrel to a lonesome and vulnerable man. Although sometimes confusing, this shifting character is always dazzling, intelligent, witty. The accounts of his suffering sometimes seem confessional, but there is an impudent, boisterous quality behind Henry that keeps him alive. A disciple of Yeats and Auden, Berryman wrestles with the problem of syntax within the poetic line. The poems are formal in that they follow stanza patterns with some rhyme, yet they always sound colloquial in tone.

Berryman's Sonnets (1967) contains 115 sonnets written to his mistress many years before. They show many of the roots for the "Dream Songs" such as complex diction, archaic spelling, and a witty attitude. Although occasionally freer than the Petrarchan sonnet, these poems generally adhere to the form.

His Toy, His Dream, His Rest: 308 Dream Songs (1968) carries Henry through eleven more years of public and private life. Henry is still restless and dynamic, a live character whose wit, melancholy, and rage are well communicated to the reader. Again the person shifts, as Henry talks about himself in the first, second, and third persons. But Henry here is not as jaunty as the earlier man; he has been saddened by the death of too many friends over the eleven-year span. There are painful elegies for some of Berryman's friends, yet we are reminded of the earlier wit as the book opens with "Op. psth. no. 1" when Henry is in his grave and later resurrects himself. Things are seen from the point of view of dying in the midst of life. Although Berryman denies that he is Henry, Henry portrays much of the author's life.

W. H. Auden (1907–   ). Son of a physician in York, England, Wystan Hugh Auden was educated at Christ Church, Oxford. After travels in Germany he settled down as a schoolmaster and poet until the Spanish Civil War drew him to serve on the Loyalist side as an ambulance driver. In 1935 he married Erika Mann, daughter of the German novelist Thomas Mann. In 1939 he established residence in the United States, becoming an American citizen in 1946. Since 1950 he has taught and lectured at many American universities, and has lived abroad for periods of several months.

Auden had been hailed as the outstanding native poet of England in the twentieth century before he transplanted himself to America. His change of residence is inextricably bound to a change in his viewpoint. The British Auden believed that the secular earthly paradise could be obtained in the Old World by political radicalism. The American Auden has dropped such hopes in favor of an existential Christianity. He sees salvation as an individual rather than a collective problem. "In America," he has stated, "to move on and make a fresh start somewhere else is still the normal reaction to dissatisfaction." His own dissatisfaction has caused him to search for the hidden God desperately needed by the isolated soul and to proclaim the City of God formed by men of good will.

The Age of Anxiety: A Baroque Eclogue (1947). The central concept is the *angst*, or anguish, of modern society; to Auden's mind a feeling whose source is fundamentally religious. The loss of belief and tradition, the anonymity of mass man in an industrialized culture have stirred the lonely individual to seek escape from his own purgatory.

In structure the poem owes much to Dante's *Divine Comedy*. "Baroque" refers to the incongruities and contrasts characteristic of a period of stress.

Part I, as well as the next three parts, takes place in a Third Avenue bar on All-Hallows Eve. There are four characters with alcohol-inspired visions:

Malin, a Canadian aviator, disclaiming any faith, is the most intelligent of the group and the one actually most Christian.

Rosetta, a department-store buyer, has gained financial success, but her Jewish origins enforce a profound sense of insecurity and rootlessness.

Quant, an Irish shipping clerk, is an embittered, aging widower convinced that life has absolutely no meaning.

Emble, a handsome young American naval officer, is perhaps potentially heroic but youthfully uncertain and vacillating.

At the outset each character is immersed in his own reverie until a newscast about World War II causes them to discuss the universal significance of war. Malin focuses their conversation upon the basic problem: man's desperate desire to overcome fear, guilt, and anxiety.

Part II considers Shakespeare's Seven Ages of Man. The four conversationalists unsuccessfully search for meaning in the successive stages of life only to fall back into their pathetic illusions.

Part III treats of the Seven Stages of the Quest, i.e., the search for imaginary innocence and safety, the "Regressive road to Grandmother's House." The journey through the secular, sensuous world proves equally futile.

Part IV, "The Dirge," yearns for the False Messiah, a Napoleon or a Sherlock Holmes, who will rescue man and Nature, but "Our lost dad" is a hopeless hope.

Part V takes the revelers to Rosetta's apartment to celebrate an incipient love affair between Rosetta and Emble. Although the older men recognize the illusion of Eros, they encourage the young folks and depart. Emble, however, collapses and Rosetta must resign herself to her empty loneliness.

Part VI is an epilogue counterpointing Malin's essentially Christian reflections upon love and time with Quant's insistence upon Heraclitean flux and the meaninglessness of history. Unable in this world to achieve full knowledge or full happiness, Malin says that we must look instead to Heavenly Grace for sustaining faith.

Nones (1951) through *About the House* (1965) reveal the stabilized visiting professor in Auden. The pyrotechnics and amazing variety of his earlier verse have yielded to an older man's sober intelligence and wide reading, mirrored in extremely civilized poetry, conversational in tone. Technically, Auden has worked increasingly and with consummate skill in syllabic verse, perhaps influenced by Marianne Moore. He suggests individual decorum and a reasonable attempt at brotherhood as the only logical behavior in a materialistic world that blandly ignores the City of God.

Collected Poetry (1945) brings together poems from many previous volumes.

"Musée des Beaux Arts" takes as its central image Breughel's painting "Icarus" and uses it to illustrate "how everything turns away / Quite leisurely from the disaster."

"In Memory of W. B. Yeats" attempts to be objective in its statement about death. Its structure is complicated, beginning in unrhymed free verse and moving through what seems to be syllabic verse to the final section of formally rhymed quatrains. The first section describes the day Yeats died, using the antitheses of which Yeats himself was so fond. The second part is Auden's judgment of Yeats's life and work. The final section, with its formality, seems to suggest that Auden has restrained his grief and has ordered his thoughts about Yeats and his poems.

Randall Jarrell (1914–65). A native of Nashville, Tennessee, Randall Jarrell spent most of his youth in the Southwest. He received a B.A. from Vanderbilt University in 1935 and an M.A. in 1938. He taught at Kenyon College and at the University of Texas until 1942 when he entered the Army Air Corps. From his discharge in 1946 until his death in an automobile accident, he taught at several colleges, including Princeton, Sarah Lawrence, and primarily at the University of North Carolina at Greensboro.

His volumes of poetry include *Blood for a Stranger* (1942), *Little Friend, Little Friend* (1945), *Losses* (1948), *Woman at the Washington Zoo* (1960), and *The Lost World* (1965). His essays are collected in *Poetry and the Age* (1953) and *A Sad Heart at the Supermarket*

(1962). His one novel is *Pictures from an Institution* (1954). He is also known for children's books, including *The Bat Poet* (1964).

Selected Poems (1964) reprints some poems from *Blood for a Stranger, Losses,* and *The Seven-League Crutches* (1951), with some revisions. Originally published in 1955, this volume preserves what Jarrell wanted from his first books, and includes the complete *Woman at the Washington Zoo.*

"A Girl in a Library" concerns a girl who has fallen asleep in the library of a Southern college, a woman who looks out of one of the books, and a third person, the "I" of the poem.

"The Death of the Ball Turret Gunner" is compassionate but unhesitant in its grasp of the brutalities of World War II. While Jarrell generally is very specific in details, as he is in this short poem, when an abstraction does appear, such as the "State," it has a dark and sinister quality.

"The Woman at the Washington Zoo" presents a middle-aged woman. Recognizing that the world is passing her by like the saris from the embassies, this woman reflects on her own drab life and cries, "You know what I was, / You see what I am: change me, change me!"

The Lost World (1965) consists chiefly of dramatic monologues spoken by aging women about variations of solitude and the recollections of lost childhood.

"Next Day" involves us by its suburban dailiness. The woman remembers her youthful beauty as the grocery boy pats her dog and doesn't notice her. In a way, she is saved by recognizing that others have aged with her.

"The Mockingbird," originally from *The Bat Poet,* is a remarkable comment on the making of poetry itself. The mockingbird fights to own the yard he lives in, driving away the other birds and animals. But he also learns how to imitate:

> He imitates the world he drove away
> So well that for a minute, in the moonlight,
> Which one's the mockingbird? Which one's the world?

"The Old and New Masters" begins with a reference to Auden's poem "Musée des Beaux Arts." Jarrell then goes on to describe two paintings to illustrate his point. Tracing their treatment of suffering, he describes accurately but suggests dark mysteries hidden under the paintings, and finally suggests how unimportant all that human suffering will turn out to be.

Richard Wilbur (1921–   ). Richard Purdy Wilbur is a native New Yorker. His A.B. from Amherst in 1942 was followed by an M.A. from

Harvard in 1947. He has taught at Harvard (1950–54), Wellesley (1955–57), and Wesleyan (since 1957). His first two volumes of poetry were *The Beautiful Changes* (1947) and *Ceremony* (1950). *Things of This World* (1956) seems to represent a growing trend among recent academicians to write more directly and simply than earlier tradition has dictated. Marianne Moore and Robert Frost have strongly influenced Wilbur to produce a lively but meditative poetry with the traditional subject matter. Strongest of all influences is that of Wallace Stevens.

"Love Calls Us to the Things of This World," the title poem of this volume, transforms a fleshy subject into spirit by the use and power of the imagination. The poem opens to the speaker's perception of laundry waving in the morning air. Whereas the laundry seems ethereal, the waking poet wishes that the whole world could be as *real* as this sight. With this vision, the man's spirit re-enters his waking body. The laundry becomes an emblem of love ("linen for the backs of thieves") and there is some reciprocity between love and the things of this world.

Advice to a Prophet (1961) continues Wilbur's earlier themes of direct confrontation of this world in order to transform it through the imagination. Also, like his earlier poems these are more often pictorial than dramatic.

"Advice to a Prophet," the title poem, is a classical elegiac poem. Perhaps because he aims too high, the speaker in the poem feels profound sadness and irony when he looks at the large issues of life.

Archibald MacLeish (1892–   ). A native of Glencoe, Illinois, Archibald MacLeish received his A.B. from Yale in 1915. Married in 1916, he volunteered for military service during World War I and in France rose from an army private to captain. His first volume of poetry was *Tower of Ivory* (1917). In 1919 he received the LL.B. from Harvard and briefly taught law at Harvard. Admitted to the Bar, he practiced law in Boston until 1923. From 1923 to 1928 he lived abroad, chiefly in France. A trip through Mexico, much of it on foot, provided material for *Conquistador*. MacLeish energetically supported Franklin Delano Roosevelt's administration; and he was Librarian of Congress from 1939 to 1944. Notable public service continued: MacLeish was Assistant Secretary of State (1944–45) and Chairman of the U.S. delegation to found UNESCO (1945), with subsequent high posts in UNESCO. From 1953 to 1956 he held the presidency of the American Academy of Arts and Letters. Among other activities have been many stints as a university lecturer, with honorary degrees from American and foreign institutions. Amidst all

these labors he has continued to write poetry right up to recent
years.

MacLeish's fundamental assertion is that with all the undeniable defects of the twentieth century, man can still shape a good life in
a liberal democracy.

Streets in the Moon (1926) is the first MacLeish volume to include
examples of the distinctive MacLeish idiom. Modern speech patterns are
employed in a wide range of modernist verse experiments. Many of
his best poems are included.

"The Silent Slain" likens the dead of World War I to Roland's
trapped contingent at Roncevaux, all to be mourned for, all betrayed.

"Memorial Rain" describes the memorial services for the poet's brother,
Kenneth, an aviator killed in Belgium. The banalities of the memorial
speech are swept away by the rain that cleanses the earth and bestows peace upon the buried.

"The End of the World" is a sonnet using the image of a circus
tent (setting for the later play *J.B.*) to suggest the sense of loss and
alienation in modern man. Everything explodes and there is "nothing
at all."

"Ars Poetica" represents the poet's belief that a poem should exist
for its own sake, that its truth does not exist apart from itself.

The Hamlet of A. MacLeish (1928), his first work to arouse the
attention of major critics, in some respects resembles Eliot's *The
Waste Land*. There is a suggestion of Jessie Weston's *From Ritual to
Romance* in the Holy Grail allusions and of Jules Laforgue in the
painfully introspective scrutiny of contemporary man. The themes of
broken traditions and of a sterile land dominate this poem. The
Shakespearean hero belonged to an era when evil clearly had a name
and was patently observable, but the modern man (the MacLeish-
Hamlet of our times) fences with shadows of shadows, tormented in
spirit, incapable of finding solutions.

New Found Land (1930) is about MacLeish's return to America
and his search for the meaning of the American experience.

"Cinema of a Man," in a kaleidoscopic compression of images suggested by the technique of St.-John Perse, pictures his own tearing
between the two worlds of Old and New.

"Land's End" perceives in the Eskimos a primitive folk who in elemental fashion grasp "Shapes solid and real."

Conquistador (1932) gained for MacLeish a wide reading public.
The basis for the book is the Bernal Diaz eyewitness account of the
conquest of Mexico by Cortez. The epic magnificence, combining
exotic splendor and bloody violence of an ancient land with reverie

and lyricism, grips the reader. Seeking plunder and adventure, the conquerors have demolished a whole ancient culture of humanity.

The Fall of the City (1937) is a verse drama written for American radio performance. MacLeish depicts a demoralized city which in its terror chooses capitulation rather than fighting for survival. The conqueror who takes the city without a struggle is found to be nothing more than hollow armor.

Land of the Free (1938) is an experiment in combining verse and photographs. The "sound track" of free verse ironically comments on the pictures of eroded fields, polluted rivers, evicted tenant farmers, gaunt and hopeless faces, all the remnants of a wasted land. The poem wonders whether with the raping of the continent the American dream has been buried under the tombstone.

Air Raid (1939) is also a radio verse drama. The locale, though unnamed, is Guernica, Spain, in 1937 during the Spanish Civil War. A peaceful small town is suddenly devastated by a saturation air bombardment. The announcer's utter callousness about the human obliteration is one of the most telling ironies of an age that seems to be advancing in mechanical prowess and retrogressing in human sympathies.

Actfive, and Other Poems (1948) collects verse written during active public life in the war years. Dominating the poems is the anger of a sensitive idealist over the failure of men to create the good life that is within their grasp.

"Brave New World" contrasts the courageous vision of Jefferson and his supporters with the frightened men of the Second World War years. The poet demands that his fellow Americans give living substance to the exalted words they bandy about so easily.

Collected Poems 1917–1952 (1952) contains some newly published pieces which show a movement away from the polemic verse of the Depression and war years toward a more lyrical verse.

Songs for Eve (1954), a slender volume of twenty-eight poems, is a lyrical assertion of the potentialities of man. The Eden legend is interpreted not as a fall from grace but as the emergence of man from animality into the realm of self-knowledge and conscious creativity.

J.B., a Play in Verse (1957) has elicited praise, and was very effective on the stage. The circus motif recalls the poet's early sonnet, "The End of the World."

Two broken-down actors, Zuss (Zeus) and Nickles (Old Nick), reduced to selling balloons and popcorn at the circus, observe and comment from a raised platform upon the problems of J.B. (Job) who is on the lower stage. Initially J.B. is a happy New England millionaire with an attractive wife, Sarah, and five splendid children. His innocent children all die horribly and his wealth dissolves while he is inflicted with agonizing illness. Sarah urges J.B. to "curse God and die" and leaves him, but he seeks to understand the inscrutable ways of divinity. The three comforters offer explanations. Zophar, the fat priest, interprets the torments of J.B. as arising from sin, if not from his own undiscoverable sin then from original sin. Bildad, the Marxist, argues that one man's suffering is inconsequential because justice for total humanity infinitely outweighs justice for one man. Eliphaz, the psychiatrist, suavely dismisses guilt as a "psychophenomenal situation," an illusion. J.B. refuses the choices of suicide to escape his pains, seeking submission before unjust fate, or laughing scorn at life as a brutal farce. Amidst an indifferent cosmos, J.B. and Sarah (returned to him) will assert their mutual love.

This play is poetic drama forged from American speech. When Zuss dons the God-mask and Nickles the Satan-mask they ascend to the perspective of Ultimate Good and Ultimate Evil. During the first eight scenes the circus top covers the stage, confining the problems to this little world. The three concluding scenes are without the canvas cover, and expose the action to the conundrum of time and space.

The theme is fundamental: the pointless suffering of man in a world he did not make and cannot really manage. But beneath this the play deals with larger concepts: the nature of God, the meaning of the universe, the purpose of life, good and evil. The modern Job finally triumphs over his unjust afflictions by realizing that he needs no forgiveness. Instead, freed of guilt, he forgives God.

Marianne Moore (1887–   ). Marianne Craig Moore was born in Kirkwood, Missouri, and when she was seven the family moved to Carlisle, Pennsylvania. She received her B.A. from Bryn Mawr College in 1909 and after a European visit taught at the Carlisle Indian School from 1911 to 1915. She then undertook the editorship of *The Dial,* a post she held until 1929; she helped shape it into one of the outstanding journals of American poetry of the twentieth century. Her stature as a poet has been widely recognized. She never married. She now lives in New York City.

Marianne Moore is a poet's poet. Her verse is not obscure and is marked by a cool detachment. The paradoxes of life, often expounded wittily and with astounding erudition and range, fascinate her and produce a strong moral response. She was associated with the Objectivism that also engaged William Carlos Williams, but she has consistently seen in the "thing-in-itself" analogies to support individualism and personal integrity. Disdaining masculine "logic," she works intuitively, employing what she terms "elasticity." Though a resolute experimenter, she writes meticulously restrained lines usually of "syllabic" verse, a metrical system that counts syllables rather than feet. Although she also wrote extensively during the first part of the century, she seems to belong to the present.

Collected Poems (1951) contains, with some revisions, almost all of Miss Moore's poetry to that date. The previous volumes which it collects are *Poems* (1921), *Observations* (1924), and *What Are Years* (1941).

"Part of a Novel, Part of a Poem, Part of a Play," in three sections, finds exhilarating the possibilities of life in a small, unprepossessing community. The calm and storm, security and danger, order and disorder that we constantly encounter about us nevertheless give cause for a restrained optimism.

"No Swan so Fine" sarcastically decries the artifice of Louis XV. The monarch who prized the mere decorative contrivances of art was dead before his actual demise, for the love of the false is a love of extinction.

"The Plumed Basilisk" is a detailed description of this fierce-looking lizard which, according to legend, could kill a man with a look. It first appears that the myth will evaporate when the physical reality is closely examined. But suddenly the poet begins to see a mystery in this creature, a "noiseless music" surrounding it, a great terrifying silence in its eyes. At this point the imagination could easily make the leap from reality to myth.

"In the Days of Prismatic Color" asserts that early in creation color was "fine," exemplifying pristine simplicity, while now it has become trapped in "complexity." With her sensible femininity she denounces intricacy and darkness for their own sakes.

"Marriage" presents a modern Adam and Eve, both restive under the marital yoke. Here, as elsewhere throughout life, we must strive simultaneously for union and for freedom, for the physical and the spiritual. Though the ideal can never be realized, the paradoxes of marriage can be harmoniously balanced by mutual love and understanding.

"To a Steam Roller" likens the ponderous crushing of the machine to impersonal dogmatists with vast inflexible systems. The huge bulk of the machine is suddenly made absurd by contrasting it with the flickering beauty and imaginative freedom of a butterfly.

"What Are Years?" admits the entrapment of life, but although "satisfaction" in so much of our existence is impossible, we may assert the will to struggle and find joy in the spirit of man.

"Nevertheless" finds in the plant world examples of courageous survival
in the face of apparently insuperable obstacles.

"Elephants" suggests that these giant beasts even in captivity have attained a serenity unknown to man. Like humans, elephants live in a
world they did not make and cannot reshape; they wisely accept it.
The Fables of La Fontaine (1954) is one of the major poetic translations into English and is highly praised by fellow poets. Miss Moore's
version is quite free and imaginative in its urbane and conversational
handling of the original. She was especially drawn to La Fontaine from
her own extensive use of animals to exemplify traits of character and
behavior, and from her shared conviction with the Frenchman that art
depicts not the world we might desire but the world we inhabit.

Like a Bulwark (1957), as well as her subsequent verse into the
1960s, has maintained Miss Moore's consistent themes. Her dazzling
range and catholicity of interests are well demonstrated in "Baseball
and Writing" (1961), which in a penetrating display of wit compares
the subleties and vicissitudes of baseball with the task of writing. She
sees the delight that can be found in both endeavors if they are faced
with courage and skill.

OTHER IMPORTANT POETS
OF THE MID-TWENTIETH CENTURY

Karl Shapiro (1913–   ). Karl Jay Shapiro was born in Baltimore,
Maryland, and was educated at Johns Hopkins University. Recollections
of his army service from 1941 to 1945 appear from time to time in his
verse; *V-Letter* (1944) appeared while he was stationed in the South
Pacific. He was a poetry consultant at the Library of Congress (1946–
47) and a professor at Johns Hopkins (1947–50). From 1956 until
recently he has taught at the University of Nebraska. He is a notable
scholar of modern verse (*Prose Keys to Modern Poetry*, in 1962) and of
English prosody (*A Prosody Handbook*, in 1965). Some of his volumes
of poetry are *Poems* (1935), *Person, Place, and Thing* (1942), and
The Bourgeois Poet (1964).

Poems, 1940–1953 (1953), composed for the most part of conventional verse forms, is resolute in concentrating upon everyday contemporary situations. His own nature compels a deep, unsentimental sympathy with all life. A reverence for life pervades his most memorable
war verse such as "Elegy for a Dead Soldier." Like Delmore Schwartz,
in his later work he has found religious strength in Jewish traditions but
conforms to no orthodoxy.

Delmore Schwartz (1913–66). Delmore Schwartz was born in
Brooklyn and was educated at Wisconsin, New York University (B.A.

in 1935), and Harvard. He taught at Harvard from 1940 to 1947 and later lectured at many American universities. As an undergraduate he had already established a reputation for significant verse, and in 1960 he became the youngest poet ever to receive the Bollingen Prize. *The World Is a Wedding* (1948) collects his notable short stories, mostly about Jewish life in New York City.

Summer Knowledge: New and Selected Poems, 1938–1958 (1959) employs, as few other modern poets are able to do, traditional philosophical concepts in startlingly contemporary situations (e.g., "In the Naked Bed, in Plato's Cave" explores the cave image of Plato's *Republic* from a bed in a house upon a busy city street). Shakespeare is a major influence upon Schwartz (he identifies himself with the playwright's hero in the long poem, "Coriolanus and His Mother"). His chief theme is the struggle between the individual and time—its maturings and its ravagings. All his verse manifests tremendous gusto, exuberant language and images, eloquent lyricism. His later verse emphasized joy in religious faith.

Richard Eberhart (1904–   ). A native of Austin, Minnesota, Richard Eberhart received his A.B. from Dartmouth in 1926. He then went on to Cambridge University in England for another A.B. in 1929 and an M.A. in 1933. During 1930 and 1931 he was tutor to the son of the King of Siam. After teaching in New England preparatory schools he served in the U. S. Navy 1942–46, rising to lieutenant commander. Since the war he has followed two divergent careers. As a business executive he has risen to the directorship of several commercial firms. As a teacher and lecturer he has been on the staff of Princeton, Dartmouth, and other universities.

Selected Poems 1930–1965 (1965) reveals Eberhart to be a traditionalist among mid-twentieth-century American poets. He tends toward conservative literary-philosophical diction and toward conventional verse forms. His poetry has a strong moral element and his major themes are God, sin, and human mortality. Much in the manner of the nineteenth-century Romantics, he finds solace in divine Nature, childhood intuitions, and the mystic revelation. His best-known piece, "The Fury of Aerial Bombardment," sees the war as an inevitable outcropping of original sin.

Peter Viereck (1916–   ). Peter Robert Edwin Viereck, born in New York City, is the son of George Sylvester Viereck, a well-known novelist, essayist, and editor. Peter Viereck's Harvard training led to a Ph.D. in 1942. His Harvard teaching was broken off in the same year to permit army service in Africa and Italy. He taught at Smith College, 1947–48, and after that at Mount Holyoke. The astounding range of Viereck's work includes Russian history, German culture, geopolitics.

Politically he is a spokesman for the "New Conservatism" which he calls "a revolt against revolt," opposing equally fascism, communism, and floundering liberalism.

Terror and Decorum (1948) was his first volume of poetry. Witty and skillful, he insists upon clarity instead of the "private message" of much current verse. Viereck stands out from other notable war poets in his sense of the romantic element in war, especially in "Kilroy," based upon the epigraph "Kilroy was here," scrawled throughout the world by American soldiers in World War II.

Kenneth Patchen (1911–   ). Born in Niles, Ohio, Kenneth Patchen at seventeen went to work with his father's crew in the steel mills. When out of work he briefly attended the University of Wisconsin, 1929–30. Thereafter he drifted from one end of the continent to the other working at odd jobs until he received a Guggenheim fellowship. He published his first poetry volume in 1936. In addition to his poetic skill, Patchen is a highly competent illustrator.

Before the Brave (1936) to *But Even So* (1963). Patchen's nightmare world shrieks with crescendos of noise and ugliness and bleak, sterile promontories of modern tawdriness. Much of his work resembles the daring experiments of James Joyce. Few poets match the savage intensity of Patchen, but his powerful vignettes of contemporary life are also remarkably full of subtlety and nuances. Probably his most famous poem is "Do the Dead Know What Time It Is?" in which the narrator's conversation in a bar with a philosophical drunk is interrupted by a harlot's solicitation.

Léonie Adams (1899–   ). Born in Brooklyn, Léonie Fuller Adams was educated at Barnard. She has taught English at several Eastern universities.

Poems: A Selection (1954) reveals Miss Adams to be one of the outstanding metaphysicians among modern twentieth-century poets in English. "Country Summer," for instance, which appears in numerous anthologies, displays simultaneously a passionate intensity and sharp intellectuality toward Nature. Her technical mastery and richly textured imagery have won her the Bollingen Prize.

Stanley Kunitz (1905–   ). From Worcester, Massachusetts, Stanley Jasspon Kunitz proceeded to Harvard and then to many years as a reference-book compiler, chiefly for the H. W. Wilson Company. After World War II service with the Air Corps, he taught at Bennington, Brandeis, and other American colleges.

Selected Poems, 1928–1958 (1958) brought belated recognition, including a Pulitzer Prize, to this long-practicing poet of distinction. Though often classified as "metaphysical," Kunitz has a much wider range than Léonie Adams, from the mysticism of "Invocation" to the realistic picture of a victimized tourist in Rome in "The Thief." His favorite form is the rhymed quatrain where much like Emily Dickinson he enjoys the challenge of a tight form to express a sudden and witty apprehension of the pleasure and pain in everyday experience.

Elizabeth Bishop (1911–   ). A native of Worcester, Massachusetts, Elizabeth Bishop graduated from Vassar in 1934. She has held many poetry fellowships and has won the Pulitzer Prize. In recent years she has resided in Brazil.

Poems: North & South. A Cold Spring (1955) establishes her as one of the excellent poets of this era. Miss Bishop owes much to the intellectual poetry of Marianne Moore but in her own right is perhaps the most distinguished of poetic impressionists today. She creates a sharp, clean-cut impression in "The Fish," "The Weed," "The Monument," and suggests the moral implications to the individual who in the lonely modern world must fabricate his own integrity. Her poems are restrained yet show great ingenuity.

Muriel Rukeyser (1913–   ). A native New Yorker, Muriel Rukeyser never completed a college degree, although she attended Vassar and Columbia, but the latter conferred upon her an honorary doctorate in 1961. Since 1932 she has thrown herself vigorously into liberal and humanitarian causes. Working for a London magazine in Spain, she was in Barcelona on the day that the Spanish Civil War erupted. Since 1956 she has been on the faculty of Sarah Lawrence College. Her first book of poems was *Theory of Flight* (1935).

Selected Poems (1951) and subsequent poetry have united a passionate social protest with a mystical certainty that justice and freedom are realistic goals. Strongly romantic and melodic, her verses employ the imagery of modern technology and urban life. Typical is her long poem *The Soul and Body of John Brown* (1940), which envisages the American hero as heir to the Hebrew prophets of freedom and intensified life.

Dudley Fitts (1903–68). A Bostonian by birth and a Harvard graduate (1925), Dudley Fitts has taught at Choate School, Phillips Academy, Princeton University, and the Bread Loaf Writers' Conference. He was editor of the Yale Series of Younger Poets from 1960 until his death.

Aristophanes' Lysistrata (1954) and many subsequent translations place Fitts in the forefront of twentieth-century translators from Greek into English. Fitts's work unites genuine poetic skill with the modern mind and the modern idiom to produce translations that are fresh and exciting, while still impeccable in scholarship.

Yvor Winters (1900–68). Born in Chicago, Arthur Yvor Winters attended the University of Chicago in 1917–18 until he went to the

Southwest—New Mexico—for his health. In 1925 he received his A.B. and M.A. from the University of Colorado, and in 1934, his Ph.D. from Stanford University. He taught English at Stanford for many years. A noted traditionalist in verse, he received the Bollingen Prize in 1960. His volumes of poetry include *The Immobile Wind* (1921) and *The Bare Hills* (1927). His critical works are also well known; see Chapter 8.

Collected Poems (1952) contains only a small portion of Winters' complete work, but it encompasses all that he wished to keep, and outlines the evolution of his style. All of these poems show strictness of rhymes and of metrics, but within their disciplined form great energy is evident. Although Winters seems to insist on rational principles in his poetry, he is capable of creating images that go beyond the powers of the mind. Beneath the austere tone, there is a man often capable of tenderness.

"A Prayer for My Son" illustrates this last point. The poem is very formal, being addressed to "Eternal Spirit." The diction is restrained, the metrics and rhyme, regular. But under this seeming detachment is the father who says, "Pity this small and new / Bright soul on hands and knees."

John Ciardi (1916–   ). In his native Boston, John Ciardi was a *magna cum laude* graduate of Tufts College in 1938. In the next year he earned an M.A. from the University of Michigan. From 1940 to 1942 he taught at the University of Kansas City and then served in the Air Corps from 1942 to 1946. Since the war he has taught at Harvard and Rutgers. His recent volumes of poetry include *I Marry You* (1958) and *In the Stoneworks* (1961). Perhaps his major influence has been in criticism, especially as an editor of the *Saturday Review* since 1956.

Ciardi has a notable reputation as a translator. *The Inferno of Dante* (1954), *Dante's Purgatorio* (1961), and *Dante's Paradiso* (1971) are masterful translations of the *Divine Comedy* into English *terza rima*. Ciardi translations have vitality and exhibit his great ability to render poetry into poetry.

THE BLACK MOUNTAIN SCHOOL—THE PROJECTIVISTS. In the early fifties a group of poets led by Charles Olson of Black Mountain College began a minor revolt against the formal techniques of the more academic "neo-stylists" who had dominated poetry since the war. Olson in the essay "Projective Verse" described many of the principles of the Black Mountain group. He rejected traditional metric patterns, syntax and stanza form, and conceived of a verse that would correspond to the rhythms of the poet's breathing during the time when he was writing. The projectivist verse is characterized by an irregular spacing of lines and words, somewhat in the manner of e. e. cummings. There is also a strong tendency toward a collage-like effect, a juxtaposition and a piling up of perceptions. The form of the projectivist verse was also influenced by the improvisational jazz that was becoming popular in the early fifties.

Charles Olson (1910–   ). A native of Worcester, Massachusetts, Charles Olson holds a master's degree from Harvard and has taught at Clark, Harvard, and Black Mountain College. At the latter institution he was the acknowledged leader during the 1950s of the "projectivist" group of poets who published much work in *Black Mountain Review* and *Origin*. A notable piece of Olson scholarship was *Call Me Ishmael* (1947), a study of literary influences upon Herman Melville.

Maximus Poems (separate parts in 1953, 1956, and 1960) may be said to keynote "projectivist" poetry writing. Free verse is the medium for an undressed scrutiny of contemporary American life in colloquial, scornful, and freewheeling diction. Nonetheless, the erudition of Olson constantly peeps through. His affinity to his academic peers is shown in his attitude and learning, but is disguised by his freer style.

Robert Creeley (1926–   ). Robert Creeley was born in Arlington, Massachusetts. He was editor of the *Black Mountain Review* and is also a novelist.

For Love; Poems 1950–1960 (1962).

"Kore" tells of a man who met Chance upon a road and sat down with him "to move later if and as I might." When he does move and sumbits to Chance, he sees a wondrous thing—a mythical group—a lady with a flute accompanied by goat men. The poem expresses the Black Mountain group's concern with chance form and variation and the spontaneity and the wonderful visions that may come if one enters the realm of chance.

Robert Duncan (1919–   ). Born in Oakland, California, Robert Duncan has worked as a critic and an editor. His verse is characterized by its collage-like structure and juxtaposition of images. Works by Duncan include *Selected Poems* (1959) and *Roots and Branches* (1964).

The Opening of the Field (1960).

The poem "Ingmar Bergman's *Seventh Seal*" was inspired by this movie by Bergman. Like the clown in the movie, the poet sees that the answer to life is not to question suffering or sorrow over the crucified Christ, or fear the "Angel of Wrath." One should meet life with a happy innocence, for to be concerned with death and the hereafter, whether one fears them or scorns them, is to miss the joy of life.

THE SAN FRANCISCO SCHOOL—THE BEATS. San Francisco has long been a haven for American poets but it has often been overshadowed by the schools of poetry in New York. However, in the mid-fifties a distinctive San Francisco school was formed under the leadership of

Lawrence Ferlinghetti. The "Beat" movement received a great amount of publicity and for several years Ferlinghetti, Allen Ginsburg, and Gregory Corso enjoyed widespread popularity. Kenneth Rexroth was also for a time associated with the Beats. The Beat movement was an avowed rebellion against the values and institutions of the middle-class society of the fifties, and the rebellion took many forms. The Beat poets and writers were constantly on the road searching for new spiritual values yet somehow always despairing of finding them. Their interests ranged from drugs and jazz to Zen Buddhism, and these activities gave them a certain exotic flavor that was quickly imitated by many young people. The best examples of Beat poetry were Ferlinghetti's *A Coney Island of the Mind* and Ginsberg's *Howl*, both of which have had an extraordinarily large circulation. Perhaps the most important of the contributions of the Beats was in their many poetry readings in coffeehouses and in parks, a practice that brought poetry out of academic circles and to a public which had never before been so closely involved with it.

Allen Ginsberg (1926–   ). A Columbia graduate (1948), Allen Ginsberg, a native of Paterson, New Jersey, proudly points to his jobs as dishwasher, spot welder, stevedore, and porter. He has read his verse in many countries and it has been translated into many languages. William Carlos Williams, also from Paterson, wrote the introduction to *Howl*.

Howl, and Other Poems (1956) has as its title piece an exceptionally widely read poem. The rhythms of the Old Testament and of Whitman's poetry serve as vehicles for an impassioned diatribe against a dehumanized commercial culture which annihilates the creative artistry of man. The first section pictures the blighted lives of "the best minds of my generation." Without stability or worth-while values, the modern artist is driven to suffering and destruction. The second section blames the worship of Moloch (coarse materialistic greed) for the betrayal of the American myth and the persecution of the sensitive, perceptive soul. The third section addresses Carl Solomon (to whom the whole poem is dedicated) to identify the poet with all suffering mankind. The conclusion asserts the holiness of all life, however debased and thwarted. Ginsberg's other major work is *Kaddish and Other Poems 1958–1960* (1961).

Lawrence Ferlinghetti (1919–   ). A native of Yonkers, New York, Lawrence Ferlinghetti holds an A.B. from the University of North Carolina, an M.A. from Columbia, and a doctorate from the Sorbonne in Paris. He has been a leader of the "San Francisco Renaissance," making the North Beach a literary haven for young artists. His bookshop, City Lights Books, consistently published new authors to whom other publishers' doors were closed. Ferlinghetti is also an accomplished painter.

A Coney Island of the Mind (1958) has appealed, as the poet hoped, to a wide audience, many of whom are not regular readers of verse. The major influences upon his poetry seem to be e. e. cummings and two French poets, Jacques Prévert and Guillaume Apollinaire. In denunciation of the sterility and cheapness of the modern world, Ferlinghetti is both biting and ingeniously witty.

Kenneth Rexroth (1905–   ). A native of South Bend, Indiana, Kenneth Rexroth is largely self-educated and has mastered an extraordinary variety of foreign languages, ancient and modern. He has been one of the chief artists in the San Francisco School of the fifties and sixties. Initially Rexroth supported the Beats, although he later abandoned them. He is skillful in both original and translated poetry. Notable are *One Hundred Poems from the Japanese* (1954), *One Hundred Poems from the Chinese* (1956), *Thirty Spanish Poems of Love and Exile* (1956).

Gregory Corso (1930–   ). A native of New York City, Gregory Nunzio Corso had a difficult youth on the Lower East Side. He served a sentence in a reform school at age sixteen. When he returned to New York later, he became identified with Jack Kerouac, Allen Ginsberg, and their friends. He has taught at Buffalo University and published several books of poems, beginning with *Vestal Lady on Brattle* (1955) and including *Happy Birthday of Death* (1960), *Long Live Man* (1962), and *Selected Poems* (1962).

Gasoline (1958) contains a number of poems which are as impudent and irreverent as any of the other Beat poets. Corso's poems demonstrate verbal facility as well as intellectual content.

THE BLACK POETS. Although for a long time only infrequently taught in schools and universities, the work of black poets has developed along parallel lines with the work of other Americans of this century. The poetic resurgence in America and England after World War I was accompanied by the "Harlem Renaissance" which produced such outstanding poets as Langston Hughes and Countee Cullen, who have already been discussed in Chapter 2.

The black poets work in a wide variety of styles; many stay within the bounds of traditional English verse, while others make use of the rhythms and speech patterns of Negro folk songs, ballads, and blues. They speak of life in the urban slums, in the Southern countryside, or write historical narratives. Perhaps the only common ground among these poets is their consciousness of being black.

Robert Hayden (1913–   ). Robert Hayden was born in Detroit, Michigan, and graduated from Wayne State University. He received his M.A. from the University of Michigan and taught English there for two years. In 1946 he began teaching at Fisk University.

Selected Poems (1966).

"Frederick Douglass" invokes the spirit of the ex-slave who became a leading fighter for Negro freedom. Hayden describes freedom "as needful to man as air"; and when this freedom belongs to all, Douglass will be remembered not only with speeches and poems "but with the lives grown out of his life, and lives / fleshing his dream of the beautiful, needful thing."

Gwendolyn Brooks (1917–   ). Gwendolyn Brooks was born in Topeka, Kansas, and was raised and educated in Chicago. She has taught creative writing at several colleges, published three volumes of poetry, and written a short novel. In 1950 she won the Pulitzer Prize for her volume of poems *Annie Allen*.

Selected Poems (1963).

"Children of the Poor" expresses in beautifully precise language the fears of a mother for her child, fears which those without children can never know. The child is always reaching for things and she is afraid for him in a world where reaching out always leads to failure and despair. But she cannot suppress these instincts, for "reaching is his rule."

Sterling Brown (1901–   ). Born in Washington, D.C., Sterling Brown did his undergraduate work at Williams College and received his M.A. from Harvard in 1923. He has since taught at Howard University, published two volumes of literary criticism and written many essays. Brown has shown a remarkable ability in transforming Negro folk stories and ballads into a sharply biting poetry. Many of his early poems are collected in *Southern Road* (1932).

"Slim in Hell" tells of Slim Greer who goes to Heaven and then visits Hell to make a report on it at the request of St. Peter. Slim starts walking through Hell and it begins to look more and more like the South until finally Slim meets Satan who "turned into a cracker / Wid a sheriff's star." Slim manages to get back to Heaven where he wonders about whether he was in Hell or in Dixie. St. Peter sends him back to Earth until he can understand that they are one and the same place.

LeRoi Jones (1934–   ). LeRoi Jones was born in Newark, New Jersey, received his B.A. at Howard University, and did graduate work at The New School for Social Research and Columbia University. He is a successful playwright and critic and is an outspoken and active leader in the black nationalist movement.

Preface to a Twenty Volume Suicide Note (1961).

"Look for You Yesterday, Here You Come Today," in a languorous confessional style captures the mood of inaction and alienation of the poet in the city. He sees the loneliness and lack of passion around him and "The hours of the atmosphere / grind their teeth like hags"; his thoughts are "cold and lifeless / as subway rails." He thinks that his dilemma could be solved simply by a return to the joyful and oblivious desires of childhood, but he suddenly realizes that he can no longer understand how he felt then.

AMERICAN INDIAN POETRY. Until the latter part of the nineteenth century American Indian poetry, so integrally part of the original native American culture, was practically unknown to Western man. The first large-scale effort to translate Indian poetry was made by Henry Rowe Schoolcraft, whose major work, *Historical and Statistical Information Respecting . . . the Indian Tribes of the United States* (6 vols., 1851–57), encouraged many others to begin studies of the Indians and of their poetry.

The task of collection and translation of Indian poetry became the work of anthropologists, ethnologists, and linguists, in collaboration with native translators. This condition arose from the fact that translations of primitive poetry are impossible without a rather complete and systematic understanding of the culture and beliefs of the makers of the poetry. While poets have done some translation of American Indian poetry, the great body of work has been done by the kind of social scientist mentioned above. Through the excellence of the translations that we now possess these workers have shown themselves to be proficient and sensitive communicators of the Indian way of life.

Like all primitive poetry, the vast majority of Indian poetry had a definite purpose—the communication with supernatural forces in order to gain power over nature. The poems were sung and were often connected with rituals. Thus there can be found ceremonial chants, hymns, prayers, incantations, songs inspired by visions and dreams, songs connected with the hunt and with the harvest, and most commonly, songs of healing. There were humorous songs as well, but even these had religious significance. Poetry permeated every aspect of Indian life.

While the songs were strongly influenced by the natural environment in which the Indian lived, there is nothing in Indian poetry like the lyric ode to nature which is to be found in Western romantic poetry. Not only was the Indian's perception of nature greatly different from that of the poet of European tradition, but to engage in poetic outpourings of the soul was, to him, simply not the function of the word. The word had a sacred function and to use it for lesser purposes was considered wasteful.

The subject matter of a piece of Indian poetry varied widely according to the particular culture and locale in which it was written. To the desert-dwelling tribes of the Southwest, the rain was the most important element; in many of their songs images of rain, thunder, and lightning abound. Some of the tribes of the Pacific Northwest reveal their concepts of wealth and private property. The songs of other Indian groups reflect their customs, beliefs, and life styles. The songs were of course further differentiated by the minds of the individual poets.

Perhaps the most important characteristic in the structure of Indian poetry is its highly rhythmic quality. The singing and chanting, especially in rituals, almost always followed the rhythm set by drums or other percussive instruments. Like the symbology of Indian poetry, its meter is quite foreign to Western ears, and to translate the metrical patterns into English while keeping the sense is considered impossible. However, the larger rhythmic qualities such as the repetition of phrases and refrains can be readily translated.

Among the anthologies, *The Winged Serpent* (1946) by Margaret Astrov, *The Sky Clears* (1951) by A. Grove Day, and *Technicians of the Sacred* (1969) by Jerome Rothenberg are particularly valuable. The most comprehensive collection of Indian poetry is to be found in the Bureau of American Ethnology collection, which is available in all good libraries.

SOME RECENT POETS

May Swenson (1919–   ). Born in Logan, Utah, May Swenson attended Utah State University. She has been an editor of *New Directions*. Two of her volumes of poetry are *A Cage of Spines* (1958) and *To Mix with Time. New and Selected Poems* (1963).

"The Centaur" from *A Cage of Spines,* like most of Miss Swenson's poems, is energetic and direct. The exact details of a small girl pretending to be a horse suggest a mysterious world hidden behind the surface picture. The images are clearly drawn and beguiling, but the story, too, captures the reader.

W. D. Snodgrass (1926–   ). William DeWitt Snodgrass was born in Wilkinsburg, Pennsylvania. He attended the State University of Iowa where he earned a B.A. in 1949, an M.A. in 1951, and an M.F.A. in 1953. He has taught at Cornell University and Wayne State University. His first volume, *Heart's Needle* (1959), won the Pulitzer Prize. Snodgrass published only a very few poems until 1968, when his second book appeared, entitled *After Experience.*

Heart's Needle (1959) contains a number of highly personal poems dealing with his life and problems, but suggesting a much wider scope.

"April Inventory" is written in a complicated formal stanzaic form which helps to contain its emotion. Characterizing the professor who has not made an academic success of himself but who has also avoided the ulcers that go with success, Snodgrass still recognizes he is aging. He finds that there are things he must force himself to do that once were natural. But yet, he is happy that he has enjoyed life. Realizing that "trees turn bare and girls turn wives," he can still wish, "There is a loveliness exists, / Preserve us, not for special lists."

After Experience (1968) reveals a great deal of the man Snodgrass in his poetry. The experiences after which these poems were written are often painful, but still lovely and within reach of the reader. His diction is simultaneously both sentimental and tough. His phrases seem simple, but they are well grounded in fact. Snodgrass understands what he describes.

Sylvia Plath (1932–63). Born in Boston, Massachusetts, Sylvia Plath earned her B.A. *summa cum laude* from Smith College in 1955 and her M.A. in 1957 from Newnham College, Cambridge, where she was a Fulbright scholar. She was married to the British poet Ted Hughes. Her poems were widely published in magazines. Her volumes include *The Colossus* (1960), *Uncollected Poems* (1965), and a novel, *The Bell Jar*, first published under the pseudonym Victoria Lucas.

Ariel (1966) encompasses a group of poems written in the last months of Miss Plath's life. The birth of her son in 1962 triggered a creative period in which she would rise at four in the morning to write. The poems are very personal and confessional, but their tone is controlled. The book makes poetry and death inseparable. Like Robert Lowell, she shatters herself and looks for a new self, but in her case, the only outlet seemed to be suicide.

"Ariel," the title poem, although suggesting Shakespeare's blithe spirit, is about Miss Plath's horse. Both horse and rider need rapid motion, yet what emerges is not a feeling of pure force but the sense of her control over the horse, the poem, and her own life.

"Daddy," one of the last poems she wrote, translates her private search for her father into a general statement. Miss Plath, it seems, had to re-enact her father's death to be freed from its burden.

Anne Sexton (1928–   ). Born in Newton, Massachusetts, Anne Sexton was at one time a fashion model and later a disciple of the "confessional" school of poetry of Robert Lowell and W. D. Snodgrass. *All My Pretty Ones* (1962).

"The Starry Night," inspired by a painting by Van Gogh, captures the mystical power and furious wheeling of the stars which canopy the bleak and silent earth. The heavens seem alive and the sleeping town below "does not exist." The poet feels a great longing to die and fly "into that rushing beast of the night."

Denise Levertov (1923–   ). Denise Levertov was born in England but settled in the United States in 1948. She has worked as an editor and college lecturer and was associated with the Black Mountain group of poets. Volumes by Miss Levertov include *With Eyes at the Back of*

Our Heads (1959), *The Jacob's Ladder* (1961) and *O Taste and See* (1964).

Overland to the Islands (1958).

"Pure Products" tells of an old couple who came in their last years to California. They seem slightly ridiculous in their dress and mannerisms but the poet does not scorn them. She sees a strangely basic drive within them. "To the Sea some force has driven them away from a lifetime." As they prepare to die they have come to the original source of life.

Anthony Hecht (1923–   ). Born in New York City, Anthony Evan Hecht received his B.A. in 1944 from Bard College and his M.A. in 1950 from Columbia University. He has taught at Kenyon College, New York University, Bard College, and elsewhere. Many awards have been bestowed upon him, including the Prix de Rome in 1951 and Guggenheim fellowships in 1954 and 1959. In addition to his own poems, he has translated from both French and German poets.

A Summoning of Stones (1954), Hecht's first book of poems, reveals the poet as one interested in coordinating the different parts of a poem so that the meaning is supported by the metrical form. Some of the poems are breathy, romantic statements in complex syntax, but most of the poems work like a musical fugue toward a resolution where all the strains of meaning and form converge.

"The Origin of Centaurs" exhibits technical brilliance—the metrics and rhyme patterns are complicated but well handled. Retelling the Greek story of Ixion and Hera whose union resulted in the Centaur, this poem plays upon opposites. The interplay of art and nature, the contrast between the ephemeral and the solid worldly objects help to express the union of man and spirit.

The Hard Hours (1967) contains a selection of fifteen poems reprinted from his first book and some new poems. Relying on the metaphysical tradition, Hecht displays a sharp and formal wit. In some cases the poems seem so skillful or learned that they lose their emotional attachment. But most of the poems are well controlled and still powerful so that the reader submits to the experience itself.

James Dickey (1923–   ). Born in Atlanta, Georgia, James Dickey received his B.A. *magna cum laude* in 1949, and his M.A. in 1950 from Vanderbilt University. He was a night-fighter pilot in World War II and the Korean conflict. After being an advertising executive in New York City and Atlanta, Dickey taught at various colleges including Rice Institute, the University of Florida, and Reed College. He has published several volumes of poetry, including *Drowning With Others* (1962), *Helmets* (1964), and *Poems 1957–1967* (1967).

Poems 1957–1967 (1967) includes a number of new poems as well as some which appeared earlier in four previous books. In the new poems, he continues to confront themes of suburbia—home, youth, sports—but fails to engage in social problems. In spite of his apparent indifference to others and his concentration on himself, however, he does seem to head for a truth of his own. He experiments with the "split line" of Anglo-Saxon poetry which revolves around a central caesura and relies on alliteration.

"Falling," one of the new poems in this volume, takes as its subject a frequent preoccupation of Dickey—violence treated with characteristic American commercialism. The poem begins with a quotation from the New York *Times* about a stewardess who fell from a plane in flight. "Americans are both attracted / fascinated and troubled / repelled by this type of headline." The poem follows the girl as she falls, twisting, shedding her regulation clothing, to land, back broken, on the field in Kansas. Dickey transforms ordinary experiences of life, like undressing, like falling, into something frightening and unusual by changing the setting. Following the girl to her death, Dickey imagines her thoughts, actions, and sensations, showing the same mixed sense of attraction and fear that readers do.

James Wright (1927–   ). James Wright was born in Martins Ferry, Ohio, and became a member of "The Sixties" group with Robert Bly and others. He has written for magazines and has published several volumes of poetry translations. His poetry volumes include *The Green Wall* (1957) and *The Branch Will Not Break* (1963).

Saint Judas (1959).

"Saint Judas" tells of the traitor to Christ as he is on his way to commit suicide. He sees a man being beaten by hoodlums, and for no reason that he can fathom he runs and "held the man for nothing in my arms." It is a perfectly selfless act by a condemned man who has nothing to gain.

Robert Bly (1926–   ). Robert Bly was born in Madison, Minnesota. He has worked as a translator and has edited the magazine *The Sixties*. With James Wright and James Dickey he has tried to create a new poetry with great simplicity and a deep psychological imagery.

Silence in the Snowy Fields (1962).

"Snowfall in the Afternoon" describes an ordinary scene but invests it with a strange urgency and a sense of foreboding. With a heightened sense of reality Bly tells of a thick, almost material darkness which huddles by the earth and of a house and barn which seem to move together as protection from the cold.

CHAPTER SEVEN

The Drama in the Mid-Twentieth Century

NEW TENDENCIES IN THE DRAMA

The American drama in mid-century has two main focal points. The late forties and the fifties brought outstanding plays of great individuality by Arthur Miller and Tennessee Williams. They and other playwrights, each in his own way, expressed strong feelings of hopelessness and disillusionment about the condition of man in the modern world. The playwrights turned inward, and drama became more personal and subjective. The second focal point is the theater of the sixties, with the impact of the plays of Edward Albee. Some of Albee's plays are marked by overwhelming vitality, others by a searching and reflective quality. His work, although different in emphasis, expression, and theme, is like that of the other mid-century dramatists in being essentially personal and subjective.

The mainly amateur little theaters which had been such an important proving ground for new playwrights had largely disappeared. Nevertheless, in the fifties the off-Broadway movement began in New York's Greenwich Village and provided a needed forum for new playwrights. Soon a great many lofts, old union halls, and church cellars were converted into small playhouses. Professional actors performing for reduced pay in relatively inexpensive productions enabled the off-Broadway theaters to be as versatile and creative as the little theaters of the twenties. Albee's first plays were seen off Broadway, and recognition led to his later successes on Broadway. Another outlet for new creative work was provided by foundation grants to resident companies in various parts of the country. Staffed largely by professionals, these regional theaters have delighted out-of-town audiences with excellent productions of both the classics and the avant-garde.

The theater at present is moving in many different directions, and it is difficult to say where it is headed. Like most of the arts, drama is now in an experimental period, which hopefully will bring it new strength and new freshness.

MAJOR DRAMATISTS OF THE FIRST PART OF THE PERIOD

Tennessee Williams (1914–). Thomas Lanier Williams was born in Columbus, Mississippi. When Williams was twelve, his father took the family to St. Louis, where meager family finances during the Depression forced young Tom (Tennessee) to work as a clerk in a shoe warehouse. His education included courses at the University of Missouri and Washington University (St. Louis). He worked his way through the University of Iowa, receiving his A.B. in 1938. In adopting his pen name in 1939 he may have had in mind his ancestors who fought Indians in Tennessee.

The plays of Williams have a double fascination in their skillful construction and their frequent emphasis upon violence and sexuality. A recurring Williams theme is the study of a trapped character caught up in the decaying civilization of the South. Williams is deeply concerned with evil in the world, its roots in the rejection of life and sexuality. A true romantic, he is fascinated by the raw primitivism surging beneath the thin veneer of civilization.

The Glass Menagerie (1945), the first major play by Williams and continuously one of the most admired, is a strongly autobiographical work set in the 1930s.

Deserted by her husband, Amanda Wingfield pretends amidst lower middle-class life in St. Louis that she had been a vivacious, much-sought-after Southern belle. Her son, Tom, is disgusted with his monotonous clerical job in a shoe warehouse. Daughter Laura, a cripple, is abnormally shy, retreating from the world to live with her collection of small glass figurines. Continually urged by his mother to produce a suitor for Laura, Tom brings Jim O'Connor to dinner. Jim is polite to Laura, but he is already engaged to be married. Enraged by the failure of her elaborate preparations, Amanda tongue-lashes Tom to flight, leaving the two women in their unreal dream world.

The delicate fragility of the glass animals symbolizes Laura, a recluse from an indifferent world. She is sensitive, misunderstood, incapable of full engagement with life. For a few brief moments, to the surprise of Tom, she blossoms before Jim, whom she had known in high school and idolized. Laura is not the severely punished failure that many later Williams women are, because as the innocent she does not reject but is rejected. Always a remarkable portrayer of women, Williams creates a superb role in Amanda, a curious balance of the preposterous and the noble. She enunciates a theme which was to become a preoccupation with Williams: the struggle between an idealistic desire to recapture a lost world of dignity and the necessity to survive in the sordid, hostile present. Amanda, with the charm of a former Southern belle, tries to create an atmosphere of graciousness and civility. Tom is the poet that Williams himself had been at that age, shackled to a dull, tedious job and to a frustrated mother and sister, dwellers in another universe. His strength lies in his patience with Amanda and Laura, and especially in his highly sensitive understanding of Laura and deep affection for her. As foil to the perceptive Tom, Jim is average and unimaginative, yet appealing in his fumbling half-understanding of and kindness toward Laura.

Unity in *The Glass Menagerie* is achieved not by conventional techniques but by the pervasive mood and intense emotional excitement of the drama. There is a great freshness, too, and a poetic tenderness which sets this early play apart from Williams' later works marked by violent action.

A Streetcar Named Desire (1947) is one of the most powerful and striking works of the American theater.

Blanche DuBois arrives in New Orleans to visit her sister, Stella, and Stella's husband, Stanley Kowalski. Blanche clings to her aristocratic heritage and tries to maintain an air of delicacy and good breeding, even though she has lost her home and money. She immediately comes into conflict with the crude and frank animal nature of Stanley. Stanley investigates her earlier life and reveals that she had been a prostitute and had also seduced a boy in the school where she taught. Blanche is attracted to Mitch, a friend of Stanley, but Mitch deserts her when he hears about her past. The central conflict of the play is between the starkly realistic attitude of Stanley and the imaginative dreaminess of Blanche. While Stella is in the hospital giving birth to a child, Stanley insists upon sexual intimacy with Blanche. Then, with her pretensions destroyed, Blanche loses her mental balance and is sent to an asylum. The height of crisis occurs in an argument between Stanley and Stella, and it seems for a moment that Stella will side with Blanche and leave Stanley. In the end Stanley and Stella accept the stronger realities of their life together.

Summer and Smoke (1948) has a more abstract quality.

At the town park before the stone angel named Eternity, Alma Winemiller, daughter of the Episcopalian clergyman, and John Buchanan, son of the town physician, hold a childhood tryst. Alma grows up to be a prim young woman, while John combines medicine and philandering. Alma tries to prevent John's consorting with Rosa Gonzales, daughter of a Mexican gambler. Standing before an anatomy chart in the doctor's office, John gives Alma a lecture on the body. By stemming an epidemic in a nearby community, John becomes a hero and crowns his new image of respectability by marrying Nellie Ewell. Forlorn Alma picks up a traveling salesman.

The opposing symbols are the statue (spirit) and the anatomy chart (body). Apparently his anatomy lesson converts Alma from the spirit to the flesh, while worldly success brings new seriousness to John. The play's dominating note, with its element of pathos, is the failure of communication between the central characters, as seen in the groping but always thwarted attempts of Alma and John to establish a viable relationship.

The Rose Tattoo (1951) has as its setting a Sicilian colony on the Gulf Coast between Mobile and New Orleans. Much of the play was written in Italy.

Serafina delle Rose adores her husband, Rosario, not realizing that he is a smuggler having an affair with Estelle Hohengarten, blackjack dealer at the local gambling casino. After Rosario's death Serafina laments her husband as a saint and puritanically guards her daughter, Rosa, against Jack Hunter, an innocent youth. Learning of her husband's infidelity, Serafina takes up with Alvaro Mangiacavallo; and Rosa, with this example from her mother, races to Jack, who is about to ship out as a sailor. Displaying a rose tattoo upon his chest, Alvaro proclaims his liaison with Serafina to the entire community.

Williams' tone has changed in this play from tragic to comic. His obvious intent is a joyous hymn to robust natural love, to Italian gaiety and warmth. The language is American Southern with a Sicilian flavor. Serafina lives for sex. Various erotic symbols—a bleating goat, a squawking parrot, distant Negro laughter, mounting volume from a "blues piano"—serve as accompaniment. Contrasted to the outgoing, vital life are frustrated people like Rosa's prim high-school teacher. Then, too, the death of Rosario early in the play contrasts with the earthy comedy which soon develops.

Camino Real (1953) is an expressionistic drama. It is recounted as a dream of the idealist Don Quixote, who finds a modern world of heartless materialism and universal decay. The one wholesome character is the irrepressible all-American boy Kilroy, cursed with a weak heart and eventually dying at the hands of street cleaners. Many characters roam through this drama, some offering moments of hope, but most suggesting perversion and degeneracy. The playwright says that *Camino*

Real (Royal Road) "is nothing more or less than my conception of the time and world that I live in." To critics, appalled by what they deemed the Williams universe of ultimate corruption, the playwright quoted a line from Don Quixote in the play: "Life is an unanswered question, but let's still believe in the dignity and importance of the question." The last words of the play, "The violets have broken the rocks," seem to imply that fragile life with its imaginative beauty and natural love will somehow triumph over the cruelty and ugliness of the modern age.

Cat on a Hot Tin Roof (1955) exists in two versions—the first as originally written by Williams and the second as modified by him for production under the urging of Elia Kazan, the director.

Big Daddy, master of the Pollitt plantation, is dying of cancer, although he is deceived into believing that all he has is a "spastic colon." His older son, Gooper, and Gooper's wife, Mae, and their five children have descended on the house to await his death and their inheritance. Big Daddy's younger son, Brick, a former athlete and sports announcer turned alcoholic, is in a state of despair because of the atmosphere of lies and hypocrisy which he has been forced to live in. He has given up sleeping with his wife, Maggie, and his only goal is to drink every day until he feels that "click" in his head which turns on a mellow world in which he can find peace. Yet it is Brick who is closest to Big Daddy, and the talk which they have in the second act is the climax of the play. Big Daddy brings up the unspoken subject of Brick's past friendship with Skipper, a fellow athlete. The details of the friendship are never clearly revealed, but there were rumors that it had developed into a homosexual affair. Innuendos on this subject by Maggie had caused Skipper to drink himself to death; and to escape the burden of rumors and lies, Brick became an alcoholic. Brick, in the frank spirit of his father's statements, tells Big Daddy what the doctors have said, that he is dying of cancer. In the original version the last we see of Big Daddy is at the end of the second act when he exits cursing his family. In the production version Big Daddy returns briefly and seems more reconciled to his fate. Maggie lies that she and Brick are going to have a child (that they are childless has been another source of conflict in their lives); and in the end there is a possibility that Brick will make her wish come true.

The dominant mood of the play is one of social and familial disintegration. A more positive emphasis, illustrated in the climactic second act, is on the need for a moment when those unnamable truths that are an undercurrent in the lives of most families are brought into the open.

Sweet Bird of Youth (1959) tells of an actress past her prime who seeks to retain her grasp upon the things which mean most to her through an intimate relation with a handsome young gigolo. The first act has the poetic and searching quality often characteristic of Williams. The second act, concerning other events in the young man's life, is nightmarish, sordid, depressing. The last act, though marked by disillusionment, recaptures some of the original theme suggested by the title.

The Night of the Iguana (1962), like *Summer and Smoke*, has a rather abstract quality.

Lawrence Shannon, an unfrocked cleric, conducts tours through Mexico. At the Costa Verde Hotel the lecherous Shannon seems logical prey for the proprietress, the widowed Maxine Faulk. However, Shannon seduces sixteen-year-old Charlotte Goodall in spite of the vehement opposition of spinsterish Miss Judith Fellowes. More gently, Hannah Jelkes converses with Shannon. Hannah is a penniless sketch artist who draws portraits in nightclubs and cabarets, while her aged grandfather, Nonno, recites his second-rate poems. Completing his last poem, Nonno dies. Hannah persuades Shannon to release an iguana which Maxine had planned to eat.

Shannon's freeing of the iguana symbolizes his own release. He had been guilt-ridden by the thought of his sins of lust. He frees himself from Maxine and Charlotte. Hannah suggests that he turn to true compassion. A profoundly good woman, Hannah resists Shannon's attempt to corrupt her through sensuality. Shannon is finally able to perceive others not as means to his sensual gratification, but indeed as fellow human beings.

Arthur Miller (1915–   ). Arthur Miller graduated from high school in his native New York in 1932, and in the Depression days worked for two years in an automobile-parts warehouse to obtain money for college. He studied at the University of Michigan, and after graduating in 1938 returned to New York.

Arthur Miller senses more than any other American dramatist the painful insecurity of man in the twentieth-century industrial world. His plays reveal his moral earnestness and profound commitment to social responsibility. "There is a world to make," he declares, "a civilization to create that will move toward the only goal the humanistic, democratic mind can ever attempt with honor."

All My Sons (1947) was Miller's first important play.

During the war Joe Keller and Mr. Deever were partners in a concern making airplane parts for the Army Air Force. Defective cylinder heads (twenty-one flyers died from this negligence) resulted in trials in which Joe was exonerated, while Deever went to prison. And also during the war Joe's son Larry was listed as "missing in action." Joe's other son, Chris, now (three and a half years later) loves Ann Deever, formerly engaged to Larry. His mother demurs, hoping that Larry is still alive. Chris learns that it was his father and not Deever who had been guilty in the matter of the defective cylinders. To win permission for her marriage to Chris, Ann shows the letter written to her by Larry on the day of his death, in which he plans suicide at chagrin over his father's crime. Learning the truth, Joe Keller kills himself.

Another dramatist might have made Joe merely an unscrupulous profiteer. Miller creates a far more impressive and universalized character in the simple, well-intentioned man who cut a few corners to meet an exacting production schedule. When Ann reveals Larry's last letter, Joe comprehends how Larry saw him as the betrayer of twenty-one other American sons who lost their lives because of his carelessness. Gazing at the letter from his dead boy, the slowly comprehending Joe says: "Sure, he was my son. But I think to him they were all my sons. And I guess they were, I guess they were."

Death of a Salesman (1949) is unquestionably one of the most notable modern American dramas.

All his life Willy Loman has been a traveling salesman in New England, working out of the home office in New York. Tired at the age of sixty-three and mentally disturbed, he breaks off his wonted circuit and wearily comes home, hopeful that the company will give him an office job. Willy is particularly disappointed in his older son, Biff, a high-school football hero but now a drifter. The shiftlessness of Biff actually dates from his surprise visit to his father's hotel room, where Biff found Willy with a prostitute; his idealization of his father destroyed, Biff has accomplished nothing since. Willy tries to get Biff started in a sporting-goods store along with Happy, his younger brother, but this scheme falls through as do all Biff's enterprises. Howard Wagner, Willy's boss, dismisses him because the aging man is no longer truly competent. Willy borrows money from his neighbor Charley but refuses a nonsales job offered by Charley. Biff forces his father to confront the truth: The whole trio of Loman males are failures. To give his family the $20,000 of his life insurance, Willy commits suicide. Linda, Willy's wife, cannot understand why Willy killed himself. She has just made the last payment on the house, and at last they would be free.

Willy Loman is the victim of a world in which the structure of society has changed too rapidly and old values have been too quickly destroyed for him to understand. Willy's roots are in the old America with its ideals of rugged individualism and an ever-present frontier. Wherever he turns he sees machines and men who think like machines, and he retreats to a dream world of the past. But the pattern is suddenly broken when Biff tells Willy that he loves him. Willy is deeply touched, and rouses himself, feeling a need for action. Willy's car is the instrument of his livelihood and its moods are constantly plaguing him, and it fittingly becomes the instrument of his destruction. Whether his suicide can be interpreted as a free act or an act of desperation by a demented soul is left to the audience to decide.

The Crucible (1953), set in Salem, Massachusetts, in 1692, suggests a parallel between colonial witch-hunting and the political "witch-hunting" during the McCarthy era of the early fifties. When witch mania seizes Salem, one of the young women, Abigail, who yearns for farmer John Proctor, accuses Elizabeth, Proctor's wife, of witchcraft; Abigail hopes thus to win Proctor for herself. Proctor tries to get his servant girl, Mary Warren, to testify that the charges are false, but the ignorant girl, mercilessly badgered on the witness stand, in her confusion accuses Proctor himself of witchcraft. Proctor is told by the judge that his life will be spared if he will identify other witches, but he refuses and goes to his execution.

Proctor is a truly human man, guilty of minor sins as all men are, and aghast at mass madness that indiscriminately chops down innocent people. In refusing to compromise his integrity and in trying by his own death to bring a halt to the prevailing insanity, he reaches genuinely heroic stature.

Throughout the play the conflict between good and evil reveals the dangerous effect of negative forces upon positive goals in modern life.

A View From the Bridge (1955) is set in the Red Hook section of Brooklyn. Miller had heard of this episode in his youth.

Eddie Carbone, a longshoreman, lives a relatively happy life with his wife, Beatrice, and their adopted niece, Catherine. Two cousins of Beatrice, Marco and Rodolpho, arrive illegally from Sicily and are harbored by Eddie in their apartment. When Rodolpho and Catherine fall in love, Eddie is crushed. He tries to talk them out of it, threatens Rodolpho, and implies that he is a homosexual. Eddie goes to the lawyer Alfieri to see if there is some legal action that he can take, but Alfieri tells him that nature is simply running its course and there is nothing he or anyone can do. Finally, in despair, Eddie informs on Marco and Rodolpho to the immigration authorities. Marco curses Eddie for the betrayal. They fight, and Eddie is killed.

Originally the play was written as a verse tragedy and much of the dialogue remains poetry printed as prose. The lawyer Alfieri comments on the action from time to time, gives warnings, and intensifies the feeling of impending doom. He makes clear that these tragic yet seemingly ordinary events are part of man's present pattern of life, with a significance broader than that of individual lives.

After the Fall (1964) is a bluntly confessional drama of Arthur Miller's life with Marilyn Monroe. Miller married Marilyn Monroe in 1956 when she was one of Hollywood's most publicized glamour girls. Miller's first marriage, from 1940 to 1956, had ended in divorce. Of this play Miller said that the action takes place "in the mind, thought, and memory of Quentin."

The first act of *After the Fall* examines the origins of insecurity and guilt feelings in Quentin. His mother, Rose, had left him alone once in his childhood while she pursued her pleasures in Atlantic City. Quentin feels ashamed of his failure to rally behind a friend pilloried during the "un-American" investigations. His first wife, Louise, in her demands makes no rapprochement with him.

The second act recounts the harrowing second marriage of Quentin, this time to Maggie. As an immensely publicized popular singer, she is a national sex symbol, gradually becoming incapable of finding her true self amidst her mythical build-up. Maggie's mother once tried to kill her. She has pitifully sought security with many men, and under Quentin's scrutiny she increasingly feels guilty and still essentially unwanted. Maggie commits suicide, and leaves Quentin to Holga, a German girl purified through the persecution of a Nazi concentration camp.

Autobiographical as much of the play is, Quentin is certainly not portrayed flatteringly. He wishes Maggie to conceive of him as a rescuer, yet he sees her as scapegoat for his sense of guilt and inadequacy. Presumably, only through suffering and understanding could a viable marital relationship be established.

An early work of Miller on a personal and social theme is the novel *Focus* (1945).

William Inge (1913–   ). Born in Independence, Kansas, William Inge received an A.B. from the University of Kansas in 1935 and an M.A. from Peabody Teachers College in 1938. From the latter year until 1943 he taught at Stephens College, Missouri. From 1943 to 1946 he was drama critic for the St. Louis *Star-Times*. Witnessing and admiring Tennessee Williams' *The Glass Menagerie*, he decided to turn to playwriting himself. From 1946 to 1949 he taught at Washington University in St. Louis. The next year his Broadway career began.

Inge's concern has been with middle-class life in the Midwest, finding "surprising depths of feeling that lie just below the public surface of human personality." The search for mutual love provides the nearest thing to security for his characters, who thus can obtain some relief from their failures and frustrations. Inge's plays are largely in the realistic tradition.

Come Back, Little Sheba (1950) was Inge's first play to win acclaim.

Doc Delaney had made Lola pregnant while he was in medical school. He dropped his studies to marry her, and practiced as a chiropractor. He became an alcoholic but took the cure and hasn't had a drink in a long time. Doc and Lola's only child died at birth, and Doc now takes a protective interest in their coed boarder, Marie. But Doc becomes disillusioned when he discovers that Turk, a husky athlete, has spent the night with Marie, and he goes on a drunken spree during which he tries to kill Lola. Marie leaves to get married to Bruce, who has just arrived. Doc returns from a cure in the hospital, to begin life again with Lola.

Doc is tortured throughout the play by guilt feelings. He is further troubled by his mixed sexual and fatherly feelings toward Marie, and he considers the innocent sensuality of his wife not becoming in a wife. The title of the play refers to Lola's constantly calling for her lost dog, Little Sheba, symbolic of the youthful dreams which she has not yet let go of. But as the play ends she has a dream that Sheba has died, and suddenly she looks at Doc and at her own life in a new and realistic way and joyfully decides to embrace this new reality.

Picnic (1953), perhaps Inge's best play, again has for its subject matter the lives of middle-class people in a Midwestern community.

Hal Carter, a former college football star and now a drifter, enters into the lives of the middle-class characters in a small Kansas town. He lures Madge Owens away from her boy friend Alan Seymour and disrupts and changes the lives of the other characters. Hal is unjustly accused of car theft and is forced to leave town on a freight train. Madge decides to follow him.

The theme of the play, like that of others of Inge's plays, is the sharp contrast between the ideal and the real, the course that life is expected to take and the course that it really does take. Flo, Madge's mother, wants a comfortable and stable middle-class life for her daughter. She is at first despondent but finally resigned to the burst of passion by Madge which suddenly reverses her well-laid plans. Hal has affected each of the characters in different ways. The schoolteacher loses her feeling of haughty independence and realizes she needs male companionship. Mrs. Potts feels a new experience of warmth and life. Most of the women in the town had become lonely, and the men were thinking only of their work. The brief visit of Hal has awakened dormant passions within these townsfolk, and has given them a new eagerness for living.

Bus Stop (1955) employs the old dramatic device of throwing together a bizarre assembly of widely different personalities.

A restaurant thirty miles from Kansas City is the refuge for a motley group during a blizzard. The cast includes the worldly-wise and widowed proprietress, the small-town sheriff, an aged roué, a friendly but innocent waitress, a cowboy and his side-kick, a brassy night-club singer with the inevitable heart of gold, and the coarse and lecherous bus driver. During the enforced wait most of their lives are changed. Elma, the waitress, has an important lesson in handling an old reprobate like Gerald Lyman. Grace, owner of the bus stop, reaches an understanding with Carl, the bus driver. Cherie, the entertainer, changes from a reluctant captive of Bo, the cowpoke, into his loving admirer. Bo's pal, Virgil, leaves when he realizes that Bo is going to be married. This play is not actually melodrama. The characters are unromanticized people with unexciting careers. None of them can ever reach the rainbow's end, but they prove tolerantly capable of making the best of life's ambiguous bargains.

The Dark at the Top of the Stairs (1957) marks an Inge move toward more poetic symbolism. The title is Inge's metaphor for any man's fear about the uncertain future.

Rubin Flood is a traveling salesman whose product, harnesses, is becoming increasingly unprofitable. Seldom at home, he leaves the training of ten-year-old Sonny and sixteen-year-old Reenie to his wife, Cora. Quarreling over the high-priced party gown of Reenie, Rubin leaves Cora. Reenie has chosen her escort, Sammy, a Jewish boy. Later reflecting upon the anti-Semitic attitude at the country club, Sammy commits suicide. Reenie is deeply saddened. Sonny begins to grow up, trying to comfort his sister. Rubin returns, now selling agricultural machinery. He and Cora are reunited.

Sonny is afraid to climb alone the stairway leading to a darkened upper hall. Each of the characters in this drama has his own dreaded stairway to climb. While other characters, such as Lottie, Cora's sister, fail to make the symbolic climb, each of the Floods succeeds.

OTHER NOTABLE DRAMATISTS

Robert Anderson (1917–   ). A native New Yorker, Robert Woodruff Anderson attended Phillips Exeter Academy and graduated from Harvard in 1939. While an undergraduate and subsequently while teaching English at Harvard, he wrote dramas. From 1942 to 1946 he served in the U. S. Navy. He has been active in teaching and in writing scripts for television and the movies.

Tea and Sympathy (1953) takes its title from the twofold responsibility usually assumed by the wives of masters in preparatory schools.

Tom Lee, a student at a boy's boarding school, is looked upon as different by the other boys because he is more interested in music and poetry than in sports. After a time, he is accused, unjustly, of a homosexual affair with one of his teachers. The teacher is dismissed, and Tom is subjected to the verbal abuse of his schoolmates. But his chief tormenter is Bill Reynolds, the master of the house in which Tom resides. Tom's only real friend is Laura, Bill's wife. Bill is jealous of Laura's affection for Tom, and this goads him on to further vindictiveness toward the boy. At the suggestion of Al, his roommate, Tom, to prove his manhood, makes an excursion to the local prostitute, Ellie Martin. But he cannot force himself to make love to her. Since Ellie's place is out of bounds to the students, Tom is to be expelled from the school. There is a confrontation between Laura and Bill in which Laura brings out the possibility that Bill is accusing Tom of a condition which he unconsciously fears is within himself. Laura tells Bill that she is going to leave him. But first she must somehow reassure Tom that he is normal. She enters his room, locks the door, and begins to make love to him as the curtain comes down.

Laura is the one character whose concept of right and wrong flows from within rather than from the dictates of convention. In focusing on her and Tom, Anderson makes clear his point that society must be broader in its tolerance.

Later Robert Anderson wrote a group of four short plays produced together under the title *You Know I Can't Hear You When the Water's Running* (1967). Imbued with the comic spirit suggested by the title, these plays add a new dimension to Anderson's work, and give much pleasure to the audience. A more recent Anderson play is *I Never Sang for My Father* (1968).

Arthur Laurents (1918–). Born in Brooklyn, Arthur Laurents studied playwriting at Cornell and radio script writing at New York University. Before entering the Army, he was already a well-known writer for radio.

Home of the Brave (1945), written while Laurents was still in the Army, is one of the few good plays about World War II to hit Broadway.

While fighting the Japanese, Peter Coen's comrade, Finch, dies in Coen's arms. Elation at his own survival quickly changes to guilt sensations in Coen, and he is unable to use his legs. Sodium amytal treatments recall his previous life, and he comes to believe that his feelings are associated with his Jewish origin. But a casual admittance to similar feelings by Mingo, another of his soldier associates, causes Coen to realize that he is a normal human being, and he is cured of his temporary disability.

The Time of the Cuckoo (1952), a by-product of a Laurents tour of Europe, has been his most popular play.

American schoolmarm Leona Samish is attracted in Venice to Renato Di Rossi, an antique dealer. Her feelings are repressed at first. Then finding that he is married, she is repelled at his advances. But when she meets an American artist, Eddie Yeager, and finds that he has been unfaithful to his wife, June, Leona yields to Di Rossi. Di Rossi breaks off the affair not from any moral scruples but because Leona's responses are complex, rather than direct.

Two cultural viewpoints are neatly contrasted. After this one exotic interlude, Leona returns home and falls back into her conventional attitudes and existence, with only an occasional furtive, happy memory of the days in Venice.

The excellent movie *Summertime* (1955) is based on this play.

A Clearing in the Woods (1957) is Laurents' most experimental play. At a clearing in the woods (i.e., at a point of illumination amidst the forest of error) mature Virginia meets three women of different ages. Not initially recognizing them, she gradually learns that all three are herself at various stages of her life. She also sees again: George, with whom she trifled; Andy, a fiancé whom she discarded because of his inability to make money; and Pete, her ex-husband, whom she dismissed as weak.

Virginia is the American woman seen through her metamorphoses as sweetheart, fiancée, and wife. Laurents diagnoses her as infected with "the loneliness afoot in this country." She relentlessly demands of others perfection in their achievements and devoted love to bestow on her. She comes to realize that she has indeed been loved, and always by completely normal human beings. She, too, is an imperfect mortal who must accept the world and herself as they actually are.

Laurents wrote the libretto for the musical *West Side Story* (1957), with music by Leonard Bernstein.

Paddy Chayefsky (1923–   ). Sidney Chayevsky was born in New York City and received his B.S. from C.C.N.Y. in 1943. He served in the U. S. Army, 1943–45. In 1952 he began a meteoric career in television script writing. His *Marty* (1953) was the first television script to be made into a motion picture.

Chayefsky turned successfully from television to drama for the theater.

The Tenth Man (1959) is a modern play, drawing in some respects from a Yiddish theater classic, *The Dybbuk* by Solomon Ansky. A *dybbuk* is the soul of a dead man who experienced injustice in life and inhabits the body of a living being until the wrong is righted. The entire action of *The Tenth Man* occurs in a shabby New York Orthodox synagogue against the background of Jewish prayers and ceremonial rites.

Evelyn must undergo exorcism for the dybbuk possessing her (it is the spirit of a woman seduced by her grandfather in Europe). Her cynical boy friend Arthur, a young lawyer, deems a psychiatrist more useful. In the ceremony that he unwillingly attends, exorcism takes place in him. He returns to consciousness with a "desire to wake in the morning, a passion for the things of life." Arthur and Evelyn leave, bonded in love.

The original Ansky drama breathed the folklore world of East European Jewry, with an undercurrent of hostility to Orthodoxy. Chayefsky's modern adaptation assails the cynicism of today's intellectuals and offers redemption through love.

Gideon (1961) was written after intensive travels and study in Israel. Disguised as The Angel, but too frequently lapsing into calling himself God, the deity raises cloddish Gideon to save Israel. In spite of miraculous interventions, God is piqued to find Gideon unwilling to ascribe all his victories to the deity. Gideon suggests to his people a "historical, economic, sociopsychological, and cultural" explanation for his successes. Though somewhat ruffled, God shrugs and says to the audience:

> "Man believes the best he can
> Which means, it seems, belief in man."

Like Archibald MacLeish in *J.B.*, which is an outstanding and moving recent drama about religion (see Chapter 6, page 331), Chayefsky proclaims that man must develop beyond God, assume God's grandeur, and construct a human morality. Chayefsky remarked: "I don't want to compare it with *J.B.* My play is not about God testing Gideon. It's about Gideon testing God."

A MORE RECENT MAJOR DRAMATIST

Edward Albee (1928–). Born in Washington, D.C., Edward Franklin Albee was an adopted child of the Albee family. He graduated from Choate School but left Trinity College, Connecticut, before completing his sophomore year. He tried a variety of New York jobs ranging from counterman in a luncheonette to continuity writer for a radio station. In 1953 Thornton Wilder suggested that he turn to playwriting. *Fam and Yam* (1960) was one of his earliest-written dramas.

Albee is the most individual and exciting recent dramatic talent in the American theater. Like the early O'Neill, Albee brings a vitality which is influenced to some extent by qualities of recent European drama, especially as expressed in the works of Eugène Ionesco, Samuel Beckett, and Jean Genêt, exponents of the Theater of the Absurd. Ionesco defines the concept of the movement: "Absurd is that which is devoid of purpose. . . . Cut off from his religious, metaphysical, and transcendental roots, man is lost; all his actions become senseless, absurd, useless." The dramatists of the absurd attempt a unity of the theme with irrational form and with "slice-of-life" dialogue, often apparently pedestrian and unpredictable. Albee insists that "the responsibility of the playwright is to comment boldly and relentlessly on his time."

The Zoo Story (1959), a one-act play, was first staged in Berlin.

Since its first New York performance it has frequently been played in this country.

Peter, an executive in a small publishing house, is sitting on a bench in Central Park when he is approached by Jerry, who attempts to get Peter involved in a conversation. Peter is reluctant to deal with the rather seedy-looking character and would much prefer to be left alone with his book; but Jerry is insistent. Jerry pries into Peter's personal life, asking him about his job, his family, and other matters. Jerry freely tells of his own life style—that he is a homosexual and that he lives in a tiny room in a brownstone boardinghouse. He gives detailed descriptions of the objects in his room, his neighbors, and of his encounter with his landlady's dog. Jerry has been hinting all along that something happened to him at the zoo, where he had been before he encountered Peter. He always seems to be on the point of relating this zoo story when he gets off onto another subject. Now he sits beside Peter and tries to take the whole bench for himself. Peter protests, but Jerry keeps shoving him further down the bench. They scuffle, and Jerry takes out a knife and throws it at Peter's feet. He taunts Peter into picking it up, and then Jerry runs on the blade himself. Dying, he finally tells what happened at the zoo: "I think that while I was at the zoo I decided that I would walk north . . . northerly, rather . . . until I found you . . . or some-body . . . and I decided that I would talk to you . . . I would tell you things." Jerry finishes, wipes the knife clean of fingerprints, and dies. The distracted Peter rushes off.

Jerry is trying to establish contact with Peter through defensive walls that people build around themselves. Jerry is in despair over the im-possibility of communicating in the large city. He feels a great need to love and to touch another person. He is determined to make another person feel something toward him whether it be hate or love; and Peter is the person that he has chanced upon. All his efforts at involving Peter in his life fail until he suddenly realizes that his words are getting him nowhere and that somehow he must act.

Who's Afraid of Virginia Woolf? (1962) takes place in a small college in New England.

It is late Saturday night when George, a history teacher, and Martha, his wife, arrive home from a faculty party given by her father, the president of the college. A few minutes later, much to George's surprise, Nick, a biology teacher, and his wife, Honey, arrive. Martha had invited them to come over after the party. For the rest of the play Nick and Honey are to be witnesses and unwilling participants in the vicious psychological warfare between George and Martha. Martha tries to humiliate George by mocking his failures in the history department and his attempts at being a writer. George retaliates by telling of Martha's voracious and perverted sexual appetites. Nick at one point confides in George his real reason for marrying Honey—that she had had an "hysterical pregnancy" which after they were married turned out to be a false alarm. George reveals this fact when they are all in the room together, and humiliates both the guests. Martha gets even with George by making love to Nick while Honey is too drunk to understand what is going on. The games continue until Martha breaks a rule. She mentions the subject of her and George's son, whom, it later becomes clear, they had invented because they could not have children. They had mutually agreed only to mention him between themselves, and Martha's breaking of this rule makes George devise the final trick that will end the games. He announces that a telegram has arrived saying their son was killed in an auto crash. The news crushes Martha. After Honey and Nick leave, it appears that perhaps George and Martha will have a better life together now that they will no longer depend upon the unreality of references to their imaginary son. At last they have only their love for each other, and it may or may not be enough.

Tiny Alice (1964) in a very different mood demonstrates Albee's amazing eloquence in writing dramatic language, as well as his freshness of concept.

The Cardinal receives the Lawyer in his garden. They had gone to school together and even then they had loathed each other. Now they make no effort to conceal their mutual hatred and their preliminary remarks are articulate and deeply biting. They shortly get down to business. The Lawyer represents a Miss Alice and has come to inform the Cardinal that she desires to give the Church $100 million a year for the next twenty years. Upon hearing this the Cardinal has a difficult time concealing his greed, and agrees to the Lawyer's stipulation that the Cardinal will send his secretary, Brother Julian, to the mansion of Miss Alice to act as intermediary in the negotiations. Brother Julian arrives at the home of Miss Alice and is greeted by the Butler. Julian meets Miss Alice and for most of the rest of the play is subjected by her to a series of physical and spiritual temptations. Julian is fascinated by the scale model of the mansion which rests on a table in the library. This tiny house evidently represents a deeper reality of which the large house is only the appearance. In the same way there must be somewhere a Tiny Alice who is truer to life's reality than the Miss Alice of the play's action.

Through the windows of the tiny house, the large house is seen to be reproduced exactly—in miniature. And seemingly there is a *tinier* house in the library of the tiny house. A fire begins in the chapel of the tiny house, and simultaneously a fire begins in the chapel of the mansion. The others in the group, which includes the Cardinal and the Lawyer, seem to accept such an event as being natural. It is only Julian who cannot understand this and the other mysteries which are gradually closing in on him. Through Miss Alice he discovers the earthly pleasures which he has so long denied himself—delicate food and old wine, leisure, and finally Miss Alice herself. They are married, and Julian believes that they are to begin a normal life. He only gradually becomes aware that the Lawyer and the Butler and Miss Alice are representatives of some vastly intelligent evil force which is determined to possess his soul. When the full realization hits him he tries to escape and is shot by the Lawyer. Julian is left alone dying, and speaks a long rambling soliloquy in which he tries to understand what has been happening.

OTHER IMPORTANT RECENT DRAMATISTS

Lorraine Hansberry (1930–65). Lorraine Hansberry was born in Chicago and attended the University of Wisconsin and Roosevelt College. She was one of the first Negro dramatists to win a wide audience, and the fine quality of her writing was immediately recognized.

A Raisin in the Sun (1959) employs an all-Negro cast except for the part of Lindner.

The play opens in the crowded Younger apartment in the South Side of Chicago. There is a nervous tension between Walter Younger and his wife, Ruth. The reason for this is the insurance check for $10,000 which Mama Younger, Walter's mother, is going to receive the next day. Walter wants the money to invest in a liquor business with friends of his. He has had quite enough of being a chauffeur, and he wants Ruth to ask Mama to give him the money. In the opening scene we are also introduced to Beneatha Younger, Walter's sister. She is a college student intent upon becoming a doctor. She is of a quite different generation from Walter, and is passionately involved in the cause of black identity and equality. Mama Younger is of an older school of thought. She asks no more than peaceful coexistence with white society and is proud of what she has been able to accomplish against the many barriers that she has encountered. Walter takes a midway attitude. He is torn between the necessity of providing a decent living for his wife and his son, Travis, and the psychological necessity of proving to himself that he is a free man.

When the check arrives, Mama makes a down payment on a house in a white neighborhood. Walter is enraged by this, for he believed that he could have made better use of the money. He slips into a mood of depression, stops going to work, and begins hanging around the streets. Mama decides to give him the remaining $6500 on condition that he will put $3000 of it in a bank for Beneatha's education. Walter uses the money to invest in the liquor store with his friends. As the family is preparing to move they are approached by a Mr. Lindner of the Improvement Association of the community to which they are moving. He tries to persuade them to move somewhere else. But the Youngers are not intimidated by him, and he leaves. Meanwhile Walter and the family find out that Walter's friend, to whom he had entrusted the money for the liquor business, has suddenly left town with the money. Walter is in a distracted state, and calls Lindner and makes a deal with him to sell the house to the community at a profit to the Youngers. The other Youngers are shocked by the news that Walter would sell out to prejudice. Lindner arrives to complete the deal, but Walter has a change of heart and tells him they are going to move in after all. The last scene shows the family moving out of the old apartment.

Arthur Kopit (1937–   ). A native of Lawrence, New York, Arthur L. Kopit went to Harvard to study engineering but found that playwriting appealed to him more. As an undergraduate dramatist he displayed an extraordinary penchant for bizarre titles, such as *On the Runway of Life You Never Know What's Coming Off Next*.

Oh Dad, Poor Dad, Mamma's Hung You in the Closet and I'm Feelin' So Sad (1960) is subtitled "A Pseudoclassical Tragifarce in a Bastard French Tradition." It was first performed in London.

Immensely rich and immensely eccentric Madame Rosepettle travels about Latin America measuring yachts and shielding her son, Jonathan, from life. In Havana harbor she lures Commodore Roseabove to her cabin where she shows him in the bedroom closet the stuffed body of her husband, whom she had killed. Understandably, the Commodore decamps. Jonathan is being seduced by the lascivious baby-sitter, Rosalie, but in struggling for his virtue he strangles her. Madame Rosepettle finds the girl's body buried under a huge mound composed of Jonathan's stamp, coin, and book collections.

The play seems to be an example in drama of the school of black humor, which conceals a despairing vision of a rotting society behind the zaniest of laughter. Madame Rosepettle is the dominating mother and Rosalie the devouring female, both carried to their most ludicrous extremes. All the males are hopelessly floundering (or mummified). Under the scintillating humor is a sad, sad note of life's ghastliness.

A more recent play by Kopit, *Indians* (1969), deals sympathetically with the aspirations of the American Indians, in a pageant-like drama in which Buffalo Bill is a leading character.

Jack Gelber (1932–   ). Born in Chicago, Jack Gelber received a B.S. at the University of Illinois in 1953. From 1953 to 1955 he lived in San Francisco and thereafter in New York.

The Connection (1959) takes its name from the drug-addict's term for the seller of his narcotics. The play incorporates an unusual device to create audience participation. The imaginary producer (Jim) and the writer (Jaybird) explain to the audience that they have collected this group of addicts to improvise a play from a pattern laid down by the writer. Two photographers with lights and movie camera go back and forth between the stage and the audience.

The action of the play takes place in the apartment of Leach. A group of heroin addicts are waiting for the arrival of Cowboy, who is to bring with him the "fix" that they all need so badly. The dialogue reflects the boredom and the spiritual malaise which is at the very essence of their lives. Yet they do not ask for pity. They see the people of the "square" world equally "hooked" on various things that give them pleasure, whether it be money or new clothes. In between speeches the musicians play jazz. Finally Cowboy arrives with Sister Salvation of the Salvation Army whom he has used as an unwitting cover-up in his transportation of the drugs. One by one the junkies step into the bathroom to get a fix. Leach takes an overdose; and several of the junkies, fearing that he is going to die and get them involved with the police, decide to leave. Jaybird and Jim enter once more and comment on the failure of the play—that nothing worked out as they had planned it.

Jack Carter Richardson (1934–   ). A native New Yorker, Richardson holds an A.B. from Columbia and has also studied at the University of Paris and the University of Munich. He served in the U. S. Army for two years in Korea.

The Prodigal (1960) is a modernization of one of the greatest classic legends. To a degree it is influenced by the dramatic techniques of the French dramatists Giraudoux and Anouilh.

Agamemnon, king of Argos, pompously sets out to conquer Troy, and in his absence Aegisthus moves to power by fostering a new state religion (resembling Protestant fundamentalism) for which he composes impressive hymns and prayers. Power corrupts the wily Aegisthus. Agamemnon upon his return tries to enlist his son Orestes in deposing the entrenched usurper. Orestes refuses, and Clytemnestra goads Aegisthus into killing Agamemnon, thus forcing the hand of Orestes. The youth still tries to evade his destiny, but, all pressures operating against him, he wearily gives in and unwillingly returns to avenge his father by slaying both Aegisthus and Clytemnestra.

Orestes is equally contemptuous of the romanticism of Agamemnon and the rationalistics of Aegisthus. In a mad world he wishes only to be sane and unattached. But destiny inexorably compels him to action that he detests. It is not the divine will of ancient Greek concept or blind fate as other eras might designate it; it is the mind-set of contemporary society, all the determined nudgings of an environment from which he cannot escape, that forces Orestes to violence. "The world," Orestes insists in conclusion, "demands that we inherit the pretensions of our fathers, that we go on killing in the name of ancient illusions about ourselves, that we assume the right to punish, order, and invent philosophies to make our worst moments seem inspired."

CHAPTER EIGHT

Prose of the Mid-Twentieth Century

RECENT EMPHASIS UPON CRITICISM

In mid-century prose writing, a very creative approach to literary criticism has expressed itself in the works of an unusually large number of highly gifted critics. Some of them offer a very individual conception, while others have worked together in presenting a shared point of view. This is particularly true of the group associated with the New Criticism, which has had a dynamic effect upon much appreciation and much teaching of literature. Although the beginnings of the New Criticism go back to the earlier part of the century, many of its most influential statements fall definitely within mid-century. This chapter presents the views of various leading critics.

Although criticism by its constructiveness has achieved much prominence in recent prose, there have of course been recent prose writers in various fields whose skilled and moving works have won wide recognition. We turn to them toward the end of the chapter.

It had been our hope that we could point to new trends in prose comparable to the new directions which we have discussed in the chapter on recent poetry. There are indications that such a development is in the making. One of several examples is the work of Susan Sontag (born in New York City in 1933), whose *Against Interpretation and Other Essays* (1966) and *Styles of Radical Will* (1969) show deep understanding of key intellectual expressions of the contemporary scene and also profound concern for the pressing problems and events around us, while at the same time, like the recent poets, she achieves an appropriate form for her statements and draws strongly upon her personal convictions.

This chapter cannot attempt to forecast the further trends in prose. It aims rather to provide background material for the reader and student.

MAJOR LITERARY CRITICS OF MID-CENTURY

Richard Volney Chase, Jr. (1914–   ). A native of Lakeport, New Hampshire, Richard Volney Chase teaches literature at Columbia University. As an outstanding representative of new liberalism in criticism, he has described his efforts as attempts to "ransom liberalism from the ruinous sellouts, failures, and defeats of the Thirties." His major work is *The American Novel and Its Traditions* (1957) which posits "romance" rather than "realism" as the main line of American fiction. Refusing bondage to realistic detail, Chase says, the American novel emphasizes action rather than character and has thus been free to struggle with the violent opposites of our national make-up. Like F. O. Matthiessen (see Chapter 4), Chase finds that the finest American fiction is imbued with the tragic vision of life. *The Democratic Vista* (1959) consists of Platonic dialogues emphasizing liberal democracy as the guiding beacon of American thought and art.

Frederick J. Hoffman (1909–   ). Frederick John Hoffman was born in Port Washington, Wisconsin. He received the A.B. from Stanford University in 1934, the M.A. from the University of Minnesota in 1936, and the Ph.D. from Ohio State University in 1942. He has taught at the universities of Ohio State, Oklahoma, Wisconsin, and (since 1960) California. Hoffman has been one of the most prolific writers upon twentieth-century American literature, notably in *The Twenties* (1955).

Freudianism and the Literary Mind (1945) examines the impact of Freud's concepts upon twentieth-century authors, whether conscious students of the psychoanalyst such as Waldo Frank (see Chapter 4) or followers of Freudian teachings "by default," as Hoffman suggests Sherwood Anderson was. No doctrinaire Freudian, Hoffman sees psychoanalysis and the contemporary literary mind as complementary explorations of the Western consciousness of this era. In the 1957 revision of this work Hoffman adds a Freudian examination of *Tender Is the Night* by F. Scott Fitzgerald.

Joseph Campbell (1904–   ). At Columbia University in his native New York, Joseph Campbell received his A.B. and M.A. From 1927 to 1929 he studied in France and Germany. Since 1934 he has taught literature at Sarah Lawrence College. With Henry Morton Robinson he prepared *A Skeleton Key to Finnegans Wake* (1944).

The Hero with a Thousand Faces (1949), the first significant American study in depth of a Jungian archetype in literature, is a major achievement in myth criticism. Bearing to the task an impressive grasp of world-wide anthropology and mythology, Campbell finds one myth (monomyth) informing much of the world's literature and folklore— the myth of rebirth involving the three stages of "the separation or departure," "the trials and victories of initiation," "return and reintegration with society."

More recently Campbell has developed a very comprehensive and refreshingly incisive study of the whole range of mythmaking, in four volumes entitled as a group *The Masks of God.* These searching works in comparative mythology are: *Primitive Mythology* (1959), *Oriental Mythology* (1962), *Occidental Mythology* (1964), and *Creative Mythology* (1969).

Northrop Frye (1912–   ). Born in Sherbrooke, Quebec, Northrop Frye took his A.B. in 1933 from the University of Toronto and his M.A. from Oxford in 1940. Although ordained a clergyman in the United Church of Canada in 1936, he has spent most of his career teaching English literature at the University of Toronto. He is a frequent and influential lecturer at universities in the U.S.A., and for many years has been outstanding in educational radio and television in Canada. *Fearful Symmetry* (1947) established him as one of the most notable of all scholars concerning William Blake.

Anatomy of Criticism: Four Essays (1957) was termed a "fearful symmetry" by one reviewer. Frye apprehends criticism as "an examination of literature in terms of a conceptual framework derivable from an inductive survey of the literary field." The elaborate framework which he constructs blocks out subdivisions under "modes, symbols, myths, genres," to see all of Western literature from Homer to the present as forming one totality. Although disclaiming any preconceived system to steer through this vastness, his emphasis falls upon the archetypal symbol. An individual literary work, therefore, is not a self-contained entity (as in the New Criticism, discussed later) but a means of unifying and integrating the full experience of our entire culture. *Moby Dick,* for instance, "is absorbed into our imaginative experience of leviathans and dragons of the deep from the Old Testament onward." Rich with learning and perceptivity, this work, like that of Wellek and Warren (discussed later), seeks to encompass the whole range of literary theory.

Leslie A. Fiedler (1917–   ). Leslie Aaron Fiedler was born in Newark, New Jersey. From New York University he received the A.B. in 1938, and from the University of Wisconsin he received the M.A. in 1939 and the Ph.D. in 1941. He has taught in this country at the universities of Montana, Columbia, New York, and Princeton, and has taught abroad in the universities of Rome, Bologna, and Athens. From *An End to Innocence* (1955) to *Waiting for the End* (1964) he has been the *enfant terrible* of American literary criticism. His writings are marked by unacademic assertiveness, and the manner in which he applies psychoanalytic criticism to American literature is controversial. However, few serious critics of our time are such exciting reading.

Love and Death in the American Novel (1960) searches in American fiction for the archetypes of Eros and Thanatos mentioned in the title. With the passing of patriarchal puritanism, Fiedler says, the Oedipus complex has resulted in the American rejection of the father image. Repression, however, has prevented a full-bodied drive toward the mother figure, thus resulting in the innocuous blond maiden of so much American fiction and a notorious lack of adequate female characters in the American novel. The standard resolution has been the creation of a male-male relationship, writes Fiedler, "haunting almost all our major writers of fiction" from Cooper to Hemingway and producing such pairings as Bumppo and Chingachgook, Huck and Jim. This eventuates in the love of sterility and death. Even the most antagonistic readers of Fiedler are forced to acknowledge numerous surprising insights afforded by his psychoanalytical approach.

Kenneth Burke (1897–   ). Kenneth Duva Burke was born in Pittsburgh, Pennsylvania, and educated at Ohio State and Columbia. In his earlier years he was a notable translator of German literature and wrote extensively for "little magazines" such as *Broom, Secession,* and *Dial.* He has lectured widely: University of Chicago, New School for Social Research, Bennington College, Drew University, Pennsylvania State University, and University of California.

Leading critics are practically unanimous in praising Burke's approach and viewpoint, but many readers find his involved syntax and highly technical vocabulary rough going. Burke's focal point lies in "symbolic action." All art, he believes, results from a psychological impulse for the "arousing and fulfillment of desires." As differentiated from a practical act, a symbolic act is "the dancing of an attitude"; but it is a symbol to impel action, as a primitive rain dance seeks to induce action from Nature and a sophisticated modern dance is often highly suggestive of action to both observer and participant.

As an "integrative" critic Burke has attempted beyond most other critics to reconcile in one system all critical approaches (e.g., Marxism and Freudianism, sociological and humanistic) and to trace in literature the human responses that embrace all our life from primitive ritual to scientific research.

Attitudes Toward History (1937) is Burke's first definitive study of symbolic action, although the concept is adumbrated in previous works. In spite of the title, literature is the major concern. In reaction to "the curve of history," says Burke, authors express one of three attitudes. "Acceptance" produces orthodox philosophies such as those of Emerson and Whitman, and genres such as the epic, lyric, comedy, and tragedy in support of the Establishment. "Rejection" produces rebellious philosophies such as those of Marx and Nietzsche, and genres of derision such as satire and burlesque. "Acceptance-rejection," balancing the two previous attitudes, represents an ironic or humanistic attitude, perhaps most familiar to us today in writers such as Faulkner.

The thoughtful critic scrutinizes literary works for the "cues" and "clusters" that will reveal symbolic action and attitude regardless of the "official front" presented to the world. Like Blake, Burke would see Milton as essentially "of the Devil's party," because contrary to his professed orthodoxy he portrays Satan and disorder with far greater vividness and imagery than he does God and order.

The Philosophy of Literary Form—Studies in Symbolic Action (1941) finds in all art three ingredients: dream, prayer, chart. Dream is the vision, generally from the deep unconscious, that emblems the author's attitude toward experience. Prayer is the communicative faculty, urging artist and perceiver of art to action. Chart is the realistic-rationalistic sizing up and application to the tangible world. Burke employs his scheme of dream, prayer, chart (or symbol, rhetoric, and grammar) to explore a multitude of writings from Homer and Aeschylus to Steinbeck and Robert Penn Warren.

A Grammar of Motives (1945) begins a trilogy "on human relations," probably unique in its attempt to construct a total system of human behavior from the starting point of literary theory. By his integrative scheme, every piece of writing and every human action can be analyzed as "dramatism" under five "key terms": act, scene, agent, agency, purpose. All human behavior (dramatism) arises from the linguistic symbolism of man. Language creates the negative in human perception. Thus man builds hierarchy, an elaborate system of "thou-shalt-nots." Since no one can fulfill perfectly every provision of the hierarchical covenant, each man experiences a sense of guilt. Removal of the sense of guilt requires catharsis, which operates through mortification, or victimage. Either attempt at purification produces a final alleviation of guilt, a redemption. Burke ranges through the entire realm of man's achievement, finding his principle of dramatism applicable widely; two examples would be Keats's "Ode on a Grecian Urn" and the American Constitution. Burke's all-inclusive analysis of human behavior has thus shifted from the earlier basis of literary criticism to a survey of linguistic act, a study which he has subsequently labeled as "Logology." *A Rhetoric of Motives* (1950), second in the trilogy, concentrates upon the audience impact of utterances. Rhetoric is the persuasive attempt of language to evoke identification in reader and hearer. *Language as Symbolic Action* (1966) treats of the psychology of expression, finding four elements in all human utterances: poetry (pure symbolism), grammar (knowledge), rhetoric (catharsis leading to redemption), and ethics (self and social delineation).

THE NEW CRITICISM. The term "New Criticism" as used in mid-twentieth-century American thinking and teaching derives from the point of view of the Agrarian poets whom we have discussed in Chapter 2: John Crowe Ransom, Allen Tate, Robert Penn Warren, and with them the noted scholar and teacher Cleanth Brooks. The three Agrarian poets have biographical sketches in the first poetry chapter (Chapter 2).

Ransom popularized the label when he called a collection of essays that he edited *The New Criticism* (1941). The New Critics center their whole attention upon the primary aesthetic achievement of an individual literary work. They consider the study of the background of a work—biographical, historical, sociological, psychological, and other factors in the poet's or author's development—as relatively unimportant. They emphasize close textual analysis, and explore "irony," "paradox," and "tension" as creating within poetry an "equilibrium of opposed forces."

John Crowe Ransom makes his chief critical statement in *The World's Body* (1938), which attacks science in the name of poetry. Through its method, Ransom states, science "skeletonizes" the world, while poetry re-establishes its "body." Ransom calls for a return to the traditional values of society that would humanize man and elevate him to the realm of the aesthetic. **Allen Tate** states his position in an essay "Tension in Poetry" included in his *Collected Essays* (1959). Tate avers: "The meaning of poetry is in its tension, the full, organized body of all the extension and intention that we can find in it." By extension he refers to the denotative aspect of the poetic language; by intention he refers to the connotative aspect. **Robert Penn Warren** is an analytic critic with a broader view than that of his fellow Agrarians. Especially noted among his essays is "A Poem of Pure Imagination," dealing with Coleridge's "The Rime of the Ancient Mariner."

We shall consider now a number of the other important critics associated with or sympathetic to the New Criticism.

Cleanth Brooks (1906–   ). Born in Murray, Kentucky, Cleanth Brooks received an A.B. from Vanderbilt (where he studied under Ransom) in 1928 and an A.M. from Tulane in 1929. As a Rhodes scholar he proceeded to Oxford where he earned a B.Litt. in 1932.

In the latter year he started a collegiate teaching career at Louisiana State University that subsequently took him to the universities of Texas, Southern California, and Yale.

Modern Poetry and the Tradition (1939) perhaps more than any other single work establishes the premises of New Criticism. To Brooks the "tradition" is the centuries-old union within poetry of intellect and emotion to explore the total cultural experience. The Romantics have tried to break the tradition by emphasizing individual emotion. Brooks finds ties between seventeenth-century metaphysical poetry and our contemporary verse in concise, sensuous imagery. Like Donne, modern poets such as Yeats, Eliot, Ransom, Tate, and Warren have restored the full range available to poetry and have displayed the tension, irony, and concreteness requisite to significant verse. At close range Brooks probes poetry not as edifying message or revelation or sociological condition but as the aesthetic experience in itself.

The Well-Wrought Urn: Studies in the Structure of Poetry (1947) exemplifies the theory of New Criticism in scrutiny of several special poems. Although perhaps the best-known explication is that of "Ode on a Grecian Urn" by Keats, the title more broadly suggests the artistic structuring of any competent piece of art. Most criticism, Brooks asserts, suffers from the "heresy of paraphrase" by which some rationalistic summary is proffered instead of "the real core of meaning which constitutes the essence of the poem." The essence of the poem is not such a logical statement but "a pattern of resolved stresses" manipulating symbol or myth by paradox and ambiguity to convey a total knowledge of human experience. Other critics sometimes find Brooks supersubtle in excavating hidden meanings and deeply concealed artistry, but few deny the value of his insistence upon coming to grips with the art object itself, seeking the actual aesthetic perceptivity of the poet.

Perhaps Cleanth Brooks's most widespread influence has been exerted in collaboration with Robert Penn Warren, with whom he edited *Southern Review* (1935–42) and prepared memorable textbooks, beginning with *An Approach to Literature* (1936, and many subsequent editions) that have carried the tenets of New Criticism to several decades of American college students and have greatly influenced the teaching of creative literature.

René Wellek (1903–   ). Born in Vienna, Austria, René Wellek received the Ph.D. from Charles University in Prague, Czechoslovakia, in 1926. He continued advanced studies at Princeton and taught at various universities in this country and in Europe until settling down in 1946 as professor of Slavic and of comparative literature at Yale. He has received many honors for service to the humanities, and has been president of the American Association of Comparative Literature and the International Association of Comparative Literature.

Theory of Literature (1949), in collaboration with Austin Warren (Professor of English at the University of Michigan), has probably been the most influential work of this century upon the methods of literary study. The first major section of the volume, "The Extrinsic Approach to the Study of Literature," scrutinizes the historical, biographical, sociological, and other approaches that the authors consider valuable but essentially peripheral to the basic interpretation of creative literature. "The Intrinsic Study of Literature" supports the fundamentals of the New Criticism. Literature may communicate certain knowledge and truth, but its prime function is "fidelity to its own nature."

Wellek's four-volume *History of Modern Criticism* (1955–65) is a major independent work.

Yvor Winters (1900–68). For a biographical sketch, see the discussion of Winters' poetry in Chapter 6.

The Function of Criticism (1957) demonstrates Winters' essential allegiance to the analytical technique of the New Critics but also his great difference from them in his emphasis upon the moral and rational nature of poetry. Although one of the avowed opponents of New Humanism in his contributions to *The Critique of Humanism* (1930), he nonetheless shares in the conservative and aristocratic attitude of Irving Babbitt, who represented the New Humanism in an earlier generation. Hostile to both romanticism and science, Winters exalts poetry as the means of enriching our perception of human experience, increasing our intellectual grasp, and bolstering our moral fiber. An earlier work is *In Defense of Reason* (1947).

R. P. Blackmur (1904–   ). Richard Palmer Blackmur, a native of Springfield, Massachusetts, did not study for an undergraduate degree. Rutgers University awarded him an honorary Litt.D., and Blackmur has been a resident fellow at Princeton. He began critical writing for *The Hound and Horn* in Cambridge, Massachusetts, in 1927, and after the discontinuance of that publication in 1934 he wrote regularly in journals associated with the New Criticism.

The Double Agent, Essays in Craft and Elucidation (1935), the first collection of Blackmur's critical pieces, exemplifies his fundamental qualities. He differs from his fellow New Critics in asserting critical relativism. In "The Critic's Job of Work" he declares that "any rational approach to literature is valid and may properly be called critical which fastens at any point upon the work itself." Notable in the collection is a highly appreciative scrutiny of the verse of Wallace Stevens, whose language is praised as precisely controlled rhetoric and not mere ornamentation, and a denunciation of e. e. cummings for vague sentimental phrasings.

The Lion and the Honeycomb: Essays in Solicitude and Critique (1955), as well as books of the two previous decades, carries on the quiet, meticulous Blackmur criticism. He is especially appreciative of Henry James and Henry Adams. "A Burden for Critics" is one of the most balanced and impressive contemporary statements of the proper role of the critic. Blackmur sees the burden of critics in this chaotic age as the necessity to "make bridges between the society and the arts: to prepare the audience for its art and to prepare the arts for their artists." He insists that art must not exist *in vacuo.* In this age of cultural disintegration he ascribes to criticism the vital function of producing "a sequence of rational critical judgments upon the art of our time as an aid in determining the identity, the meaning in itself, of present society."

NEO-ARISTOTELIANISM. This group, the Neo-Aristotelians, is often called the Chicago Aristotelians, or the Chicago Critics, because of the origin and focus of this school at the University of Chicago. Although hostile to historical and sociological approaches, the movement is essentially a reaction against the New Criticism, which, claim the Chicagoans, unduly ignores traditional poetics. The *Poetics* of Aristotle is advanced as the soundest foundation upon which to erect a structure of purely literary criticism.

Ronald S. Crane (1886–   ). Ronald Salmon Crane was born in Tecumseh, Michigan. He received the A.B. from the University of Michigan in 1908 and the Ph.D. from the University of Pennsylvania in 1911. He taught English at Northwestern University from 1911 to 1924 and at the University of Chicago from 1924 until his retirement in 1951. Thereafter his eminence as scholar-critic took him as visiting professor to universities throughout the country.

Critics and Criticism: Ancient and Modern (1952), edited by Crane, consists of twenty essays by Crane and his confreres. In 1948 Crane had called for a return by critics to Aristotelian principles, and this work is the fruit of his urgings. In his introduction Crane says that New Critics lose sight of the reality of literary genre and the relationship of whole works to other wholes. The Aristotelian principles are advanced because they supply a controlling viewpoint, uniform procedure, and consistent standards of judgment.

The Languages of Criticism and the Structure of Poetry (1953) consists of Crane lectures at the University of Toronto and represents probably the most definitive, as well as the most broadly tolerant, enunciation of Neo-Aristotelianism. Crane recognizes virtues in the many paths of literary criticism but insists upon the examination of total structure and form as a corrective to the fragmentary minutiae-hunting of much recent criticism.

IMPORTANT MID-CENTURY PROSE STYLISTS IN VARIOUS FIELDS

Thomas Merton (1915–68). The son of a British landscape painter father and an American Quaker mother, Thomas Merton was born in Prades, France. After education in France and England, he secured the A.B. (1938) and the M.A. (1939) from Columbia University. In 1938 he became a convert to Roman Catholicism. He entered the Trappist monastery of Our Lady of Gethsemani, Kentucky, in 1941 and in 1949 was ordained a priest.

The Seven-Storey Mountain (1948), Merton's spiritual autobiography, was widely read and widely acclaimed for its intense concentration upon the mystical religious experience. Such spiritual autobiographies are extraordinarily rare; for a counterpart to Merton's work, Americans have to leaf all the way back to Woolman's eighteenth-century *Journal*.

Rachel Carson (1907–64). Rachel Louise Carson was born in Springdale, Pennsylvania, and attended Johns Hopkins where she received an M.A. in 1932. Her primary field of study was marine biology, and she wrote three books on the sea—*Under the Sea-Wind* (1941) *The Sea Around Us* (1951), and *The Edge of the Sea* (1955). Her deep concern about all of nature caused her to turn in her last book, *Silent Spring*, to the immensely troubling matter of the danger of the widespread use of insecticides aimed at pests but actually attacking and killing birds and other precious forms of animal life.

The Sea Around Us (1951) is a scientifically accurate and beautifully written study of the oceans—their history, geography, composition, and the creatures which live in them. Miss Carson begins by describing theories on the creation of the seas. Billions of years ago when the Earth was a spinning ball of molten iron a great hunk of this material was torn away and sent spinning into space to become the Moon. The resulting hole in the earth was the basin which, after centuries of rainfall, the Pacific Ocean would fill. Miss Carson also describes the shape of the bottom of the oceans—consisting of great mountains, valleys, and trenches—which have been partially mapped by sonar. She tells of the creatures of the sea, the differences between the characteristics of the sea life at different depths, and how these creatures experience the seasons in much the same way as do land creatures. The overwhelming impression that one gets from the book is the great sense of mystery which the author feels toward the sea, and her desire to impart this feeling to the reader.

Silent Spring (1962) aroused the public to problems resulting from the use of chemical insecticides.

Miss Carson traces the development of the insecticides from the end of World War II, when they first came into widespread use, through the fifties. She gives a clear description of the nature of the various chemicals as well as explanations of how they are employed. She attacks the irresponsibility of various agencies of the federal government for permitting indiscriminate employment of these chemicals. The effect that they have had upon the land and the wildlife, as well as upon man, demonstrates the lack of understanding of nature on the part of many in government and in industry. It is ironic that the insects which the chemicals aim to control or destroy largely continue to thrive, whereas a great number of bird species have largely disappeared from parts of America, rivers have been polluted, and the ecology of whole regions has been upset. In fact, through the process of natural selection, the insect pests gradually become immune to the chemicals, and it happens that since the chemicals destroy many of the predatory insects, the prey insects often increase in number. Miss Carson offers some positive alternatives to the chemical control of insects. She suggests proven methods of biological control such as the introduction into a region of other insects which will prey on the unwanted insects. And she insists that we must rid ourselves of the idea that we can control nature. We must accept the idea that we are sharing a planet with other creatures, rather than dominating it.

Edwin Way Teale (1899–   ). Born in Joliet, Illinois, Edwin Way Teale received an A.B. (1922) from Earlham College, and an M.A. (1926) from Columbia. After various teaching and journalistic activities he became a free-lance writer in 1941. Among his numerous honors is presidency in 1958 of the Thoreau Society.

North with the Spring (1951) employs a concept that Thoreau would have applauded. Teale begins in lower Florida and follows emergent spring all the way up the Atlantic Coast through New England. Carefully avoiding transcendental musings as he faithfully chronicles the wondrous awakening of new life, Teale nonetheless gives ringing affirmation to the theme of eternal renewal. Across the great rolling land and even in the midst of the concreted cities, Nature denies death and lifts the world from its winter slumber to vibrant life.

The majestic theme of Teale's *North with the Spring* might hopefully be transferred from the vast continent itself to its human inhabitants and their culture, offering the hope of new creative gifts as we embark upon the last third of the twentieth century.

Index

DOUBLEDAY COLLEGE COURSE GUIDES